MEDIAPOLITIK

MEDIAPOLITIK

How the Mass Media Have
Transformed World Politics

LEE EDWARDS

THE CATHOLIC UNIVERSITY
OF AMERICA PRESS

WASHINGTON, D.C.

Copyright ©2001
The Catholic University of America Press
All rights reserved
Printed in the United States of America

The paper used in this publication meets the minimum requirements of American National
Standards for Information Science — Permanence of Paper for Printed Library Materials.
ANSI Z39-48-1984.

LIBRARY OF CONGRESS CATALOGING-IN-PUBLICATION DATA

Edwards, Lee.
  Mediapolitik : how the mass media have transformed world politics / Lee Edwards.
    p. cm.
  Includes bibliographical references and index.
  ISBN 0-8132-0991-9 (alk. paper) — ISBN 0-8132-0992-7 (pbk. : alk. paper)
    1. Mass media—Political aspects.   2. Mass media policy.   3. Mass media—Influ-
  ence.   4. World politics—1989–   I. Title.
  P95.8 .E34   2001
  302.23—dc21

                                                                    00-026076

TO
M. Stanton Evans

CONTENTS

ACKNOWLEDGMENTS

This book grew out of my undergraduate and graduate classes in the Department of Politics at The Catholic University of America. In and out of the classroom, my students helped me develop the theory of *mediapolitik*. I wish to thank the past and present chairmen of the department, Steve Schneck and David Walsh, for affording me the opportunity to teach at a wonderful university. And I thank Adele Chwalek, director of the Mullen Library, and her staff for their always professional assistance.

I am indebted to the Earhart Foundation and the Wilbur Foundation for their generous support. Bluntly put, academics cannot write textbooks without the help of such foundations.

Research assistance was provided by Leda Rose, Jason Boffetti, Sarah Simmons, and William Connery. I am grateful to David McGonagle, director of The Catholic University of America Press, for agreeing to publish this, my first textbook.

Lee Edwards
Alexandria, Virginia

INTRODUCTION

WHEN THE POLISH UNION LEADER Lech Walesa was asked what effect Radio Free Europe had had on Solidarity's activities in Communist Poland, he responded, "Would there be earth without the sun?" The East German Communist Party boss Walter Ulbricht said of the TV antennas on apartment houses, "The enemy of the people stands on the roof." A spokesman for the democratic "No" opposition that upset the Chilean dictator Augusto Pinochet in a plebiscite remarked, "In fifteen minutes of television time, we destroyed fifteen years of government publicity for the dictatorship." The Chinese Communist Party General Secretary Jiang Zemin stated that Tiananmen Square illustrated the "chaos" that will result "if the tools of public opinion are not tightly controlled in the hands of true Marxists." In an address at Harvard University, Alexander Solzhenitsyn declared that "the press has become the greatest power within the Western countries, more powerful than the legislature, the executive, and the judiciary."[1] Leaders of every nation, north and south, rich and poor, free and not free, acknowledge the power of the mass media to influence and shape the politics of their nation.

1. *Proceedings* of "The Failure of Communism: The Western Response," an international conference sponsored by Radio Free Europe/Radio Liberty, November 15, 1989 (Munich, Germany: RFE/RL Fund, 1989) p. 47; Elaubem Attias, "Liberation on the Airwaves," *Christian Science Monitor*, February 14, 1991; Leonard R. Sussman, *Power, the Press and the Technology of Freedom: The Coming Age of ISND* (New York: Freedom House, 1989), p. 227; Robert Delfs, "Speak No Evil," *Far Eastern Economic Review*, December 14, 1989, p. 27; Alexander Solzhenitsyn, "The Exhausted West," *Harvard Magazine*, July–August 1978, p. 23.

There is no denying that the mass media are everywhere. With over one billion television sets and two-and-a-half portable radios in the world, how could it be otherwise? "Teleplomacy" often replaces diplomacy at summits as each head of state tries to put the best spin on the final communique. Wars are fought on television as well as on the ground. Iraqi President Saddam Hussein's attempts to influence world opinion during the Persian Gulf War were clumsy and crude—patting the heads of the children of Western "guests," inviting inspection of a bombed-out "milk" factory—but his calculated efforts in the middle of a shooting war underscored the critical role of the mass media in today's information-driven world.

Television has contracted time in world politics. No longer do diplomats have a week or even a day to draft a response to a crisis. More often their deadline is only an hour away, when Cable News Network (CNN) presents its next edition of *Headline News*. Leaders of democratic and nondemocratic nations alike seek to influence the course of events through the use of the mass media, to a degree that is just beginning to be measured seriously. It is no coincidence that at the height of the cold war, the three nations with the largest communications systems were the three most powerful nations in the world—the United States, the Soviet Union, and the People's Republic of China.

Like every other technology developed by man, the mass media can be employed to improve or impair the human condition. They have been used to further tyranny, as in the former Soviet Union or in present-day Iraq. They have also preserved freedom, as in the United States and other Western democracies. And they have helped to extend freedom, as in Central Europe, South Africa, and Latin America. On balance, the history of the twentieth century demonstrates that the mass media are a liberating force when and if they are joined with democratic principles and institutions. Some scholars have written of the innate freedom-making power of the media, but the mass media are a means to, not a guarantee of, freedom, as dictators from Lenin and Hitler to Fidel Castro and Saddam Hussein have shown.[2]

Given the mass media's ever-increasing significance, a need has arisen for a theory to describe world politics and the mass media as they are now and are likely to be for the foreseeable future. Such a theory recognizes

2. See Sussman, *Power, the Press and Technology of Freedom;* and George Gilder, *Life after Television* (New York: Norton, 1992).

that the world has entered the Cyber Age, in which mass communication depends as much on the personal computer and fiber optics as on a television or radio set and the microchip. The futurist Alvin Toffler's metaphor of a "third wave" is, however, misleading insofar as it implies that cyber-communication will sweep away the older means of communication.[3] On the contrary, the Cyber Age will not replace but will build on the media developments of the preceding ages—the Gutenberg Age and the Electronic Age. For our information in the twenty-first century, we will be able to call upon a wide variety of media, ranging from the newspaper to the TV to the PC.

I call this new interrelationship between the mass media and world politics *mediapolitik*.[4] There are three basic models: liberal democratic, authoritarian, and totalitarian. In the liberal democratic model, both the politics and the mass media of a country are free of government control. At their optimum, politicians and journalists operate within a framework of responsibility and accountability. Because of Founders like George Washington, James Madison, and Thomas Jefferson, the leading national example of the liberal democratic model is the United States, whose *mediapolitik* is rooted in free speech and a free press.

In the authoritarian model, politics and mass media are regulated by the government, while the economy and culture are usually unregulated. Politicians and journalists operate within a framework of *realpolitik*, which allows the government, not the people, to determine how free institutions shall be. National examples of the authoritarian model are Saudi Arabia, Singapore, and Chile under Pinochet.

In the totalitarian model, politics and mass media are controlled absolutely by the government. All institutions operate within a utopian framework calculated to shape the entire society in the image of the ruling party. National examples of the totalitarian model are Iraq and North Korea.

3. Alvin Toffler, *The Third Wave* (New York: Bantam Books, 1980), pp. 156–58. Toffler writes, "The Third Wave does more than simply accelerate the information flows; it *transforms* [emphasis added] the deep structure of information on which our daily actions depend" (p. 158).

4. The term "mediapolitik" was used in 1981 by *Washington Post* media critic Tom Shales when discussing a CBS movie about the efforts of Skokie, Illinois, citizens to prevent a 1978 march by American Nazis in their city. Shales suggested that the subject would have been better handled by journalists, rather than docudramatists, commenting, "The games of mediapolitik go on, and not in terribly encouraging ways." Tom Shales, "The Nazis and Skokie," *Washington Post,* November 17, 1981. I have used *mediapolitik* in a much broader sense to describe the interaction of world politics and the mass media.

ALL POLITICS IS GLOBAL

The mass media have made all of us participants in world politics. In 1776, news of the signing of the Declaration of Independence took one month to travel from Philadelphia to Savannah, a distance of 750 miles. In 1991, Cable News Network enabled us to watch the beginning of the Persian Gulf War in our living rooms in prime time. Political leaders from Washington to Moscow to Tokyo make daily use of media power. We may mock Saddam Hussein's or Slobodan Milosevic's heavy-handed attempts at propaganda, but would World War II have ended in total victory for the Allies if Adolf Hitler had had daily access to a global television system like CNN? Images do matter. Senator John McCain (R-Ariz.), a prisoner of war during the Vietnam conflict, argues that "World War I wouldn't have lasted three months if people had known what was going on in that conflict."[5] That is, pictures of the senseless carnage of trench warfare would have produced a public demand for an end to the fighting that could not have been resisted. In the age of instant information, then, all politics is global.

In this interdependent world, the U.S. mass media are the most important media because, first, the United States is the most powerful nation—economically, militarily, politically—in the world. Wall Street determines economic trends, the Pentagon dictates military decisions, Washington approves or disapproves political solutions around the world, and American TV networks (especially CNN) and major publications influence the flow of news and information on every continent. Twenty-five years ago, the British sociologist Jeremy Tunstall concluded, in a widely praised work, that "the media are American." Asked in the mid-1990s whether that was still true, Tunstall responded that "the United States is the only media superpower."[6]

Second, the U.S. media have always had a major influence on the conduct of American foreign policy (and therefore the foreign policy of all

5. Jacqueline Sharkey, "When Pictures Drive Foreign Policy," *American Journalism Review,* December 1993, p. 19.

6. Jeremy Tunstall, "Are the Media Still American?" *Media Studies Journal,* fall 1995, p. 16. Tunstall first states that the U.S. "slice" of the "world media pie is still growing" but later says that America is a media superpower "in gradual decline." However, his careful overview of the workings of the mass media around the world, and the degree to which the United States dominates them, confirms his opening sentence: "There is still much truth in the assertion that the media are American," pp. 7, 16.

nations) because our policy makers depend heavily upon the media to make their decisions. As one State Department official put it, "The first thing we do [each morning] is read the newspaper—*the* newspaper—the *New York Times*. You can't work in the State Department without the *New York Times*."[7] The same is true for the major electronic media that often take their lead from the *Times*.

The media's influential role in foreign policy is reinforced by the American public's ethnocentric character, its tendency to be more interested in what happens within rather than outside the borders of the United States. American parochialism is diminishing under the impact of global economics and environmentalism, but it is still strong and widespread. It usually takes a conflict involving U.S. forces or a major disaster like an earthquake or a famine to shift the attention of most Americans to foreign news. They tend otherwise to leave the monitoring of the world to the president and the foreign policy establishment (including media like the *New York Times*).

When NBC News broadcast a prime-time, hour-long interview with the Soviet leader Mikhail Gorbachev in December 1987—just before an important U.S.-Soviet meeting on the reduction of nuclear weapons— only 15 percent of the nation tuned in. Half of the viewers who normally watched NBC switched to other networks, preferring, for example, a popular situation comedy, *Kate and Allie*, to Gorbachev's discussing how to reduce the danger of nuclear war.[8] Of the top twenty-five news stories between 1986 and 1996, just six stories dealt with overseas events: the end of the Persian Gulf War, Iraq's invasion of Kuwait, Iraq's occupation of Kuwait, the invasion of Panama, the U.S. air strike on Libya, and the sending of U.S. forces into Somalia. As will be noted, four of those stories concerned American military actions.[9]

But there are limits to the ability of television to influence government decision making. The harrowing situation of Bosnian Muslims in Srebrenica in the spring of 1993 did not persuade the permanent members of the U.N. Security Council to act to rescue them. Nevertheless, aroused by the televised horrors of what was happening to the city's residents, the

7. Doris A. Graber, *Mass Media and American Politics,* 4th ed. (Washington: CQ Press, 1993), p. 362.

8. Ibid., p. 361.

9. Kimberly Parker and Claudia Deane, "Ten Years of the Pew News Interest Index," (paper presented at the annual meeting of the American Association for Public Opinion Research, Washington, May 17, 1997), p. 2.

nonaligned nations on the security council forced passage of a resolution creating safe areas in Bosnia. Television pictures are more likely to produce a *tactical* response than a *strategic* change in overall policy.[10]

Thus, despite widespread coverage of the Bosnian war by all networks for several years, a strong majority of the American people in mid-1995 still did not believe that the United States had a direct responsibility to end the fighting in the Balkans. Their reasoning was simple: U.S. strategic interests were not involved. Yet by a margin of 58 percent, Americans believed that the United Nations had a responsibility to do something about the fighting there.[11] Public skepticism about America's role was reflected in the House of Representatives, which voted in November 1995 to bar President Clinton from sending U.S. ground troops to enforce a Bosnian peace agreement unless Congress approved.[12]

The 1999 war in Kosovo burst onto the front pages and evening telecasts without any warning. In the 1991 Persian Gulf War, there was an eight-month buildup after Iraq's invasion of Kuwait, followed by thirty days of air strikes and a weeklong ground war, all of which gave the American people time, explained Barbara Cochran of the Radio and Television News Directors Association, "to see what was at stake."[13]

In contrast, few Americans had heard of the troubled Serbian province until the U.S.-led NATO forces began bombing Kosovo in late March 1999. But President Clinton's constant references to Serbia's "ethnic cleansing" and his comparison of its leader Slobodan Milosevic to Adolf Hitler, plus heartbreaking pictures of exhausted and frightened refugees, caught the nation's attention. And when CNN broadcast Serbian television footage of three young American soldiers captured near the Kosovo border, along with live interviews of their families, the American people were aroused. Public support for NATO's bombing raids topped 60 percent, while support for sending ground troops into Kosovo went from 31 percent to 47 percent in just two weeks.[14] Across the Atlantic, the earlier uneasiness

10. Nik Gowing, "Behind the CNN Factor," *Washington Post*, July 31, 1994. Also see Nik Gowing, "Real-Time Television Coverage of Armed Conflicts and Diplomatic Crises: Does It Pressure or Distort Foreign Policy Decisions?" working paper 94-1, The Joan Shorenstein Barone Center on the Press, Politics and Public Policy, John F. Kennedy School of Government, Harvard University, June 1994.

11. News release, Times Mirror Center for the People and the Press, June 25, 1995.

12. Helen Dewar and Michael Dobbs, "House Votes to Bar Sending Troops to Bosnia without Hill Approval," *Washington Post*, November 18, 1995.

13. Jennifer Harper, "Media Educate America on War," *Washington Times*, April 2, 1999.

14. Alexandra Marks, "Public Support Grows for War with Yugoslavia," *Christian Science Monitor*, April 9, 1999.

about the first aerial combat in Europe in fifty years was replaced by public concern for the Kosovar refugees and revulsion at how they had been forced from their homeland.

So, which comes first in wartime—the policy or the pictures? As this book will show, there is a strong but always shifting correlation among government, journalism, and public opinion in foreign policy making. "Image in and of itself does not drive policy," states Marvin Kalb, director of the Joan Shorenstein Barone Center at Harvard University. "Image heightens existing factors."[15]

POWER AND RESPONSIBILITY

Given the enormous influence of the mass media on world politics, we must ask: How responsibly are journalists wielding their power? The question is particularly appropriate for those editors and reporters who live and work in a free or partly free country, or those in about two-thirds of the world.

In its 1998 survey of press freedom, Freedom House reported that in sixty-six countries—35 percent of the 186 nations examined—the press was not free and had little or no authority beyond what it was given by the government. The nonfree countries included most of Africa and much of the Middle East and Asia, including the most populous nation of all, China. In fifty-two countries—28 percent of the total—the press was partly free. Examples ranged from Russia to Brazil. In sixty-eight countries—36 percent—the news media were free. Examples included the United States, all of Europe, much of the Caribbean, and many of the island nations of Asia.[16] The French media watchdog group, *Reporters sans frontiers*, summed up its 1998 report: more than two billion people lived in countries where there was no media freedom at all, while two billion more lived in countries where the government routinely restricted or harassed journalists.[17]

There is, however, a growing dichotomy in spirit and in performance between those journalists who have long enjoyed freedom and those who have recently achieved freedom. The former, as in the United States, expend much of their energy seeking increased ratings and circulation,

15. Jacqueline Sharkey, "When Pictures Drive Foreign Policy," *American Journalism Review,* December 1993, p. 18.

16. Leonard R. Sussman, "'Pressticide' and Press Ethics," *Freedom Review* 26, no. 1 (January–February 1995): p. 64–66.

17. Paul Goble, "Victories and Defeats on the Media Front," Radio Free Europe/Radio Liberty commentary, January 4, 1999.

higher salaries and profits, and greater personal status in their profession and in society at large. The latter journalists, as in the Czech Republic and Poland, are less concerned about their own future than they are about the future of their country.

This kind of disinterested journalistic zeal is found less and less often in the United States and other long-established Western democracies. One result has been a discernible decline in the quality of the news operations of America's mass media, particularly in television. Thirty years ago, CBS's Edward R. Murrow, a reluctant Jeremiah, warned TV news directors that television was headed toward "decadence, escapism and insulation from the realities of the world."[18] Today, the American media's emphasis on, even obsession with, the tawdry and the trivial is deeply troubling. The former New York Times columnist A. M. Rosenthal laments the "exploding movement in newspapers, magazines and TV toward the specialized form of garbage collection known as gossip."[19]

Many in the U.S. media seem to have made a Faustian bargain, trading long-term trust and integrity for immediate ratings and circulation. The television critic Walter Goodman charges that television coverage of politics has been reduced to "stirring up emotions and shutting down minds."[20] Andrew Lack, president of NBC News, said bluntly that TV news, "wittingly or unwittingly, is contributing to the dumbing down of America. . . . We're tapping viewers' emotions instead of their brains."[21] The media analyst Kiku Adatto, for example, documented that the average length of a presidential statement on a network evening news broadcast fell from forty-two seconds in 1968 to less than ten seconds in 1988. Responding to widespread criticism of "sound-bite journalism," TV network executives promised that the news would return to covering the issues and lengthening the statements of presidential candidates. But it was an empty promise: in 1992, George Bush and Bill Clinton could be heard, on average, for less than nine seconds at a time.[22] The average length of the statements of President Clinton and Bob Dole in 1996 was even shorter.

18. Daniel Schorr, "TV's 'Magazines': A Different Kind of Reality," USA Today, January 12, 1995.

19. A. M. Rosenthal, "Journalists as Performers," New York Times, January 15, 1995.

20. Walter Goodman, "What's Bad for Politics Is Great for Television," New York Times, November 27, 1994.

21. Andrew Lack, "TV News Heads Downhill," USA Today, September 14, 1995.

22. James Q. Wilson, "Stagestruck," The New Republic, June 21, 1993, p. 31. For an extended examination of the shrinking soundbite, see Kiku Adatto, Picture Perfect: The Art and Artifice of Public Image Making (New York: Basic Books, 1993).

The attitude of American journalists has also changed significantly in the last thirty years. "Cynicism has replaced a necessary skepticism," said the *New York Times*' William Glaberson, "as the core of American journalism."[23] Robert MacNeil, creator of PBS's celebrated *MacNeil/Lehrer News-Hour*, is scathing about the obsessive coverage of the O. J. Simpson trial by the broadcast networks, especially CBS and NBC. He sees the "O. J.-ification" of the news as dangerous for democracy, substituting ratings-driven entertainment for information that might be useful to the electorate. He also deplores the increasingly negative tone of the news, which often treats elected officials as guilty until proven innocent. "Every journalist in this country," he says, "has a stake in the democratic system working."[24]

Media cynicism and negativism have unquestionably affected American politics. The University of Michigan has been surveying public confidence in U.S. institutions since the end of World War II. For the twenty-year period between 1972 and 1992, the proportion of people expressing "great confidence" in the executive branch fell from 29 percent to 12 percent, while those with "hardly any confidence" rose from 18 percent to 32 percent. Congress fared worse: "great confidence" among the public plummeted from 24 percent to 7 percent, while "hardly any confidence" nearly tripled, from 15 percent to 41 percent. The figures improved some after the Republicans captured control of Congress in 1994. But in 1999, the Pew Research Center for the People and the Press reported that just 28 percent of the public said they trusted the federal government to do what was right "most of the time." Nearly 60 percent responded that they trusted Washington only "some of the time."[25]

Robert D. Putnam, a Harvard professor, contends that television has profoundly undermined the nation's culture. In "Bowling Alone" and in subsequent writings, Putnam suggests that television has been a major factor in the decline in public trust and participation, or what he calls the nation's "social capital." Over the last thirty years, there has been a sharp drop in the percentage of people joining groups of all kinds—political, choral, fraternal, church, hobby. Even those who bowl now tend to bowl alone instead of joining leagues. In a *Washington Post* interview, Putnam

23. William Glaberson, "Raking Mud; The New Press Criticism: News as the Enemy of Hope," *New York Times*, October 9, 1994.

24. Elizabeth Kolbert, "Robert MacNeil Gives a Thoughtful Goodbye," *New York Times*, October 15, 1995.

25. Everett Carll Ladd and Karlyn H. Bowman, *What's Wrong: A Survey of American Satisfaction and Complaint* (Washington: AEI Press, 1999), pp. 105–8.

said, "The social fabric is becoming visibly thinner, our connections among one another are becoming visibly thinner. We don't trust one another as much, and we don't know one another as much. And, of course, that is behind the deterioration of the political dialogue, the deterioration of the political debate."[26]

Generally unaware of the conclusions of scholars like Putnam, the U.S. public places a significant measure of the blame for the decline in American institutions on the mass media. When the Times Mirror Center for the People and the Press asked in a 1994 survey whether the news media help or hinder society in solving its problems, an amazing 71 percent responded that the media get in the way. Only 25 percent said that the media help society solve its problems. When the center, renamed the Pew Research Center for the People and the Press, asked in 1999 whether the news media protected or hurt democracy, 38 percent said the media "hurt" democracy, up from 23 percent in 1985.[27] The media scholar Roy Peter Clark laments the public's low regard for journalists: "They assume we would celebrate a death for a good story."[28]

As a result, public confidence in the media has also declined precipitously over the last two decades, from 23 percent to 11 percent for the print press, from 19 percent to 12 percent for television.[29] According to the Pew Research Center, 58 percent of the public doubts the general accuracy of news reports.[30] Kathleen Hall Jamieson, head of the Annenberg School of Communications at the University of Pennsylvania, warns that "journalists are now creating the coverage that is going to lead to their own destruction. If you cover the world cynically . . . you invite your readers and viewers to reject journalism as a mode of communication because it must be cynical too."[31]

26. Thomas B. Edsall, "TV Tattered Nation's Social Fabric, Political Scientist Contends," *Washington Post,* September 3, 1995.

27. Paul H. Weaver, *News and the Culture of Lying* (New York: The Free Press, 1994), pp. 20–21; "The People, the Press & Politics: The New Political Landscape," Times Mirror Center for the People and the Press, Washington, September 21, 1994, p. 160; "Public Votes for Continuity and Change in 2000," Pew Research Center for the People and the Press, February 1999, p. 2 of summary.

28. Roy Peter Clark, "Natural Born Killers," *New York Times,* October 14, 1994.

29. Karlyn Bowman and Everett Carll Ladd, "Public Opinion toward Congress: A Historical Look," *Congress, the Press, and the Public* (Washington: American Enterprise Institute and the Brookings Institution, 1994), p. 54.

30. "Public Votes for Continuity and Change in 2000," The Pew Research Center for the People and the Press, February 1999, p. 5 of summary.

31. Glaberson, "Raking Mud."

DECIDING THE NEWS

How do American journalists make their decisions? Scholars have written extensively of the economic, political, and technical influences on the news-making process, but have paid far less attention to the roles of ethics and philosophy.[32] According to the political scientist Doris Graber, most journalists in free countries follow either a libertarian or a social responsibility philosophy.[33] Libertarians argue that they must be free to report whatever they can discover. Radical libertarians insist that the public has a right to know everything about everything. Their motto is, "Let the chips fall where they may," even if the falling "chips" turn out to be reputations and even lives. CBS's Mike Wallace admitted at a Harvard media conference that he believed it would be appropriate for him to accompany enemy troops into battle, even if they ambushed and killed American soldiers.[34]

Most libertarians are practitioners of what has been called the New Journalism, which encourages cynicism and confrontation in the pursuit of a story and often produces enmity between the media and government. Media antagonism toward government was spawned by the government's lies during the Vietnam War on everything from the chances of victory to the number of American men killed and wounded. Media distrust of government was reinforced by the Watergate scandal that finally forced President Richard Nixon to resign rather than be impeached for lying and abusing the powers of the presidency. Media cynicism about government was deepened by President Bill Clinton's repeated public lies about his sexual relationship with Monica Lewinsky.

Other journalists adhere to a philosophy of social responsibility. They insist that they better society by encouraging their audiences to behave in more socially responsible ways. They seek to influence social behavior and

32. For a traditional analysis, see Graber, *Mass Media and American Politics;* Edward Jay Epstein, *News from Nowhere: Television and the News* (New York: Random House, 1973); Michael Parenti, *Inventing Reality: The Politics of News Media* (New York: St. Martin's Press, 1993); Herbert Gans, *Deciding What's News: A Study of CBS Evening News, NBC Nightly News, Newsweek and Time* (New York: Vintage Books, 1979); J. Herbert Altschull, *Agents of Power: The Media and Public Policy* (White Plains, N.Y.: Longman Publishers, 1994). A more philosophical approach is taken by John C. Merrill in *The Dialectic in Journalism: Toward a Responsible Use of Press Freedom* (Baton Rouge: Louisiana State University Press, 1989).

33. Graber, *Mass Media and American Politics,* pp. 20–21.

34. John Corry, "TV News and the Neutrality Principle," *Commentary,* May 1991, p. 24.

thought for a common "good." They claim a higher standard than libertarian journalists, openly advocating, for example, civil rights at home and human rights abroad. But they often wind up reflecting the public impulse of the moment, promoting, for example, a politically correct candidate like Jesse Jackson for president or Mikhail Gorbachev as the "Man of the Decade." Such social responsibility (relentlessly utilitarian and even relativistic) often degenerates into social correctness. Critics point out that journalists have not been given a public mandate to act as the arbiters of values and policies in our pluralistic society. Reporters and editors "lack the legitimacy," the media scholar Doris Graber says, that comes from being elected by the people or appointed by elected officials.[35]

Yet there is no denying the unique and celebrated position of journalists in American society. The First Amendment guarantees the media freedom and power unlike that accorded any other American institution. But the Founders hoped that the media would use their liberty and power prudently and toward the preservation of a constitutional republic. The First Amendment is not a license to make money, win Pulitzer Prizes, or form a fourth branch of government. The First Amendment is intended to protect the press from government censorship. It is there to ensure that the people will receive the information they need to make intelligent, reasoned decisions about their government and their politics. Madison affirmed that "a popular government without popular information, or the means of acquiring it, is but a prologue to a farce or a tragedy; or perhaps both. Knowledge will forever govern ignorance." Jefferson was equally emphatic about the connection between a free press and a free government, stating: "I am . . . for freedom of the press, and against all violations of the Constitution to silence by force and not by reason the complaints or criticism, just or unjust, of our citizens against the conduct of their agents."[36]

But the U.S. media of the last decade have too often blurred the lines between news and opinion, offered entertainment rather than information, and, in the words of Peter Kann, publisher of the *Wall Street Journal*, stressed the "bizarre, the perverse, and the pathological."[37] What is urgently needed as a corrective is a renewed emphasis on responsibility and ac-

35. Graber, *Mass Media and American Politics*, p. 24.

36. James Madison to W. T. Barry, August 4, 1822, in *The Writings of James Madison*, ed. Gaillard Hunt, vol. 9 (New York, 1904), p. 103; Thomas Jefferson to Elbridge Gerry, January 26, 1799, in *The Life and Selected Writings of Thomas Jefferson*, ed. Adrienne Koch and William Peden (New York: Modern Library, 1944), p. 545.

37. Sussman, "'Pressticide' and Press Ethics," p. 68.

countability among individual journalists and in journalism as a profession.

Individual responsibility stresses the virtues of wisdom, courage, justice, and, above all, prudence. It encourages reason rather than emotion in decision making. It rejects sound-bite explanations of complex problems and positions. Individual accountability leads a journalist to admit his mistakes readily and publicly. The British historian and former journalist Paul Johnson has proposed ten commandments for all who exercise media power and influence. The second commandment is that journalists always think through the consequences of their reporting, asking themselves: "What will legitimately inform and what will corrupt?"[38]

Institutional responsibility stresses duties as well as rights, order as well as liberty. It strengthens the constitutional framework that protects the rights of all citizens, including journalists. The media must act more responsibly, not only out of their own self-interest but for the good of the free society which guarantees their interests and those of every other citizen. Institutional accountability leads a media organization, for example, to establish the office of ombudsman and to offer its readers or viewers the opportunity to challenge publicly that organization's coverage, or lack of coverage, of an individual or event.

Responsibility and accountability vary from country to country. Protective of the First Amendment, U.S. courts have traditionally held that the freedom of the *print* media to determine what they will or will not publish is almost absolute (see *Miami Herald Publishing Company v. Tornillo*, 1974). Private citizens may ask to respond to an article or editorial but have no right to demand publication of their response. The public, however, has specific access rights to the electronic media as defined by Section 315 of the Communications Act of 1934. The act's equal-time provision requires broadcasters to give all candidates for the same political office equal opportunity to campaign on their stations. The right of rebuttal requires that an attack on the honesty, character, or integrity of an individual or group entitles the object of the attack to a reply.[39] The laws regarding the Internet are a work in progress, with some legal experts urging a libertarian approach, others one of social responsibility.

---

38. Paul Johnson, "Morality and the Mass Media" (address given at conference of the World Media Association, Seoul, South Korea, August 1992), excerpted in *Washington Times*, September 7, 1992.

39. Graber, *Mass Media and American Politics*, pp. 66–71.

In contrast, France has long had a law authorizing the right of reply in all mass media, and the Council of Europe has recommended its institution for its members. As it has on other questions, the U.S. Supreme Court could change its position on the right of reply, influenced by the renewed emphasis on the rights of states, several of which have mandated the right of reply. Such a wrenching reversal would probably not be necessary if the American media candidly acknowledged the widespread public dissatisfaction about them and took steps to improve their performance.

Yet, a 1995 survey by the Times Mirror Center for the People and the Press showed that most American journalists think they are doing a good job. When asked to consider the news media, journalists graded them fair to good, an average of C+. Younger journalists graded the news media, particularly television news, even higher than older journalists. Almost two out of three (64 percent) of those under thirty-five years of age graded network news "A/B."[40] Four years later, however, journalists were more willing to agree with public criticism of their profession and the quality of their work. Journalists shared the public's unease about the way they implemented their watchdog role. Some 45 percent of those in the national news media and 39 percent of those in the local media said that the press "drives controversies" with its intensive coverage of the personal and ethical behavior of public figures.[41]

Any reform of American journalism is difficult because of its sprawling, decentralized infrastructure—1,500 daily newspapers, 7,500 weekly newspapers, 12,000 magazines, 1,100 commercial TV stations, 360 noncommercial TV stations, over 11,000 cable TV systems, 11,000 radio stations, and 10,000 journalists in Washington alone.[42] There is also a professional divide between print and broadcast journalism. Perhaps because of their historical roots, print journalists are more often willing to criticize themselves than are broadcast journalists: while there are ombudsmen at about forty major daily newspapers in America, not one TV broadcast network has an ombudsman, although CBS's top-rated *60 Minutes,* for ex-

40. "The People, the Press & Their Leaders 1995," published by The Times Mirror Center for the People and the Press, Washington, May 1995, p. 18.

41. "Striking the Balance: Audience Interests, Business Pressures, and Journalists' Values," The Pew Research Center for the People and the Press, February 1999, p. 1 of section 1.

42. Herbert Strentz and Vernon Keel, "North America," in *Global Journalism: Survey of International Communication,* 3d ed., ed. John C. Merrill (White Plains, N.Y.: Longman Publishers, 1995), pp. 381–86; *TV and Cable Fact Book, Cable Volume* (Washington: Warren Publishing Co., 1998), introduction.

ample, frequently offers viewer reactions. But self-criticism, regardless of the medium, is tolerated only so far. When ABC News apologized on-air for erroneously stating (during its program *DayOne*) that Philip Morris "artificially spikes" and "fortifies" its cigarettes with nicotine, several journalists and media critics expressed concern about the "chilling effect" of the apology. "It sends the message," commented Jane Kirtley of the Reporters Committee for Freedom of the Press, "that corporate America can use a libel suit to discourage investigative reporting." Nearly drowned out among the cries of concern was the common sense reaction of Lawrence Grossman, the former president of NBC News, who said, "I think we ought to do a lot more of admitting when we're wrong."[43]

Attempts at reform also come up against the different perspectives of editor and reporter. Because of their gatekeeping responsibilities, editors are less libertarian and more socially conscious than reporters. And there are other important differences among journalists. Journalists in the larger metropolitan areas are usually more cynical (they prefer the word "sophisticated") than those in medium-sized markets. Because the economic stakes are often higher, television-network journalists are more apt to shape programming for dramatic impact in pursuit of high ratings than their colleagues at local TV stations. Given its diverse, multifaceted nature, American journalism, in the eyes of some critics, resembles not so much a Leviathan as a giant Medusa.

Still, for all the cynicism, there is a growing awareness among many journalists that something must be done about the media half of American *mediapolitik*. Emblematic is James Fallows's *Breaking the News*, in which the former editor of *U.S. News & World Report* says flatly that "the institution of journalism . . . is irresponsible with its power." The Pew Research Center's 1999 survey of journalists' attitudes about their profession revealed an increased willingness to admit shortcomings; most conceded they were "out of touch with the public."[44] Sydney H. Schanberg, who received a Pulitzer Prize for his coverage of the fall of Cambodia in 1975, has described American journalism as "slipshod" and "reckless." Every journalist, he wrote on the front page of the *Washington Post*'s "Outlook" sec-

43. "Apology Accepted," full-page advertisement published by Philip Morris Companies, *USA Today*, August 25, 1995; Alan Bash, "Media Reaction Mixed to ABC's Tobacco Apology," *USA Today*, August 23, 1995.

44. James Fallows, *Breaking the News: How the Media Undermine American Democracy* (New York: Pantheon Books, 1996), p. 9; "Striking the Balance," p. 2 of main summary.

tion, knows that "the old-time standards . . . have been weakened if not discarded."[45]

The responses of nearly one hundred leading reporters, editors, ombudsmen, and media critics to a survey by this author indicates that a more open, and urgent, attitude toward reform is forming in the U.S. mass media. The survey results are analyzed in detail in chapter 11, but among the more pertinent:

An overwhelming majority (72 percent) agree that "many" journalists have become cynical rather than skeptical in their coverage. As large a number (73 percent) agree that the media have "significantly" lowered standards in pursuit of greater circulation and higher ratings. And 87 percent state that there is a place for "moral" responsibility in modern journalism, as an antidote to cynicism and excessive skepticism,

Among the specific reforms endorsed by these leading journalists are a nongovernmental National Media Council, ombudsmen at all the TV networks, free TV time for all major political candidates, and more exacting standards for political advertisements. By a narrow margin (56 to 44 percent), the respondents reject restrictions on outside income for journalists.[46]

FREE VERSUS NOT FREE

Journalists in newly free countries have different problems from their compatriots in the United States and settled Western democracies—like staying alive. Vladislav Listyev, the director of Russian Public Television, was murdered in February 1995, the suspected victim of a "hit" by organized crime. Speculation about the motive for his death ranged from the network's planned banning of commercials to a struggle for control of its vast influence and resources, including the only television channel to reach all the former Soviet republics. "I believe," said Alexander Yakovlev, the board chairman of Ostankino, from which the new network was created, "that in the final analysis, this was a political assassination."[47] Russian

45. Sydney H. Schanberg, "The News No One Dares to Cover," *Washington Post*, August 29, 1999.

46. A three-page questionnaire was prepared and mailed by the author in April 1995 to approximately 200 leading American journalists. Ninety-five journalists responded from April through June 1995. See Appendix for the full text of the questionnaire and a tabulation of the responses.

47. Angela Charlton, "Russians Wonder Who's Next," *Washington Times*, March 3, 1995; Margaret Shapiro, "Yeltsin Fires Moscow's Police Chief, Prosecutor," *Washington Post*, March 3, 1995.

journalists openly wondered who would be next and pointed to the brutal murder, in October 1994, of Dmitry Kholodov, a newspaper reporter who was investigating army corruption. Fifteen journalists were killed in the former Soviet Union in 1994, five in Russia.[48] Five years later, the numbers had barely changed: four journalists were murdered in Russia, including Larisa Yudina, editor of the daily newspaper *Sovetskaya Kalmykia Segognya,* who was investigating allegations of embezzlement by the president of Kalmyk, Kirsan Ilyumzhinov.[49]

Such tragic incidents are likely to keep occurring in new democracies until tolerance toward opposing views and respect for the political process become commonplace. The development of such attitudes is difficult in formerly totalitarian societies where politics was a charade, and dissidence usually resulted in a one-way ticket to the Gulag. It will take years to build a lasting framework of democratic principles and practices in these once-Communist countries that will assure open politics and free media.

The process is complicated by the fact that the continuing struggle between government and media over the flow of information in partly free, and even in free, countries is so unevenly matched. The government has many more powerful weapons than the media. The media analyst Leonard R. Sussman has estimated that the state has eighty-seven different ways— physical, psychological, editorial, legal, and financial—through which to control the media. They range from assassination, banning, and jamming broadcasts to censorship, confiscation of facilities, and bribes. In contrast, the media have only nineteen ways to resist government pressure and maintain their independence. The media's "weapons" include the exposure of wrongdoing, denial of coverage to political figures, and setting the agenda.[50]

Journalists do have one other significant asset—each other. Journalists in established democracies can teach their newly free colleagues the need for tolerance, the importance of dissent, and the role of skepticism, not cynicism. Journalists in new democracies can remind Western reporters and editors not to take freedom for granted and to renew their sense of purpose and passion. Journalists in old and new democracies alike can acknowledge that freedom requires that man be responsible and accountable not simply to himself but to society. Both should acknowledge that

---

48. Sussman, " 'Pressticide' and Press Ethics," p. 64.
49. Paul Goble, "Victories and Defeats on the Media Front."
50. Sussman, *Power, the Press and the Technology of Freedom,* pp. 162–65.

the best *mediapolitik* is one in which politicians and journalists serve the people and each other in the cause of liberty.

WHAT KIND OF WORLD POLITICS?

The way the world works has changed because the mass media have changed not our nature, but the practice of our politics. People are much the same as they were in 500 B.C., 1776, or 1941, but the tools of communication are radically different. One man on television can make a difference, for good or for evil, around the world. The world has become not a global village in which the media foster a "common consciousness," as Marshall McLuhan once famously declared, but rather a *mediapolis*—a gigantic, sprawling global city with many different neighborhoods, rich, poor, or middle-class, safe or dangerous, handsome or ugly, in which the mass media provide competing and often contradictory images of society.[51] We cannot be absolutely certain whether the mass media will help produce a world politics modeled after George Orwell's *1984* or Thomas Jefferson's Declaration of Independence. It depends on the ends to which the media's unprecedented power is used. To understand the global politics of this century and to anticipate the politics of the next, we must study carefully the ever-increasing impact of *mediapolitik* on all of us.

This book offers case studies of the different models of *mediapolitik* around the world, led by the most influential media of all, the American mass media. Sometimes the government and the media compete democratically over the flow of information, as in the Persian Gulf War and Kosovo. Sometimes a government deliberately exercises media power to influence events and people's perceptions of events, as Beijing did after the massacre in Tiananmen Square. Sometimes media power slips loose of government control and helps to bring down a seemingly secure regime, as happened in the former Soviet Union. Sometimes external mass media influence the course of events, as in Poland and Czechoslovakia. Sometimes internal media make a profound difference in political outcomes, as in Chile and South Africa. But in every circumstance, in every nation, the mass media have become an indispensable part of world politics.

51. I am endebted to Lance Morrow for the image of "a global city," which he used in a *Time* essay about Sarajevo. See "The Ruin of a Cat, the Ghost of a Dog," *Time*, December 14, 1992, p. 38.

CHAPTER 1

THE MEDIA BECOME TRULY MASS

UNLIKE TRADITIONAL ELEMENTS of national power like economic resources and military strength, the mass media are a recent development in political history. Johann Gutenberg invented the letter press in the latter part of the fifteenth century, but there were no true "mass" media until the American and French Revolutions of the eighteenth century.

The two revolutions offer instructive contrasts in the vital role of the mass media, free and not free, in the practice of politics. Fiery Samuel Adams, America's first political journalist, declared: "There is nothing so fretting and vexatious, nothing so justly terrible to tyrants, and their tools and abettors, as a Free Press."[1] The Massachusetts Committee of Correspondence, headquartered in Boston under the direction of Adams, channeled a flow of essential information to the Sons of Liberty in every colony. Colonial newspapers were in the front lines of the Revolution, helping to produce the radical change in the "principles, opinions, sentiments, and affections" of the people that John Adams called "the real American Revolution."[2]

From 1765, when the hated Stamp Act was passed, to 1775, when the first shots were fired at Concord and Lexington, American newspapers led the struggle against British tyranny. They printed the names of those "Enemies to their Country" who imported outlawed British goods. British offi-

1. Samuel Adams, writing as "Populus," *Boston Gazette,* March 14, 1768.
2. John Adams to Hezekiah Niles, Feb. 13, 1818, in *The Works of John Adams,* ed. Charles Francis Adams (Boston, 1850–56), vol. 10, pp. 282–83.

cials and their supporters were described as "serpents," "guileful betray-
ers," "diabolical Tools of Tyrants," and "Men totally abandoned to Wicked-
ness." The Boston Tea Party was planned in the house of an editor of the
Boston Gazette. News coverage was politicized, with papers throughout
the colonies detailing the outrages of British troops, real and alleged. A
Son of Liberty wrote in the *Providence Gazette* that "the press hath never
done greater service since its first invention." In the pre-Revolutionary period, the media had essentially been controlled by government. Now the
people freely used the media to express opinions and disseminate information against government control. Half a million copies of Thomas
Paine's incendiary pamphlet *Common Sense* were sold in the thirteen
colonies, which had a total population of only three million. Equivalent
sales in today's America would be an astounding forty-two million. As
usual, Benjamin Franklin offered an appropriate epigram: The press not
only can "strike while the iron is hot," it can "heat it by continually striking."[3]

The colonial newspapers were not all rhetoric. They also provided reasoned arguments against the British attempts to control its wayward
colonies. John Dickinson, writing as the "Pennsylvania Farmer," pointed
out that the English Parliament had no legal right to impose the Towns-
hend Acts because their primary purpose was to raise revenue, not regulate imperial trade.[4]

In addition to galvanizing public opposition against an autocratic, arrogant British government, the American press helped produce a new national consciousness. On the eve of the Revolution, colonists thought of
themselves not only as citizens of New York, Virginia, or Pennsylvania, but
as "Americans." They felt they were Americans because of a conjunction of
democratic principles as enunciated by brilliant, dedicated leaders like
Samuel Adams, Patrick Henry, George Washington, Benjamin Franklin,
John Adams, James Madison, and Thomas Jefferson, and of an independent press committed to democratic principles. The profound influence of
the American press on the Revolution was also made possible by the failure of the British government to exercise strict control over the press, a
mistake the French monarchy was determined not to repeat.

3. Mitchell Stephens, *A History of News* (New York: Penguin Books, 1988), pp. 188–92; A.
J. Langguth, *Patriots: The Men Who Started the American Revolution* (New York: Simon and
Schuster, 1988), p. 341.

4. See Edwin Emery and Henry Ladd Smith, *The Press in America* (New York: Prentice-
Hall, 1954), pp. 95–98; also Arthur M. Schlesinger, *Prelude to Independence: The Newspaper
War on Britain, 1764–1776* (Boston: Northeastern University Press, 1980), pp. 87–90.

CONTENTED AND CORRUPT

French newspapers were among the most sophisticated in the world, inspired by the words of Voltaire: "It is as much a natural right to use one's pen as it is to use one's tongue."[5] They were also among the most controlled in the world. Licensed by the king, they were forbidden on penalty of death to attack religion, infringe on the authority of the government, or disturb public order and tranquillity. In vivid contrast to the American press's abiding concern about the future of a young nation, the French press was most interested in its own future. Louis XVI maintained a corps of contented, corrupt journalists who reported only favorable news in the official press—even omitting any mention of the storming of the Bastille when it occurred on July 14, 1789. Having no principles, democratic or otherwise, these journalists cynically traded independence for security, and wound up with neither.

On the other hand, as the historian Simon Schama points out, Versailles shops openly sold the most subversive publications, including Rousseau's *Confessions* and the London muckraking sheet *English Spy*. And the King's own younger brother was said to protect professional sellers of seditious materials. Such practices validate Alexis de Tocqueville's view that the Old Regime helped to bring about its own undoing by flirting with ideas it found diverting but only half understood.[6]

The result of this uneven government control was a frustrated public that rejected what it read in the official press and depended, in large part, on an angry underground press *(libelles)* that was so antisociety it even alarmed the iconoclastic Voltaire. "There has just appeared," he wrote, "one of those satanic works where everyone from the monarch to the last citizen is insulted with furor, where the most atrocious and most absurd calumny spreads a horrible poison on everything one respects and loves."[7] The violent rhetoric of the *libelles* undoubtedly contributed to the violent nature of the French Revolution. Like the revolution itself, the revolutionary French press ran roughshod over anyone who got in its way. The bloody results of the French Revolution confirm that the media, if they are to contribute to the furtherance of representative government and dem-

5. Stephens, *A History of News*, p. 193.

6. Simon Schama, *Citizens: A Chronicle of the French Revolution* (New York: Alfred A. Knopf, 1989), pp. 174–75.

7. Robert Darnton, *The Literary Underground of the Old Regime* (Cambridge, Mass.: Harvard University Press, 1982), p. 36.

ocracy, must practice self-discipline and moral as well as social responsibility.

Because of France's well-maintained network of canals and rivers, the *libelles* were read not only in Paris but in Lyon, Rouen, Marseilles, and Bordeaux. Their impact was heightened by the fact that the rate of literacy in late eighteenth-century France was high, reportedly higher than in early twentieth-century America. Whatever their location and social and economic station, French citizens became united in "their scorn of the ostentation of the mighty, passionate in their patriotism and enraged at the abuses of despotism."[8] They were ripe for revolution and revolutionary ideas. "It was not want," wrote de Tocqueville, "but ideas, that brought about that great revolution."[9]

Writing from exile in Switzerland, Louis-Sebastien Mercier, an apostle of Rousseau, saw royal France rushing toward its doom and declared with satisfaction: "In two minutes the work of centuries would be overturned. Palaces and houses destroyed, churches overturned, their vaults torn asunder."[10] Having no respect for the past and little understanding of the present, the French radicals waged all on the future. The French press, once the lapdog of the king, allowed itself to be taken over by revolutionaries and then controlled by anarchists who destroyed first the monarchy, then the republic, and finally themselves.

Ironically, the revolution that brought down the Old Regime was caused, in part, by false news. The crowd that marched on the Bastille was inspired by an erroneous report that thirty thousand royalist troops were about to march on Paris. Outside Paris, country people heard exaggerated accounts of riots and destruction in the towns and assumed mistakenly that armies of brigands would soon descend on them. The Great Fear of the summer of 1789, which spread the revolution to the countryside, was created by the lack of reliable information and by the absence of authority at the heart of the French government.[11]

But the most important difference between the two revolutions lay in their goals. The American Revolution was an orderly transition to a new form of government rather than a violent break with the past social order. It sought freedom rooted in law rather than a tyranny subject to the im-

8. Schama, *Citizens*, pp. 181–82.
9. Alexis de Tocqueville, *The Old Regime and the French Revolution*, trans. John Bonner (New York: Doubleday, 1955), p. viii.
10. Schama, *Citizens*, pp. 198–99.
11. Stephens, *A History of News*, pp. 196–97; Schama, *Citizens*, pp.401, 432–34.

pulse of the moment. It guaranteed the concrete rights of property rather than the abstract rights of man. The American Revolution was a rational revolution. It "was caused by a mature and thoughtful taste for freedom," wrote de Tocqueville, "not by some vague, undefined instinct for independence. . . . No disorderly passion drove it on; on the contrary, it proceeded hand in hand with a love of order and legality."[12]

In contrast, the French Revolution quickly turned irrational because it flowed from an unbridled passion for independence that rejected all inhibitions. The American press contributed significantly to the success of the American Revolution by respecting inalienable rights like life, liberty, and property, while the French press quickened the demise of the French Revolution by promoting utopian notions like the perfectability of man, total democracy, and collectivism. The essential distinction between the American and French Revolutions was repeated in the twentieth century in the protracted conflict between freedom and democracy on the one hand and fascism and communism on the other.

THE FIRST AMENDMENT

The Founders of the American Republic had a classical concept of democracy based on the notion that the power to govern and to decide political issues rested in the people. They believed that citizens can discover and maintain a common good through rational argument and debate. In this view of democracy, the media played a key role as middlemen between the government and the governed. The Founders essentially agreed with Jefferson when he wrote: "Were it left to me to decide whether we should have a government without newspapers, or newspapers without a government, I should not hesitate to prefer the latter."[13]

Included in the First Amendment of the Constitution was the unprecedented pledge: "Congress shall make no law . . . abridging the freedom of speech, or of the press," which made the American media the freest in the world. But what did the Founders mean by "freedom of the press"?

James Madison's original draft of the First Amendment, as offered in

12. Martin Diamond, *The Revolution of Sober Expectations* (Washington: American Enterprise Institute, 1974), p. 11.

13. For an excellent discussion of the media's "middleman" role, see Gary Orren, "Thinking about the Press and Government," in *Impact: How the Press Affects Federal Policymaking,* by Martin Linsky (New York: W. W. Norton & Company, 1986), p. 7; Thomas Jefferson to Edward Carrington, January 16, 1787, as quoted in Saul K. Padover, *Thomas Jefferson on Democracy* (New York: Penguin Books, 1939), pp. 92–93.

the first Congress of 1789, was unqualified: "The people shall not be deprived or abridged of their right to speak, to write, or to publish their sentiments; and the freedom of the press, as one of the great bulwarks of liberty, shall be inviolable." He intended that such freedoms be protected against state as well as federal action, adding, "No state shall violate equal rights of conscience, or the freedom of the press, or the trial by jury in criminal cases."[14] As adopted by the House of Representatives, the amendment read, "the equal rights of conscience, the freedom of speech or of the press, and the right of trial by jury in criminal cases, shall not be infringed by any state." To Madison's disappointment, the Senate struck out the provision restricting the power of the states, a move in which the House later concurred.[15]

The Founders, however, did not believe that freedom of speech and the press should be absolute, either in promise or practice. They accepted the traditional English law based on Blackstone that freedom of the press meant freedom from prior restraint and that the press was subject to the same laws as everyone else—i.e., to penalties for criminal libel. During a Pennsylvania debate on ratifying the Constitution, James Wilson said that "what is meant by the liberty of the press is that there should be no antecedent restraint upon it; but that every author is responsible when he attacks the security or welfare of the government, or the safety, character and property of the individual." Leonard Levy, a political scientist, has described the Founders' position as "an unbridled passion for a bridled liberty of speech."[16] A clever phrase, but to put it more prosaically the authors of the First Amendment were practical men who sought balance and prudence in all things, including freedom of speech and of the press.

A decade later, following the passage of the controversial Alien and Sedition Acts of 1798, a much more liberal, even libertarian, theory of speech and press ultimately emerged. The acts were said to be designed to protect the country against alien opinion and aliens themselves. The Sedition Act, for example, did not forbid criticism of the government, "only" malicious and false statements that defamed officials. The historians Ed-

14. James Madison to Edmund Randolph, May 31, 1789, in *The Writings of James Madison*, ed. Gaillard Hunt, vol. 5 (New York, 1904), p. 377.

15. Edward G. Hudon, *Freedom of Speech and Press in America* (Washington: Public Affairs Press, 1963), p. 6.

16. Walter Berns, *The First Amendment and the Future of American Democracy* (New York: Basic Books, 1976), p. 84; Leonard W. Levy, *Legacy of Suppression: Freedom of Speech and Press in Early American History* (Cambridge, Mass.: Harvard University Press, 1960), p. 105.

win Emery and Henry Ladd Smith ask, "Why *should* an editor be allowed to defame public figures, thereby discouraging decent men and women from assuming civic responsibilities in their communities?"[17] It is a question relevant in our own times, when the mass media are so prone to feeding frenzies in their coverage of public figures.

Aside from serious questions of constitutionality, the Alien and Sedition Acts lent themselves to prejudicial administration. Reacting to the bitter rhetoric generated by the Jay Treaty of 1794 (a treaty of peace with England which did not, however, stop the British practice of impressing American seamen) and the XYZ Affair (a scandal provoked by French Foreign Minister Talleyrand, who informed U.S. diplomats he would receive them as accredited ministers only after they had paid him a bribe), the Federalists, led by John Adams, unwisely used the acts to silence their Republican opponents, led by Jefferson. There was deliberate provocation on both sides. Not even the unrestrained tabloid journalism of the 1990s matched the venom and vitriol of the 1790s press. Benjamin Franklin Bache, William Duane, and James Callender wielded the poison pens for the Republicans (who later became the Democrats), while William Cobbett and John Ward Fenno responded in kind for the Federalists. Callender called George Washington and John Adams "poltroons" and "venal." And he described President Adams as a "libeller" whose "hands are reeking with the blood of the poor, friendless Connecticut sailor," a liar whose office was a "scene of profligacy and . . . usury," and a "hoary headed incendiary" whose purpose was to "embroil this country [in a war] with France." Cobbett called his Republican opponents "the refuse of nations" and "frog-eating, man-eating, blood drinking cannibals."[18]

The Alien and Sedition Acts were soon denounced in resolutions adopted by the Virginia and Kentucky legislatures and written, respectively, by Madison and Jefferson. The two resolutions emphasized the central role of a free press in a democracy and declared that the press must be free from legislative as well as prior restraint. Blackstone's definition of a free press was not appropriate to the United States. There was an essential difference between the British government and the American Constitution that necessitated "a different degree of freedom in the use of the press." Because in the United States the people, "not the government, possess the absolute sovereignty," it was necessary to secure "the great and essential right of the people . . . against legislative as well as executive ambition." Free-

17. Emery and Smith, *The Press in America*, p. 156.
18. Walter Berns, *The First Amendment*, p. 87.

dom of speech and of press were accorded constitutional protection because they are essential elements of the process whereby the people choose the members of the government. And "the right of electing the members of the government constitutes . . . the essence of a free and responsible government."[19] In a report to the Virginia General Assembly justifying the original resolution, Madison wrote:

This security of the freedom of the press requires that it should be exempt, not only from previous restraint of the executive, as in Great Britain; but from legislative restraint also; and this exemption, to be effectual, must be an exemption, not only from the previous inspection of licensers, but from the subsequent penalty of laws.[20]

Going far beyond the little he had said at the time of the Constitutional Convention and subsequently, Madison now declared that "no power whatever over the press was supposed to be delegated by the Constitution" and that the First Amendment "was intended as a positive and absolute reservation" of the freedom of the press. Conceding that there would be abuses of this freedom by the press, Madison nevertheless declared that "it is better to leave a few of its noxious branches to this luxuriant growth, than, by pruning them away, to injure the vigor of those yielding the proper fruits."[21] The wisdom of such a policy, he argued, had been proved by the many contributions of the press to the creation of the United States as "a free and independent nation." Had there been Sedition Acts a decade or two earlier, he said, might not the United States now be languishing "under the infirmities of a sickly Confederation" or "groaning under a foreign yoke?"[22]

At the same time, Madison made it clear that he and other Republicans opposed the acts because the limits on the freedom of political speech were imposed by the national rather than the state government. As Jefferson later wrote to Abigail Adams: "While we deny that Congress has a right to control the freedom of the press, we have ever asserted the right of the states and their exclusive right to do so."[23]

19. James Madison, *Writings*, vol. 6, pp. 387–88.

20. Marvin Meyers, ed., *The Mind of the Founder: Sources of the Political Thought of James Madison* (Hanover, Mass.: Brandeis University Press, 1981), p. 257.

21. Ibid., pp. 261, 259.

22. Ibid., p. 259.

23. Thomas Jefferson to Abigail Adams, September 4, 1804, in *Writings of Thomas Jefferson*, ed. Paul Leicester Ford (New York: G. P. Putnam's Sons, 1892–99), vol. 10, p. 90.

The Virginia Report became the classic statement of the Republican opposition to the Alien and Sedition Acts and led to a new libertarian interpretation of the First Amendment that would flourish in the next century. Because it emphasized the constitutional means of "interposition" open to the states, the report would also be used by proponents of states' rights and nullification in the pre–Civil War period. For all the sound and fury they generated, the Sedition Acts were not repealed but simply lapsed at the end of the two-year limitation period.

Levy argues that the new theory regarding freedom of the press encouraged "absolute freedom of political expression" and laid down the principle that only "injurious conduct" as manifested by "overt acts" or deeds should be criminally liable. It reinforced the idea that free government "depends for its very existence and security on freedom of political discourse."[24] It is intrinsic to a republican government that its public servants be of the highest conduct and character and that a press point out, without fear of reprisal, any and all derelictions by those servants.

But the First Amendment is not, as many modern journalists seem to think, a one-way street—all liberty and no accountability. True republican government requires journalists who take their responsibilities as citizens as seriously as do public servants. St. George Tucker, a prominent Jeffersonian, stated that a reporter "is bound to adhere strictly to the truth. . . . In his strictures on the conduct of men, in public stations, he is bound to do justice to their characters, and not to criminate them without substantial reason. The right of character is a sacred and invaluable right, and is not forfeited by accepting a public employment."[25] The Americans of the founding generation were not radical libertarians, the political scientist Walter Berns points out: they well understood the difference between liberty and licentiousness. While they agreed that "freedom of discussion and the law of libel [inherited from Britain] were simply incompatible," they insisted that freedom of discussion and a law that provided for the punishment of the libel of public officials were not incompatible.[26]

Although there is no extended discussion by the Founders of the functions of a free press, the Continental Congress did address the issue in the period leading up to the Declaration of Independence. In the Quebec

24. Levy, *Legacy of Suppression*, pp. lxxv–lxxvi.
25. St. George Tucker, ed., *Blackstone's Commentaries: With Notes of Reference to the Constitution and Laws of the Federal Government of the United States; and of the Commonwealth of Virginia* (Philadelphia, 1803), vol. 1, pp. 29–30.
26. Berns, *The First Amendment*, pp. 144–45.

Statement of 1774, the Congress, whose members included George Washington, Patrick Henry, Samuel Adams, and John Adams, discussed the importance of the press as the principled middleman between the people and their government:

The last right we shall mention regards the freedom of the press. The importance of this consists, besides the advancement of truth, science, morality and arts in general, in its diffusion of liberal sentiments on the administration of government, in ready communication of thoughts between subjects, and in its consequential promotion of union among them, whereby oppressive officials are shamed or intimidated into more honorable and just modes of conducting affairs.[27]

The intent of the Founders was clear: Freedom of the press is an essential condition of republican government, imposing responsibilities as well as rights. It requires journalists who practice prudence rather than prurience, ensure liberty rather than licentiousness, exhibit courage rather than compromise, and seek justice rather than personal or political gain. Because of the power and privilege they enjoy under the First Amendment, American journalists must be held to the highest, not the lowest, standards of citizenship.

Alexis de Tocqueville, who visited America in the 1830s, referred, in his classic work, *Democracy in America,* to "the inestimable benefits that the liberty of the press ensures." He gave the following reasons for the press's "immense" influence on public opinion and politics:

It causes political life to circulate through all the parts of that vast territory. Its eye is constantly open to detect the secret springs of political designs and to summon the leaders of all parties in turn to the bar of public opinion. It rallies the interests of the community round certain principles and draws up the creed of every party; for it affords a means of intercourse between those who hear and address each other without ever coming into immediate contact. When many organs of the press adopt the same line of conduct, their influence in the long run becomes irresistible, and public opinion, perpetually assailed from the same side, eventually yields to the attack. In the United States each separate journal exercises but little authority; but the power of the periodical press is second only to that of the people.[28]

27. "To the Inhabitants of the Province of Quebec," October 24, 1774, in *Journals of the Continental Congress, 1774–1789,* ed. Worthington Chauncey Ford et al., vol. 1 (Washington: U.S. Government Printing Office, 1904), p. 108.

28. Alexis de Tocqueville, *Democracy in America,* vol. 1 (New York: Vintage Books, 1945), pp. 192, 195.

De Tocqueville perceived that despite its frequent coarseness and tendency toward license, the American press played an essential role in American democracy, being the main provider of information to the people about their politics and government. "When the right of every citizen to a share in the government of society is acknowledged," he wrote, "everyone must be presumed to be able to choose between the various opinions of his contemporaries and to appreciate the different facts from which inferences may be drawn. The sovereignty of the people and the liberty of the press may therefore be regarded as correlative."[29] The French political philosopher was restating the conviction of the Founders that the press should be an honest broker of information, providing the people with the facts about the actions of their government and elected representatives, and should also be a vigilant watchdog of the same government and representatives, calling immediate attention to errors, excesses, or illegal acts. In so doing, the press acts in the national interest as well as its own self-interest, seeking to preserve a free and democratic society as well as a free and responsible press. De Tocqueville believed that "the principle of self-interest rightly understood" was the best suited of all philosophical theories to "our time" because it disciplined people in "habits of regularity, temperance, moderation, foresight, self-command"—habits that are unevenly cultivated in much of the modern mass media.[30]

THE TOTALITARIAN PRINCIPLE

At the dawn of the twentieth century, the Russian revolutionary Vladimir Lenin began applying totalitarian politics to the mass media. In the first issues of his new newspaper, *Iskra (The Spark)*, published in December 1900, Lenin defined a revolutionary newspaper as "an organization ready at any time to support every protest and every outbreak and use it to build up and consolidate the fighting forces suitable for the decisive struggle." He declared: "A newspaper is not only a collective propagandist and a collective agitator, it is also a collective organizer."[31]

Unwilling to wait patiently for the "inevitable" triumph of communism as outlined by Karl Marx, Lenin stated that mass movements must be pro-

29. Ibid., p. 190.

30. Ibid., vol. 2, pp. 129–32.

31. Vladimir Lenin, *Collected Works*, vol. 5 (Moscow: Foreign Languages Publishing House, 1961), p. 23. For an extended analysis of Lenin's views about the press by a sympathetic observer, see J. Herbert Altschull, *Agents of Power: The Media and Public Policy* (White Plains, N.Y.: Longman, 1995), pp. 209–23.

moted, especially through the mass media. He asserted that the ideas behind the media are more important than the media themselves. Reporters
and editors should be "professional revolutionaries who will give not their
spare evenings but the whole of their lives" to political organizing that will
reshape all of human society. With such a cadre, Lenin promised, more
than a decade before the October Revolution of 1917, "I will turn Russia
upside down."[32]

The mutiny of the Russian army and the uprising of the peasants during the autumn of 1917 paralyzed but did not overthrow the Provisional
Government headed by Kerensky. The final blow was struck by some three
million city workers on whom the Bolsheviks had concentrated their revolutionary propaganda from the beginning. Lenin personally wrote and
had distributed to local Bolshevik Party organizations and the Petrograd
and Moscow Party committees dozens of letters, messages, and pamphlets
that set forth the Bolshevik program and rebutted the arguments of the
opposition. The key battleground was Petrograd (now St. Petersburg),
within which the Bolsheviks distributed specialized newspapers like *Worker's Road* and *Soldier* as well as the national Party newspaper, *Pravda*.
Every edition was emblazoned with the bold slogan: "Peace, land to the
peasants, workers' control in industry, all power to the Soviets." William
Henry Chamberlin wrote in his classic study of the Russian Revolution:

This nationwide sweep of Bolshevism did not mean that a hundred and fifty million people of various races and languages had suddenly been converted to the
ideas that more or less clearly animated the 300,000 organized Bolsheviki of that
time. . . . But the magic of the slogan "Peace and Land" was sufficient for the time
being to carry the Soviet banner triumphantly from the factory quarters of Petrograd to the rolling steppes of Ukraina to the Far Eastern port of Vladivostok.[33]

In a brilliant application of totalitarian *mediapolitik,* Lenin used the
Bolshevik-controlled media outside the Kerensky government to bring
down the government. Once he assumed power, Lenin turned around and
used the government to control the media and the media to control the
government. One of his first acts was to publish a decree that any newspa-

32. For further discussion of *Iskra* and Lenin's famous pamphlet, *What Is to Be Done?*
see Bertram D. Wolfe's definitive *Three Who Made a Revolution* (New York: The Dial Press,
1948), pp. 156–60, and Eugene Methvin, *The Riot Makers* (New Rochelle, N.Y.: Arlington
House, 1970), pp. 125–29.

33. William Henry Chamberlin, *The Russian Revolution: 1917–1921* (New York: Grosset &
Dunlap, 1935), p. 350.

per "calling for open resistance or insubordination to the Workers' or Peasants' Government" or "sowing sedition through demonstrably slanderous distortions of fact" would be suppressed and their editors put on trial.[34] Management of the news, carefully selected to advance the Bolshevik cause, was given primarily to Party-controlled organs like *Pravda* and *Isvestia*.

As Jeffrey Brooks, a historian of Russia, has written, the Bolsheviks did two things with their newspapers: they reiterated, in excruciating detail, their successes in governing and problem solving for themselves and their followers, and they concealed and distorted the wider social world—to produce, by the end of the 1920s, "a grandiose system of public lying."[35]

For Lenin, the guiding principle of the totalitarian model of *mediapolitik* was the same as that of Marxism-Leninism: any means is permissible in order to seize and maintain power. Lenin held high the banner of "the dictatorship of the proletariat," but reserved for the Bolshevik Party the exclusive leadership of the proletariat. For Lenin, the political historian Bertram D. Wolfe wrote, centralism was "a revolutionary virtue per se for all lands and all circumstances of struggle."[36] Lenin called his absolutist doctrine "democratic centralism," but it was as far removed from democracy as the Kremlin was from the White House.

THE HISTORIC DIVIDING LINE

World War I was the dividing line between the old age of print media and the new age of electronic media. Before the guns of August 1914 began firing, national leaders essentially depended upon personal couriers, the postal service and the telegraph, and newspapers to communicate with each other and the public. Shortly after the signing of the Treaty of Versailles in 1920, diplomats and politicians began to realize that it was possible to communicate directly with the people—through radio.

During World War I, both the Allies and the Germans circulated military claims and political arguments to the rest of the world, but news from Berlin had to travel through London because the British had cut the German Atlantic cable shortly after the war began. German attempts to use

34. Paul Johnson, *Modern Times: The World from the Twenties to the Eighties* (New York: Harper & Row, 1990), pp. 64–65.

35. Jeffrey Brooks, "*Pravda* and the Language of Power in Soviet Russia, 1917–28," in *Media and Revolution*, ed. Jeremy D. Popkin (Lexington: University of Kentucky Press, 1995), p. 157.

36. Wolfe, *Three Who Made a Revolution*, p. 259.

the wireless for news transmission were relatively unsuccessful. The United States and other nations depended for most of their news and information upon English newspapers, which were censored under the Defense of the Realm Act. Even in the land of the Magna Carta, the public had only a limited right to know during wartime.

The unfolding course of events in Europe (like the sack of Louvain and the near encirclement of Paris) strengthened pro-Allied sentiment in the United States, which began to see the war as a historic conflict between Western democracy and German authoritarianism. A decisive event was the German torpedoing of the English ship *Lusitania* in May 1915, with the loss of 1,198 of the 1,924 persons on board, including 114 Americans. When Germany publicly celebrated the victory of its U-boat captain, many American newspapers, civic leaders, and groups that had previously been neutral joined the Allied side.

The sinking of three American ships by German U-boats in March 1917 brought President Woodrow Wilson's ringing call, "The world must be made safe for democracy," and the declaration of war on April 6. Wilson demonstrated frequently during his presidency that he was a master of rhetoric. His denunciation of eleven U.S. Senators who filibustered against the arming of merchant ships in early March as "a little group of willful men" effectively discredited the isolationist arguments of opponents of the war.[37]

Pragmatic as well as idealistic, Wilson initiated a system of what might be called democratic censorship. One week after the war began, he appointed the Committee on Public Information. The committee's functions were to disseminate facts about the war, coordinate government propaganda efforts, and serve as the government's liaison with newspapers. George Creel, the newspaperman appointed to head the committee, candidly explained that "it was a plain publicity proposition, a vast enterprise in salesmanship, the world's greatest adventure in advertising."[38] It was also an explicit acknowledgment of the critical importance of the mass media in the science of war.

Consistent with the Madisonian argument that the people will more enthusiastically support that which they understand, Creel worked hard to open up government channels to correspondents. He insisted that only news of troop movements, ship sailings, and other events of a strictly mil-

37. Emery and Smith, *The Press in America*, pp. 583–86.
38. George Creel, *How We Advertised America* (New York: Harper & Brothers, 1920), p. 4.

itary nature should be withheld by government offices. In a telling demonstration of liberal democratic *mediapolitik,* he published a code calling on newspapers to censor such news themselves, voluntarily. What was needed, said Creel, was not censorship or suppression of news but "unparalleled openness" about the mighty accomplishments of the United States, "the arsenal of democracy."[39]

The Wilson administration used the dissemination of news as a basic weapon to achieve their propaganda objectives: the mobilization of the American people against the enemy, the preservation of the friendship and morale of America's allies, the winning over of neutral nations and peoples, and the demoralization of the enemy.[40] In May 1917, the Committee on Public Information began publishing the *Official Bulletin,* in which information about the war was reprinted in newspaper form; before the war ended, the bulletin reached a daily circulation of 118,000. A historian who studied the accuracy of committee information noted how remarkable it was that, "of the more than 6,000 news stories it issued, so few were called into question at all. It may be doubted that the CPI's record for honesty will ever be equalled in the official war news of a major power."[41]

The exemplary record of the Committee on Public Information during World War I shows that even in wartime, it is possible for the liberal democratic model of *mediapolitik* to serve both the interests of the people and the government. Further proof that formal government censorship was an instrument of last resort was provided by the Wilson administration's hands-off treatment of the Hearst newspapers, which bitterly opposed U.S. entry into the war and continued to be anti-Ally, although they supported the American war effort itself. Former President Theodore Roosevelt, a fiery supporter of the war, demanded to know why the Hearst papers were not denied mail privileges. But the government took no action against William Randolph Hearst, the king of the yellow journalists, content to leave the rebuttal to other newspapers like the *New York Tribune,* which published a cartoon showing a snake coiled in the flag, with the snake's body spelling the word, "Hears-ss-ss-t."[42]

39. Emery and Smith, *The Press in America,* p. 588.

40. Ibid., p. 588.

41. Walton E. Bean, "The Accuracy of Creel Committee News, 1917–1919: An Examination of Cases," *Journalism Quarterly* 18 (September 1941): 272.

42. Emery and Smith, *The Press in America,* p. 594.

THE OTHER TOTALITARIAN

Following the war, Adolf Hitler used the new medium of radio and practiced his totalitarian brand of *mediapolitik* more effectively than any other dictator of the 1920s and 1930s. That Hitler was an admirer and imitator of Leninism is clear from a study of Lenin's classic work, *What Is To Be Done?* and the Nazi leader's *Mein Kampf.* In *Mein Kampf,* Hitler admits that he carefully studied the propaganda and mass demonstration techniques of the Viennese radicals whose members formed the Austrian Communist Party: "I saw that the Marxist Socialists had mastered and applied the propaganda instrument with astounding skill. And I soon realized that the correct use of propaganda is a true art which has remained practically unknown to the bourgeois parties."[43] Like Lenin, Hitler viewed the media as a means of propaganda, not as a forum for debate or a provider of information to the German people.

In many respects, Nazism and Leninism were Janus-like, similar in their dependence on a centralized political structure and on constant agitation and propaganda, differing most radically in the main object of their hostility: "the Jew" for the Nazi, "the capitalist" for the Communist. In *Mein Kampf,* Hitler lauds the Leninists of Germany, signaling his future intention to use their tactics:

What has won the millions of workers for Marxism is . . . the indefatigable and truly enormous propaganda work of tens of thousands of untiring agitators, from the great agitator down to the small trade-union official and the shop steward and discussion speaker. . . . It consisted, furthermore, in the gigantic mass demonstrations . . . which burned into the small, wretched individual the proud conviction that, paltry worm as he was, he was nevertheless a part of a great dragon, beneath whose burning breath the hated bourgeois would some day go up in fire and flame and the proletarian dictatorship would celebrate its ultimate final victory.[44]

Each year from 1923 to 1939 the Nazis staged huge rallies for as many as 500,000 people who marched and celebrated and pledged their loyalty to Nazism and the man whose inflammatory oratory lifted them out of themselves. "Doctrine, ceremony and ritual," wrote the American diplomat Adolph A. Berle, "were employed to bind men to a single leader and to a common cause."[45] Hitler was the first politician to maximize the use

43. Methvin, *The Riot Makers*, p. 162.
44. Adolf Hitler, *Mein Kampf* (Boston: Houghton Mifflin, 1943), pp. 472–73.
45. Adolf A. Berle, preface to *The Nuremberg Party Rallies: 1923–39*, by Hamilton T. Burden (New York: Praeger, 1968).

of electronic amplification at mass rallies. The largest crowd for any of the Lincoln-Douglas debates in 1858 was twenty thousand, the upper limit that the unaided human voice can reach. In 1932, Hitler addressed a crowd of 120,000 inside a Berlin stadium while another 100,000 outside heard his voice by loudspeakers and millions more listened by radio. Film was also used brilliantly by the Nazis, most notably in the hypnotic *Triumph of the Will*, directed by Leni Riefenstahl. Combining music, photography, and myth, the film portrayed in documentary style *der Fuhrer* and his party as political saviors of Germany.

Hitler did not overlook the importance of the press in so literate and educated a country as Germany. Although traditionally among the most independent and prosperous in Europe, German newspapers and magazines were experiencing grave weaknesses by the early 1930s, including economic foundations seriously eroded by the Depression; growing influence by special interest groups, political and economic; a serious rift between reporters and publishers that blocked cooperation; and a sharp reduction of press freedom by emergency decrees of pre-Hitler governments that too often saw newspapers as a threat to rather than a guarantor of freedom.

Hitler, for his part, saw the press as a guarantor of political power. In the revolutionary period that began with Hitler's appointment as chancellor, the historian Oron J. Hale points out, the working press was one of the first bodies to be "cleansed," coordinated, and subjected to state control through Joseph Goebbels and his Ministry of Propaganda.[46]

A totalitarian system must control all means of mass communication. In the Soviet Union, the press became a part of the state and the Party; in Fascist Italy, the journalists were organized in a state-controlled union subservient to the political regime. In Nazi Germany, journalists were controlled and the property of publishers was absorbed in order to employ the press for propaganda and as an instrument of social control and integration. Representative democracy depends upon an informed electorate with easy access to information about its government's activities; it requires an open society. Totalitarian systems, like the Soviet Union and Nazi Germany, require a regulated people with controlled access to information about their government; they demand a closed society.

46. Oron J. Hale, *The Captive Press in the Third Reich* (Princeton: Princeton University Press, 1964), p. 13.

THE DEMOCRATIC MODEL

Democratic as well as totalitarian leaders used the mass media in the 1930s, but with vastly different objectives in mind. In March 1933, President Franklin D. Roosevelt, newly inaugurated, closed the nation's banks to prevent a run on them. Just before reopening the banks, he delivered a speech to the American people to assure them that their savings were safe. He decided to use radio for his message, which was described by the CBS announcer who introduced the president as a "fireside chat."

Just as the Founders used the press to communicate directly with the people about the American Revolution, so Roosevelt used radio to talk directly to the American public about the Great Depression. Unlike Hitler, who spewed anger and hatred to bring out the worst in the German people, Roosevelt exuded confidence and optimism that brought out the best in the American people. Hitler was heir to the French Revolution and its Reign of Terror; Roosevelt was heir to the American Revolution and its commitment to freedom and equality. Roosevelt inspired confidence in his listeners when he said: "Let us unite in banishing fear. . . . It is your problem no less than it is mine. Together we cannot fail."[47] Roosevelt, with his dynamic, vibrant voice, was a masterful communicator with the people and the press. During his presidency, Roosevelt held almost a thousand press conferences, although none of them was carried by radio. His special communications weapon was the radio address, which enabled him to speak directly to the American people, without interpretation, comment, or analysis by anyone else. He shrewdly rationed them for maximum impact, giving only thirty "fireside chats" during his thirteen years in office, an average of just one radio address every five months.[48]

Winston Churchill was not the first European leader to exploit the possibilities of radio—Hitler had been manipulating the medium even before he became chancellor in 1933. But Churchill was the first democratic statesman of Europe to reach people in their homes and to move them as deeply as Roosevelt did in his radio talks. The impact of the British leader's words was strengthened by the fact that they were uttered during wartime. Until he entered the war cabinet, Churchill's audiences had been

47. Robert E. Sherwood, *Roosevelt and Hopkins* (New York: Harper & Brothers, 1948), p. 43.
48. Edward Bliss, Jr., *Now the News: The Story of Broadcast Journalism* (New York: Columbia University Press, 1991), pp. 50–52.

limited to Parliament, lecture halls, and political rallies. But with Great Britain at war, William Manchester recounts, millions now heard "his rich voice, resonant with urgency, dramatically heightened by his tempo, pauses, and crashing consonants which, one listener wrote, actually made his radio vibrate."[49] After the fall of Poland, when Hitler told the Western democracies to choose between a negotiated peace with him or "the views of Churchill and his following," British Prime Minister Neville Chamberlain gave the official response, but England heard Churchill's reply on radio.

In May 1940, barely one week after he was named prime minister and while the Nazi blitzkreig was slashing across France toward a panic-filled Paris, Churchill decided to reassure an anxious nation over the British Broadcasting Corporation. Using something close to blank verse, he told the country that he had formed a unique government:

> We have differed and quarreled in the past;
> but now one bond unites us all—
> to wage war until victory is won,
> and never to surrender ourselves to servitude and shame,
> whatever the cost and agony may be.[50]

A month later, when France was close to falling and newspapers were wondering whether England might also quit, Churchill again took to the airwaves to vow, in that indomitable voice that was to become so familiar to the world, that Britain, if necessary, would continue the battle alone:

> Upon this battle depends the survival of Christian civilization.
> Upon it depends our own British life,
> and the long continuity of our institutions and our Empire. . . .
> Let us therefore brace ourselves to our duties,
> and so bear ourselves
> that if the British Empire and its Commonwealth
> last a thousand years,
> Men will say:
> "*This* was their finest hour."[51]

49. William Manchester, *The Last Lion, Winston Spencer Churchill: Alone 1932–1940* (Boston: Little Brown and Company, 1988), p. 600.

50. Ibid., p. 685.

51. Ibid., p. 686.

With the outbreak of war, Americans, including millions whose descendants came from Europe, listened to broadcast news as never before. As television later made the Vietnam conflict, in Michael J. Arlen's phrase, "the living room war," radio brought World War II directly into the lives of this earlier generation.[52] People did not have to wait until the morning newspaper; they could almost hear the war as it was fought, due to radio correspondents like Edward R. Murrow and William L. Shirer. The reports of Murrow and others raised the consciousness of the nation about the uncertain fate of Britain and enabled President Roosevelt to persuade a reluctant Congress to help a beleaguered ally despite a strong impulse toward isolationism in the United States.

These electronic pioneers were not objective reporters in pursuit of a dramatic story; they were heralds warning America that Western civilization was in deadly peril. Archibald MacLeish, the Librarian of Congress, told Murrow that he had accomplished a miracle: "You destroyed a superstition . . . the superstition that what is done beyond 3,000 miles of water is not really done at all. . . . You burned the city of London in our houses, and we felt the flames that burned it. You laid the dead of London at our doors."[53]

When the Japanese attacked Pearl Harbor on the morning of December 7, 1941, there were no evening newspapers to report the event, as it was Sunday. From the first bulletin at 2:22 P.M. EST—which interrupted a football game on Mutual Radio—until Monday morning, the war was a radio exclusive. Two days later, Roosevelt delivered a fireside chat, carried by all three radio networks, to the American people, telling them, "We are now in this war. We are all in it—all the way." An estimated ninety million people, the largest audience in America and probably the world up to that time, heard the president.[54]

The war and the urgent need to know about it as soon as possible increased the power of radio. Millions now regularly tuned into radio news reports as they had entertainment programs like *Amos 'n' Andy*. Radio became America's first national news medium, challenging the influence of powerful regional newspapers like the *New York Times* and the *Chicago Tribune* and the motion picture news shorts. A giant step was taken toward creating a national American culture that began to homogenize a traditionally diverse people. The presence of the national radio networks

52. Bliss, *Now the News*, p. 106.   53. Ibid., p. 134.
54. Ibid., p. 138.

also spurred the growth of federal political power in the 1930s and 1940s. Through radio, a president had more direct and immediate access to the voters than any other political leader. An enormous potential for good or evil was created. In a time of great crisis, like a depression or a war, unrestricted access to the media by the president is necessary and appropriate. But in more normal times, it is possible for a chief executive to misuse them and thereby disrupt the checks and balances of representative democracy.

INSTRUMENTS OF WAR

World War II was the first major conflict in which the mass media became instruments of war. Among the Allies, the historian George N. Gordon writes, the press, radio, and films were employed to maintain civilian morale and support and to provide military instruction and information for the armed forces in training and in the field. Mass communications figured in battle in new ways: when a fighting unit captured or liberated a town, one of its first acts was to seize the local radio station or newspaper. Military commanders quickly learned that people responded to radio voices, whether of conquering heroes or resistance groups. Just as the British people rallied to the eloquent voice of Churchill over the BBC, so the Soviet people stiffened their heroic defense of Stalingrad and Leningrad against Nazi forces because of Soviet radio broadcasting.[55]

There was also the historic need for censorship regarding news about battle plans, troop movements, and other military actions. *A Code of Wartime Practices for the American Press* was issued on January 15, 1942, outlining to U.S. newspapers and magazines what would constitute improper handling of news dealing with troops, planes, ships, war production, armaments, military installations, and weather. Similar instructions were distributed to radio stations. An Office of Censorship was established by President Roosevelt to coordinate the efforts of the American press and radio to voluntarily refrain from publishing or broadcasting military and other information of value to the enemy. The office concerned itself only with news about the war, taking the position that information released by a government official or member of Congress was publishable. Thus it "avoided becoming a censor of the government."[56]

---

55. George N. Gordon, *The Communications Revolution: A History of Mass Media in the United States* (New York: Hastings House, 1977), pp. 205–7.
56. Emery and Smith, *The Press in America*, pp. 604–5.

The cooperative wartime effort between government and the mass media was remarkably successful. Not a word about the development of the atomic bomb was published or broadcast, and all details about the preparations for the D-Day invasion were kept from the Germans. Journalists censored and delayed stories about the sinking of American ships so that Berlin could not evaluate the effectiveness of their U-boat campaign in 1942—it was far more successful than the Germans ever realized.[57]

Meanwhile, the government's propaganda efforts and the job of originating news were handled by a separate agency. In early 1942, the United States created the Office of War Information under Elmer Davis, a veteran newsman. Like the Committee on Public Information during World War I, the Office of War Information provided safe but reliable information about the war to newspapers and radio stations across the country. Operating as a gigantic public relations agency, the office also coordinated the release of news and advertising, as well as campaigns for the sale of war bonds, rallies, and similar activities. Two-thirds of the office's annual budget of $36 million was allotted for overseas operations, mainly the Voice of America, which was soon beaming 2,700 programs a week to Europe and Africa in twenty-four different languages.

"Coverage of World War II by the American press," according to historians Emery and Smith, "was considered by most observers to be the best and fullest the world had ever seen." Gordon agrees that, "in spite of the censorship imposed . . . no nation in history was quite as up to date on the progress of any war as the American public during World War II, and this included much bad as well as good news."[58]

Unlike Nazi Germany, the United States believed that a government's lies always catch up with it, and that telling the truth about the war without jeopardizing national security was good policy and good politics. Hitler kept insisting over radio and in the press that Germany was winning the war, but the wounded and crippled troops returning from the Russian front told a far different story of the battles of Stalingrad and Leningrad. As a result, the credibility of all the German media was irretrievably damaged. In Nazi Germany, as later in Eastern Europe during the cold war, people risked their lives to listen to the short-wave broadcasts of the BCC and the Voice of America to learn the truth. Words, whether disseminated by newspapers, radio, or television, are critical to the conduct

---

57. Ibid., p. 605.
58. Ibid., p. 612; Gordon, *The Communications Revolution*, p. 226.

of modern warfare. Although military actions speak more loudly than words, they remain silent without words.

The impact of radio carried far beyond the war. Just as had the newspapers at the time of the founding of the Republic, the radio broadcasts of the 1930s and 1940s bonded Americans, enabling them to remain, no matter where they were physically, in contact with their leaders and with each other. Radio listeners became residents of a national village; it remained for television to make them part of a global community.

CHAPTER 2

REALITY AND TV REALITY

THE DEVELOPMENT OF American television was delayed by World War II, but three years after the shooting stopped, about one hundred TV stations were broadcasting across the country. Coverage of events was limited by the bulkiness of cameras and the time-consuming process of developing film, but it quickly became clear to politicians and journalists alike that television possessed a far greater power to create events, and move audiences, than radio. Television transformed *mediapolitik* in America, drastically reducing the power of political parties, dominating the selection of candidates, particularly at the national level, and even forcing presidents to make policy decisions based on TV coverage. In the beginning of television, a democratic liberal model of *mediapolitik*, consistent with the principles and beliefs of the American Founders, prevailed. But the Vietnam War and Watergate, along with the rise of a counterculture, produced a "new journalism" that raised questions about media power and responsibility that persist to this day.

MAKING A DIFFERENCE

In 1948, all three TV networks launched nightly fifteen-minute news programs and covered both national political conventions. The first live TV coverage of a congressional hearing occurred in 1951, when Senator Estes Kefauver of Tennessee investigated organized crime in the United States. Some scholars have described the hearings as a "pseudo-event," but Americans were fascinated by the Mafia boss Frank Costello, whose objection to pictures of his face forced cameramen to focus on his nervously moving hands. Buoyed by the favorable public reaction, the previously unknown Kefauver entered and won twelve of the fourteen Democratic presidential primaries the following spring, seriously challenging the party favorite and eventual nominee, Adlai Stevenson.

In the fall of 1952, after being accused of having personally benefitted from a secret "slush fund," Richard Nixon successfully defended himself and saved his vice presidential place on the Republican ticket by delivering a televised address—his famous "Checkers" speech—to the nation. The political historian Paul F. Boller has written that Republican strategists relied heavily on television to present Dwight Eisenhower to the voters in the 1952 presidential campaign, making extensive use of commercials and televising some forty of his speeches.[1] Although still in its infancy, television was already making a significant difference in U.S. presidential politics as both politicians and journalists experimented with the new medium.

Like Pearl Harbor, the Korean War began on a Sunday, when there were no evening newspapers; radio and TV correspondents had the story all to themselves. Borrowing from Roosevelt and Churchill, President Truman used a television address to explain to the nation why the United States, as part of a United Nations operation, had to act against Communist aggression. Sessions in the UN Security Council and General Assembly made dramatic television viewing and provided convincing evidence that the Communists had been the aggressors. The Voice of America reported what was happening in twenty-four languages, including Korean, while Radio Free Europe expanded its programming to countries behind the Iron Curtain. The Korean War was the first war covered by television, although it sometimes took as long as four days to fly film to New York for broadcasting. The pictures did not have the impact of those about the Vietnam conflict because, the TV correspondent George Herman explained, the "film was black and white, shot in newsreel style rather than in the intimate close-up style TV later developed. . . . Radio too was more in the cool factual style of World War II than in the personal suffering style of Vietnam."[2] Still, the bloody reality of war drew closer to an American people that increasingly depended upon television for its news and information.

1. Paul F. Boller, Jr., *Presidential Campaigns* (New York: Oxford University Press, 1984), pp. 282–84.

2. Edward Bliss, Jr., *Now the News: The Story of Broadcast Journalism* (New York: Columbia University Press, 1991), pp. 264–65.

MURROW AND MCCARTHY

The most famous single television program of these early years was Edward R. Murrow's *See It Now* documentary about Senator Joseph R. McCarthy of Wisconsin, broadcast on March 9, 1954. Skillfully editing film clips of McCarthy as committee chairman and public speaker, Murrow portrayed the militantly anti-Communist senator as a ruthless, unprincipled demagogue. Gilbert Seldes, a liberal media critic and an outspoken opponent of McCarthy, candidly described the Murrow program as "a hatchet job"—biased, slanted, inaccurate in parts, and editorially distorted.[3] But he and other observers argued that the objective of bringing down a man so dangerous to society justified the means of bias and distortion; that is, it was permissible to use McCarthyism against McCarthy.

Thousands of telephone calls and letters poured into CBS headquarters praising the Murrow program, but a Machiavellian standard had been established, to be used when the media establishment felt it was necessary to do so for the common good. A key question was not addressed: Who should define the common good? Determining what is best for society is sometimes obvious but more often difficult and even perilous. In the 1960s, the mass media made heroes of Martin Luther King, Jr., and other leaders of the civil rights movement, contributing to a more just America. But in the 1970s, the mass media, in the name of social responsibility, treated school busing as an extension of the civil rights cause, although a majority of black parents as well as white strongly opposed the practice. The end result was social dislocation and heated debate to this day as to whether the education of minorities is improved by forced integration of schools.[4]

Following the airing of the Murrow documentary, public opinion turned sharply against Senator McCarthy, whose descent into political oblivion was hastened by television coverage of the Army-McCarthy hearings in the spring of 1954. For thirty-five days, ABC broadcast the hearings live while CBS and NBC carried digests of each session in the evening. An entranced audience of millions watched the political duel between the

---

3. George N. Gordon, *The Communications Revolution: A History of Mass Media in the United States* (New York: Hastings House, 1977), p. 271.

4. For an extended discussion of this controversial subject, see S. Robert Lichter, Stanley Rothman, and Linda S. Lichter, *The Media Elite: America's New Powerbrokers* (Bethesda, Md.: Adler & Adler, 1986), pp. 220–53.

beetle-browed Midwest senator and the suave Boston lawyer, Joseph Welch. The climax of the hearings came when McCarthy questioned the background of a young lawyer and colleague of Welch, who interrupted to ask if McCarthy had "no sense of decency," adding: "If it were in my power to forgive you . . . I would do so. I like to think I am a gentleman, but your forgiveness will have to come from someone other than me."[5] The hearing room erupted into applause, and the curtain began to fall on McCarthy, who in December was censured by the U.S. Senate for conduct "contrary to senatorial traditions." In short, the mass media helped to create a climate of public opinion in which the Senate could censure a colleague who only two years earlier had been so powerful that even President Eisenhower had chosen not to criticize him publicly.

The 1960s saw the emergence of television as the dominant medium of political power and public opinion in America. John Kennedy defeated Richard Nixon in the first televised presidential debates in the fall of 1960, establishing television as the medium of choice in every succeeding presidential campaign. Because of television and radio, 90 percent of the American people knew of Kennedy's assassination on November 22, 1963, ninety minutes after it happened; the American penchant for wanting to know what was happening without delay was reinforced. Two days later, Lee Harvey Oswald, Kennedy's assassin, was murdered in the Dallas police station before the disbelieving eyes of millions of Sunday morning TV viewers, lending a new meaning to the phrase, "live television." The civil rights movement came of age on television. Sympathetic coverage of freedom marches and civil rights struggles in Little Rock, Selma, and Oxford, Mississippi, helped prepare legislators and the people for passage of the Civil Rights Act of 1964.

The 1960s left a deep imprint on the practice of *mediapolitik* in America, changing the voice of the reporter from outside narrator to informed participant and the role of the politician from party leader to public communicator. Politicians and journalists had coexisted peacefully within a liberal democratic framework for a long time, but their relationship now became increasingly adversarial and confrontational.

Other democracies began adjusting to the new reality of television. In England, the nonprofit British Broadcasting Corporation, controlled by a board of governors appointed by the government and financed by an an-

5. Thomas C. Reeves, *The Life and Times of Joe McCarthy: A Biography* (New York: Stein and Day, 1982), pp. 631–32.

nual license fee on radio and television sets, maintained a generally objective tone, leaving partisanship and ideology to the print media. In France, television journalists were more open proponents or opponents of government policies. President Charles de Gaulle, although reared in a Gutenberg atmosphere, understood the importance of the new medium in French politics, once explaining, "My enemies have the press, so I keep television."[6]

WHAT IS REALITY?

Television viewers live in a more full-of-wonders world than their parents and grandparents did. They can talk about famous people they have not met, enjoy famous places they have not visited, discuss famous events they have not participated in, all through television. In Marshall McLuhan's terminology, television has "extended" dramatically our access to the world, but reliance on television reality, on images alone, may have weakened our interest in true reality, which is grounded in institutions like the family, the community, and the nation.

For many viewers, television reality is the only reality. If television is not there to record and transmit, the tree did not fall in the forest, the demonstration did not happen, the candidate did not speak, the election did not occur. But even if television is there, does the event it is recording have true meaning or is it a pseudo-event created for the media? In an authoritarian or totalitarian society, such a question is not important because the government determines what is and is not real; *realpolitik* prevails. But in a democracy, the need to distinguish between real reality and television reality is imperative.

As Madison, Jefferson, and other Founders insisted, representative democracy requires an informed people who can make informed decisions about their government. Because of Ted Turner and his Cable News Network, we now have television reality twenty-four hours a day. But are the viewers of CNN truly informed or simply inundated with information? The growing ubiquity of the Internet reinforces the urgency of the question. Libertarians argue that too much news of the world is better than too little. Traditionalists respond that there can be too much of anything, even the "truth," and quote Henry Thoreau:

We are eager to tunnel under the Atlantic and bring the Old World some weeks nearer to the New; but perchance the first news that will leak through into the

6. Mitchell Stephens, *A History of News* (New York: Penguin Books, 1988), pp. 282–83.

broad, flapping American ear will be that Princess Adelaide has the whooping cough.[7]

How much is enough news and information? These pages argue that the answer lies in the liberal democratic model of *mediapolitik,* which respects the classic end of politics—the maintaining of a good and just society through a proper balance of freedom and responsibility.

CHOICE VERSUS CONTROL

Governments have attempted to control television by various methods, depending upon the nature of the government. Some countries, like Israel and South Africa, have even attempted to do without television at all. The political scientist George Quester writes that Israeli opposition to television came from religious groups that feared desecration of the Sabbath and other erosions of the country's religious nature. The old white South African regime feared an influx of American programs that showed blacks and whites as social and even intellectual equals. In both Israel and South Africa, the outright banning of television proved impossible to maintain.[8]

Because it was easy to receive Arab signals from Egypt, Jordan, and Lebanon, many Israelis imported television sets tuned to Arab wavelengths. Much of the programming was in English with Arabic subtitles so that the many Israelis who spoke English could understand the programs. Arab citizens of Israel welcomed the Arab-language programming and the Arab propaganda. Some observers argue that the Palestinians within Israel, and their campaign for independence, were sustained by the transborder programming of political as well as cultural ideas. *The New York Times* reported: "It is . . . clear that the Intifada could only thrive . . . because of the miracles of mass communication."[9]

Responding to Arab competition, the Israeli government relented enough to allow educational television, but not on the Sabbath. Consumer demand, however, eventually forced the addition of entertainment programs and an abandonment of the ban on Sabbath broadcasting as well. By the 1980s, the one remaining restriction was to limit broadcasting to black and white, but because color receivers could easily be imported, that prohibition too was essentially meaningless. The result has been a

7. Henry David Thoreau, *Walden* (New York, 1951), p. 67.
8. George Quester, *The International Politics of Television* (Lexington, Mass.: Lexington Books, 1990), p. 30.
9. Michael Widlanski, "A Televised War of Attrition," *New York Times,* March 18, 1990.

Middle East television system that resembles Joseph's coat of many colors: Jordan offers a newscast in Hebrew while Lebanese stations carry commercials for European products that are on sale in Haifa but not Beirut.[10] Politically, television has enhanced pan-Arabism—and the stature of Palestinian leader Yasser Arafat—in the Middle East. It has also presented Israel with a new variation on an old dilemma: how to maintain a democratic system under siege while applying censorship in the name of national security.

When the *intifada* began in 1988, the media scholar Leonard R. Sussman points out, television coverage in the West showed stone-throwing Palestinian youths arrayed against armed Israeli soldiers. Foreign criticism flared up when Israeli armed forces killed several young Palestinians. These pictures did not appear on government-controlled Israeli television, but the press reported the incidents, arousing Israeli public concern over the government's policy and the country's image abroad. The combination of press attention and public questioning had its impact: the tactics of the Israeli Defense Force abruptly changed, with beatings and rubber bullets replacing the use of live ammunition in most cases. The government also prohibited the press from visiting areas of combat, particularly in the occupied territories, but foreign criticism of and domestic uneasiness with the brutal handling of the Palestinian uprising persisted. Government attempts to shift the reason for the violence from itself were dismissed, even by usually sympathetic newspapers like the conservative *Ma'ariv,* which editorialized: "The blame attributed to the media for inciting unrest by reporting what is happening is a pathetic attempt to block off reality."[11] The appearance of such a critical editorial suggests that, despite the continuing Arab-Israeli conflict, a liberal democratic model of *mediapolitik* prevails in Israel.

THE SOUTH AFRICAN DIFFERENCE

Nervous about the liberating impact of a Sidney Poitier film or a Bill Cosby television program on the country's black population, the white South African government prohibited television until 1976, although it was the first African country to introduce radio broadcasting, in 1920. As would be expected of the dominant economic and military power in sub-

---

10. Quester, *The International Politics of Television,* p. 31.

11. Leonard R. Sussman, *Power, the Press and the Technology of Freedom: The Coming Age of ISDN* (New York: Freedom House, 1989), pp. 269–70.

Saharan Africa, South Africa had the most extensive radio programming in the region, with nine full-time services broadcasting in eighteen languages for a total of nearly three thousand hours a week.[12] Pretoria's ban on television was ultimately defeated, not so much by transmissions from neighboring countries like Lesotho or Botswana, but by the widespread import of VCRs (videocassette recorders) and rental films and programs. Government policy was overcome by market capitalism.

But then in the mid-1980s, violent events within its borders persuaded the South African government to invoke media censorship. Incensed by critical newscasts about bloody riots in Soweto and other black cities, Pretoria banned all cameras and photographers from such areas. The hostile standoff between government and the news media continued until 1990 when the new president, F. W. De Klerk, began using the media to reverse the negative global image of his nation and persuade a reluctant white populace to back his antiapartheid program (see chapter 10, "The Ending of Apartheid"). De Klerk carefully orchestrated the release from prison of Nelson Mandela, the African National Congress leader, into the media event of the year. Subsequently, he used media techniques, including sophisticated television commercials, to convince two-thirds of the white voters to endorse an irrevocable end to apartheid. De Klerk, that is, abandoned the old authoritarian model of *mediapolitik* and adopted the liberal democratic model to demonstrate to the world and to the black majority in South Africa that he was firmly committed to what he called a "new" South Africa.

THE SCANDINAVIAN APPROACH

Consistent with their socialist philosophy, Scandinavian governments initially followed a policy of controlled television programming, believing that they knew best what the people should watch. Their elitist mix consisted of some entertainment but mostly culture, education, and news, supposedly edifying but more often deadly dull. As recently as the early 1980s, Norway and Iceland offered only a single channel; Sweden added a second channel about the same time. To safeguard the socialist vision, Sweden prohibited television during the evening meal as well as early in the morning and late in the evening. But in Scandinavia as elsewhere, governments eventually acceded to the wishes of viewers and advertisers and

12. John C. Merrill, ed., *Global Journalism: Survey of International Communication,* 2d ed. (New York: Longman, 1991), pp. 182–85.

increasingly allowed popular feature films and programs and commercials
to be aired. The perceptions of the people were so expanded that Swedish
voters turned out the Socialist Party in 1991 after more than forty years
in power, attesting, at least in part, to the impact of liberal democratic
mediapolitik.

Government control of television stood in stark contrast to the freedom that the Scandinavian press has always enjoyed. It was in Scandinavia
that the right of reply by the reader was institutionalized, press councils
were refined, and the concept of the press ombudsman or watchdog origi-
nated. The government, however, did not keep its financial distance from
the press, setting up a widespread system of subsidies, ostensibly to preserve editorial pluralism. The subsidies ranged from tax and postal dis-
counts to direct payments through grants and government advertising.[13]
The press insisted that the millions of dollars in support made no difference in its coverage of government policies and programs, but the practice
suggests a Scandinavian variation on the Golden Rule in which he who
has the gold rules.

THE AMERICAN MODEL

Regardless of geography and political system, more and more governments all over the world are adopting some variation of the American media model with its adherence to the principles of political and economic
freedom. These principles presuppose that a man is a free, rational individual. Without this premise, modern media are merely technology, a random element of national power to be used by a government as it chooses.
But when linked with democratic politics, the mass media become a
strong, even irresistible, force for freedom and the common good.

As Aristotle stated, man is by nature a political—i.e., a communicating—animal. The mass media, particularly television, are the most powerful communicating instruments that the world has ever known, because
they can transmit the same message at the same time to so many different
people. But the real power of the mass media rests not in the medium but
in the message. The mass media contribute to the advancement of freedom when the information they provide distinguishes between the practices of free and unfree governments. Totalitarian as well as authoritarian
governments and even some socialist governments use the media to deny

13. Manny Paraschos, "Europe," in Merrill, *Global Journalism,* p. 96.

the differences between regimes. To them, and to many of today's journalists, there are no significant differences among states—power is all. They have no consistent understanding of the essential nature of man as a free, rational being.

The power and influence of the mass media in a nation are determined by their relationship to the politics of that nation. Whether they are grounded in power and profit or in reason and responsibility determines whether the media are a force for freedom or tyranny in world politics. The more free the government and the people, the more free the media. But if the media do not believe that freedom should be balanced with responsibility as a basic principle, if they see every choice as equally valid, they will not be able to help the people and the government to be free. In such a circumstance, not only will the media no longer be a liberating influence, they will degrade the politics of liberal democracy.

There are disturbing signs of media degradation in the United States, including the increase of "trash journalism" on television, the influence of supermarket tabloids on campaigns, the constant polling that produces a kind of political hypochondria requiring the nation's political pulse to be taken every day, the emphasis on "horserace journalism" rather than in-depth analysis of policies and programs—all justified by the public's right to know. But the American public does not want to know everything. As we will see in chapter 3, the overwhelming majority of the American people believed they knew all they needed to know about the course and conduct of the Persian Gulf War, despite media arguments that the public needed to know more.

How, then, do we ensure an independent, principled media—and a principled, responsive government? It depends, as it always has, upon the people's having the best possible understanding of government. If people are well educated and believe in the Good (as defined in classical political philosophy and as understood in most religions), they can contribute to and insist on good government and good media. If not, we get the corrupt politicians and biased journalists we deserve.

The present global dominance of the American media is nothing new. The twentieth century was indeed the American Century, in Henry Luce's phrase, if we consider the impact of the silent films of Hollywood in the 1920s (the Weimar Republic restricted the number of American films that could be shown in a theater in a week), the spread of American newspaper techniques around the world, a second peak of Hollywood filmmaking after World War II, the invasion of television starting in the 1960s, and the explosion of the Internet in the 1990s. The political impact of American television has been profound and undeniable:

Whether a popular program is about space adventure, crime in the streets, a vicious family dynasty, or western adventures, viewers in an economically underdeveloped society are still likely to come away from the screen a little more restless with their own traditional lot in life and viewers in Communist-governed states are likely to become even more discontented.[14]

And discontent can develop into revolution as the collapse of Communism in Eastern and Central Europe and in the former Soviet Union demonstrated.

MEDIA MODELS

One of the best explanations about the interrelationship between the state and the media was written in the 1950s by political scientists Fred Siebert, Theodore Peterson, and Wilbur Schramm, who argued that "the press always takes on the form and coloration of the social and political structures within which it operates." That is, there are different press systems because there are different social systems based on a society's basic assumptions about the nature of man and the relation of man to the state. The authors offer four models: authoritarian, libertarian, Soviet Communist, and social responsibility. Actually, they say there are only two, authoritarian and libertarian, with the Soviet Communist model developing from the former, and the social responsibility model a modification of the latter.[15]

According to Siebert, Peterson, and Schramm, the authoritarian model came into being in the late Renaissance, soon after the invention of printing, and was based on the absolute power of the monarch. Because the purpose of the press was to support the state, no criticism of the power structure was allowed. The media were owned by the king, a political party, or private parties. The intellectual progenitors of the authoritarian model were Hobbes and Machiavelli; later, its most prominent intellectual supporter was Hegel. Today this model obtains, for example, in Iran and Singapore.

The libertarian model, the authors maintain, reversed the position of

14. Quester, *The International Politics of Television*, p. 46.
15. Fred S. Siebert, Theodore Peterson, and Wilbur Schramm, *Four Theories of the Press* (Urbana: University of Illinois Press, 1956), pp. 1–2.

man and the state as reflected in authoritarian theory. It arose in England in the late seventeenth century as a result of Milton's *Areopagitica* and John Locke's writings and spread to the United States and Europe. Stemming from the Enlightenment and the concept of natural rights, the purpose of the media was to find and present the truth, regardless of the consequences. The media were controlled by the dictates of the free market and the courts. Other intellectual proponents included John Stuart Mill and Adam Smith. National examples of the libertarian model today are the United States, Japan, and Germany.

The Soviet Communist model, say Siebert, Peterson, and Schramm, was born in early twentieth-century Russia. Grounded in Marxist determinism and the dictatorship of the proletariat, the Communist media operated as a tool of the ruling power as did the older authoritarian media, but with one major difference: they were always state-owned rather than privately owned. They could not and did not criticize Communist Party objectives unless directed to do so—as Khrushchev did with his famous denunciation of Stalin at the Twentieth Party Congress in 1956. Authors of the Soviet Communist model included Marx and Lenin. It prevails today in Cuba and North Korea.

The social responsibility model, Siebert, Peterson and Schramm state, was based on the belief that the growing power and potential private monopoly of the media imposed an obligation that all sides are fairly presented and that the public is given sufficient information to make informed decisions about its politics and government. It stemmed from the 1947 report of the Hutchins Commission on Freedom of the Press and other American critics of libertarian theory. The Hutchins Commission decried what it called the decline of widespread press responsibility and the concentration of media power in too few private hands and warned: "If [the agencies of mass communication] are irresponsible, not even the First Amendment will protect their freedom from governmental control. The amendment will be amended."

A decade later, Siefert, Peterson, and Schramm reinforced the warning, speculating that if the media do not honor their responsibility, "it may be necessary for some other agency of the public to enforce it."[16] Social responsibility theory had far less confidence in the rationality of man than libertarian theory, suggesting that while human beings are certainly capa-

16. Commission on Freedom of the Press, *A Free and Responsible Press* (Chicago, 1947), p. 80; Siebert, Peterson, and Schramm, *Four Theories of the Press*, p. 5.

ble of using reason, they are often unwilling to do so. This model prevails in Scandinavia, which with its social democratic roots, agrees that man, and woman, must often be goaded into seeking truth and exercising reason, as defined by the state rather than the people.

One serious flaw in the Siebert-Peterson-Schramm thesis is the argument that the media of a nation *always* take on the form and coloration of the social and political structures within which they operate. That could be argued forty years ago, when there were no satellites, VCRs, fax machines, minicams, or PCs, but today the internal media of a nation are often influenced and even shaped by external media, often assuming a form that is at variance with the political and sometimes the social structures of that nation (as we have seen in Israel and South Africa and will see in Poland and other parts of Eastern and Central Europe). Because even totalitarian governments cannot successfully exclude external media as they formerly did, they cannot control internal media with the same firmness as in the past. Even the Chinese Communist government, with its formidable propaganda resources, including a sixty-million-member Communist Party, has not been able to convince all of the Chinese people, particularly those who live in the cities, that there was no massacre in Tiananmen Square. For decades, the German Democratic Republic's Communist leaders insisted that the people of East Germany lived a better life than their West German brothers and sisters. In 1989, after viewing the truth about east and west for decades, the East German people rejected Communism and demanded unification under Bonn and its democratic capitalist philosophy. In today's electronically connected world, national barriers cannot be permanently maintained; inevitably they are breached by pictures and sounds from without.

Even before Siebert, Peterson, and Schramm, the political scientists Harold Lasswell and Charles Wright explored the role of the mass media in society. They suggested that there were four basic media functions: surveillance of the environment, correlation of how society responds to the environment, the transmission of culture from one generation to the next, and entertainment. "Surveillance" informs and provides news about such matters as the economy or a potentially dangerous military situation. "Correlation" selects and interprets information, checking, for example, on the actions of government, monitoring public opinion, conferring status on a political leader. "Transmission" provides cultural continuity between generations, increasing social cohesion and reducing anomie. "Entertainment" creates a mass culture and provides private relaxation.

Lasswell and Wright point out that the media have dysfunctions as well as functions: too much surveillance (information) can lead to apathy and passivity; incorrect correlation (interpretation) can extend power and impede change; the wrong cultural transmission can lead to mass society and depersonalization; entertainment of the lowest common denominator can encourage escapism and corrupt fine art. Lasswell anticipated C. Wright Mills's *The Power Elite* when he spoke of how "ruling elements" in society were especially alert to each other and relied upon communication (the media) "as a means of preserving power."[17]

In the years since Siebert, Peterson, and Schramm wrote *Four Theories of the Press*, other scholars have offered their philosophies of the media. In his useful survey, the political scientist Whitney R. Mundt lists Ralph Lowenstein, who emphasizes the importance of ownership as well as philosophy; John Merrill, who reduces the models to two, authoritarian-tending and libertarian-tending; William Hachten, who adds two new models, revolutionary and developmental; J. Herbert Altschull, who, using economic analysis, divides the world into market, Marxist, and advancing, while insisting that truth is a goal of the press in all three philosophies; Robert Picard, who elevates a democratic socialist model to coequal status with revolutionary and developmental models; and Sydney Head, who suggests there are three models of government-media relationships in international broadcasting: permissive (United States), paternalistic (Great Britain), and authoritarian (USSR).[18] Mention should also be made of George Quester's theory that the great debate in international television is whether choice or control shall prevail.

COMMUNITARIAN ETHICS

In 1993, three communications scholars, Clifford Christians, John P. Ferre, and Mark Fackler, wrote *Good News: Social Ethics and the Press*, which built upon the social responsibility theory of the Hutchins Com-

17. See Werner J. Severin and James W. Tankard, Jr., *Communication Theories: Origins, Methods, and Uses in the Mass Media* (New York: Longman, 1992), pp. 293–98, for an excellent summary of Lasswell and Wright. Also C. R. Wright, "Functional Analysis in Mass Communication," *Public Opinion Quarterly* 24 (1960): 605–20; C. R. Wright, *Mass Communication: A Sociological Perspective* (New York: Random House, 1986), pp. 4–6; H. D. Lasswell, "The Structure and Function of Communication in Society," in W. Schramm, *Mass Communication* (Urbana: University of Illinois, 1960), pp. 117–30. Also C. Wright Mills, *The Power Elite* (New York: Oxford University Press, 1956).

18. Whitney R. Mundt, "Global Media Philosophies," in Merrill, *Global Journalism*, pp. 11–27.

mission. They sought, Edmund B. Lambeth, a journalism professor, has pointed out, to replace the classical liberalism of the Enlightenment with a social ethics that emphasized people as interdependent and in need of co-operation. "The telos of communitarian journalism," the authors of *Good News* write, "has distinctive features: justice, covenant and empowerment." Their central argument is:

When the axis of the press's content is shifted from individual autonomy to communitarianism, its mission is fundamentally reoriented. In this reformulation, the goal of reporting becomes civic transformation. Operating within a communitarian world view itself, the news media seek to engender a like-minded philosophy among the public. A revitalized citizenship shaped by community norms becomes the press's aim—not merely readers and audiences provided with data, but morally literate persons.[19]

The Christians-Ferre-Fackler book is formidable in its research (450 books and articles in the bibliography, 37 pages of endnotes) and argumentation, quoting thinkers from St. Augustine to Paul Tillich, Richard Rorty, and Michael Sandel. Their delineation of the flaws of what they call "individualistic liberalism" is sound, but they never explain how an amorphous mass called a "community" can, with any certainty, produce a set of "ethics" consistent with traditional virtues and liberal democracy. Nor do they attempt to resolve the yawning difference between their theoretical construct of a "world-view pluralism [that] is the axis of communitarian democracy" and the reality of international organizations like the United Nations, which routinely condemns "Zionism" (i.e., Israel) for being racist; the Organization of American States, which declines to inspect the totalitarian excesses of Fidel Castro; or the Organization of African Unity, which remains silent about the mass murders perpetrated by Idi Amin and other black dictators.

When Christians, Ferre, and Fackler write that "world views are never individually generated but express communal life," they are taking sides in a philosophical debate that has endured for more than two thousand years: Does a good society produce good citizens, or do good citizens produce a good society? In his *Politics,* Aristotle claims that the *polis* or state precedes the family and the individual "since the whole is of necessity prior to the part." But Daniel N. Robinson, a professor of philosophy, states, Aristotle also laid the foundation for an ethics of personal responsibility

19. Clifford G. Christians, John P. Ferre, and P. Mark Fackler, *Good News: Social Ethics and the Press* (New York: Oxford University Press, 1993), p. 89.

and for a jurisprudence centered on the individual. Aristotle noted that there remains a persistent tension between the recognition of persons as fully responsible individuals and, at the same time, "products of the cultures into which they are born."[20]

Western history favors the dominant role of the individual rather than the state. Certainly the American experience demonstrates that Founders like Washington and Jefferson were responsible for the political miracle that became the United States rather than the reverse; that the leadership of Abraham Lincoln, Ulysses Grant, and others saved the Union, not that the fractured American community saved itself; that Franklin Roosevelt and the New Dealers, not some kind of spontaneous self-regeneration, got the country to work itself out of the Great Depression.

Christians, Ferre, and Sackler offer "normative pluralism" as a third way between the rationalism of Aristotle and the nihilism of Nietzsche.[21] But communitarian ethics, "grounded in community, aiming for civic transformation, and operating by the principle of mutuality," is flawed because its essentially collectivist approach is at odds with the post-Communist world, which has rejected collectivism and is turning toward liberal democracy.[22] On every continent, people are increasingly depending upon what the authors dismiss as "individualistic liberalism" to guide their decisions.

"COMMITTED" JOURNALISM

In his widely praised work, *Committed Journalism: An Ethic for the Profession,* Edmund B. Lambeth points out that scholars like John Merrill in the 1970s and J. Herbert Altschull in the 1980s attacked social responsibility theory as meaningless or dangerous. Altschull argued that the term "social responsibility" did not specify the source or direction of the journalist's obligations. From Altschull's Marxist perspective, it was too subjective, too prone to be guided by the journalist's individual whims and prejudices. Merrill protested that the doctrine of social responsibility would inevitably lead to governmental restrictions on the press that would curb its freedom.[23] From Merrill's libertarian view, it was too collectivist.

Lambeth suggests a framework for journalistic principles based on the

20. Daniel N. Robinson, "Races and Persons," *The World & I,* February 1992, pp. 485–86.

21. Christians, Ferre, and Fackler, *Good News,* p. 194.

22. Ibid., p. 15.

23. Edmund B. Lambeth, *Committed Journalism: An Ethic for the Profession,* 2d ed. (Bloomington: Indiana University Press, 1992), p. 7.

values of Judeo-Christian and classical Greek civilizations, since "journalism is not a disembodied occupation." After all, he says, journalists are members of the human race—"no system should suggest that they inhabit a special moral universe which requires a special ethical stance." He proposes five rules for a practitioner of journalism in a constitutional democracy: telling the truth, behaving justly, respecting and protecting independence and freedom, acting humanely, and being a good steward of the resources, especially the First Amendment, that protect journalism and a free society.[24] All of Lambeth's rules emphasize the critical reality that a journalist, in the modern era of *mediapolitik,* is not an isolated individual liable only to himself but a responsible member of a powerful profession (rather than an occupation) that is at the very heart of government and society.[25]

Lambeth quotes approvingly from *Habits of the Heart,* by Robert N. Bellah, Richard Madsen, William M. Sullivan, Ann Swidler, and Steven M. Tipton, who contend that the historic role of the news media as "the mortise" that links the sundry sectors of American society into a civic whole is fast eroding. Bellah and the others take issue with the individualistic utilitarianism that prevails in American life, especially among journalists; they point out that journalism is, after all, a communitarian enterprise. At the same time, Lambeth criticizes the authors of *Habits* (as he does the authors of *Good News*) for neglecting the tradition of free expression as a means of fostering and defining community.[26] He stresses that *Habits* largely ignores John Stuart Mill as well as John Locke and the framers of the U.S. Constitution, who designed a way to protect communities with a system of law and "bounded government." *Habits,* Lambeth says, views classical liberalism as a negative tradition of freedom—freedom "from" rather than freedom "to"—"that fails to provide much help for Americans wrestling with moral issues in public life."[27]

What Lambeth is proposing, with his "committed" journalism, is an acceptance of the necessary balance between the rights of the individual and

24. Ibid., p. 24.
25. Wilbert E. Moore has identified six characteristics of a profession: it must be a full-time occupation; it must be a "calling" that involves deep commitment; it must have a formal organization that sets professional standards; it must have professionals who have prepared for their calling through long and special preparation; it must serve society; it must deserve and require autonomy. See Wilbert E. Moore, *The Professions* (New York: Russell Sage, 1970), pp. 4–22.
26. Lambeth, *Committed Journalism,* pp. 189–90.
27. Ibid., p. 202.

the responsibilities of the community. He takes his notion of what constitutes a community from *Habits:* It "is a group of people who are socially interdependent, who participate together in discussion and decision making, and who share certain practices . . . that both define the community and are nurtured by it. Such a community is not quickly formed. It almost always has a history and also a community of memory, defined in part by its past and its memory of its past." Quoting approvingly the neo-Aristotelian philosopher, Alasdair MacIntyre, and *Habits of the Heart,* Lambeth calls for journalistic practices that "are not undertaken as means to an end but are ethically good in themselves."[28]

Investigative journalism, he suggests, is a practice that, in the hands of some reporters, has gone out of control. Although there are examples of good investigative journalism: Seymour Hersh won a Pulitzer Prize for his exposure of an Army massacre of innocent civilians in the Vietnamese village of My Lai. The dogged coverage of Watergate by *Washington Post* reporters Bob Woodward and Carl Bernstein forced President Richard Nixon to resign. But CBS News was forced to apologize to General William C. Westmoreland after he filed a libel suit against the network for a slanted documentary about the Vietnam War. Two *Los Angeles Times* reporters almost found themselves in contempt of court after being caught trying to listen to a closed San Diego proceeding. And the *Washington Post* returned a Pulitzer Prize after editors discovered that a series of riveting articles about a seven-year-old heroin addict was fiction and not fact.[29]

ROUND PEGS AND SQUARE HOLES

Lambeth's theory, however, as perceptive as it is, is limited to the American experience; it does not help us when we consider the politics and media of other nations or the impact of the U.S. media on global politics. Furthermore, all of the above theories suffer from the intellectual vice of trying to fit every nation into one or another category. For example, where do you put Cuba, which is both a Marxist and a third world nation? Or Japan, which is market-oriented and adheres to a philosophy of social responsibility? Or Saudi Arabia, which is capitalist, third world, and authoritarian?

As important as the Siebert-Peterson-Schramm thesis was forty years ago and as hard as all the subsequent theories try, none of them adequately describes today's world politics and mass media, particularly in the

28. Ibid., p. 203.
29. Ibid., p. 179.

wake of the collapse of Communism in the former Soviet Union and Eastern and Central Europe and the spread of democracy across the world.
Existing media theories tend to be one-way, focusing more on the media
than on politics, considering, for example, press freedom rather than press
influence. While it is important to examine the economic, political, and
other weapons that a government uses to control the media, it is no less
important to gauge how much the media, either as an instrument of the
government or as an independent force, affect the course of politics in a
nation and in the world.

Some writers have examined the development of the media as a participant as well as an observer of the politics of a nation. Quester asserts that
television influences politics in three ways: (1) in a democracy, it helps in-
cumbents retain power by reelection; (2) in both electoral democracies
and nonelected dictatorships, it empowers candidates and political figures
who are telegenic; and (3) in both, it focuses public attention on issues and
ideas that are visual and graphic rather than subtle and thoughtful.
Quester suggests that the latter impact may work against incumbent administrations by creating an appetite for "bad news," which leads the public to blame, and remove, those in charge. But he weakens his argument by
offering as an example of the latter Walter Cronkite, who ended each CBS
News evening broadcast during 1980 by counting the number of days that
the American hostages had been held in Tehran. Quester says that without
television, the average American might not have paid so much attention to
the hostages and they thus might have been released sooner—a badly
skewed reading of the Ayatollah Khomeini's deep animus toward the "satanic" United States and the American people's equally deep concern
about the plight of their fellow citizens.[30] With or without television pictures of the mass demonstrations outside the U.S. Embassy, with or without the nightly Cronkite countdown, the reality of the captivity of the
hostages would have remained in the public consciousness. In this instance, TV reality as provided by Cronkite and real reality as provided by
the Ayatollah were one and the same.

A NEW MODEL

There is a need for a theory that presents a picture of politics and media as they are likely to be in the first part of the twenty-first century. Such
a theory requires the use of broad models that are philosophically, not

---

30. Quester, *The International Politics of Television*, pp. 66–69.

simply economically or geographically, based. It discards nation labels like Soviet and third world. It rejects dated political terms like communist. And it is not satisfied with the sensual determinism of Marshall McLuhan, who described television as a visual, aural, and tactile medium whose content does not matter.[31] I call it *mediapolitik*.

This new theory depends on only three basic models: liberal democratic, authoritarian, and totalitarian. In the *liberal democratic model*, both the politics and the mass media are free of government control. Politics and media serve the governed not the government. Their rights are protected by law and sometimes, as in the United States, by constitution. They have a philosophical base rooted in the classical political thinkers of Western civilization: Plato, Aristotle, Augustine, Aquinas, Locke, and Mill. At their best, they operate within a framework of moral and political as well as societal responsibility. The leading example of this model is the United States, which, because of Founders like Madison and Jefferson, provides us with a *mediapolitik* rooted in democratic principles. Other examples include Great Britain and Germany.

In the *authoritarian model*, politics and mass media are regulated by the government, but the economy and the culture are usually not regulated. Politics and media serve the government, which may be controlled by an individual or a political party; in either case, the government is nationalist and has few imperialist ambitions. Rights are nominally guaranteed by laws which may be suspended in time of crisis. The philosophical base of this model is Machiavellian. Politicians and journalists operate within a framework of *realpolitik*, which allows the government to determine how free institutions shall be. Examples of the authoritarian model are Singapore and Chile under Pinochet.

In the *totalitarian model*, politics and mass media are controlled absolutely by the government. Politics and media serve the state in the name of the people, but the needs of the state always come first. Rights are defined by the party that runs the state. The philosophical base of this model is Hegelian and Leninist-Marxist. Institutions operate within a utopian framework calculated to shape the entire society in the image of the ruling party. Examples of the totalitarian model are Iraq, Cuba, and North Korea.

Just how large a role the mass media play in national politics depends upon the following criteria:

31. Marshall McLuhan, *Understanding Media: The Extensions of Man* (New York: McGraw-Hill, 1964), p. 18.

First, there must be a significant media infrastructure, including television and radio networks and national newspapers and magazines. Such an infrastructure exists in all of the Western democracies, by public demand, as well as in major Communist countries like China and Cuba, by government policy.

Second, there must be a sufficiently large reading or viewing audience to make the media truly mass. The Western democracies have long since ceded to consumer demand for diverse media, while the government of the former Soviet Union believed—and the government of the present People's Republic of China believes—that the media can be manipulated to Communist ends. The critical role of the mass media in both free and unfree modern nations is aided by the fact that the Gutenberg age demanded a certain level of literacy, while the television age requires only good eyesight and hearing. On the positive side, the mass media now reach more people, who can therefore make decisions and be more involved in local, national, and global politics. On the negative side, if citizens rely exclusively on television to the near-exclusion of reading and more careful analysis of events and personalities, they will be less likely to use rational thought in making responsible political decisions. People might accept what they see without reflecting upon it or comparing it with some alternative means of information. How can we guard against this potential *1984* scenario? By ensuring that both politics and media abide by democratic principles.

Third, public officials must spend a considerable portion of their time planning for and working with the media. In his study of how the press affects U.S. policymaking, Martin Linsky found that six out of ten successful public officials devoted as much as 25 percent of their time to the press. Based on his examination of several hundred high-ranking federal officials over a period of twenty years, he concluded that "to be successful in their jobs policymakers must move toward a theory of press relations which is deliberative and strategic in character."[32] There is solid evidence, much of it offered for the first time in this book, that public officials all over the world have adopted just such a strategy. This strategy strengthens democratic regimes and weakens nondemocratic regimes by encouraging the "ombudsman" role of the media as the watchdog of the people.

Fourth, the media must have the potential power to be able to change

32. Martin Linsky, *Impact: How the Press Affects Federal Policymaking* (New York: W. W. Norton & Company, 1986), pp. 85, 217.

the process or the direction of a policy, either for good or bad. This can be done in several different ways: by framing the issue (tyranny versus democracy, reform versus status quo); setting the agenda (placing an issue on the front page or at the beginning of a newscast); forcing a government to react more quickly to an event (CNN and the Internet have made all public officials practitioners of the instant response); involving high-ranking rather than low-ranking officials in the policymaking process (prime-time television has a way of attracting the attention of presidents, prime ministers, and even dictators).

As we shall see, Boris Yeltsin overcame the Moscow coup plotters in August 1991 in large measure because he used the mass media to solidify public support for himself inside and outside the Soviet Union. East Germany was able to cast off Communism through a bloodless revolution in the fall of 1989 because West German television had long since convinced the East German people that Marxism-Leninism was an empty ideology that would never be able to deliver on its promises. Western mass media encouraged Chinese students in their heroic efforts to create a democracy movement in the spring of 1989, but were unable to prevent the Chinese Communist leadership from sending the tanks into Tiananmen Square and massacring hundreds of people.

The following chapters offer case studies of the different models of *mediapolitik* in the United States, Iraq, Serbia, Eastern and Central Europe, the former Soviet Union, China, Japan, Chile, and South Africa. Taken together, they demonstrate that the mass media are indeed a liberating force when and if they are joined with democratic principles and institutions.

CHAPTER 3

TELEWAR AND TELEPEACE

IN THE AGE OF *mediapolitik*, old-style personal diplomacy is supplemented by new-style public diplomacy. In the age of Gutenberg, monarchs usually conducted negotiations and signed treaties behind closed doors. Today, national leaders prefer to let the sunshine in, using the mass media to achieve their goals. The challenge is to maintain the right mix of traditional diplomacy and modern "teleplomacy," a challenge complicated by television correspondents who do not hesitate to participate in the diplomatic process.

One of the best-known instances of teleplomacy, as practiced by members of the media, began in November 1977 when CBS anchorman Walter Cronkite became what the media scholar Doris Graber calls a Middle East "peacemaker."[1] During a television satellite interview, Cronkite elicited from Egyptian President Anwar el Sadat a public promise that he would go to Jerusalem if it would further peace. No Arab leader had ever before made such a public commitment. In a separate televised interview, Cronkite secured a pledge from Israeli Prime Minister Menachem Begin that he would personally welcome Sadat at Ben Gurion Airport if he came. No Israeli leader had ever before made such a public promise. The means for a historic Egyptian-Israeli meeting were created because (1) Cronkite was pursuing a scoop (in line with libertarian journalism), (2) Cronkite wanted to help advance the cause of peace in the Middle East

1. Doris A. Graber, *Mass Media and American Politics*, 3d ed. (Washington: CQ Press, 1989), p. 337.

64

(reflecting social responsibility journalism), and (3) President Jimmy Carter had laid the necessary foundation through his foreign policy initiatives.

When Sadat arrived in Israel on November 19, 1977, the mass media continued to play a major role. Anchormen from all three American television networks accompanied him, and some two thousand journalists from all over the world were at the airport to record his arrival. The Sadat-Begin meeting was carried live on U.S. television and radio, and in the weeks that followed tens of millions of Americans (and many millions more worldwide) watched the peacemaking process.

The following spring, when the talks moved to the United States, both Egyptian and Israeli leaders skillfully practiced teleplomacy. Upon arriving in America, Sadat immediately made himself available for a television interview, and in a televised address to the National Press Club accused the Israelis of delaying the negotiations. Israel responded to the Arab propaganda offensive by sending Foreign Minister Moshe Dayan (with his dramatic black eye patch) on a ten-day speaking tour of American cities to win support for the Israeli side. Graber says that "little thought" is given to the political ramifications that ensue when foreign heads of state use the American press as a platform, but Sadat and Begin knew what they were doing and provided a lesson in teleplomacy subsequently followed by every foreign leader: Take full advantage of the First Amendment of the U.S. Constitution to communicate directly with the American people in the hope of enlisting their support.[2] The 1978 teleplomacy had another clear impact: Sadat and Begin so raised international expectations of an Egyptian-Israeli agreement that the Camp David accord, with Carter's considerable assistance, became almost inevitable.

THE GREAT COMMUNICATOR

One particularly skilled practitioner of teleplomacy was President Ronald Reagan, a former film and television star whose national political career was launched with a televised address in support of Barry Goldwater, the Republican presidential nominee, in 1964. What some critics do not understand about Reagan's success as "the great communicator" during his presidency is that it depended upon content as well as form. Reagan was elected and reelected president by landslide margins because of *what* he proposed—less government, fewer regulations, lower taxes, and a

2. Ibid., p. 338.

stronger national defense—not *how* he proposed his programs. He did not ignore appearances, but he knew that in the media age, a wise politician puts content first and form second, while a weak politician will do precisely the opposite.

Because Reagan was so skillful a speaker, some observers were caught up in the mechanics. Barbara Matusow, a journalist, has described how the 1984 London Conference of the seven leading industrial nations (the G-7) was "masterfully" managed by the Reagan White House.[3] Reagan aide Michael Deaver, his staff, and selected journalists visited Europe several times to inspect each site that the president would visit. It was arranged that each major American official scheduled to attend the summit would appear on television talk shows and give background briefings to journalists. The president met with reporters from the six other nations whose leaders would be at the meeting. The White House provided journalists with a steady flow of news events and photo opportunities at the summit, but Reagan already had his eye fixed on the Normandy beaches, where he intended to remind the world of the difference between freedom and tyranny and of man's right to be free.[4]

Not since the Allies planned the invasion of France in 1944, perhaps, had the Normandy coast been so carefully inspected as it was for Reagan's address on the fortieth anniversary of D-Day; the site selected was the Omaha Beach Memorial overlooking the water at Pointe du Hoc. In the course of the preparations, the White House received a letter from a young California woman whose father had fought at Normandy as a twenty-year-old private in the U.S. Army. She had written the president that she was determined to make a pilgrimage to France to honor her father. In a characteristically generous gesture, Reagan paid her way to France, and when he spoke on the cliff, she was standing close by. At one moment he read from a poignant letter to her father: "I'm going there, Dad, and I'll see the beaches and the barricades and the monuments. I'll see the graves and I'll put flowers there just like you wanted to do. I'll never forget what you went through, Dad, nor will I let anyone else forget. And, Dad, I'll always be proud."[5] The young woman wept as she listened and so almost did the president, who ended his remarks with these words:

3. Barbara Matusow, "Abroad: The White House Writes the Lead," *Washington Journalism Review*, September 1984, pp. 43–46.

4. Charles Press and Kenneth Verburg, *American Politicians and Journalists* (Glenview, Ill.: Scott, Foresman and Company, 1988), p. 280.

5. Robert J. Donovan and Ray Scherer, *Unsilent Revolution: Television News and American Public Life* (New York: Cambridge University Press, 1992), p. 190.

A D-day veteran has shown us the meaning for this day far better than any president can. It is enough for us to say about Private Zanatta and all the men of honor and courage who fought beside him four decades ago: We will always remember. We will always be proud. We will always be prepared, so we may always be free.[6]

It was teleplomacy of an elevated kind, reflecting Reagan's ability to communicate American ideals.

The president also relied on the mass media, particularly television, to help him win political battles. In February 1982, for example, Reagan proposed an initiative to expand trade and commerce in the Caribbean. One survey, for example, found that 35 percent of television viewers in Columbus, Ohio, supported the proposal; after the president delivered a televised address explaining how the plan would help our neighbors to the south as well as the U.S. economy, 64 percent of the Columbus viewers supported the initiative. In April 1983, Reagan discussed the crisis in Central America in a televised address to Congress. ABC asked viewers to call in: of 336,462 calls received, 258,943, or 76 percent, agreed with the president that events in the region threatened the United States.

In May 1984, the day before a House vote on economic and military aid to El Salvador, Reagan went on television to urge passage of a Republican rather than a Democratic bill. The House, which had a comfortable Democratic majority, approved the Republican version by 212 to 208. Robert J. Donovan and Ray Scherer, political journalists, conclude that time and again Reagan's television broadcasts resulted in the passage of conservative legislation over the opposition of the liberal House Democratic leadership.[7] The political scientist Richard E. Neustadt has written that presidential power is essentially the power to persuade an audience that the policy a president is proposing is in the best interest of that audience; in the media age, television is *the* medium of presidential persuasion.[8]

STRANGE BEDFELLOWS

Like politics, *mediapolitik* makes strange bedfellows—for example, the director of the Central Intelligence Agency, a United States senator, a well-known American columnist, and an Asian dictator. In the fall of 1985, an embattled President Ferdinand Marcos was trying to retain power in an increasingly unstable Philippines. U.S. officials, including CIA Director

6. Ronald Reagan, *An American Life* (New York: Simon and Schuster, 1990), p. 376.
7. Donovan and Scherer, *Unsilent Revolution*, p. 194.
8. Richard E. Neustadt, *Presidential Power: The Politics of Leadership from FDR to Carter* (New York: John Wiley & Sons, 1980), p. 10.

William J. Casey, had been pressuring Marcos for months to hold elections to reestablish his authority. At the time, a friendly Philippines was vital to American strategic interests in the Far East. On the advice of U.S. Senator Paul Laxalt, a friend of Marcos and an even closer friend of President Reagan, Marcos announced his decision to call an election on ABC's Sunday morning public affairs program, *This Week with David Brinkley*, rather than in a broadcast to the Philippine people. Laxalt told Marcos that making his announcement on the Brinkley program "would be very effective for American consumption." By prearrangement, the Washington columnist George Will asked Marcos: "Some people wonder if it would not be possible for you to call an early election to set a new mandate." Marcos responded grandly: "If all these childish claims to popularity on both sides have to be settled, I think we had better settle it by calling an election right now." After proposing a sixty-day campaign, Marcos exclaimed, "I'm ready, I'm ready."[9]

The dictator was ready for anything—but defeat. When the February 7 returns favored his challenger, Corazon Aquino, rather than himself, Marcos charged vote fraud and threatened to use military power to stay in office. In fact, there had been massive ballot tampering—by Marcos supporters—and Senator Richard Lugar of Indiana, a conservative Republican and chairman of the Senator Foreign Relations Committee, had personally witnessed the fraud as head of a U.S. delegation monitoring the fairness of the Philippine election. When President Reagan, who had known the militantly anti-Communist Marcos since Reagan was governor of California, suggested there had been fraud on both sides, Lugar publicly declared that the president was "not well informed." Lugar decided to practice some *mediapolitik* of his own and appeared the following Sunday, February 23, 1986, on all three network television shows: NBC's *Meet the Press*, CBS's *Face the Nation*, and ABC's *This Week with David Brinkley*.

Politicians and journalists called Lugar's appearances the "hat trick"— the feat of scoring three goals in one hockey game, rare in hockey, almost unheard of in public affairs television. From his electronic platform, Lugar called on Reagan to ask Marcos to resign, and the next day, Senator Laxalt, clearly on orders from the White House, telephoned the Philippine leader, saying, "I think the time has come" to resign.[10] Without U.S. backing,

---

9. Hedrick Smith, *The Power Game: How Washington Works* (New York: Random House, 1988), p. 43.

10. Ibid., p. 44.

Marcos knew he was through, and over the strong protests of his support-ers he went into political exile. He was an authoritarian ruler who failed to appreciate that he might not win a free and open election conducted un-der the watchful eye of a free and open mass media.

THE MEDIA AT WAR

In time of war, the historian Loren B. Thompson states, "the military imperative to maintain secrecy and the journalistic imperative to convey truth will always be in tension." So it has been throughout American his-tory. During the Civil War, Secretary of War Edwin M. Stanton ordered a reporter for the *New York Tribune* to be shot for refusing to hand over a dispatch. The reporter was spared when other cabinet members (and President Lincoln) argued for a more lenient policy, declaring that the support of the press was essential to the war effort. Despite inconsistent censorship, often-hostile commanders, and a multifront war, journalists covered the war brilliantly, establishing a new standard for wartime jour-nalism "that would influence the reporting of all future conflicts."[11]

The questions that confronted the government and the media in the Civil War have resurfaced in every succeeding conflict. What is the proper role of the journalist in wartime? Should he always be an impartial ob-server, without regard for the consequences of his dispatches? Or does he have a duty to society not to report everything he sees and hears? What are the obligations of the government to help the journalist carry out his job? What are the government's responsibilities to the people in a war? What kind of censorship should there be—voluntary, mandatory, some combi-nation of the two? What happens when there is no formal declaration of war?

In many ways, World War I created the system of news coverage that is the journalistic half of *mediapolitik*. Modern techniques of communica-tion transmitted stories. The "pooling" of correspondents became stan-dard procedure, setting a precedent for the pack journalism that covers much of national and world politics today. Government censorship was institutionalized. One week after the United States' entry into the war, President Wilson appointed a Committee on Public Information to dis-seminate facts about the war and liaise with the press. George Creel, a newspaperman named to head the Committee, asked editors and re-

11. Loren B. Thompson, "The Press and the Pentagon: Old Battles, New Skirmishes," *The American Enterprise*, January/February 1992, p. 14.

porters to censor themselves voluntarily about troop movements, ship sailings, and other military events. The press generally cooperated because there had been a formal declaration of war by Congress. During World War I, the media were not subjected to the kind of government censorship and control that characterized the Civil War. Indeed, the Creel Committee, in the opinion of one expert, "remains one of the most liberal and least oppressive governmental wartime propaganda and censorship bodies found anywhere on the globe during this century."[12]

World War II was the first truly global war in history, affecting everyone on earth, even citizens of allegedly neutral countries like Sweden and Switzerland. It was also the first global conflict, the media historian George N. Gordon says, to employ mass communications as a means of public persuasion and propaganda, for military instruction and education, and as weapons themselves. The radio service of the British Broadcasting Corporation strengthened English resistance to Nazi Germany's nightly air raids during the Battle of Britain, counteracting Hitler's efforts, through propagandists like "Lord Haw-Haw," to weaken civilian morale. The Soviet Union used radio broadcasting to reinforce public resolve during the prolonged Nazi attacks on Stalingrad and Leningrad. In France, Holland, and Denmark, underground newspapers and broadcasters sprang up, with writers like Jean Paul Sartre and Albert Camus fighting a propaganda war in tandem with the military resistance.[13]

In the United States, the Roosevelt administration asked journalists to enlist in the war effort, and an overwhelming majority agreed, making possible, as in World War I, a system of voluntary censorship. The consensus on the righteousness of the war was so universal that few of the 2,600 correspondents accredited by the Navy and War Departments protested against review of their copy. Journalists of that generation were part of the American mainstream, staunch defenders of liberal democracy and market capitalism. They acknowledged the serious threat of fascist tyranny and the high stakes of the war, and they reported responsibly. Determined to combat Josef Goebbels's Ministry of Propaganda in Berlin with the truth, the United States created the Office of War Information under the direction of Elmer Davis, a veteran newsman and CBS news commentator. A major operation of the OWI was the Voice of America, which

---

12. George N. Gordon, *The Communications Revolution: A History of Mass Media in the United States* (New York: Hastings House, 1977), p. 144.

13. Ibid., pp. 205–7.

broadcast news programs about the progress of the war overseas and also engaged in psychological warfare against the enemy. The broadcasts aimed at Italy, Germany, and Japan were often combined with massive airdrops of leaflets on enemy troops, declaring that the war was lost and promising good treatment if they surrendered.[14]

In Germany, tight censorship was maintained by the Nazi regime, which told the people only good news, but even Hitler could not prevent the soldiers returning from the Russian front from revealing that they had been decisively defeated. The credibility of the German news services, newspapers, and radio broadcasts was seriously damaged. Paralleling later practice during the cold war, an increasing number of German citizens, risking death if caught, listened to the shortwave broadcasts (in German) of the BBC and the Voice of America. Germany's censorship failed because the people were able to determine the truth through word of mouth (the SS were not omnipresent) and through foreign broadcasts (Germany's radio jamming facilities were inadequate). During the cold war, the Communist governments of the Soviet Union and China were more thorough in their propaganda and their censorship and therefore more successful in retaining power.

KOREA: A LACK OF CONSENSUS

The sense of shared purpose that suffused military-media relations during World War II did not prevail in the Korean War, only five years later. A basic reason for the lack of consensus was that there was never a formal declaration of war against North Korea. Republican isolationists joined with Democratic pacifists in Congress to question American involvement. To forestall criticism, President Truman worked through the United Nations, which condemned North Korea's aggression in June 1950 and asked U.S. forces to help South Korea repel the invasion. At least in the beginning, Truman received media support. In the face of Communist aggression in Korea and elsewhere, the free world had no choice, stated the *New York Times*, but to build up its own armed strength to the point "which will enable it both to deter Russia from going to war and to nip in the bud or crush by overwhelming force any aggression by Soviet satellites acting as Moscow's cat's-paws."[15]

When critics contended that South Korea was a peripheral, not a major,

14. Ibid., pp. 210–11.
15. Editorial, *New York Times*, July 17, 1950.

strategic interest, the White House responded that if the United States stood by while South Korea fell, it would demonstrate to the world that the leader of the free world was either afraid of the U.S.S.R. or indifferent to the fate of its allies. Meanwhile, the U.S. commander in Korea, General Douglas MacArthur, initially depended upon a voluntary system of censorship like that used in World War II. But after numerous disagreements, a more formal approach was adopted, and as a result dispatches were often delayed or heavily censored. Resentment among journalists intensified when the military openly complained that negative reporting was hurting the war effort, which it saw as U.S. resolve in the face of Communist aggression.[16]

But as the war dragged on and casualties mounted, public and media support for the war declined sharply, and Truman's approval ratings sagged. In the fall of 1952, Dwight D. Eisenhower, the Republican presidential nominee, attacked Truman for his handling of the war and promised that, if elected, he would go to Korea for a personal assessment of the situation. This pledge by the World War II hero and a dramatic television speech in support of Eisenhower by General MacArthur, who had been fired for insubordination by Truman, helped end the Democratic hold on the White House.

VIETNAM: A LIMITED CONFLICT

Like Korea, Vietnam was a limited war, without any official sanction by Congress (except for the disputed Tonkin Gulf Resolution of August 1964), which engendered initial approval, then widespread discussion, and finally strong opposition at home. President John F. Kennedy played down U.S. involvement, but President Lyndon B. Johnson quickly escalated the American role in the war and tried to enlist the media, as his mentor FDR had done during World War II, to help achieve victory. Johnson also quoted his assassinated predecessor on the key supportive role of the media in times of "clear and present danger." In a 1961 speech before the American Newspaper Publishers Association, shortly after the Bay of Pigs failure, President Kennedy had said:

I am asking the members of the newspaper profession and the industry in this country to reexamine their own responsibilities—to consider the degree and nature of the present danger—and to heed the duty of self-restraint which that danger imposes upon all of us. Every newspaper now asks itself with respect to every

16. Thompson, "The Press and the Pentagon," p. 15.

story: "Is it news?" All I suggest is that you add the question: "Is it in the interest of national security?"[17]

Most of the U.S. mass media supported the stated goals of the Vietnamese conflict (prevent the Communist takeover of South Vietnam and block any domino effect in the rest of Southeast Asia), until the surprising Tet offensive of January 1968. Although the North Vietnamese and the Viet Cong suffered a major military defeat during the offensive, the fact that they were able to carry the war into Saigon and even threaten the American Embassy there, created serious doubts in the minds of a growing segment of the public and the media about the Johnson administration's ability to stop Communist aggression in South Vietnam. The enormous impact of Tet was summed up by a gloomy Walter Cronkite in a CBS television special on February 27:

It seems now more certain than ever that the bloody experience of Vietnam is to end in a stalemate. . . . It is increasingly clear to this reporter that the only rational way out . . . [is] to negotiate, not as victors, but as an honorable people who lived up to their pledge to defend democracy, and did the best they could.[18]

Yet, for all his pessimism, Cronkite viewed the conflict as a legitimate struggle for democracy and not an imperialist war, as critics then and revisionist historians since have described the Vietnam War. For Cronkite, Vietnam was a just war but, unhappily, one that America could not win.

After viewing the telecast (Johnson had three television sets installed in the Oval Office so he could monitor all the networks whenever he wanted), the president is alleged to have remarked to his press secretary, George Christian, that if he had lost Walter Cronkite, he had lost Mr. Average Citizen. In a testimonial to the power of *mediapolitik*, the author and journalist David Halberstam wrote that "it was the first time in American history a war had been declared over by an anchorman."[19] Robert Elegant, who

17. *Public Papers of the Presidents of the United States, John F. Kennedy, 1961* (Washington: Government Printing Office, 1961), pp. 336–37. For a sharply critical view of "unconstitutional" government pressure on and manipulation of the mass media, see Ted Galen Carpenter, *The Captive Press: Foreign Policy Crises and the First Amendment* (Washington: The Cato Institute, 1995). Carpenter argues that if the government "co-opts, censors, intimidates, or otherwise silences the news media, it can virtually preclude meaningful debate on its policies" (pp. 10–11).

18. Peter Braestrup, *Big Story: How the American Press and Television Reported and Interpreted the Crisis of Tet 1968 in Vietnam and Washington* (Garden City, N.Y.: Anchor Books, 1978), p. 134.

19. David Halberstam, *The Powers That Be* (New York: Alfred A. Knopf, 1979), p. 514.

covered the war for *The Los Angeles Times,* agreed with Halberstam's assessment, writing that "the outcome of the war was determined not on the battlefield, but on the printed page, and above all on the television screen."[20] A month later, Johnson announced his decision not to seek re-election—on television.

In late 1968, an NBC producer suggested a three-part series showing that Tet had been a military victory for America and that the media had greatly exaggerated the view that it was a defeat for South Vietnam. The idea was rejected because Tet was already established "in the public's mind as a defeat, and therefore it was an American defeat."[21] General Vo Nguyen Giap, North Vietnam's most famous general, later confirmed the critical psychological role of the Tet offensive, commenting: "The war was fought on many fronts. At that time, the most important front was American public opinion."[22]

News coverage of the Vietnam War differed from that of previous conflicts in two important ways: (1) television brought the often-bloody war into the living rooms of Americans; and (2) journalists were allowed to travel throughout the country without a military escort and to report whatever they saw as long as they did not disclose militarily sensitive information. No important secrets were revealed, but many correspondents gave highly negative assessments of the U.S. military's performance, producing bitter recriminations about "Who lost Vietnam?"—the military or the media—that have persisted to this day.[23]

The attitude of many in the media and Congress might have been different if President Johnson had chosen to mobilize the American people, to invoke the national will, for the Vietnam War. But as the Pentagon official in charge of public affairs commented: "There was not once a significant organized effort by the Executive Branch of the federal government to put across its side." According to Doris Kearns Goodwin, a Johnson biographer, the president's decision not to mobilize the public was based on his fears that it would jeopardize his Great Society programs.[24] Johnson ap-

20. Reed Irvine and Joe Goulden, "Old Tactics of Vietnam," *Washington Times,* January 30, 1991.

21. Braestrup, *Big Story,* p. 509.

22. Ibid.

23. For an extended analysis of television's impact on the American public's attitude about Vietnam, see Michael Arlen, *The Living Room War* (New York: Viking Press, 1969).

24. Harry G. Summers, Jr., *On Strategy: A Critical Analysis of the Vietnam War* (New York: Dell, 1984), pp. 34–35; Doris Kearns [Goodwin], *Lyndon Johnson and the American Dream* (New York: Harper & Row, 1976), pp. 251–53.

parently did not perceive the fallacy of committing the military without first committing the American people.

Tom Shales, *The Washington Post*'s television critic, argues that the media coverage of the war had a lasting cultural impact on America, and that, in fact, "Vietnam made us a television nation." During the two world wars and the Korean War, the mass media, led by the press, played its historic role as middleman between the government and the people, providing news and information and serving as a mediating institution. There was always time for people and government to consider what had happened, to place the event in its proper context in life and society. But during the Vietnam years, Americans watched the war in their living rooms as it happened, much as they watched a parade march down Main Street or Mickey Mantle hit a home run. In vivid color, television showed the dead and the wounded, the burning villages, the faces of terrified children.

Reflection became difficult, and then impossible. Americans began making up their minds immediately about the significance of events, with help from an increasingly skeptical media corps, which abandoned the role of mediator for that of partisan. Journalists commented and analyzed as battles were fought and huts were burned and soldiers were killed. The war was transformed from a necessary defense of freedom into an unnecessary involvement in someone else's civil war. Americans saw one president declare he would not seek reelection and another president resign his office on television. "We lived through years of darkness and emerged from them media-wise," Shales sums up, "even media-obsessed." Sounding like Marshall McLuhan, Shales comments: "Television itself was the light at the end of the tunnel."[25]

But like McLuhan, Shales went too far. Television is inanimate, it cannot reason or make decisions. It does what its gatekeepers tell it to do. And if its gatekeepers—its editors, anchors, reporters—do not have a solid understanding of their responsibilities as well as their rights, television can mislead rather than enlighten the American people.

THE PERSIAN GULF WAR

On June 1, 1980, five years after the fall of South Vietnam, a flamboyant Atlanta businessman started the Cable News Network (CNN), a network that would influence world politics more than any other media institution of the late twentieth century. In the age of *mediapolitik*, Ted Turner rea-

25. Tom Shales, "The War That Came in from the Tube," *Washington Post*, April 21, 1985.

soned that there was a large market at home and abroad for a twenty-four-hour-a-day news service. Ridiculed by the old-line broadcast networks and plagued by amateurish production and programming, CNN initially suffered heavy financial losses that almost forced Turner to shut down his perpetual news machine. After a $20 million loss in 1984, a CNN executive wrote: "We have depended on the news to do our producing for us. When the news is dramatic and compelling, CNN is. When the news is not, CNN is not."[26] Over the next several years, CNN became steadily more professional and its ratings dramatically improved with the rise to power of Gorbachev in the Soviet Union, the Iran-contra affair, the Reagan-Gorbachev summits, the 1988 national political conventions (which CNN carried gavel-to-gavel), the Tiananmen Square massacre, and the collapse of Communism in Eastern and Central Europe. Turner shrewdly expanded the network's operations into Japan and Western Europe, which had large English-speaking populations and their own cable systems. CNN earned an estimated $134 million in 1989 and $170 million in 1992, confirming that it was no longer the plaything of an eccentric entrepreneur but a media organization to be reckoned with. CNN became a world-class media power with the Persian Gulf War.

On the evening of January 16, 1991, in prime time, a U.S.-led military coalition hit targets in Iraq and Kuwait, initiating the six-week Gulf War. While ABC was the first network to report that the bombing had begun, CNN dominated the coverage as its correspondents in Baghdad reported the shelling of strategic targets through their hotel windows. At a Pentagon press briefing that evening, Defense Secretary Dick Cheney commented: "The best reporting that I've seen on what transpired in Baghdad was on CNN." The cable network received a telling compliment when NBC's Tom Brokaw interviewed CNN's Bernard Shaw by telephone and then remarked: "CNN used to be called the little network that could. It's no longer a little network."[27] The network's dramatic pictures of antiaircraft artillery lighting up the sky over Baghdad was carried live that first night to 105 countries. In the United States, the network's coverage reached eleven million households, not counting network affiliates with access to CNN—only 1.6 million households less than the redoubtable CBS.

The U.S. military waged a two-front war: one against Iraq's armed

26. Edwin Diamond, "How CNN Does It," *New York,* February 11, 1991, p. 38.
27. Tom Shales, "Television, Eyewitness on the Front Line," *Washington Post,* January 17, 1991.

forces and a second to enlist the mass media in support of the war effort. Remembering the bitter fruit of unrestrained media freedom in Vietnam, the Pentagon laid down new guidelines that required print and broadcast reporters to work in pools, to be accompanied by information officers when in the field, and to submit their copy to military editors. Pete Williams, the spokesman for the Pentagon, explained that the rules were needed because a small army of eight hundred journalists was in Saudi Arabia demanding to cover the war from the front lines, a logistical impossibility. Despite protests by the media, a national poll showed that nearly eight of ten Americans supported the Defense Department's restrictions. In fact, almost six in ten surveyed said the military should exert "more control" over the media.[28]

This wide gap between the media and the public regarding war news suggests that the public, following months-long congressional debate and then approval of Operation Desert Storm, firmly supported the war effort, as in World War II, while many in the media adopted a skeptical stance, as in the latter days of the Vietnam War. The American people accepted that in a war, when the lives of individual soldiers as well as national security are at stake, a free press can be legitimately if reasonably restricted. They expected the mass media to acknowledge their power to affect the course of a conflict and to accept responsibility for their actions and their mistakes, if any. To the question why the American people rank the media so low, their self-righteous attitude in wartime offers one explanation.

The British news media, in contrast, submitted to far more severe censorship than their American counterparts. Guidelines laid down by the Ministry of Defense in London forbade journalists to mention specific locations, troop numbers, and operational techniques unless officially authorized to do so. The ministry used the experience of the Falkland Islands War in 1982 as a standard for its media approach to the Gulf crisis. During the Falklands War, bitter disputes arose between the Thatcher government and the news media about what the public had a right to know, and the British public supported the firm line taken by the government.[29]

28. Howard Kurtz, "Media's Mixed Reviews," *Washington Post,* January 31, 1991.

29. "Government Sets Rules for Media Coverage of Gulf War," *Christian Science Monitor,* January 17, 1991.

THE "NEUTRAL" JOURNALIST

The American public's concern about the conduct of the media in the Persian Gulf War was heightened when on several occasions American reporters provided tactical intelligence about the conflict not only to the public but to the enemy. On the first night of the war, David Green, a CBS cameraman traveling between Khafji and the border with Kuwait, told anchorman Dan Rather that there were no Saudi troops between his position and the border and that the Iraqis could "just walk in here . . . if they wanted." Apparently, the Iraqis were listening because the battle for Khafji followed. The same night, all the networks announced the start of the allied air assault some fifteen minutes before many pilots reached their targets. Presumably, the Iraqis, like everyone else in the Middle East, were monitoring CNN and the other networks and alerted their antiaircraft batteries.

A turning point had been reached in war journalism, wrote the media critic John Corry: the old ideal of objectivity was replaced by a new standard of "neutrality" by which a reporter stood midway between two opposing sides, even when one of the sides was his own. In the past, the majority of the media endorsed the basic principles of American democracy—representative government, individual responsibility, a market economy—while only a minority of iconoclasts and sensationalists dissented. The majority did not agree on everything, but they did agree that the American system, with all its imperfections, was the best in the world. Today a growing number of journalists have a markedly different set of beliefs from those of mainstream America. Unlike the working-class hero of *The Front Page*, the modern journalist is usually well educated and well paid, cosmopolitan in background, socially liberal in outlook, and firmly antiestablishment. Modern American journalists, conclude media analysts S. Robert Lichter, Stanley Rothman, and Linda S. Richter, have become "an elite in terms of economic status, public perception, and social influence."[30] Such an elite will be at best skeptical and at worst hostile toward a highly structured, traditional institution like the military.

CBS's Mike Wallace proclaimed the new principle of media neutrality at a 1987 conference on the military and the press when he said it would be appropriate for him as a journalist to accompany enemy troops into bat-

---

30. S. Robert Lichter, Stanley Rothman, and Linda S. Richter, *The Media Elite: America's New Powerbrokers* (Bethesda, Md.: Adler & Adler, 1986), p. 53.

tle, even if they ambushed (and presumably killed) American soldiers. During the Persian Gulf War, CNN's Bernard Shaw refused to be debriefed by American officers after he left Baghdad because, he said, reporters must be "neutral."[31] Being "neutral" apparently means refusing not only to take sides but also to make distinctions. There was a critical distinction between the strategy of the United States and that of Iraq, the media scholar Stephen Hess points out: "Saddam Hussein's targets were [Kuwaiti] civilians while the U.S. targets were [Iraqi] military, in which unfortunately civilians may have died."[32]

There is deep irony in Shaw's declaration of neutrality, since he and other modern correspondents are fond of describing Edward R. Murrow as their hero and model. Yet, in the Battle of Britain and other World War II battles, Murrow made it clear which side he was on. Certainly, he would never have traveled to Berlin, checked into the Grand Hotel, and reported, without comment, Adolf Hitler's fulminations about the war. Ed Turner, when he was CNN executive vice president, had a far different perspective, declaring that if the American media had had the requisite technology during World War II, "You would have seen Eva Braun on the *Donahue* show and Hitler on *Meet the Press*."[33]

The notion of media "neutrality" raises a plethora of questions about media performance in and out of wartime. If a neutral journalist does not owe a higher duty to his country, where does his higher duty lie? Would Turner and Shaw have broadcast the battle plans of U.S. troops against Iraq if they had obtained the information? Would they have published the facts about the Bay of Pigs invasion in the spring of 1961—as James Reston of the *New York Times* did not, after receiving a personal plea from President Kennedy? Would they have printed revealing photographs of a polio-crippled President Roosevelt during World War II—as all U.S. newspapers, even the Roosevelt-hating *Chicago Tribune*, did not?

If a neutral journalist insists that he has no higher duty to his country, then all the more reason for him to practice moral and political, not simply social, responsibility in his reporting. It is not enough for him to follow a libertarian philosophy when human security, let alone the nation's

---

31. John Corry, "TV News and the Neutrality Principle," *Commentary*, May 1991, p. 24.

32. "Bashing the Media: Why the Public Outrage?" *Defense Media Monitor*, February 28, 1991, p. 2.

33. E. J. Dionne, Jr., "Mainstream Reporting and Middle East Extremities," *Washington Post*, September 1, 1990.

security, is in question. Lyle Denniston of the *Baltimore Sun* is a libertarian absolutist who insists that the "only" reason for his, and other journalists', existence is to "get the news." He says that journalists "should stop trying to play God because we care about the outcome of a story. We should stop caring about outcomes."[34] But Denniston sets up a false premise. It is not necessary for journalists to play God to be concerned about whether the impact of their stories advances the good or the bad, democracy or totalitarianism. To be indifferent to outcomes is to be indifferent to life—and liberty.

CNN's ace war correspondent, Peter Arnett, explained his "neutralism" during the Persian Gulf War this way: "I am sick of wars, and I am here [in Baghdad] because maybe my contribution will somehow lessen the hostilities, if not this time, maybe next time."[35] Accordingly, when Arnett visited what had been Baghdad's two main power plants, destroyed by bombs and missiles, he spoke of "relentless attacks on civilian installations." He did not add that the installations had been covered in camouflage paint. When he reported on the famous target that the Pentagon said was a biological weapons factory and the Iraqis claimed was a "baby-milk plant" ("innocent enough from what we could see," commented Arnett), he did not mention its camouflage either. But visiting German peace activists did notice the camouflage and their comments were widely reported in the European press.

CNN viewers saw and heard an angry woman beside a crater screaming, in perfect English: "All of you are responsible, all of you, bombing the people for the sake of oil." The same woman also appeared on French television speaking excellent French. Several days later, a CNN anchor identified her as an employee of the Iraqi Foreign Ministry—i.e., a trained propagandist in the telewar being conducted by Saddam Hussein.[36] Peter Braestrup, the author of *Big Story*, the classic study of media coverage of the Vietnam War, maintained that CNN was clearly being used by Iraqi officials and that, for all his professionalism, Arnett was "America's first journalistic POW."[37]

CNN also aired audio soundtracks from what Iraqi television called

34. Lyle Denniston, "In Defense of Journalistic Competence," *The Long Term View* 1, no. 2 (summer 1992): p. 22.

35. Ibid., p. 24.

36. Ibid., pp. 25–26.

37. Don Kowet, "CNN's Baghdad Reports Draw Fire as Propaganda," *Washington Times*, January 28, 1991.

"interviews" with American prisoners of war captured in air attacks. One pilot said, "I think our leaders and our people have wrongly attacked the peaceful people of Iraq." CNN noted that the interviews were "recorded in captivity" and were "cleared by Iraqi censors," but were these broadcasts news or propaganda? ABC refused to air the audiotapes, explaining that it had had "a lot of experience with statements made by people who are being held against their will . . . [Such people] are often forced to read statements under threat of their lives."[38]

SADDAM'S MEDIA TARGETS

What was Saddam's target audience for his propaganda? The United States and the West? The Arabic world? His own Iraqi people? The likely answer: all three. In August 1990, when the Iraqi dictator was seen awkwardly tousling the hair of a frightened five-year-old British hostage, Western viewers were repulsed and angered. Yet Middle Eastern viewers may well have reacted differently because the boy was obviously well fed and had access to medical care. "In that part of the world," the director of the Center for International Journalism commented, "that can be more important than freedom of speech and movement."[39] Saddam understood the authoritarian nature of Islamic politics but not the democratic nature of Western politics. He badly miscalculated, shortly after the war started, when Iraqi television displayed pictures of U.S. prisoners of war, pilots whose bruised and swollen faces left no doubt they had been beaten. Far from demonstrating Saddam's magnanimity, the images "reinforced the 'Butcher of Baghdad' image."[40]

Saddam nevertheless kept trying; he decided he could win a round in the media war after U.S. bombs hit a suburban Baghdad bunker and left possibly hundreds of civilians dead. Iraqi officials took American television journalists to the site to see the burned bodies and hear the cries of grieving relatives. The Iraqis contended that the carnage was proof of America's barbarism in the war. U.S. officials quickly responded that the pictures were misleading and that Iraq was responsible for placing civilians in what was clearly a military installation, complete with camou-

---

38. Tom Shales, "The Toll of Running Round the Clock," *Washington Post*, January 21, 1991.

39. David Lieberman, "How Saddam Manipulates TV as a Weapon of War," *TV Guide*, March 15, 1991, p. 15. Comment is by Scott Armstrong, director, Center for International Journalism, American University.

40. Ibid.

flaged roof. The American people agreed: a *USA Today* poll revealed that an overwhelming 84 percent of Americans blamed Saddam Hussein for the deaths. Although the Iraqi dictator's attempt to use the media failed, the U.S. military was so concerned about public reaction at home and abroad that it adjusted its bombing strategy to concentrate less on the cities and more on military targets in southern Iraq.[41] American generals were acting on a basic maxim of telewar: "The media is really a battlefield, and you have to win on it."[42]

The Defense Department even deliberately used the mass media to mislead the Iraqi army. A few weeks before the war began, the U.S. Marines held practice amphibious maneuvers in the Persian Gulf south of Kuwait. Heavy media coverage of Operation Imminent Thunder helped persuade Iraq to station a large part of its army along the Kuwaiti coast, opening the way for allied forces to carry out the "left hook" flanking attack that led to a stunning victory. Pete Williams, the Pentagon spokesman, admitted that the military had conducted operations designed to fool the Iraqis.[43] Saddam Hussein was certain to get the misleading message—three offices in his presidential palace were wired to receive CNN.

In one sense, Saddam's totalitarian rule has been one long, televised Orwellian event. His decrees and deeds led the news over Iraqi television night after night, and his frequent trips to the countryside were portrayed on the state-controlled media as "dynamic, problem-solving missions." He even commissioned a television docudrama of his life and had a son-in-law play him as a young man. Seeking to position himself as the deserving heir of the region's many riches, ancient and modern, Saddam set about to rebuild the ancient city of Babylon as it may have existed during the reign of King Nebuchadnezzar, the fabled ruler of Babylonia in the sixth century B.C. During one evening celebration, the faces of Nebuchadnezzar and Saddam were projected into the sky, side by side.[44] As self-serving and heavy-handed as the propaganda was, most Iraqis brought their children up to applaud it; they had no other choice in Saddam's Big Brother dictatorship.[45]

41. Ibid.

42. "U.S. Used Press as a Weapon," *Wall Street Journal,* February 28, 1991. Statement was made by a senior Army officer.

43. CBS Evening News, April 10, 1992.

44. Judith Miller and Laurie Mylroie, *Saddam Hussein and the Crisis in the Gulf* (New York: Times Books, 1990), pp. 57–58.

45. Glenn Frankel, "Bush, Hussein Waging Psychological Warfare through Media," *Washington Post,* September 2, 1990.

THE HITLER PARALLELS

Like Hitler, Saddam controls all the reins of political power: he is president, secretary-general of the Iraqi Baath Party, commander in chief, head of the government, and chairman of the Revolutionary Command Council. He has replaced the state with the party and then the party with himself as the giver of life and death. Like Hitler, he has murdered not only former opponents and rivals but old colleagues and associates who might lead a future coup d'etat against him. Like Hitler, he has constructed a vast network of government informers, prompting one diplomat to remark, "There is a feeling that at least three million Iraqis are watching the eleven million others."[46]

Like Hitler, Saddam has carried out a policy of genocide against a religious group within Iraq—the Kurds. Largely Sunni Moslem but non-Arab, the Kurds make up about 20 percent of the population. Saddam's use of chemical weapons against the Kurds makes Iraq the only state in the world ever to have used such terrible weapons against its own citizens. Like Hitler, Saddam uses terror as a deliberate instrument of state policy to suppress all centers or potential centers of opposition. And like Hitler, he is constantly intimidating other states to project an aura of invincibility at home, and to keep his enormous army—still the largest in the Middle East—occupied. As Plato wrote, a tyrant "will continue to stir up war in order that the people may continue to need a leader."[47]

The Iraqi leader's favorite medium of communication with the West has always been CNN. In September 1990, as President Bush and Soviet President Gorbachev were meeting in Helsinki, Saddam launched a verbal attack clearly aimed at dividing the two leaders, an attack he knew would be relayed over CNN, which was hooked up to Bush's hotel suite. On another occasion, the network aired an interview with the Arab terrorist Abul Abbas, who made death threats against Egyptian President Hosni Mubarak and others. Bush aides admitted that the president took the threats as seriously "as if they had been delivered through official channels."[48]

While a CNN correspondent denied that "we are practicing diplomacy or that we are active diplomats," the willingness of the network to be a

46. Miller and Mylroie, *Saddam Hussein and the Crisis in the Gulf*, p. 46.

47. Plato, *The Republic*, translated with an introduction by Desmond Lee, 2d ed. (New York: Penguin Books, 1981), p. 388.

48. Steve Berg, "CNN Talks; Saddam Listens," *Washington Times*, January 10, 1991.

"real-time conduit of information and government policy" has made it an active, not a passive, practitioner of teleplomacy. Heads of state had exchanged messages through the media long before broadcast and cable television, but now satellites "have speeded up this communication by a quantum leap."[49] National leaders and diplomats have far less time—sometimes only minutes—in which to consider the content of a communique or message and to frame their response. If a head of state does not provide an answer to the impatient media and the waiting world, he projects an image of vacillation and weakness, a risky signal when dealing with a dictator, large or small. In the age of *mediapolitik*, silence is not golden but dangerous.

Even before the war started, Saddam Hussein tried to arouse popular Muslim sentiment against the allied governments, especially Saudi Arabia and Egypt. Using Iraqi television and Holy Mecca Radio as policy instruments, Baghdad did its best to convince Middle Easterners that Kuwait deserved to be seized, that Saudi Arabia had betrayed the holy cities of Islam, and that America had come to control the region's oil resources and humiliate Arabs. Saddam explained that he had conquered Kuwait to stop its corrupt rulers from spending billions "on their lust and on gambling in the West." He accused Emir Jabir, Kuwait's ruler, of keeping seventy wives and marrying a virgin every Thursday. A special target of Saddam's invective was Saudi King Fahd. When Fahd called for Saudi women to join the armed forces (which women have done for years in Iraq), Holy Mecca Radio asked if the king thought that "our honor is so trivial to us that we will allow our daughters to stand next to Zionist and U.S. soldiers—pork eaters, sinners, and AIDS victims." The radio accused Fahd of "turning our women into instruments of pleasure for Bush's pigs and Shamir's tigers." Americans in Mecca and Medina were said to "drink and party with semi-nude dancers," thereby desecrating the Islamic holy cities.[50]

Anti-American media repeated the Iraqi charges. A radical Tehran newspaper accused the Saudis of footing the bill for American debauchery. A pro-Iraqi daily newspaper in Jordan detailed the astronomical amounts of alcohol consumed by American soldiers. But these grossly exaggerated stories were not picked up by other Middle East media, confirming that popular anger against the U.S.-Arab alliance, at least within the Gulf countries, was limited. The failure of Saddam's propaganda bar-

49. Ibid.
50. Daniel Pipes, "On Holy Mecca Radio," *Washington Times*, January 24, 1991.

rage to sow any significant dissension among Muslims enabled the U.S.-led coalition to take more aggressive action on the battlefield.[51]

Among the laser-directed bombs, Tomahawk cruise missiles, and other high-technology weapons of the war fluttered millions of old-fashioned "paper bullets," propaganda leaflets intended to break the Iraqi soldier's will to fight. Their message was uncomplicated: If you cease resistance, "you will not die." Radio broadcasts and loudspeakers on the front lines told the Iraqis how to use the leaflets as "safe conduct passes" when they surrendered. Leaflet droppers, popularly known as "confetti soldiers," had often been used in previous conflicts; at one point during the Vietnam War, an estimated one *billion* leaflets were dropped by American forces on the Viet Cong every month.

One leaflet aimed at Iraqi troops provided written instructions for surrender on one side and featured drawings on the other side, including a scene of three Iraqi prisoners sitting down to a meal of fruit, a powerful image for hungry men. The leaflets urged the troops to "cease resistance," language that emerged from World War II when Japanese soldiers rejected a leaflet that contained the humiliating words "I surrender," but accepted the more honorable phrase "I cease resistance." A second Gulf War leaflet pictured an elderly Arab couple—ostensibly a soldier's parents—lamenting their son's plight. "Oh my son," reads the Arabic script near the father, "when will you return?" The mother is imagining her son bandaged and mangled. It was calculated that the emotional appeal of the family at home and the stark warning of injury and death would help convince Iraqi soldiers to wave a white flag as soon as allied forces came into view. When thousands of Saddam's men quickly surrendered, psychological warfare experts took credit for persuading allied generals to aim a "drumfire of printed paper" as well as bombs and missiles at the enemy.[52] That so many Iraqis laid down their arms also suggests the universal appeal of and desire for freedom, even among Moslems brought up under the totalitarian regime of Saddam Hussein.

THE TYRANNY OF TIME

How captive the mass media are to time and how addicted they have become to pack journalism was proved in their coverage of Iraq's false peace offer on February 15, made nearly two weeks before it finally surren-

51. Ibid.
52. Charles Paul Freund, "War's 'Paper Bullets,'" *Washington Post*, February 10, 1991.

dered. A CNN anchor read one of the first dispatches about the alleged peace proposal at 6:41 A.M., saying: "Iraq is ready to cooperate with U.N. Security Council Resolution 660 for an honorable political solution in the gulf including a withdrawal from Kuwait." Bryant Gumbel began NBC's *Today* show with the "very hopeful news" that "Iraq is prepared to withdraw from Kuwait." Harry Smith, co-anchor of CBS *This Morning*, waxed the most euphoric, declaring from Saudi Arabia that "this war, for a lot of intents and purposes, is over."

It was not until 10 A.M. that a CNN correspondent in Moscow read all of Iraq's conditions, most of them unacceptable to the United States and its allies. Shortly thereafter, President Bush held a special news conference to announce flatly, "There is nothing new. It is a hoax." The networks spent the rest of the day lamenting that hopes for peace had been raised and dashed without adding, Tom Shales pointed out, that they had been primarily responsible for raising and dashing them. Such egregious lapses in elementary journalism are certain to keep happening because (1) in the rush to be first, news now often reaches the air not only unedited but unverified; (2) when one news source reports something that is very newsworthy, every other news medium rushes to join the pack.[53] The media have always been prone to rush into print or to go on the air with a story. What is different today is their willingness to rush to judgment, often concluding that the U.S. government and its representatives rather than the other side are at fault.

As the Persian Gulf War drew to a close, President Bush followed the media tenets of a presidential campaign: "Answer everything quickly and aggressively, put no trust in your opponent, and prevent him from ever gaining the initiative."[54] When the Soviets announced on Thursday, February 21, that Iraq had agreed to "unconditional withdrawal," the White House immediately indicated that President Bush had serious reservations and within a few hours began saying that the Soviet plan to end the war was "unacceptable." White House officials knew they had to react quickly or the Soviet proposal would go unchallenged, at least in the mass media, and gain some support in Europe.

The next morning, Bush bypassed the State Department and diplomatic channels and chose the Rose Garden to announce, via televised news

53. Tom Shales, "TV's Brief Peace," *Washington Post*, February 16, 1991.
54. Ann Devroy and Dan Balz, "White House Wages War of Words Like Political Race," *Washington Post*, February 27, 1991.

conference, a list of strict conditions that Saddam Hussein would have to meet within twenty-four hours to avoid a ground war; in the meantime, said the president, the war would continue with "undiminished intensity." On Monday night, when Baghdad Radio (not the Iraqi Foreign Ministry) reported that Saddam had ordered a withdrawal of troops from Kuwait, the White House swiftly countered, before the evening television news programs ended, with a statement that "the war goes on." A White House official explained that the uncompromising message was aimed at the United Nations, where officials were going into a late-night session, and came so quickly because "we did not want the Baghdad Radio report to hang out [unanswered] for 10 or 12 hours."[55]

Bush's hard-line strategy was proved correct when on Tuesday, February 26, the Iraqi leader announced, over state radio, an immediate pullout from Kuwait, but also described the war as a moral victory for the Iraqi people and did not renounce his country's claim to Kuwait. With his troops routed, his capital city pockmarked with bomb craters, and his seizure of a neighboring country reversed, Saddam still exhorted his people and Muslims throughout the Middle East: "The band of infidels will ultimately be defeated, and God's good people will inherit the land." Bush's televised response was delivered in blunt language far removed from the realm of diplomacy but perfect for the sound-bite world of the mass media: "Saddam's most recent speech is an outrage. He is not withdrawing. His defeated forces are retreating. He is trying to claim victory in the midst of a rout. And he is not voluntarily giving up Kuwait."[56] Thus, down to the last shot fired in the Persian Gulf War, Bush and Saddam fought each other off the battlefield as well as on, acutely aware that in the age of *mediapolitik,* the course of war can be affected by the deployment of media as well as armed forces.

The war heightened the historic struggle over information between the mass media and the military, which do not, after all, have much in common. "Given the media's focus on conflict, deviance, and melodrama," wrote Peter Braestrup, "most senior military men do not see the media as allies of civic peace and virtue. . . . There is no counterpart in journalism to 'duty, honor, country,' or to the military leader's ultimate responsibility

---

55. Ibid.
56. Nora Boustang, "Saddam Tells Iraqis of Pullout but Claims 'Dignified' Victory"; statements by Saddam Hussein, "Iraqis 'Have Won with Right over Wrong,'" and George Bush, "'Saddam Is Not Interested in Peace . . .,'" *Washington Post,* February 27, 1991.

for life and death and the nation's security." There is certainly no equivalence as to objectives; as Henry Allen commented, "When the military makes a mistake in combat, its own people die. When the press makes a mistake, it runs a correction."[57]

Driven by bottom-line journalism and as usual brandishing the First Amendment, media executives complained bitterly about the restrictions placed on journalists in the Persian Gulf War, charging censorship by delay, blackouts of the "ugly parts," and leakproof pools. They protested that the media had been manipulated when the Pentagon disseminated "disinformation" about an amphibious assault against Iraq that was really a ruse to mislead the Iraqis. Representatives of leading media organizations proposed that pools should not replace independent coverage; journalists should be provided access to all major military units; stories and pictures should not be subject to prior military review; and military escorts should not interfere with reporting. Summed up one disgruntled reporter: "Don't just take us along. Leave us alone."[58] Yet, when a group of American journalists was captured in Iraq after the cease-fire, media neutrality was abruptly abandoned. Four media executives immediately wrote to President Bush, urging that no U.S. forces withdraw from Iraq until the safety of the journalists was assured.

Although Richard Harwood, the *Washington Post* ombudsman, concluded that nothing of significance to the public interest had been suppressed in the war, the Pentagon did adopt, after a year of study, less-restrictive war-zone rules for journalists, conscious of its responsibility in a democracy to keep the public reasonably informed.[59] The new guidelines were an attempt to fuse military realism and journalistic idealism. They allowed wider access to battlefields, fighting units, and military personnel; discouraged the use of small pools of journalists who must share their reporting with all of the media; and prohibited escort officers from interfering with news gathering. The military retained the right to review stories, photos, and videotape for material that could jeopardize troops or missions.[60] The more liberal rules, which included nine of ten recommendations made by network and newspaper executives after the war, sur-

57. Henry Allen, "The Gulf between Media and Military," *Washington Post*, February 21, 1991.

58. Howard Kurtz, "News Media Ask Freer Hand in Future Conflicts," *Washington Post*, July 1, 1991; Michael Getler, "Do Americans Really Want to Censor War Coverage This Way?" *Washington Post*, March 17, 1991.

59. Richard Harwood, "News from the Front," *Washington Post*, February 10, 1991.

60. James Cox, "Military Revamps Press Rules," *USA Today*, April 17, 1992.

prised some journalists and scholars, but should not have. In modern tele-war, the U.S. military needs the mass media to learn what the enemy is doing, to inform the American public what it is doing, and sometimes to tell the enemy what it is not doing. The military understands that in the age of *mediapolitik*, the mass media can be as vital to victory or defeat in a conflict as the most sophisticated weapon.

THE HAITI "INVASION"

Cooperation rather than confrontation between the government and the mass media was evident in the U.S. occupation of Haiti in September 1994. Coverage began with a nationally televised address and warning to Haiti's military junta by President Bill Clinton, followed by network anchors discussing the imminent invasion with retired military officers. CBS's Dan Rather scooped the other networks by interviewing Lt. General Raoul Cedras, the head of the Haitian junta, in Port-au-Prince. Determined not to be left out of the action, all four major networks (ABC, NBC, CBS, CNN) placed correspondents with independent communications links at key installations in Haiti. Military experts provided detailed descriptions of the invasion plans, including inventories of troops and equipment, lists of targets, and maps of invasion routes.

Former Secretary of State Henry Kissinger speculated that the detailed revelations on television, especially CNN, might have helped the U.S. negotiations (led by former President Jimmy Carter; General Colin Powell, former chairman of the Joint Chiefs of Staff; and Senator Sam Nunn of Georgia) with the Haitian military and prevented a pitched battle between American and Haitian forces. It was quite possible, wrote the *New York Times*' media critic, that CNN's broadcasts "served the same purpose as the air campaign in the Persian Gulf War: weakening the enemy's resolve before the ground invasion."[61]

The Pentagon's media plan in Haiti was to be as open as possible. The media pool was given classified information by high-ranking officers, including Lt. General Henry Hugh Shelton, commander of the operation. Other than an embargo until the actual start of the invasion, wrote correspondent Andrew Schneider, "there were no restrictions on what we could report or how we could report it."[62]

61. John Tierney, "'The Press Was Here,' but Not the Enemy," *New York Times*, September 20, 1994.
62. Jacqueline Sharkey, "The Shallow End of the Pool?" *American Journalism Review*, December 1994, p. 44.

The new cooperative spirit between government and military was confirmed when all four network news divisions revealed that they had voluntarily withheld information that American planes had taken off for an invasion of Haiti until the invasion was called off and the Pentagon agreed the news could be broadcast. The networks emphasized that they acted out of concern for the safety of American troops. For the same reason, no network correspondent informed Haitian officials that an invasion was under way. Laying aside his mantle of "neutrality," CNN Vice President Ed Turner said that "the well-being of the [U.S.] troops and the safety of the mission is paramount."[63]

In another example of the role of *mediapolitik* in Haiti, the mass media gave extensive coverage to Randall Robinson, head of the lobbying group TransAfrica, when he began a hunger strike in the spring of 1994 protesting Clinton's policy of repatriating Haitian boat people and thereby endangering their lives. Pictures of a weak Robinson lying in his bed were shown around the world and helped persuade the president to rethink his policy, adopt an openly antijunta position, and direct his foreign-policy team to prepare for an invasion.[64]

Tension between the government and the media in wartime is nevertheless bound to continue, exacerbated by the presence of an international network instantaneously covering the news—CNN—and the accelerating influence of the Internet. All the discussion about less restrictive rules and more access seems almost irrelevant when television correspondents are broadcasting live from the capital of an enemy or the front lines of a battle. Not only is CNN here to stay, but other CNNs are on the way. Private corporations (like the one headed by Rupert Murdoch) and government-led entities in Germany, Japan, and other nations are launching satellite news operations. The debate about media exclusion and inclusion in war can never be completely resolved, but it can be alleviated by a greater sense of responsibility among the media. The question remains: How can this responsibility be encouraged and inculcated?

63. Bill Carter, "Networks Held Back News That Invasion Had Begun," *New York Times,* September 20, 1994; Howard Kurtz, "White House, Networks Agree on 1-Hour Blackout," *Washington Post,* September 18, 1994.
64. "How Did We Get Here?" *Newsweek,* September 26, 1994, pp. 28, 30.

TEN COMMANDMENTS FOR THE MEDIA

The British historian and former journalist Paul Johnson has proposed ten commandments—rules of moral conduct—for all who exercise media power and influence. The first imperative is the desire to discover and tell the truth, making it clear to readers and viewers that the truth is not always simple. The second commandment is that journalists must always "think through the consequences of what they tell," asking themselves, What will legitimately inform and what will corrupt? The third is that truth telling is not enough and can be dangerous without an "informed judgment." Journalists, says Johnson, should always be deepening and broadening their knowledge of the world and its peoples so that they can make informed judgments about what to report and what not to report.[65]

The fourth commandment is that men and women of the mass media should have a missionary urge to educate—to tell the public not only what it wants to know but what it needs to know. The fifth commandment, says Johnson, is in some ways the most difficult and most important to follow: those in charge of the media must distinguish between the reasoned "public opinion" that assures liberal democracy and the transitory, volatile phenomenon that is "popular opinion." In a republic, as James Madison said in Federalist 50, it ought to be the reason, not the passions, of the public that sits in judgment.[66]

The sixth commandment is that the media must show the willingness to lead—to make an unpopular but principled decision. In so doing, "the risk of losing readers and viewers must be taken." The seventh commandment is to display courage, which Johnson calls the greatest of all virtues "and the one most lacking in the media." Courage is required of all in journalism—from the lowest reporter, who must morally evaluate his orders, to the richest tycoon, who should risk his fortune to make his media outlets better and more responsible.

The eighth commandment is the willingness to admit error. The unforced admission of error demonstrates that a newspaper or a television network has a sense of honor and a conscience. The ninth commandment

---

65. Paul Johnson, "Morality and the Mass Media" (address given at a conference of the World Media Association, Seoul, South Korea, August 1992), excerpted in *Washington Times*, September 7, 1992.

66. James Madison, *The Federalist Papers*, No. 50 (New York: New American Library, 1961), p. 317.

is the ability to be habitually fair—to see and tolerate other points of view and to exercise "temperance and restraint in expressing your own." The tenth and last commandment is to respect, treasure, and honor the intrinsic power of words. Echoing Czech President Vaclav Havel, Johnson states that words can enlighten and uplift or they can kill. They are the basic coinage of all culture, "the essential units on which a civilization rests." To discharge their enormous power responsibly, therefore, the mass media must be a moral media, conducted by people with an abiding sense of their moral obligations to society.[67]

67. Paul Johnson, "Morality and the Mass Media," excerpted in *Washington Times,* September 7, 1992.

CHAPTER 4

ETHNIC CLEANSING
AND WARRING CLANS

IT WAS EARLY 1994 in Bosnia, and the television images revealed a war-torn land filled with mass graves and mass destruction. Headless corpses were eaten by pigs and dogs. Infants were killed by sniper fire. Legless children on crutches hobbled down cratered streets. Mortar shells blew up markets, shops, cemeteries, people. In the three-and-a-half years of the war, more than 200,000 Bosnians died or disappeared; more than one million became refugees outside Bosnia; another 1.5 million were displaced within the nation by the Bosnian Serbs.[1]

On a quiet Saturday morning, a 120-mm mortar shell hit an open-air market in Sarajevo, and sixty-eight civilians died in the attack. Over two hundred were wounded. The February 1994 attack was one of the bloodiest incidents in the Bosnian war. The assault occurred only one block from the May 1992 "bread-line massacre" that killed twenty people. "You must send greetings to all those politicians out there sitting in their armchairs," screamed a woman who had been shopping at the market when the mortar shell hit.[2]

Sarajevo had been shelled before. In fact, it had been hit by more than a million shells. Perhaps five thousand children had been killed in the city since the Bosnian war began in 1992.[3] The bloody horror of the 1994 mar-

1. *Country Reports on Human Rights Practices for 1993*, U.S. State Department, February 1994, p. 806.
2. "Blood Bath," *Newsweek*, February 14, 1994, p. 20.
3. Slavenka Drakulic, "Death, Live," *The New Republic*, June 21, 1993, pp. 12–13.

ketplace massacre, however, globally telecast by CNN, forced President Bill Clinton and his advisers to review what the United States could do to stop the killing. Reluctant to approve air strikes or other military initiatives, like President Bush before him, Clinton sanctioned the air evacuation of Sarajevo's latest casualties. In the age of TV diplomacy, as *Newsweek* put it, "the medical-evacuation plan at least ensured images of U.S. planes landing in Bosnia."[4] Shortly thereafter, NATO warned the Serbs to stop the shelling and withdraw their heavy weapons to a 12.5-mile radius from Sarajevo or face air strikes. The Serbs reluctantly complied, but continued their ethnic cleansing elsewhere.

It is important, however, to remember that the Serbs were not doing all the killing in Bosnia. Ethnic hatred was everywhere, as the following story illustrates:

A Serb, a Croat, and a Muslim go fishing and catch a frog. It's wartime and all the golden fish have left. "If you set me free," says the frog, "you can have three wishes."

After a fierce argument, the three bitter enemies decide the best way to divide the wishes is to have one wish each. "I wish," says the Croat, "that all Serbs were dead. They have taken one-third of our country, and we really hate them. They deserve to die." The frog just croaks.

"I wish," says the Serb, "that all Croats were dead. They deserve to die for what they did to us during World War II." The frog just croaks.

"Have you granted those two wishes?" asks the Muslim. "Are all the Serbs and Croats dead?"

"Yes," says the frog.

"In that case," says the Muslim, "I'll just have a cup of coffee."

Still, it is true that the Serbs committed most of the atrocities in the Bosnian war, a fact amply documented by the mass media. When TV pictures of emaciated prisoners, their hollow stares framed by the barbed wire of a Serbian detention camp, were flashed around the globe in August 1992, the world reacted with anger. Because of media exposure, Serbian authorities were obliged to close down the prisoner camps. Yet, misinformation regarding Serb victims also circulated, as Peter Brock, a foreign correspondent, has amply documented:

• *Time*'s cover photo of August 17, 1992, depicted a skeletal "Muslim" in a Serbian detention camp. The "Muslim" was later identified as a Serb, suffering from tuberculosis.

4. "Blood Bath," p. 22.

• The BCC in 1992 filmed an elderly Bosnian Muslim POW in a Serb concentration camp. He was later revealed to be a Serb POW in a Muslim detention camp.

• Stories were aired of wounded Muslim children aboard a Sarajevo bus hit by sniper fire in August 1992. Several of the children were Serbian.

• *Newsweek* published a photo on January 4, 1993, of several bodies allegedly mutilated by Serbs. The bodies were subsequently identified as Serbs.[5]

THE PERILS OF PACK JOURNALISM

As they are wont to do on a "hot" story, the media engaged in pack journalism in Bosnia, presenting the Orthodox Serbs as the "bad guys" and the Muslims and, to a lesser extent the Croats, as the "good guys." The reality was far more complicated and admittedly more difficult to portray within the time constraints of television. But on balance, the mass media, led by television, followed a liberal democratic model of *mediapolitik* in Bosnia. Almost nightly and always graphically, they presented the presumed facts of the Bosnian conflict to the American public and their leaders.

In so reporting, they contradicted some media scholars who assert that foreign news is selected primarily for audience appeal rather than political significance. The sociologist Herbert Gans examined foreign affairs news in TV newscasts and news magazines nearly two decades ago and identified the subjects aired most often.[6] They included, in order of frequency: (1) American activities in foreign countries, especially visits by presidents and secretaries of state; (2) events that directly affect Americans, such as embargoes, G-7 meetings, and other matters that transcend national boundaries; (3) U.S. relations with totalitarian and formerly totalitarian countries (i.e., adversaries or potential adversaries); (4) changes in the leadership of foreign countries and the activities of European, particularly British, royalty; (5) dramatic political conflicts like wars or revolutions; (6) catastrophic events such as earthquakes, floods, and famines. (According to the media critic Edwin Diamond, the relative importance of a catastrophe is measured as follows: "10,000 deaths in Nepal equals 100 deaths in

---

5. Peter Brock, "Dateline Yugoslavia: The Partisan Press," *Foreign Policy,* no. 93 (winter 1993/4): pp. 153–54.

6. Herbert J. Gans, *Deciding What's News: A Study of CBS Evening News, NBC Nightly News, Newsweek and Time* (New York: Pantheon Books, 1979), pp. 30–36.

Wales equals 10 deaths in West Virginia equals one death next door.")[7] The seventh area of coverage, according to Gans, involved the excesses of foreign dictators—such as the wholesale murders of Uganda's Idi Amin, the death squads of Latin American caudillos, and the massacre in China's Tiananmen Square.

On the Gans scale, the Bosnian war would rank no higher than number five as an event worthy of extensive coverage, but instead the American media chose to highlight Bosnia, treating it as much more than a simple catastrophe story. Nor did the media automatically reflect the Clinton administration's foreign policy position. CNN, *Time*, the *New York Times*, and other media kept pushing Bosnia as a major story, forcing the White House and the State Department to devote more attention to the conflict than they otherwise would have.

Lloyd Cutler, White House counsel under President Carter, has stated that TV coverage of international events has made policy making irrational. He argues that television can force the president's hand, creating a "political need" for a prompt response. If the president delays, he is portrayed as indecisive and is attacked by opponents seeking political advantage. If the president selects an unpopular policy, he creates a negative reaction. TV reporting, according to Cutler, does not wait for a national consensus to emerge behind the president in a time of crisis.[8]

Cutler's comments reflect the Carter administration's humiliating experience during the Iranian hostage crisis, when TV news programs nightly announced how many days the American hostages had been held in Tehran. Cutler called the daily announcement the "TV doomsday clock" and likened it to a Chinese water torture for President Carter.[9] But what of the torture that the hostages were going through? Should the U.S. media have remained silent and not mentioned the plight of the imprisoned Americans?

With their unflagging coverage of the Iranian hostage crisis, the U.S. media were practicing both libertarian (it was a highly dramatic story) and social responsibility journalism (the publicity would increase public pressure on both the U.S. and Iranian governments to free the hostages).

7. Edwin Diamond, *The Tin Kazoo: Television, Politics, and the News* (Cambridge, Mass.: MIT Press, 1975), p. 94.
8. Charles Press and Kenneth Verburg, *American Politicians and Journalists* (Glenview, Ill.: Scott, Foresman, 1988), p. 289.
9. Ibid.

In covering Bosnia, most of the American media hewed to a social responsibility philosophy more than a libertarian one. The TV networks and other media would probably have moved on to some other D&D (death and destruction) story—there were some thirty conflicts worldwide in 1994, including Sudan, Angola, Tajikistan, and Georgia—except that the media believed that the West had a moral as well as a social responsibility to try to end the fighting in Bosnia. Typical headlines in *Time* and *Newsweek* read: "The U.S. and Europe can no longer look away." "Will we strike Bosnia?" "Shocking images from battered Bosnia put pressure on Clinton to decide what America should do—or can do—to stop the nightmare." "Why is the West scared?"[10]

In effect, the media took their cue from Elie Wiesel, a Holocaust survivor: standing before Washington's new memorial museum to Hitler's victims, Wiesel turned to President Clinton and pleaded, "As a Jew, I am saying that we must do something to stop the bloodshed in [Bosnia]."[11]

U.S. RELUCTANCE AND EUROPEAN INDECISION

Why, then, was the United States so reluctant to intervene directly in Bosnia? Why was there no European unity over a course of action to end the war, as opposed to endless discussions and fruitless negotiations? Some political scientists have argued that the power of the mass media has become so immense that the mere transmission of TV pictures will provoke an international response to end a war, a famine, or other man-made crisis. But the shocking images poured forth from Bosnia for more than three years, and no end to the war emerged. Why?

Is it possible that there was too much coverage of the Bosnian war? People can become desensitized to suffering, particularly when it happens "over there." As the U.S. Committee for Refugees wrote:

Rather than disbelieving accounts of mass atrocities, we simply don't react to them. We no longer have room in our hearts to accommodate the world's suffering, especially when we believe that nothing we feel or do will make a difference anyway.[12]

According to the *Newsweek* correspondent Michael Elliott, intellectuals on both sides of the Atlantic protested the siege of Sarajevo, but there was

10. *Newsweek*, May 10, 1993; *Time*, June 8, 1992; *Newsweek*, February 21, 1994; *Newsweek*, August 17, 1992; *Newsweek*, February 14, 1994.

11. Mark Whitaker, "Getting Tough at Last," *Newsweek*, May 10, 1993, p. 22.

12. *World Refugee Survey 1988* (New York: U.S. Committee for Refugees, 1989), pp. 14–15.

"no outpouring of support for Bosnia like that which rallied to the cause of the Republicans in Spain" in the 1930s.[13] It has been suggested that West Europeans had grown so accustomed to not fighting in the fifty years since the end of World War II that they did not see the Bosnian conflict as one in which they wanted to risk their lives. The Germans are a special case: because of their recent "history" (i.e., Hitler and the Third Reich), they are reluctant to use their military power.

In America, the explanation of inaction begins with the Vietnam War, which still discourages U.S. involvement in any conflict. Professional soldiers and ordinary citizens alike are exceedingly wary of armed interventions that have a vague political purpose and an indeterminate end. Additionally, there was no personal connection between Bosnia and America. There was no large, vocal Bosnian American constituency demanding that the United States "do something" about the continuing carnage in their motherland. Simply put, most Americans saw Bosnia as a "European" problem. In the summer of 1995, according to a survey by the Times Mirror Center for the People and the Press, a strong majority (61 percent) continued to oppose the use of U.S. military forces to help end the fighting in Bosnia, a rise from 55 percent a year earlier.[14]

Undergirding all the talk about what to do and what not to do in Bosnia was one simple fact: the cold war was over. No Communist dominoes were at risk in the Balkans, no freedom fighters were being heralded. The region seemed to be a hopeless tangle of Serbs, Bosnians, and Croats; of Orthodox Christians, Roman Catholics, and Muslims. During World War II, Croats backed the Nazis and Serbs became Communist guerrillas. As one newsmagazine put it, "Religion and nationality make the Balkans more a flash point than a melting pot."[15] The "new world order" proclaimed by President Bush received its fifteen minutes of fame with the success of the Persian Gulf War but quickly disappeared. Nothing, yet, has come along to take its place, except, perhaps, a growing realization by Americans that the United States is the only superpower in the world and must sometimes, somehow, act like one, even at some cost to itself and its citizens.

In such an era of transition, *mediapolitik* can help us understand why

---

13. Michael Elliott, "Why Is the West Scared?" *Newsweek*, February 14, 1994, p. 24.

14. "Bosnia, the Use of Force and the Clinton Administration," news release distributed by the Times Mirror Center for the People and the Press, June 25, 1995.

15. "Ethnic Cleansing," *Newsweek*, August 17, 1992, p. 18.

things happen or do not happen in world politics. As we have seen, the mass media provided news and information about the Bosnian conflict which, while sometimes flawed in their black-and-white depiction of the guilty and the innocent, made the war a major issue that had to be addressed.

A BALKAN SWITZERLAND?

It should be noted that a conference of European ministers, meeting in Lisbon in March 1992, did come up with a peace plan shortly after Bosnia-Herzegovina declared its independence. The plan divided the country into seven regions, primarily governed through Switzerland-like cantons. It gave the Muslims 44 percent of the land, the Serbs 44 percent, and the Croats 12 percent. The Bosnian Serb leader Radovan Karadzic called the Lisbon plan a "Balkan Switzerland" and signed it. Suspicious of Karadzic's approval, Muslims and Croats recanted their acceptance and demanded more land. One month later, the Serbs, who had rejected Bosnia's independence, took up arms, and the Bosnian war began.[16]

In August 1995, after forty months of fighting and 220,000 dead, a new ethnic map of Bosnia began to emerge, created not at the diplomatic table but on the battlefield. Following the Serb conquest of several Muslim enclaves in the east and Muslim and Croat gains over the Serbs in the west, the United States suggested a new plan—the fourth since the 1992 Lisbon meeting. The proposed division of land was 49 percent for the Serbs, 51 percent for a Muslim-Croat federation. One international relations expert described the American plan as saying to all sides, "This is the best you're going to get and [you'd better] accept it."[17]

The diplomatic initiative was strengthened by several weeks of NATO air strikes against the Bosnian Serbs, who once again had launched a mortar shell into the central Sarajevo market, killing at least thirty-eight people and wounding eighty-five. The evening network newscasts and the front pages of the daily newspapers were filled with pictures of the dead and the wounded and the grieving. The *New York Times* reported that "the scene was familiar, but the horrified frenzy among an exhausted population was still intense."[18] This time, there was little hesitation or disagree-

16. Tom Squitieri, "In Bosnia, It's Back to the Drawing Board," *USA Today*, August 29, 1995.

17. Ibid.

18. Roger Cohen, "Shelling Kills Dozens in Sarajevo; U.S. Urges NATO to Strike Serbs," *New York Times*, August 29, 1995.

ment about an appropriate response. The West dispatched an armada of U.S., French, British, and Dutch jets against Serb military positions around Sarajevo and throughout Bosnia. Over 3,500 aircraft sorties were flown in three weeks; it was the biggest air operation in NATO's history to that time and the largest in Europe since World War II. It signaled that the alliance's hope of obtaining an easy post–cold war diplomatic solution in Bosnia had been replaced by a more traditional reliance on force.

One person in particular had been enraged by the bloody pictures telecast by CNN: Admiral Leighton W. Smith, the commander of NATO's southern forces. He had immediately picked up a phone and informed his liaison officer to U.N. forces in the former Yugoslavia, "If that's a Bosnian Serb shell, I'm going to start the process of recommending [air] strikes."[19] Smith's swift reaction to what he saw on CNN set in motion a train of events that ran from Operation Deliberate Force—NATO's protracted air and artillery campaign—to peace talks in Ohio and the stationing of up to sixty thousand troops in Bosnia, including twenty thousand Americans.

Gone now was any Western indecision. When bad weather over Bosnia forced NATO to cancel jet strikes, a U.S. warship launched Tomahawk cruise missiles at Serb-held territory in northwest Bosnia. The shift to power politics, the reporter Michael Dobbs wrote, could be traced to the public humiliation heaped on the United States and its allies in April 1995 when the Bosnian Serbs retaliated against a limited round of Western bombing by seizing hundreds of U.N. peacekeepers. Confronted with TV pictures of Western hostages chained to posts and serving as human shields, NATO drew up plans for "a get-tough policy."[20] Its resolve was reinforced when Serbs overran so-called U.N. "safe havens" in Zepa and Srebrenica and forced U.N. peacekeepers to withdraw from another enclave in Gorazde. NATO had also been stunned when a U.S. Air Force F-16 had been shot down over northern Bosnia in early June.

As usual, the Bosnian Serbs reacted defiantly to the massive NATO bombing, with Radovan Karadzic declaring that "the people's will for [an independent Bosnian Serb] state will harden. The West's calculations about the Serbs are wrong." Serbian stubbornness was reinforced by the official media of Serbia, which never showed any of the sweeping brutality that Serbs exhibited against Muslims in Bosnia. The *New York Times'*

19. Rick Atkinson, "Air Assault Sets Stage for Broader Role," *Washington Post*, November 15, 1995.

20. Michael Dobbs, "In the Balkans, the Tables Are Turned," *Washington Post*, August 31, 1995.

Roger Cohen wrote that the Serbs wondered why they were persecuted and finally concluded that "it is all an American-led plot against them."[21] Like Iraq's Saddam Hussein, Serbian General Ratko Mladic talked tough, vowing over Bosnian Serb television, "We shall remain in our positions." But President Slobodan Milosevic of Serbia told a U.N. peace mission that the Bosnian Serb leadership had agreed to place its fate in his hands in future negotiations. The State Department's Peter Tanoff chose PBS's *MacNeil/Lehrer NewsHour*, not the department's briefing room, to respond, "It looks like Milosevic is taking matters in hand."[22]

DIVIDING UP THE PIE

Although the Clinton administration came into office vowing that it would not approve a peace settlement based on ethnic division, Richard C. Holbrooke, the assistant secretary of state for European and Canadian affairs, brokered just such an agreement in the fall of 1995. As Holbrooke put it, "Enemies must live and work together. It's happened in Europe. It's happened in Asia. It must happen in the former Yugoslavia."[23] A key provision was that Bosnia's current boundaries would be maintained, with territory divided almost equally between a Bosnian Serb state and one controlled by a federation of Croats and Muslims. But Holbrooke's success was based on several important U.S. commitments: (1) to provide twenty thousand American troops for a NATO peacekeeping force that would remain in Bosnia "at least a year"; (2) to spend an estimated $2 billion on the deployment of those American forces; (3) to contribute several hundred million dollars to a Balkans reconstruction fund; and (4) to organize a multinational effort to arm and train the Muslims in Bosnia after a peace accord was implemented.[24]

The American public's grudging acceptance of U.S. involvement in Bosnian peace-keeping was due in large measure to the mass media's constant coverage of the bloody Bosnian conflict for nearly four years. Without the graphic pictures of death, destruction, and despair in Sarajevo and elsewhere, Americans and a skeptical Congress would have rejected any

21. Roger Cohen, "Calling History to Arms: Serbs Invoke Their Past," *New York Times,* September 8, 1995.

22. John Pomfret, "Milosevic Offers Conciliatory Move," *Washington Post,* August 31, 1995; Lee Michael and Steve Komarow, "Battered Serbs Still Defiant," *USA Today,* August 31, 1995.

23. Elaine Sciolino, "What Price Peace?" *New York Times,* September 9, 1995.

24. Dana Priest and Ann Devroy, "White House to Ask $1 Billion for Bosnia Troop Deployment," *Washington Post,* September 28, 1995.

significant U.S. part in keeping the peace in Bosnia. Even so, an October 1995 poll by the *New York Times* and CBS showed that only 37 percent of Americans favored sending American ground troops to participate in a NATO-led force in Bosnia. A solid majority of 57 percent were opposed.[25]

In late October, while the presidents of Serbia, Croatia, and Bosnia were meeting in Dayton, Ohio, to try to end the war, the House of Representatives voted overwhelmingly—315 to 103—for a nonbinding resolution requiring the president to ask Congress for permission to send troops to Bosnia. Two weeks later, as the Dayton, Ohio, negotiations reached their climax, the House, on a largely party-line vote of 243 to 171, voted to bar Clinton from sending U.S. troops to enforce a Bosnian peace agreement unless Congress approved. House Speaker Newt Gingrich commented cautiously: "We should not automatically say no, nor should we automatically say yes."[26] In contrast, Senate Majority Leader Bob Dole, a World War II veteran and decorated hero, said that he supported the president's decision. "The Congress cannot stop this troop deployment from happening," he said in a Senate speech. "If we would try to cut off funds we would harm the men and women in the military who have already begun to arrive in Bosnia."[27]

It was appropriate that President Clinton used television to speak to the American people about a war whose every bloody twist and turn had been reported on television. It was only Clinton's tenth telecast from the Oval Office in nearly three years as president. Seeking to overcome the widespread public skepticism (only 35 percent believed that "vital" American interests were at stake in Bosnia), Clinton promised that "America's role will not be about fighting a war, it will be about helping the people of Bosnia to secure their own peace agreement." After acknowledging that the United States should not try to be "the world's policeman," he insisted that "there are times and places where our leadership can mean the difference between peace and war, and where we can defend our fundamental values as a people and serve our most basic strategic interests."[28]

25. Elaine Sciolino, "Soldiering On, Without an Enemy," *New York Times,* October 29, 1995.

26. "Clinton Announces Balkan Pact," Associated Press dispatch V0766, November 21, 1995.

27. Helen Dewar, "Dole's 'Old Values' Emerge on Bosnia," *Washington Post,* December 2, 1995.

28. Ann Devroy and Helen Dewar, "U.S. Troops Vital to Bosnia Peace, Clinton Says"; text of Clinton's remarks on U.S. troops in Bosnia, *Washington Post,* November 28, 1995.

Skepticism regarding a successful outcome in Bosnia was certainly warranted—the defiant attitude of Bosnian Serb leaders Karadzic and Mladic was ominous. But as the *New York Times'* Roger Cohen wrote, "the flailing of Europe . . . has made it clear that American leadership in the Balkans is irreplaceable. So America is being called on to secure a peace, guarantee it with troops and cast enough light on the past in order to build the future. It worked in Germany and Japan. It might work in Bosnia."[29]

And what was the role of the mass media in the peace accord—large, medium, minimal, none at all? Believers in traditional diplomacy, like Henry Kissinger, like to work behind closed doors, far from the madding crowds and the mass media. Kissinger's most famous act of stealth diplomacy occurred in 1971, when the White House announced that he was taking a day off during a trip to Pakistan while in fact he was flying to Beijing to make plans for President Nixon's historic visit to China the next year. Another kind of secret diplomacy happened in Oslo in 1993 when third world diplomats and academics brought Israelis and Palestinians together for informal talks. The result, the *New York Times* correspondent Elaine Sciolino wrote, was a formal peace agreement achieved without the help of the United States, which viewed the discussions "as a fairly meaningless back channel."[30]

The news media had no direct access to the Bosnia peace talks, which took place behind high-security fences at Wright-Patterson Air Force Base outside Dayton, Ohio. As a result, some correspondents were reduced to premature and embarrassing speculations, as when CNN's foreign affairs correspondent, Christiane Amanpour, announced the failure of the peace effort in a special report from Sarajevo.[31] Should we then credit the successful outcome of the Bosnian peace accord to traditional closed-door diplomacy? Not at all.

Secretary of State Warren Christopher himself violated the official gag order, giving three television interviews on the first night of the talks. Christopher was not just feeding hungry journalists but also practicing liberal *mediapolitik*, as every public official of a liberal democracy must today. Richard Holbrooke, who brokered the Dayton agreement, was

---

29. Roger Cohen, "A Cycle of War and Illusion," *New York Times,* September 24, 1995.

30. Elaine Sciolino, "Gag Orders Can Do Wonders for a Peace Talk," *New York Times,* November 5, 1995.

31. Michael Dobbs, "After Marathon Negotiations, An Extra Mile to Reach Peace," *Washington Post,* November 23, 1995.

known to be so addicted to attention from the media that as ambassador to Germany, he often called journalists in Washington in the middle of the night to chat.[32]

In summary, the peace talks in Dayton took place because the mass media, with their vivid, sustained coverage of the Bosnian fighting, made the war a priority issue that the West—especially an American president who had promised action in his 1992 campaign—had to resolve. The specific catalyst was CNN's terrible pictures of the mortar round exploding in the Sarajevo market on August 28, 1995. The scenes of limbless torsos, crimson streets, and stunned survivors so angered the commander of NATO's southern forces that he initiated a devastating air assault against the Bosnian Serbs that forced them to agree to talks.

A HUMANITARIAN IMPULSE

Some 1,500 miles to the south of Bosnia, the restless eye of the television camera came to rest, in 1992, on the small African country of Somalia. A savage civil war between rival clans raged. Tens of thousands had died due to violence, famine, and disease, including many children under the age of five. Some 4.5 million Somalis were ravaged by hunger as hundreds died daily from lack of food.

CBS's *60 Minutes* devoted a segment to the tragedy of Somalia, where corpses were buried under mounds of sand and emaciated adults received one 600-calorie bowl of gruel a day, usually made of rice and beans. On its cover, *Time* printed the haunting picture of a skeletal child, who had perished from hunger at a refugee camp in Baidoa. The United States government and private organizations began a food airlift to Somalia, but the fighting and the looting by rival clans made food and aid distribution erratic and difficult. The *Washington Post* headlined an article, "Somalia's Overshadowed Tragedy: World Anxious about Balkan Turmoil, Aloof to That in Africa." The *New York Times* columnist Anna Quindlen blamed U.S. inaction on Eurocentrism, and justified intervention in Somalia by declaring, "It is the moral thing to do."[33] President Bush wanted to intervene, but he was in the middle of a reelection campaign and feared he would be accused of playing politics if he acted.

In December 1992, having lost to Bill Clinton and no longer concerned about domestic politics, Bush offered a division of U.S. ground troops as

32. Sciolino, "Gag Orders."

33. Michael Maren, "Feeding a Famine," *Forbes MediaCritic*, fall 1994, pp. 34–35.

part of a multinational peacemaking force in Somalia. As the president dispatched the American forces, beginning Operation Restore Hope, he told them they were doing "God's work."[34] The odds on the operation's success were good. Somalia had no government that could protest intervention, no jungle or hills that could be used by guerrillas, no air force, no army, and no navy. The country, commented one newsmagazine, was "a nearly ideal laboratory in which to test the theory that high-minded application of force can right some of the world's wrong."[35] The American people seemed to agree, with 42 percent stating, in a national poll, that the United States had "a greater responsibility" than other countries to keep peace around the world and ensure humanitarian relief.[36]

HE WHO LIVES BY TV . . .

From beginning to end, Operation Restore Hope was a TV story. As Navy SEALS waded ashore at Mogadishu in the moonlight, their faces blackened with camouflage paint, they braced for possible confrontation with hostile clans. But what they were met with, and blinded by, was the glare of television lights. The only flashes came from cameras, not rifles or machine guns. The SEALS were the "stars" in the first-ever live-broadcast military landing, televised to America and around the world by CNN, ABC, NBC, CBS, and all the other networks that had been given the precise time and place of the landing by a Pentagon eager to cooperate with the media.[37]

Somalis were ecstatic over the arrival of the Americans, who they hoped would not only feed the starving but repair their broken government and reform their lawless society. Declared one mother of seven, "I'd like the U.S. troops to stay here for life."[38] Expectations were so high that disappointments and recriminations were inevitable. Bush told Congress that some 28,000 American troops would stay in Somalia "only as long as necessary to establish a secure environment" for humanitarian efforts. But U.N. Secretary General Boutros Boutros-Ghali saw the U.S. mission in broader terms, stating that the United States would have to "disarm" the warring clans and set up a military police force to preserve order. Only

34. "It's Our Fight Now," *Newsweek*, December 14, 1992, p. 31.
35. "Why Somalia?" *Newsweek*, December 7, 1992, p. 25.
36. "It's Our Fight Now," p. 35.
37. Jill Smolowe, "Great Expectations," *Time*, December 21, 1992, p. 33.
38. Ibid.

then, said the secretary general, would the U.N. provide peacekeepers to take over.[39]

As Bush departed and Clinton moved into the White House, rules for humanitarian intervention, like Operation Restore Hope, began to take shape. They included: (1) Human suffering was sufficient reason to take action. Balance of power was no longer a sine qua non for intervention. U.N. Resolution 794 stated that "the magnitude of the human tragedy" in Somalia "constitutes a threat to international security." (2) The United States was, in effect, the world's chief of police. Someone had to be in charge of each military intervention; in most instances, it would be the world's only superpower. As Bush said, "American action is often necessary as a catalyst for broader involvement of the world community." (3) Regional action was preferred. Not even the United States could police every beat in the global city. In Cambodia, for example, Asians, including Japanese troops, were trying to keep the peace. (4) Intervention should be limited to the feasible. Defense Secretary Dick Cheney commented that Somalia was "militarily doable."[40]

Few Americans disagreed that the United States should be willing to lend soldiers for humanitarian efforts like Operation Restore Hope in Somalia, or send soldiers into military operations that served national interests as in Desert Storm in Kuwait and Iraq. But whether it was humanitarian or military intervention, it was understood that the operation had to be successful, or else such actions would be sharply challenged in the future. And always, the media critic Jonathan Alter points out, information, especially that provided to hundreds of millions by television, "democratizes the process." As this book demonstrates again and again, TV mobilizes public opinion for and against a policy in ways that even the most determined leaders of totalitarian, let alone democratic, governments cannot control.[41]

Less than ten months after the Marines landed, the world watched disbelievingly as a laughing Somali crowd dragged the almost naked corpse of an American soldier through the streets of Mogadishu as young men kicked and stamped on him. They saw the bloody face, numb with fear, of Warrant Officer Michael Durant, held prisoner somewhere in the back

39. Ibid., p. 30.
40. "It's Our Fight Now," p. 35.
41. Jonathan Alter, "Did the Press Push Us into Somalia?" *Newsweek*, December 21, 1992, p. 33.

streets of a city that once rang with cheers for Americans. They learned that in an attempt to capture clan leader Mohammed Farah Aidid and three top aides, seventeen U.S. soldiers died, seventy-seven were wounded, and one pilot, Durant, was captured.

"LET'S GET OUT!"

Thousands of outraged Americans immediately telephoned and wrote their congressmen and the White House, bombarding them with angry questions. What was the United States doing in Somalia? How did a humanitarian mission that began with handshakes and smiles turn into a deadly battle with hate-filled Somalis? In just a few days, the anger had coalesced into a blunt demand: "Let's get out."[42] Members of Congress referred to the pictures—and the resulting telephone calls—in emotional speeches urging the president to bring home the boys immediately. Going on national TV, President Clinton tried to have it both ways, announcing that he was doubling the number of U.S. troops in Somalia but also promising that all American forces would leave the country by March 31, 1994.

Long before the October debacle, Operation Restore Hope had degenerated into Operation Manhunt, after Aidid's troops killed twenty-four Pakistanis in a June 1993 ambush in south Mogadishu. (The United States handed control of the mission to the United Nations in May.) A furious Boutros-Ghali pushed through a U.N. Security Council resolution calling for the arrest and punishment of those responsible for the attack on the Pakistanis. To the dismay of the Pentagon, a bounty of $25,000 was placed on Aidid's head.

An increasingly concerned United States launched a two-track policy: continue to help in the hunt for Aidid, but press Boutros-Ghali to bring the various Somali factions, including the Aidid-led clan, together. However, not only were the two tracks clearly contradictory, but Boutros-Ghali became so obsessed with capturing Aidid that, according to U.N. sources, he "was not interested in making peace with him."[43] All the contradictions came to a head in October when American Rangers charged off to the Olympic Hotel to seize Aidid and were met by murderous fire from Aidid supporters who came rushing from all over the city to join the battle.

As long as things seemed to go well in Somalia, most Americans sound-

---

42. George J. Church, "Anatomy of a Disaster," *Time*, October 18, 1993; Michael Elliott, "The Making of a Fiasco," *Newsweek*, October 18, 1993.

43. Elliott, "The Making of a Fiasco," p. 36.

ed few objections. In May 1993, for example, the House of Representatives decisively passed a resolution endorsing a nation-building mission in Somalia and favoring the use of American troops to support it, for several years if necessary.[44] Operation Restore Hope, *Time* wrote, was a new kind of American intervention, one for purely humanitarian purposes, in a country where the United States had no economic or strategic interests. The ensuing multinational mission was a new kind of U.N. intervention, intended not to oversee but to make peace, undertaken without the usual invitation from a host government and carried out not by lightly armed troops but by forces with enough weapons to fight a serious battle.[45]

But the Somali experiment in multilateral peacemaking failed for several reasons: (1) there was no clear division of command and control between U.S. and U.N. military units in Somalia; (2) the Clinton administration did not explain in sufficient detail the new nation-building mission in Somalia to the American people; (3) the U.N. secretary general became too directly involved in the Somali mission, micromanaging operations much as President Lyndon B. Johnson had dictated daily bombing sorties in the Vietnam War; and (4) U.S. policy makers did not consider, adequately, how the mass media could be a negative as well as a positive factor in the Somali mission. They did not understand clearly enough that what the mass media gives, they can also take away.

Some journalists have expressed concern about the powerful impact that pictures can have on public and congressional opinion, aware that dramatic images can oversimplify complex issues. "What sort of policy making is it," wrote the *New York Times'* Walter Goodman, "to have Washington's actions decided, even in part, on the latest affecting pictures on the evening news?" But according to *Newsday's* Patrick Sloyan, who won a Pulitzer Prize for his coverage of the Persian Gulf War, the anti-American pictures from Somalia "brought home to everybody in this country that something was wrong with the American policy."[46]

BLAMING THE MESSENGER

The retired diplomat George Kennan, who coined the word "containment" in the 1940s, sharply questioned the justification for sending Amer-

44. Church, "Anatomy of a Disaster," p. 46.
45. Ibid., p. 50.
46. Jacqueline Sharkey, "When Pictures Drive Foreign Policy," *American Journalism Review*, December 1993, p. 14.

ican forces to a distant land where the United States had no pressing national security interests. He blamed Bush's action and the American public's acceptance of his decision on the American media, particularly television. Writing in the *New York Times*. Kennan stated that if U.S. policy,
"particularly policy involving the use of our armed forces abroad, is to be
controlled by popular emotional impulses, and particularly ones provoked by the commercial television industry, then there is no place . . . for
what have been traditionally been regarded as the responsible deliberative
organs of our government."[47] Kennan's notion of the government organs
"responsible" for foreign policy and national security had always been
narrow. As head of the State Department's Planning Committee in 1947
and 1948 and throughout his long career after that, he insisted that American foreign policy should be administrated by professionals in the executive branch, not amateurs in the legislative branch. He had refused to "lob-
by" members of Congress, who he said were guilty of assorted sins,
including in later years admitting "television cameras into the legislative
chamber."[48]

Responding to Kennan in a letter to the *Times*, CBS's Dan Rather argued that it was wrong to credit television with so much influence. Some
reporters, he wrote, "may wish for the power to direct public opinion and
to guide American policy—but they don't have it." CNN's Ed Turner
agreed, stating that "it's up to the President and the State Department to
conceive policy and execute it, and if somehow we are driving them, then
maybe we need some new officials in Washington."[49] But R. W. Apple, Jr.,
the veteran head of the *New York Times*' Washington bureau, dismissed
Turner's idea of how foreign policy is made as "a fantasy." The "journalism
of images," Apple said, has always had a "tremendous impact upon public
opinion, and public opinion has always had a tremendous impact on government."[50] Apple's statement is a precise summary of a major theme of
this book.

THE BALKANS, AGAIN

In the spring of 1998, three years after the Dayton peace talks had ended
the fighting in Bosnia, civil war again broke out in a little-known area of

47. George Kennan, letter to the editor, *New York Times*, September 30, 1993.
48. George Kennan, *Around the Cragged Hill: A Personal and Political Philosophy* (New
York: W. W. Norton & Company, 1993), pp. 137–38.
49. Sharkey, "When Pictures Drive Foreign Policy," p. 16.
50. Ibid.

the Balkans. Kosovo was a rural province of two million people in Serbia, one of the six republics that Marshal Tito ruled as Yugoslavia from the end of World War II until his death in 1980. Kosovo was 90 percent ethnic Albanian and Muslim, but to the Serbian Orthodox minority it was sacred territory, as the site of a fourteenth-century battle they had lost to their historic foes—the Turks. After more than five hundred years, Serbs still considered the ethnic Albanian citizens of the province to be "Turks."

Following Tito's death, the Kosovars sought independence, but Serbian leader Slobodan Milosevic declared in a widely televised 1989 address that he would defend the rights of the Serbs and the "sacred" land of Kosovo at all costs. He then ended the autonomy granted to Kosovo and initiated a heavy-handed authoritarian rule. Militant Kosovars formed the Kosovo Liberation Army (KLA) in 1996 and in February and March 1998 attacked Serb police and troops. The Serbs retaliated in full force, killing an estimated 2,000 people and driving 200,000 Kosovars from their homes.[51] A new round of ethnic cleansing had begun.

Ambassador Richard Holbrooke, the principal architect of the Dayton accords, was dispatched to Belgrade to talk with Milosevic, who under threat of NATO air strikes, agreed to a cease-fire in Kosovo. Both the Serbs and the Kosovo Albanians attended peace talks in February and March 1999, in Rambouillet, France, but the Serbs refused to sign the agreement—which would have installed a NATO peacekeeping force in "sacred" Kosovo—and instead stepped up their drive to expel the Albanian majority from the territory.

The United States and its NATO allies had little choice but to carry out their threat and launch an air campaign to cripple the Serbian war machine in Kosovo and effect compliance with the Rambouillet peace plan. The intensive air strikes began on March 24, 1999, and continued for eleven weeks, finally forcing Milosevic to withdraw Serbian troops from Kosovo and allow NATO troops to take up peacekeeping positions within the province.

It was, wrote Blaine Harden of the *New York Times,* "a curious mismatch of a war." In one corner was NATO, the best-armed military alliance in history; in the other corner was Milosevic, a wily Balkan dictator with an antiquated but fiercely nationalist army. No less curious were the rules of combat as laid down by President Clinton on the first day, "I do not in-

51. "A Long, Complicated Agreement," *Washington Times,* June 11, 1999.

tend to put [U.S.] troops in Kosovo to fight a war."[52] Because of the American dictum, NATO was obliged to do what had never been done before—seek to win a war without risking its soldiers on the ground. The result was a 72-day air campaign that included more than 33,000 missions flown, with bombs dropped and missiles fired on about one-third of them.

To paraphrase an old medical saying, the operation was a success but the patient nearly died. About 10,000 ethnic Albanian men were murdered by Serbs. Serbian forces burned houses and other property and made some 800,000 Albanians flee for their lives. But there was not one battle-related NATO fatality because NATO kept most of its airplanes above 15,000 feet to minimize allied casualties and relied heavily upon the use of cruise missiles. Three American soldiers were captured by Serbs but were returned. A stealth fighter crashed, but the pilot was rescued. Although there were no fireworks and no one danced in the streets, it was undoubtedly a victory in what Czech President Vaclav Havel called the "first war fought for human rights rather than national interests."[53]

And as with all modern wars, it was also fought across the airwaves. Milosevic closed down or took over the independent media in Belgrade and hounded political dissidents into silence. One of the few journalists who continued to denounce the regime was shot dead in the streets of Belgrade. The state media mounted a major anti-NATO campaign claiming that the allied bombing was responsible for thousands of Serbian civilian casualties. Milosevic's aim was clear—to discredit NATO's military strategy and to depict the Serbian nation "as the victim of foreign aggression."[54] Belgrade went so far as to adopt a modern campaign technique, sending far from subtle videos to Western opinion leaders and news media. In one Serbian spot, NATO bombers flew through dark skies in the formation of a swastika.

In turn, Secretary of State Madeleine Albright and Defense Secretary William Cohen blitzed the American networks, describing Milosevic as responsible for a "humanitarian catastrophe" and "dreadful massacres." They operated in a relative vacuum created by the Serbian expulsion of most Western journalists and the lack of television pictures from the

52. Blaine Harden, "The Long Struggle That Led the Serbian Leader to Back Down," *New York Times,* June 8, 1999.

53. Reese Cleghorn, "The War and How Not to Call It," *American Journalism Review,* July/August 1999, p. 4.

54. Blaine Harden, "The Milosevic Generation," *New York Times Magazine,* August 29, 1999, p. 34; Janusz Bugajski, "The Situation in Kosovo," *The World & I,* June 1999, p. 56.

Balkan war zone—there was no real-time CNN coverage as during the Persian Gulf War. President Clinton intensified the rhetoric by comparing Milosevic to Hitler, saying of the Serbian repression, "We have seen this kind of evil conduct before in this century."[55]

Even with such stinging accusations, America's feelings about the Kosovo war were slow to surface. "Kosovo burst into the headlines without any buildup," commented Barbara Cochran, a broadcast journalist. With the Persian Gulf War, there was an eight-month troop buildup after Iraq's invasion of Kuwait followed by thirty days of air strikes and a weeklong ground war. "It gave the public time to see what was at stake," Cochran said. "That has not been the case this time around."[56]

However, as the pictures of exhausted and frightened refugees pouring out of Kosovo filled TV screens night after night, public support for the NATO air campaign steadily increased. Between late March and early April, even the number of Americans backing U.S. ground troops went from 31 percent to 47 percent—although Clinton insisted he would resist any such action. "[Milosevic]'s evil," commented one citizen, "and this kind of ethnic cleansing is really disturbing. You don't want to hurt anyone, but he should be stopped at all costs."[57]

Television images of fleeing Kosovo refugees had much the same impact on public opinion across Europe, reported the *New York Times*, turning "pacifists and anti-NATO activists of decades ago" into supporters of sustained bombing.[58] The initial disquiet about seeing air combat in Europe for the first time in fifty years was overcome by concern for the refugees and revulsion at how they had been forced from their homeland. And the parallels with Nazi Germany had far more impact in Europe. German Foreign Minister Joschka Fischer later declared that Milosevic's aggression was "a declaration of war against the policy of European integration."[59]

The Kosovo conflict was also the first war to be fought out on the Inter-

55. Howard Kurtz, "Demonizing the Enemy, Controlling the Information," *Washington Post*, March 27, 1999; "President's Strategy: 'Our Plan Is to Persist until We Prevail,'" *New York Times*, April 6, 1999.

56. Jennifer Harper, "Media Educate America on War," *Washington Times*, April 2, 1999.

57. Alexandra Marks, "Public Support Grows for War with Yugoslavia," *Christian Science Monitor*, April 9, 1999.

58. Warren Hoge, "News Reports Bolster Support for Bombings," *New York Times*, April 6, 1999.

59. Fred Hiatt, "A Chance for Democracy," *Washington Post*, June 6, 1999.

net as well as the battlefield. The Internet, through Web sites and e-mail, provided users with unmediated access to people and events. "Why should people listen to the reporting of others," reason Web users, "if they can listen to the participants directly?" But in a conflict as complicated as Kosovo, pointed out Paul Goble, a broadcast analyst, the Internet can give an even more distorted picture of events than more traditional media. One notorious use of the Internet was the appearance of the Serbian paramilitary leader known as Arkan in a chat room, prompting one journalist to write that the incident afforded users the chance to listen to "killers without context."[60]

Some analysts expressed concern that the flood of information about Kosovo on the Internet detracted attention from more traditional journalistic sources and undermined public confidence in such sources. Paradoxically, some mainstream journalists, driven by a desire not to be left behind by Internet reporting, adopted its strategy of providing instant information without adequate verification and context.

During World War I, Senator Hiram Johnson remarked that "the first casualty when war comes is truth." The Internet can certainly be a defender of truth, suggested Paul Goble, but as events in Kosovo showed, it can also be a weapon against it, "one all the more powerful because being new, its strength is largely underestimated and misunderstood."[61]

A different view was offered by analyst Jon Katz, a self-admitted "Web enthusiast," who pointed out that the most potent images of the war in Kosovo—the technobombs, the captured American soldiers, the streams of refugees—all came from the mainstream media. Kosovo, Katz wrote in *Brill's Content*, was "a politics, power, and policy story" centered in Washington, London, Berlin, and Belgrade and best covered by traditional reporting methods. The Web, Katz said, certainly helped people learn about their relatives and contribute to refugee relief. But from the first the Kosovo War was a story "overwhelmingly influenced" by conventional correspondents reporting on casualties and refugees from the war zones and on policy and strategy from the capitals.[62]

---

60. Paul Goble, "A War on the Web," Radio Free Europe/Radio Liberty analysis, April 6, 1999.
61. Ibid.
62. Jon Katz, "The Myth of the Internet War," *Brill's Content*, June 1999.

SERBIAN INCONSISTENCY

Despite the severe restrictions on domestic media, the Serbian authorities did not pursue a consistent policy toward foreign correspondents during the Kosovo War. In the Serbian capital of Belgrade, home base for most Western journalists, CBS and ABC were at first expelled, but ABC was later allowed to return. NBC was permitted to stay. CNN was singled out by Serb propaganda as a "factory of lies," but Serbian television continued to carry CNN. A *New York Times* reporter was ordered to leave but later allowed back in. A NBC News executive commented that "there seems to be no rhyme or reason" to the expulsions.[63]

Most journalists took full advantage of the technical advances of the information age—more mobile satellite dishes, more reliable cell phones, satellite phones with longer battery life. The "SATphones," according to NBC's Kevin McAuliffe, were invaluable in the early stages of the conflict, enabling reporters equipped with laptop and modem to transmit stories from wherever they were. One reporter filed his articles via e-mail in friendly mailboxes across Europe. Another sent stories from the war zone using only his laptop and a local London cell phone. A *Newsweek* editor in New York City was able to hold a conference with six reporters in different locations in the field, all via cell and SATphones.[64]

Even with the impressive display of U.S. might—defeating Serbia from the air without a single NATO casualty—much of the American public remained somewhat ambivalent about the Kosovo War. While 74 percent of Americans approved of U.S. involvement in the Gulf War, only 58 percent thought Kosovo was worthwhile. President Clinton's approval rating moved only a few points up after victory in Kosovo. Andrew Kohut, director of the Pew Research Center for the People and the Press, suggested that the public was skeptical about Clinton's "victory" because the results so far had been messy and ambiguous. "Many people," said Kohut, "are wary about what we may or may not have achieved."[65]

Considering the public ambivalence, the internationalist *Wall Street Journal* suggested editorially that Kosovo was "a lesson of interdependence" not yet fully absorbed by the politicians and the thinkers. "The

63. Kevin McAuliffe, "Kosovo: A Special Report," *Columbia Journalism Review,* May/June 1999, p. 28.

64. Ibid., p. 29.

65. John M. Broder, "Laurels Elude President as Public Judges a War," *New York Times,* June 22, 1999.

world as it exists today," the *Journal* stated, "makes a Slobodan Milosevic, a once-obscure place called Kosovo and something called ethnic cleansing a subject of dinnertime conversation in every household with a television everywhere in the world."[66] And, this author would add, the subject of diplomatic discussion in the foreign ministry of every nation in the world.

Given that TV is a constant and instant presence in all of our lives, American foreign policy must be all the more clear and consistent. It cannot give in to the impulse of the moment as shaped by the latest CNN bulletin. "If Americans had seen the battles of the Wilderness and Cold Harbor on TV screens in 1864," Lance Morrow wrote in a *Time* essay, "if they had witnessed the meat-grinding carnage of Ulysses Grant's warmaking, then public opinion would have demanded an end to the Civil War, and the Union might well have split into two countries, one of them farmed by black slaves."[67]

Simply stated, a policy must be judged on whether it is right or wrong, not whether it is popular or unpopular. Who were we trying to be in Somalia? Morrow says that first we impersonated Mother Teresa, and then John Wayne. A more appropriate model would have been Ronald Reagan, whose measured use of force in Grenada, Afghanistan, and Angola, to name three countries where the Reagan Doctrine was applied, enabled freedom fighters to overcome the forces of tyranny and to lay a foundation—in two of the countries—for liberal democracy. Few would dispute that the United States acted correctly and humanely in feeding the starving people of Somalia, but would probably agree that we erred badly when we endorsed the grandiose plans of an ambitious U.N. secretary general to build a "nation" in Somalia where one had never existed.

DIFFERENT AND YET THE SAME

It would be difficult to find two more dissimilar countries than Bosnia and Somalia, starkly different in their politics, culture, and history. But their TV images were much the same—dead men, crying women, starving children, broken cities, the inevitable detritus of war. One might have expected the world's sole superpower to either commit itself or reject involvement in these conflicts based solely on its national interest. Instead, the United States let others take the lead in the one crisis but stepped forward in the other.

66. "A Substitute for Victory," *Wall Street Journal,* June 11, 1999.
67. Lance Morrow, "The Limits of Idealism," *Time,* October 18, 1993, p. 39.

Relying on *realpolitik,* the United States declined for more than three years—despite almost daily televised pictures of Bosnian atrocities—to apply significant pressure to end the fighting in Bosnia. Yet when the United States and other NATO members carried out their sustained air strikes against the Serbs in August and September 1995, Americans endorsed the action because of the ethnic cleansing in Bosnia they had been witnessing on television for years. Similarly, the United States delayed action in Kosovo until the awful reality of Milosevic's oppression of the Albanian Kosovars filled American TV screens in 1999. In contrast, the U.S. government, moved by pictures of starving children, quickly mobilized men and materiel for a humanitarian mission in Somalia. In all three instances, television played an important—some say, too important—role in the decision-making process.

Echoing George Kennan to some extent, Everette E. Dennis, executive director of the Freedom Forum Media Studies Center, believes that "real-time coverage is a disaster" in terms of its impact on foreign policy. Public opinion used to be formed gradually over weeks or months, argues Dennis, but now "it takes only hours" for it to be galvanized to support a particular policy. "One of the obligations of leadership these days," he says, "is to try to take a somewhat measured approach in the midst of all kinds of conflicting signals and visual images that might, in fact, be wrong."[68]

Media analysts like Dennis and elitist diplomats like Kennan are right to issue warnings about the emotional impact of television on public opinion and therefore foreign policy, but they are wrong to call real-time coverage of crises a "disaster." Television is neither a disaster nor a triumph because, as these pages repeatedly argue, it is not a living thing. It is, rather, a technology that can be used for better or for worse, for good or for evil, to advance democracy or tyranny, depending upon the character and the motivations of those who control it.

In contrast to neo-Luddites like George Kennan, who scorn television and its populist impulse, telediplomats like Secretary of State Madeleine Albright strive to use television and other mass media to advance freedom and justice in our age of information. Testifying about Somalia before the Senate Foreign Relations Committee, Albright said, matter-of-factly:

Television's ability to bring graphic images of pain and outrage into our living rooms has heightened the pressure both for immediate engagement in areas of in-

68. Sharkey, "When Pictures Drive Foreign Policy," p. 19.

ternational crisis and immediate disengagement when events do not go according to plan. Because we live in a democratic society, none of us can be oblivious to those pressures.[69]

What is the correct image of U.S. foreign policy? Is it, as Marvin Kalb, the director of the Shorenstein Center on the Press, Politics and Public Policy at Harvard University, suggests, the picture of an American soldier being dragged through the streets of Mogadishu? Is it NATO warplanes bombing the Serbian installations encircling Sarajevo? Is it the open-ended deployment of 6,000 U.S. troops as part of the 50,000-strong peacekeeping force in Kosovo? Is it a smiling Arafat and Rabin shaking hands on the White House lawn? Is it Harry Wu, an American citizen, being sentenced to fifteen years in a Chinese prison for telling the truth on television about Communist China's forced labor camps? Or is the most accurate image of American foreign policy, at least during the Clinton administration, all of the above?

69. Ibid.

CHAPTER 5

THE YEAR OF MIRACLES

THE FALL OF COMMUNISM in Eastern and Central Europe in 1989 was the result of decades of political tyranny and economic backwardness. While the West enjoyed remarkable prosperity and personal freedom, the East fell into an economic and political morass from which no escape seemed possible. With no incentives to compete or modernize, Eastern Europe's industrial sector became a monument to bureaucratic inefficiency and waste, "a museum of the early industrial age." As the *New York Times* pointed out, Singapore, an Asian city-state of only two million people, exported 20 percent more machinery to the West in 1987 than all of Eastern Europe.[1] Life expectancy declined dramatically in the Soviet bloc and infant mortality rose during Communist rule. The only groups exempted from social and economic hardship were Communist Party leaders, upper military officers, and the managerial elite.

But all the while, the once-impenetrable Iron Curtain was being breached by modern communications and technology, allowing the peoples of Eastern Europe to see how the other half of Europe lived. Increasingly, Poles, Hungarians, Czechs, and East Germans demanded change and reform, not only in the marketplace but in the realm of human rights and liberties. The demands began as early as 1956, when the Polish Communist leader Wladyslaw Gomulka defied Nikita Khrushchev despite the presence of Soviet tanks, and the Hungarian Communist leader Imre Nagy was executed after a mass uprising that was brutally crushed by the

1. "Survey of East European Economies," *New York Times*, December 20, 1987.

Soviet army. In 1968, the democratic potential of the "Prague Spring" so frightened Leonid Brezhnev that he ordered the other Warsaw Pact states—except Romania—to join Moscow in invading Czechoslovakia and crushing the new freedoms. Faced with the challenge of Solidarity in 1981, the Polish Communist government declared martial law and outlawed the free trade union. Brezhnev considered invading Poland but finally let the Jaruzelski government handle the crisis, making it clear that the Soviet Union would intervene if necessary. For nearly forty years, the Communist regimes of Eastern Europe depended on the Soviets to pull their chestnuts out of any fire, but by the mid-1980s, when Gorbachev came to power, the Soviet Union could no longer afford to maintain the empire it had so carefully and expensively built.

Even those prescient few who predicted the end of Communism— "What I am describing now is . . . the march of freedom and democracy which will leave Marxism-Leninism on the ash heap of history": Ronald Reagan, 1982; "The idea of communism is essentially dead": Zbigniew Brzezinski, 1988—did not anticipate how quickly Marxism-Leninism would collapse in Eastern and Central Europe in the "miracle year" of 1989.[2] Why did the governments of these Soviet satellites, seemingly secure and in firm control of their populations, fall like so many giant dominoes in less than a year? Only a few months before it came crashing down, East German Communist boss Erich Honecker defiantly declared that the Berlin Wall would stand for at least another hundred years.[3]

Part of the answer lies in geography. Although separate and distinct, Poland, Hungary, East Germany, Czechoslovakia, and Romania were nonetheless linked. East Germany and Poland had a common border as did Czechoslovakia and Hungary. Romania was bounded on the north by Czechoslovakia and on the west by Hungary. The five Communist countries formed a tight little region, as close as the eastern seaboard states of the United States: a flight from East Berlin to Warsaw was shorter than that from Washington to Boston. Even nationalistic differences were blurred: as a result of World War II treaties, several million Germans lived in Poland and Czechoslovakia. Hungarians had settled in Slovakia and

2. Ronald Reagan, "Address to Members of the British Parliament" (Palace of Westminster, June 8, 1982), in *Speaking My Mind* (New York: Simon and Schuster, 1989), p. 118; Zbigniew Brzezinski, *The Grand Failure: The Birth and Death of Communism in the Twentieth Century* (New York: Collier Books, 1989), p. xi.

3. John Borneman, *After the Wall: East Meets West in the New Berlin* (New York: Basic Books, 1991), p. 27.

Romania. Resentment, frustration, and hope, Zbigniew Brzezinski wrote, were all inevitable in this "cluster of states with the deepest cultural ties with Western Europe."[4] What happened in one country inevitably infected the others, as witness the following chronology of 1989.[5]

IDEAS THAT COULD NOT BE SQUELCHED

In February, Vaclav Havel, the Czech dissident, was jailed in Prague for participating in human rights protests, while in Poland after months of strikes roundtable talks began between leaders of the still-outlawed Solidarity union and the Communist government. Communists had insisted that Solidarity was "a spent force," but as the Polish economy worsened and Gorbachev asserted that he would no longer honor the Brezhnev Doctrine, they were required to "reckon with ideas they could not squelch and men they could not subdue."[6] In March, 75,000 people demonstrated in Budapest on the anniversary of the 1848 revolution, demanding a withdrawal of Soviet troops and free elections. In April, Solidarity and the Polish government agreed to the first open elections since World War II; the union's legal status was restored. Havel was released from jail after serving only half his sentence. In June, Solidarity won an overwhelming victory over Communist opponents in the Soviet bloc's first free elections in forty years; the vote swept in ninety-nine of Solidarity's candidates into the one-hundred-seat Senate. Imre Nagy, who had led the 1956 Hungarian uprising against Soviet domination, was given a hero's burial in Budapest.

Gorbachev reminded the Council of Europe meeting in Strasbourg in July that he rejected the Brezhnev Doctrine: "Any interference in domestic affairs and any attempts to restrict the sovereignty of states, both friends and allies or any others, are inadmissable."[7] In August, negotiations between Solidarity and the Communists resulted in the selection of Poland's first non-Communist prime minister since the early postwar years, Solidarity official Tadeusz Mazowiecki. With summer giving way to fall, peo-

---

4. Brzezinski, *The Grand Failure*, p. 112.

5. See Bernard Gwertzman and Michael T. Kaufman, eds., *The Collapse of Communism* (New York: Times Books, 1990), and in particular Madeleine Albright, "The Glorious Revolutions of 1989," in *The New Democratic Frontier: A Country by Country Report on Elections in Central and Eastern Europe*, ed. Larry Garber and Eric Bjornlund (Washington: National Democratic Institute for International Affairs, 1992), pp. 17–18.

6. Gwertzman and Kaufman, *The Collapse of Communism*, p. 16.

7. Ivo Banc, ed., *Eastern Europe in Revolution* (Ithaca: Cornell University Press, 1992), p. 3.

ple were returning from their vacations, but this year the annual retreat led to massive migrations that "changed governments and altered the political map of the continent."[8]

In September, an East German exodus began when Hungary opened its borders with Austria for more than 13,000 Germans, while another 17,000 GDR citizens fled through West German embassies in Warsaw and Prague. Meanwhile, the Communist leadership and the opposition in Hungary agreed on the institution of a multiparty political system. In October, hundreds of thousands began demonstrating every Monday evening in East Germany, leading to the forced resignation of longtime Communist leader Erich Honecker. After Gorbachev stated that the Soviet Union had no moral or political right to interfere in the affairs of its East European neighbors, his spokesman added, "I think the Brezhnev Doctrine is dead."[9] In November, a tidal wave of East Germans poured across the border when travel restrictions were lifted, and the Berlin Wall came tumbling down. Bulgaria's Communist Party chief Todor Zhikov stepped down after thirty-five years of rule as he watched fifty thousand people gather in Sofia demanding further reforms. Millions of Czechs and Slovaks walked off their jobs and onto the streets, and the Communist government collapsed. It appeared that all the countries except Romania were "leapfrogging each other as they raced to democracy."[10]

Poland was the first to challenge the Communist Party's political power. Hungary was the first to have the Party rename itself. Bulgaria was the first to consider eliminating the constitutional guarantee of the Party's "leading role." Czechoslovakia was the first to condemn the act that validated the Communist Party's authority—the Warsaw Pact invasion in 1968. In December, proposals for free elections were advanced in Bulgaria, while mass demonstrations occurred in the Romanian cities of Timisoara and Bucharest. The year of revolutions ended with the death of the Romanian despot, Nicolae Ceausescu, and the election of Vaclev Havel as the president of Czechoslovakia's first non-Communist government since the February 1948 coup engineered by Moscow.

8. Gwertzman and Kaufman, *The Collapse of Communism*, pp. 153–54; Banc, *Eastern Europe in Revolution*, p. 3.
    9. Gwertzman and Kaufman, *The Collapse of Communism*, p. 163.
    10. Ibid., p. 300.

THE ROLE OF IDEOLOGY

Another part of the answer to why Communism in Eastern and Central Europe collapsed like a house of cards is to be found in the essential role of ideology. Millions demonstrated in the streets of Budapest, Leipzig, Prague, and other cities, calling for free elections and a free press, demanding democracy, because the leaders of their governments candidly admitted, "We no longer believe in Marxism-Leninism." Without the glue of ideology, the Communist facade of power and authority crumbled, and the people's natural desire for freedom, dammed up for more than forty years, burst forth. At the time, Gorbachev was extravagantly praised in the West for his pragmatism in admitting the profound "mistakes" of his predecessors and acknowledging the legitimacy of other social systems, but in so doing he called into question the central concepts of Communism: democratic centralism, class struggle, world revolution, Party discipline, and even the central role of the Communist Party.[11] The Marxist-Leninist governments of Eastern and Central Europe shook and shuddered with each new political and economic reform attempted by its Big Brother.

Gorbachev never resolved the innate contradictions of using *glasnost* and *perestroika* to produce a more perfect socialist world. Zbigniew Brzezinski put it well three years before the August 1991 putsch in the USSR: "Gorbachev has unleashed forces that make historical discontinuity more likely than continuity."[12] The Soviet leader preached political liberalization but practiced Leninist one-party rule. He courted Western investment but preserved an archaic command economy. He promised "new thinking" in Soviet foreign policy but continued to send massive amounts of arms and materiel to Cuba, which supported the Sandinistas in Nicaragua and the FMLN in El Salvador. These contradictions culminated in a crisis that brought about the end of Communism in the mother country, where it had prevailed for nearly seventy-five years and seemed likely to prevail for years to come.

STAGNANT AND CORRUPT

A further reason for the swift slide of Communism into oblivion was, quite literally, its inability to deliver the goods. Gorbachev became the

---

11. Serge Schmemann, "In Hope and Dismay, Lenin's Heirs Speak," in Gwertzman and Kaufman, *The Collapse of Communism*, p. 5.
12. Brzezinski, *The Grand Failure*, p. 243.

head of "a totally stagnant state dominated by a corrupt totalitarian party."[13] President Reagan pointed out in his 1982 Westminster address that although one-fifth of its population worked in agriculture, the Soviet Union was unable to feed its own people: "Were it not for the . . . tiny private sector tolerated in Soviet agriculture, the country might be on the brink of famine." Although occupying a mere 3 percent of the arable land, private farms accounted for nearly one-quarter of Soviet farm output and nearly one-third of meat products and vegetables.[14]

Communism fell because it was revealed as a fraud. It promised bread but produced food shortages and rationing. It pledged peace but sacrificed its young men in wars in far-off lands. It guaranteed the peasant land but delivered him into collectives. One of the great economic myths of the cold war was that under Communism, the German Democratic Republic had become, by 1980, the eleventh most prosperous nation in the world, with a per capita income of approximately $5,100 and an annual GNP of $100 billion. But between 1961 (when the Wall went up) and 1984, 176,714 East Germans risked death or imprisonment to escape illegally from what Honecker liked to call "a paradise" for workers. By 1989, life had become so dreary, the environment so polluted, and the *stasi* (the secret police) so omnipresent, that 1.5 million citizens had applied for exit visas and as many as five million people, out of a total population of 16.5 million, would have left East Germany if they could.[15]

MESSAGES OF FREEDOM AND DEMOCRACY

Another reason why the Iron Curtain no longer divides Europe is that the mass media sustained and spread the desire for freedom among the peoples of Eastern and Central Europe. East German reformers credit West German television and radio with informing the people how much they were being denied by Communist rule. During the difficult decade of the 1980s, Poland's Solidarity union relied heavily upon the Voice of America, Radio Free Europe, the BBC, and other Western sources for information and inspiration. Much of Czechoslovakia could receive West German and Austrian television, and as a consequence almost everyone in the country knew that the authority of the East German regime was disintegrating and the Soviets were doing little to shore it up. The long-suffer-

13. Ibid., p. 41.
14. Reagan, *Speaking My Mind*, p. 113.
15. Norman M. Naimark, "'Ich will hier raus': Emigration and the Collapse of the Germany Democratic Republic," in Banc, *Eastern Europe in Revolution*, pp. 77, 83.

ing, long-oppressed citizens of Bucharest and other Romanian cities learned from foreign radio broadcasts about the popular movements for freedom in the other satellite states and were inspired to move against Ceausescu. Far from being an impregnable Communist fortress, Eastern and Central Europe was a giant Potemkin Village with permeable frontiers that were easily penetrated by electronic messages of democracy and capitalism from the West. The Communist mass media also had to compete with the widespread use of videocassette recorders and through them the dissemination of democratic ideas and dissident voices. One 1988 estimate placed the number of VCRs at one million in Poland, 300,000 in Hungary, 150,000 in Czechoslovakia, and even 50,000 in Stalinist Bulgaria.[16]

POLAND: THE FIRST DOMINO

The fall of Communism in Eastern Europe began, appropriately enough, in the first nation to be forced by the Soviet Union to accept Communism at the end of World War II. What were the factors that made Poland the first Soviet satellite to renounce its Communist regime, establish a democratic opposition, hold partly free parliamentary elections, elect a democratic government, and institute free market reforms? First, Zbigniew Brzezinski points out, Poland's modern history has been defined by its militant opposition to Russian domination. Second, the country's fervent Roman Catholicism set it apart from its neighbors and its traditional enemy, reinforcing nationalism and Christian beliefs that were at direct variance with those of Communism. The Church was vitally important because, the Jewish poet and activist Adam Michnik says, it was the first "to provide definite proof that it was possible to be an independent institution in a totalitarian political environment." Third, in the 1970s, a new industrial proletariat, imbued with a strong, religious spirit, forged an alliance with an anti-Communist, social democratic intelligentsia. Fourth, the Communist leadership, having borrowed some $30 billion from the West, squandered almost all of it through ineptitude and corruption, preparing the way for the emergence of a genuine people's movement, *Solidarnosc,* or Solidarity, in the mid-1970s. Solidarity confronted the Communist regime on every important front: ideologically through its reliance on religion and emphasis on democracy; and organizationally through its nationwide alliance with intellectuals, young people, and especially the

16. Brzezinski, *The Grand Failure,* p. 138.

Catholic Church.[17] In every one of these areas, the mass media, internal as well as external, had a significant impact.

In December 1981, an alarmed Polish government responded to the demands for more freedoms, as totalitarians usually do, by imposing martial law and outlawing Solidarity. But it could not suppress the desire for liberty: Poland's political outlook had permanently changed. Although a Communist superstructure stood seemingly firm for another eight years, an underground Solidarity burrowed under its foundations, providing the Polish people with a political alternative, assisted by the Catholic Church and democratic forces in the West. Far from silencing the opposition, martial law produced a flood of samizdat publications: between the end of 1981 and the end of 1987, some 1,500 underground newspapers and journals and more than 2,400 books and pamphlets were published.[18]

In addition, Solidarity produced and distributed tens of thousands of illegal audiocassettes and videocassettes. In one year, according to the Solidarity leader Marian Telecki, cash in hand amounted to $300,000 from wholesale and retail distribution; catalogue titles ranged from *Death of a Priest*, the story of the murder of Father Jerzy Popieluszko, to smuggled editions of William Styron's *Sophie's Choice*. When a wave of strikes erupted in Poland in 1988, President Wojciech Jaruzelski ordered a media blackout in hopes of containing the growing rebellion. But Solidarity sent its video crews out across the country to film the strikes and the terrible working conditions that had precipitated them. Screenings of the programs were held in churches and "safe" houses and for the Western news media. These strikes finally forced Jaruzelski into the roundtable negotiations that led to elections and the country's, and the Warsaw Pact's, first non-Communist government.[19]

The blunt truthfulness of the Solidarity media contrasted sharply with the patent pseudo-reality of the official Communist media. One ex-Communist broadcaster described the "uncanny world of Communist information" as one of daily stress: "which news to publish and which to conceal, which to distort completely and which in part only." But the people

17. Ibid., pp. 114–17; Adam Michnik, "The Moral and Spiritual Origins of Solidarity," in *Without Force or Lies: Voices from the Revolution of Central Europe in 1989–90*, ed. William M. Brinton and Alan Rinzler (San Francisco: Mercury House, 1990), p. 242.

18. Brzezinski, *The Grand Failure*, p. 120.

19. Elaine Attias, "Liberation on the Airwaves," *Christian Science Monitor*, February 14, 1991.

were not fooled, as reflected in the comment of a well-known Polish satirist who described the evening news as propagating "instructions on how to cast steel, cap bottles, and pack cottage cheese." Sometimes the heavy hand of the censor had unintended consequences: in the spring of 1982, with the nation under martial law, the main news broadcast did not appear at its regularly scheduled time. Rumors quickly multiplied: had there been a coup d'etat, a journalists' revolt, sabotage, or simply a natural calamity? It was later learned that the broadcast, which finally began twenty minutes late, had been delayed because the chief censor ordered the announcer, a uniformed major, to trim his sideburns.[20]

THE IMPORTANCE OF FOREIGN RADIO

Despite the attempts of the government to control access to external mass media, many citizens regularly listened to foreign radio broadcasts in Polish aired by Radio Free Europe, the Voice of America, and the BBC. "For many decades," said Andrzej Drawicz, president of Polish Television after the fall of Communism, "the Poles learned from radio broadcasts what was really going on in their country and abroad. A true war in the air started, its participants competing for the Polish listener's consciousness." When Lech Walesa was asked in 1989 what effect Radio Free Europe had on Solidarity's activities, he said: "The degree cannot even be described. Would there be earth without the sun?"[21]

President Reagan and Pope John Paul II agreed with Walesa's assessment of the central influence of mass media. In June 1982 the United States and the Vatican secretly committed their resources to "destabilizing the Polish government and keeping the outlawed Solidarity movement alive." Over the next seven years, tons of communications equipment, including fax machines, printing presses, transmitters, telephones, shortwave radios, video cameras, photocopiers, telex machines, computers, and word processors, were smuggled into Poland through channels established by priests, American agents, and representatives of the AFL-CIO and European trade unions. A key element of the overall U.S. strategy to separate the U.S.S.R. from its captive states in the Warsaw Pact and to force reform within the Soviet empire itself was the increased use of Radio Free Europe and the Voice of America, which persistently and credibly transmitted in-

---

20. "The Shrinking World of Totalitarian TV," *Broadcasting,* September 10, 1990, p. 96.
21. "The Shrinking World of Totalitarian TV," p. 96; *Proceedings* of "The Failure of Communism: The Western Response," an international conference sponsored by Radio Free Europe/Radio Liberty, November 15, 1989 (Munich, Germany: RFE/RL Fund, 1989), p. 47.

formation and encouragement to the peoples of Eastern and Central Europe.[22]

By 1985, it was clear to every Pole that the Communist government's efforts to eliminate Solidarity had abjectly failed. More than five hundred underground periodicals were circulating in forty-six of Poland's forty-nine provinces, some with a readership of as many as eighty thousand. The Catholic Church alone published some fifty newspapers and periodicals, including one daily newspaper, with a total circulation of two million. Nearly 4,500 clandestine books and pamphlets, with circulations ranging from one thousand to seven thousand, were printed. Comic books for children rewrote Polish fables, picturing Jaruzelski "as the villain, Communism as the red dragon and Walesa as the white knight." In describing the opposition media, Piotr Szarzynski wrote:

[They] are committed to fighting the Communists to a different degree. Some openly call for a confrontation "here and now"; others publish works of fiction not directly connected to the political struggle. Some have adopted a clearly defined and comprehensive political programme; others rarely go beyond a blanket rejection of every aspect of contemporary reality and are interested mainly in "socking it to the Commies."[23]

"SOLIDARITY LIVES!"

Meanwhile, in church basements and homes, millions of viewers watched documentary television programs secretly produced by Solidarity. With broadcasting equipment supplied by the Central Intelligence Agency and the AFL-CIO, the anti-Communist opposition systematically interrupted the government's radio programs with messages like "Solidarity lives!" or "Resist!" Solidarity also disrupted television programming with audio and visual messages urging strikes and demonstrations. "There was a great moment at the halftime of the national soccer championship," recalled a Vatican official. "Just as the whistle sounded for the half, a SOLIDARITY LIVES! banner went up on the screen and a tape came on calling for resistance. What was particularly ingenious was waiting for the halftime break; had the interruption come during the actual soccer play, it could have alienated people."[24]

No longer able to call on Moscow to maintain its authority, the Com-

22. Carl Bernstein, "The Holy Alliance," *Time*, February 24, 1992, pp. 28–35.

23. Karol Jakubowicz, "Musical Chairs? The Three Public Spheres of Poland," *Media, Culture and Society* 12 (1990): p. 199.

24. Bernstein, "The Holy Alliance," p. 35.

munist government of Poland grudgingly acceded to the political, economic, and moral pressure applied by the United States and the West externally and the Church and the Solidarity movement internally. Walesa's trial for "slandering" state officials was abandoned, and the economy plummeted in the wake of strikes, demonstrations, and sanctions. On February 19, 1987, after Warsaw promised to begin a dialogue with the Church, Reagan lifted U.S. economic sanctions against Poland. That summer, Pope John Paul II was cheered wildly by millions of his countrymen as he traveled across Poland urging the granting of human rights to all and praising the still-outlawed Solidarity; his historic journey was televised throughout Poland and Eastern and Central Europe and the world. In July 1988, Gorbachev again disappointed his Communist comrades when he visited Warsaw and signaled Moscow's recognition that the Polish government could not rule without some role for Solidarity.

THE WALESA DEBATE

The final round of political change began with an enormous miscalculation by the Communist regime, which allowed Lech Walesa to debate the leader of the government labor unions over national television on November 30, 1988. The stakes were very high, like those in a U.S. presidential debate. Not since its banning in 1981 had a Solidarity leader been afforded a major forum. If Walesa failed to make a good presentation or was clearly bested, Solidarity and its cause would be dealt a serious blow. Some of the dissident union leaders feared a trap: why would the government put Walesa on national television unless it had a plan to show him up and undercut the reform movement? But as all of Poland watched, the Solidarity founder "outargued, outwitted and outcharmed" his opponent during the forty-five-minute program. Analysts compared the impact of the debate on the country with the papal visit the previous summer.[25] Though still officially illegal, Solidarity once again became a major political force and Walesa the undisputed leader of the opposition. Why had the Communists permitted the debate to take place? Because they arrogantly assumed they would win it. Out of touch with the true feelings of those whom they ruled, they believed that the people supported them and their programs. In a sense, the collapse of Communism in Eastern and Central Europe was a classic case of cognitive dissonance, with the Communist leadership un-

25. Jan T. Gross, "Poland: From Civil Society to Political Nation," in Banc, *Eastern Europe in Revolution*, p. 57.

able to accept that, after forty years of unrelenting Marxist-Leninist agitation, propaganda, and indoctrination, the people wanted democracy and a free market.

The beleaguered Polish government had no choice in the absence of the Brezhnev Doctrine and adopted a more democratic policy. Its initial notion of democratization resembled the Gorbachev reforms of 1987–88, which allowed superficial change in the Soviet Union in order for the government to retain control. In early February 1989, the Polish Communists began discussions with the banned Solidarity union about broad political and economic reforms, with the government offering to reinstate the union and give it a share of parliamentary power in exchange for support of the government's economic programs. Reflecting Poland's emerging democratic *mediapolitik*, the opening addresses of both sides were televised nationally. Walesa immediately took the offensive, blaming the Communists for Poland's sorry situation: "We know it—the country is ruined—but it wasn't some elves who ruined it, but a system of exercising authority that detaches citizens from their rights and wastes the fruits of their labor."[26] In April, when Solidarity and the government signed an agreement restoring the banned union's legal status and providing for the first free elections since the war, the announcement of the accords was broadcast on national television. Although the Communists tried to play down the notion that they had made any significant concessions, Walesa, in a ten-minute televised address, put the accords in their proper perspective: "The roundtable discussions can become the beginning of the road for democracy and a free Poland."[27]

The Polish elections provoked mixed reaction from other Communist governments. In Hungary, where there had been serious discussion about political and economic reform since the summer of 1988, the official press and television were rapt, sending an unmistakable signal to the Hungarian populace. Opposition forces reached agreement with the Hungarian Communist leadership to begin roundtable talks intended to lead to elections like those in Poland. But in East Germany and Czechoslovakia, where government resistance to change was strong and the Communist

26. John Tagliabue, "Warsaw Opens Parley with Solidarity," *New York Times*, February 6, 1989, reprinted in Gwertzman and Kaufman, *The Collapse of Communism*, p. 16.

27. John Tagliabue, "Poland Sets Free Vote in June, First since '45; Solidarity Reinstated," *New York Times*, April 5, 1992, in Gwertzman and Kaufman, *The Collapse of Communism*, p. 35.

Party seemingly in firm control, the government media's coverage of Poland was limited and negative. East Berlin's Communist Party daily newspaper *Neues Deutschland* published only one article in two weeks—a story from Poland's Communist Party paper that savaged Solidarity. And *Rude Pravo*, the Czechoslovak Party daily, reprinted several polemical attacks from the Polish Communist press on Solidarity and the Catholic Church.

The Communists' concern was justified: Solidarity swept the elections for the Senate in June 1989, while not a single government candidate for the lower house (Sejm) obtained an absolute majority of the votes cast in his district. "The people had openly and overwhelmingly repudiated Poland's Communist regime," political analyst Ivo Banac summed up. In August, the Polish parliament approved Tadeusz Mazowiekci, a leading Catholic and Solidarity activist, as the country's new prime minister. At stake was the Leninist dictum that the authority of the Communist Party cannot be reversed by peaceful or democratic means, as well as the Western notion that Communist parties "never give up power without a fight." But Marxism-Leninism was dying, and many Western experts were applying anachronistic political models to a cold war that was ending. Not only was there no longer any real Communist resistance to the democratic revolution in Poland, but the composition of Mazowiecki's cabinet confirmed that the Solidarity government, while still talking coalition with the Communists, was actually moving toward the adoption of Western economic and political models.[28] In December 1990, nine years after he was arrested and his labor union banned, and eight years after President Reagan and Pope John Paul II had forged a Holy Alliance to help the anti-Communist Polish opposition, Lech Walesa became president of Poland.

HUNGARY: REFORM FROM THE TOP

Unlike Poland, with its large, decentralized population of thirty-nine million and bottom-up politics as practiced by Solidarity, Hungary was a much smaller, more compact country whose politics were normally directed from the top down. The bloody 1956 revolution emphasized the people's strong antipathy toward Communism and the Soviet Union, but Janos Kadar, the Communist leader who succeeded the executed Imre

28. John Tagliabue, "Poland Flirts with Pluralism Today," *New York Times,* June 3, 1989, in Gwertzman and Kaufman *The Collapse of Communism,* p. 118; Banc, *Eastern Europe in Revolution,* p. 3.

Nagy, was careful to move only gradually toward a more liberal system known as "goulash Communism." Although popular for most of the 1960s and 1970s, when the country enjoyed modest prosperity, Kadar came under increasing criticism in the 1980s when Hungary, along with every other Soviet satellite, fell farther and farther behind the West in economic growth and political freedom.

By 1987, an opposition had been established, and underground publications proliferated. The Communist leadership pragmatically conceded that the opposition had a legitimate place in national affairs. Imre Pozsgay, the head of the regime's umbrella organization, the Patriotic People's Front, and perhaps the most liberal Communist in Hungary, even suggested that the current one-party dictatorship should be viewed as a "transitional" arrangement.[29] Unlike Poland, as noted, much of the impetus for reform came from the Communist leadership at the top rather than from the workers and farmers at the bottom. In May 1988, the Party moved to rejuvenate itself and control growing pressures for basic changes by replacing Kadar with the much younger, more dynamic Karoly Grosz. Reform Communist Pozsgay was given a seat in the Politboro.

To increase the role of the market in the economy and reduce societal tensions, the new Party leadership advocated weakening the direct role of the Party organization, giving a freer, but not unrestricted, hand to the press and strengthening the position of "interest organizations" like trade unions and agricultural associations. All the compromises of 1988 were underscored by the dark legacy of 1956. Although officially suppressed, memories of the bloody revolution of 1956 had lived on, and any signs of crisis inevitably conjured up the ugly past. "It was above all the *fear of society*," Laszlo Bruszt and David Stark write, "that so deeply inscribed in the Communist leadership an instinct to do everything to avoid another 1956."[30]

A key question in the process of reform in Hungary was the reaction of the Soviet Union, which had brutally intervened in 1956. If the leadership could depend upon the threat, let alone the actual use of Soviet tanks and troops as in the past, a Communist regime could still govern with relative ease in Hungary. But if Gorbachev with his implicit rejection of the Brezh-

29. Brzezinski, *The Grand Failure*, p. 136.
30. Laszlo Bruszt and David Stark, "Remaking the Political Field in Hungary: From the Politics of Confrontation to the Politics of Competition," in Banc, *Eastern Europe in Revolution*, p. 24.

nev Doctrine prevailed, who knew what changes tomorrow would bring. There might even be a revolution against Communism that succeeded. Communist hard-liners in Hungary—and in Bulgaria, Romania, Czechoslovakia, and East Germany—based their status quo plans on the departure of Gorbachev, who in the fall of 1988 was fighting for his political survival. But their hopes were dashed when Gorbachev bested the old guard Communist Egor Ligachev at the October meeting of the Central Committee of the Soviet Communist Party.[31] Although not properly appreciated at the time, Gorbachev's defeat of Ligachev was the beginning of the end of Communism in Eastern and Central Europe. Without the Brezhnev Doctrine, the Soviet satellites were on their own, and they soon discovered that their military no longer cowed and their policies no longer appeased an aroused and deeply dissatisfied people.

DIVIDE AND CONQUER

Nevertheless, from late 1988 to mid-1989, hard-line Communists in Hungary still thought they could emerge on top by creating and dominating a multiparty political system. The cornerstone of their strategy was the time-honored Leninist practice of dividing and conquering the opposition. By February 1989, it was obvious to all parties that, with Polish Communists already engaged in their own roundtable negotiations with Solidarity, some kind of national forum would have to be convened in Hungary. Naturally, said the hard-liners, the Party would act as broker.

But the opposition refused to accept such a paternalistic move and declined to attend a proposed April meeting. Arguing for compromise rather than confrontation, reformers prevailed over hard-liners within the Communist government, and formal negotiations between the renamed Communist Party—now the Hungarian Socialist Party—and the democratic opposition were set for June 13, only three days before the anniversary of the execution of Imre Nagy and other heroes of the 1956 revolution. A key event in the hardening of the democratic opposition's position and the backing down of the Communists was the March 15 celebration of the Revolution of 1848. The Communist Party hoped to fit the anniversary into its scheme of "marginalizing the opposition by incorporating it."[32] They invited non-Communist organizations to participate in their commemoration as a celebration of national unity in which everyone wanting

31. Ibid., p. 25.
32. Ibid., p. 33.

"democracy" and a "multiparty system" could march together under the Communist Party's slogans for "renewal."

But in response, twenty-four democratic groups organized their own Budapest demonstration, which attracted more than 100,000 participants and totally overshadowed the official ceremonies. The opposition obviously won the duel of the commemorations, which was televised in every Hungarian home. Ordinary citizen and Communist Party member alike could see clearly for himself which was the larger demonstration and foresee which side would grow larger in future demonstrations. Evidence of the increasing impact of the country's more democratic *mediapolitik* came only eight days later when representatives of the alternative organizations met and organized themselves into the "Opposition Round Table," seeking, as in the Polish model, to involve the people in the political process. The formation of the Round Table fundamentally altered Hungarian politics, uniting and radicalizing the opposition, whose guiding principle was not "power sharing" but genuinely free, fully contested elections.[33]

Throughout the spring, local Communist organizations defected from the official party line and an increasing number of Communist parliamentarians declared their independence. Almost every day brought the announcement in the media of another new "alternative organization." Growing desperate, more and more high-ranking Communist Party officials revealed that they had "always" been reformers. A liberated Party press scarcely concealed its derision "as it described yet another regime figure's conversion on the road to Damascus." In April, Prime Minister Miklos Nemeth, a protégé of party head Grosz, took the unprecedented step of using an evening television news program to repudiate a speech by Grosz and to distance himself from the Communist Party hierarchy. "The *government* was clearly separating itself from the *Party*," Laszlo Bruszt of the Hungarian Academy of Sciences points out.[34]

There was another contest of rallies on May 1, the sole remaining Communist holiday, with the League of Independent Trade Unions attracting at least sixty thousand and perhaps as many as one hundred thousand people to its rally, six to ten times as large as the audience of ten thousand that dutifully turned out to hear Party boss Grosz. The significant disparity in public support was again noted by the national television audience. Separate public forums were held after the rallies and televised; the inde-

33. Ibid., pp. 33–34.
34. Ibid., pp. 36–38.

pendent unions' contacts among television reporters, producers, and technicians yielded equal coverage—fifty minutes for the ruling party, fifty minutes for the united opposition—a development every bit as telling as the content of the forums.

The third and by far the most important of the three media events in the spring of 1989, which transformed the anti-Communist opposition in Hungary into a major political force, was a ceremony honoring Imre Nagy, who had led the 1956 uprising against Soviet domination. On June 16, an estimated 250,000 Hungarians filled Heroes Square in Budapest to give Nagy, who had been hanged and thrown into a prison grave, a solemn funeral and a hero's burial. After more than thirty years of passivity and subservience, the people of Hungary became truly involved in the politics of Hungary. Those present, along with the national television audience, heard the names of fallen martyrs as well as speeches honoring the executed prime minister and denouncing the still-occupying Soviet army.

In keeping with the newly expanded media freedom, the government network televised the ceremony live from 9 A.M. to 6 P.M. Four top Communist Party officials, including Minister of State Imre Pozsgay, laid wreaths and served as honorary pallbearers flanking Nagy's coffin but left before the eulogies to Nagy that condemned the Communist Party and the Soviet Union. Consequently, they did not hear a leader of the Federation of Young Democrats paying tribute to Nagy as someone who, although a lifelong Communist, "identified himself with the wishes of the Hungarian nation to put an end to the Communist taboos, blind obedience to the Russian empire and the dictatorship of a single party." The significance of the June 16 ceremonies cannot be exaggerated: only a few months earlier, Grosz had ruled out any talk about Nagy's rehabilitation, and on the thirtieth anniversary of his hanging the previous June, the police brutally broke up a small tribute organized by dissidents.[35]

MISREADING THE PEOPLE

Facing a united opposition, fearful of another 1956 uprising, and aware that it could no longer rely on Soviet force to stay in power, reform Communists led by Poszgay calculated that they could use their superior resources, organization, and nationally recognized candidates to defeat the

---

35. Henry Kamm, "Hungarian Who Led '56 Revolt Is Buried as a Hero," *New York Times*, June 16, 1989, in Gwertzman and Kaufman, *The Collapse of Communism*, pp. 133–36; Bruszt and Stark, "Remaking the Political Field," p. 39.

opposition in open elections. It was a flagrant misreading of the rapidly evolving politics and wishes of the Hungarian people, who did not want Communism with a human or any other kind of face but freedom and democracy.

The self-confidence of the reform Communists was slightly shaken that summer when they lost four parliamentary seats that fell open because of recall campaigns. Their response was to push hard for the institution of a strong presidency and early elections, believing that even if they did not gain a plurality in Parliament, their nationally recognized candidate, Imre Pozsgay, would surely win the presidency, and they would still be able to run the government and the country. An agreement to hold presidential elections in late November emerged from talks, but a group of opposition parties objected and demanded a referendum, challenging the presidential component of the agreement. Opponents also argued that the agreement had failed to abolish the Communist Party's armed workers guard and to provide a process for a public accounting of the Party's sizeable assets.

When the referendum carried by a very narrow margin over the opposition of the reform Communists, Pozsgay and his associates plunged into "a long winter of campaigning in which their opponents thrived week by week." They attempted every Leninist trick in the book, including the manipulation of government television, but their clumsy moves only exposed their false commitment to competitive politics and encouraged a more militant anti-Communism among the opposition parties. As a result, the reform Communists were "confronted at every turn with their own awkward past."[36]

Their cause was certainly damaged by "Duna-gate"—a combination of the Hungarian word for the Danube river, Duna, and the international suffix meaning political scandal—which dominated media coverage and political debate in January 1990. An officer in the Hungarian secret police, fearing that Hungarian security forces might imitate the Romanian *securitate*, which violently resisted reform, revealed that the police continued to spy on members of the opposition and to keep records of meetings and events. With the help of the officer, a television news crew, practicing a kind of investigative journalism unprecedented in Hungary, entered police headquarters in Budapest and filmed files about recent political activities of opposition parties.

The massive negative publicity and the ensuing calls for the disman-

36. Ibid., pp. 48–51.

tling of the secret police forced the government to stop monitoring the opposition. In addition, the chief of the secret police and a deputy minister of the interior were dismissed and control of the clandestine agency was placed under the prime minister. The moves were intelligent damage control, but "Duna-gate" intensified the Communist-bashing which had already characterized the campaign. One poster portrayed the back of the head of a Soviet soldier with the words, "Good Riddance!" Another depicted a trash can full of Stalinist and Communist propaganda and offered "Spring Cleaning with the MDF" (the Hungarian Democratic Forum). Desperately, the reform Communists, under their new title, the Hungarian Socialist Party, tried to improve their anti-Communist credentials through frequent public meetings with Western leaders. But the transparent ruse failed to impress many Hungarians.[37]

Once confident that they would be the first Communists to win a popular election, the Hungarian Socialist Party in the event won only 8 percent of the parliamentary seats in the March and April 1990 elections. They would not have suffered so crushing a defeat at the hands of the Hungarian Democratic Forum, which won 43 percent of the seats in Parliament, if their opposition had not engaged in shrewd democratic *mediapolitik* in the spring and summer of 1989. The nationally televised broadcast of the March 15 celebration of the Revolution of 1848, the May 1 rally by independent workers, and the June 16 commemoration of the execution of Imry Nagy enabled the opposition to carry its message of patriotism, democracy, and capitalism into the homes of the Hungarian people and present itself as an attractive political alternative to the reform Communists. Without the mass media, there would have been no peaceful transition from democratic centralism to democracy in Hungary.

Events in Poland also clearly influenced Hungary. Agreements reached in Warsaw between the government and the opposition made it imperative for Hungarian Communists to make similar concessions, while Solidarity's activities gave reformers in Hungary a standard to follow. The political process in Hungary also benefitted from the country having the region's "most benign form of Communism." By the 1980s, there were no political prisoners, entrepreneurship was encouraged, and the borders were comparatively open, allowing Hungarian citizens to come and go with relative ease. Communist leaders like Pozsgay planned to reform the system significantly although they did not know how much deviation

37. Thomas O. Melia, "Hungary," in *The New Democratic Frontier*, pp. 56–57.

from Communist orthodoxy would be tolerated by Moscow, and they certainly did not anticipate that when the voting was all over, they would be in the minority and out of power.[38]

CZECHOSLOVAKIA: FROZEN IN TIME

Since 1948 and a Soviet-engineered coup d'etat, Czechoslovakia had been one of the most repressive Communist regimes in Eastern Europe. Unlike its Communist neighbors, Poland and Hungary, Czechoslovakia by 1989 had not experienced any political liberalization or economic reform. The regime that had been imposed by Soviet tanks and troops in 1968 was still in place, its leaders and policies essentially unaltered. The revolution that began on November 17, 1989, the historian Tony R. Judt wrote, was significantly helped by (1) the growing public anger about the economic stagnation which strengthened and emboldened the opposition; and (2) the isolation of the neo-Stalinists in Prague, surrounded by eager reformers, Communist and otherwise, in Hungary, East Germany, and the Soviet Union. In addition, Czechoslovakia had deeper democratic roots than any other country in the region, having had a liberal democratic government between the two world wars. Reform developments were at first dismissed by Party officials. Then Party boss Milos Jakes received a high-level warning from Moscow in early November that failure to initiate at least some political changes could lead to an uprising like the one that forced sweeping reforms in East Germany. Public signs of fear, tension, and conflict began to appear within the hard-line Communist government, which encouraged the opposition to hold a rally for a student killed by the Nazis fifty years earlier and to call for a national general strike.[39] The impact of these mass televised demonstrations, as in Poland and Hungary, accelerated the process of change in Czechoslovakia.

During the three weeks leading up to the general strike, the Civic Forum emerged as the leading organization of the opposition and the dissident playwright Vaclav Havel as the forum's leader. The forum did not generate itself spontaneously; it built on the foundation of the well-known human rights organization Charter 77 and on the Democratic Initiative, formed two years earlier. On November 20, 1989, 200,000 people

38. Ibid., p. 62.
39. Tony R. Judt, "Metamorphosis: The Democratic Revolution," in Banc, *Eastern Europe in Revolution*, pp. 96–98; R. W. Apple, Jr., "Unease in Prague; A Soviet Warning on Foot-Dragging Is Given to Prague," *New York Times*, November 15, 1989, in Gwertzman and Kaufman, *The Collapse of Communism*, p. 204.

gathered in central Prague and marched through the city, calling for freedom and a change in government. In a country with a population of fifteen million, this was a major event. National television provided extensive coverage of the demonstration and reported similar marches in at
least three other cities. Party leader Jakes revealed his incomprehension of
the dynamics of *mediapolitik* by accusing the protest marchers of "seeking
to create chaos and anarchy." His stern warning, couched in traditional
Marxist-Leninist language, did not begin to match the emotional impact
of the march of several hundred thousand televised nationally by the station that his government controlled. Everyone understood that if the Party were truly in command, the march would not have been allowed.

"WE ARE NOT LIKE THEM"

For the next three days, crowds continuously occupied Prague, growing
to over one-third of a million in size. Havel addressed the crowds for the
first time on November 21, two days before Alexander Dubcek, the reformist leader forced from power after Soviet tanks invaded Czechoslovakia in 1968, made his first public appearance in Slovakia in two decades.
Havel told a huge gathering in Wenceslaus Square that Communist leaders had held their first talks with the Civic Forum, a telltale concession. On
the sixth consecutive day of mass protest—it would be as though Martin
Luther King, Jr., had led not one but six Marches on Washington in August
1963—Havel told cheering crowds that he sought to reach "especially all
the workers in our country who are for reform." As cheers of "Long live
the workers" echoed through the square, the defiant intellectual declared
that those who had "taken bloody vengeance against all their rivals for so
many years are now afraid of us." But he insisted that "we are not like
them. We don't want to take vengeance on anyone. We only ask to take
control of our country." For the first time, citizens were able to watch a live
broadcast from Wenceslaus Square on state-run television, another sign
that the totalitarian grip of the Party on the country was slipping away.[40]

The most powerful demonstration of national solidarity came on November 27, when millions of Czechs and Slovaks walked off their jobs and
into the streets, bringing Prague and the rest of the country to a standstill.
"It has become an unstoppable wave," commented a senior Western diplo-

---

40. Judt, "Metamorphosis," p. 99; John Tagliabue, "250,000 Czechs, Hailing Dubcek,
Urge Ouster of Hard-Line Leaders," *New York Times*, November 22, 1989, in Gwertzman
and Kaufman, *The Collapse of Communism*, pp. 233–34.

mat. Most Communists agreed that the government's authority was quickly deteriorating. *Rude Provo*, the official publication of the Communist Party, spoke of the paralysis of the Central Committee and of "political mummies" who were blocking reform. It urged the Party to prepare for "free democratic elections" by developing a new program "that will be supported by all." On a new television program called *The Government Speaks to You*, Communist ministers declared that they favored a free-market economy. State television carried pictures of participants in the national strike from all over the country.[41]

No longer able to control itself, let alone events, a divided and isolated Communist leadership made concession after concession in a desperate attempt to retain some semblance of authority. The Parliament removed the constitutional clause guaranteeing the Communist Party its "leading role." A new government was inaugurated with five non-Communist members. But Civic Forum, now given air time over Czech radio, used its visible strength in the streets of Prague to press the Communists for deeper concessions. At the same time, state television metamorphosed from a tool of the government into a vehicle for the opposition. The daily mass rallies, including calls for an end to the Communist monopoly on political power, were televised live and uncensored. Typical of the new democratic *mediapolitik* were the video programs shown in the front windows of Civic Forum headquarters. One video depicted the violent breakup by police of a student demonstration on November 17 and showed the rallies in Wenceslaus Square that followed that night of violence. Also included were interviews with opposition leaders and items from the official press that had been exposed as lies. These new forms of expression would have been cause for arrest only a few weeks before, but had become so widespread that one leader of the Communist Party was overheard asking another for the time of that day's demonstration. "I don't know," the official replied. "Why don't you go outside and check the wall."[42]

Confronted by crowds that had coalesced almost overnight into a dominant political force, the Communists caved in, accepting a new government with a non-Communist majority and expelling Jakeš and the Prague

41. R. W. Apple, "Millions of Czechoslovaks Increase Pressure on Party with Two-Hour General Strike," *New York Times*, November 27, 1989, in Gwertzman and Kaufman, *The Collapse of Communism*, pp. 257–58.

42. Esther B. Fein, "If the Party Has Its Back to the Wall, It's a Wall with New Posters on It," *New York Times*, November 26, 1989, in Gwertzman and Kaufman, *The Collapse of Communism*, pp. 255–56.

Party chief. But a hard-line Communist still remained president—for a time. It was fitting that on December 29, 1989, Vaclav Havel, who had gone from dissident playwright to the leader of the Civic Forum mass movement in less than one month, was elected president of Czechoslovakia. The students were satisfied that their demands for freedom and democracy had at last been met and halted their six-week-old strike.

The Velvet Revolution would not have occurred without the remarkable leadership of Havel, who insisted that the Civic Forum press their demands to the limit, thereby keeping the Communists on the defensive; who realized the need to avoid violence, regardless of provocation; who worked hard to keep lines of communication open to the Communists without ceding real power; and who understood the critical power of the mass media, external as well as internal, in the age of *mediapolitik*. On the day he took office as president, Havel went to the offices of the Voice of America in Prague to thank the Czech and Slovak service for "helping to bring about the peaceful revolution."[43] Earlier, he praised Radio Free Europe as "the main free independent mass medium." He freely acknowledged that without the international support and publicity generated by VOA, RFE, and other media, he and other dissident Czechs would have remained in prison "for many years."[44]

The cumulative effect of the daily broadcasts of the mass rallies, demonstrations, and strikes on Communist authority in Czechoslovakia can be compared to the impact of the daily air raids and missile attacks on Iraqi armed forces by the U.S.-led coalition during the Persian Gulf War. In both conflicts, the enemy was so devastated and demoralized that he had little option but to surrender. "The Czechs and Slovaks came from further behind," wrote Judt, "and have moved further ahead (except in economic reform) than any other formerly Communist country." Their success was in direct proportion to their strong democratic tradition supported by an economic and social infrastructure, including the media, that survived forty years of Communist dictatorship.[45]

43. Kenneth Y. Tomlinson, "Freedom's Victory: What We Owe to Faith and the Free Market," *Imprimis,* December 1991, p. 3. Tomlinson is a former director of the Voice of America.

44. Jan Obrman, "Special Report: An Interview with Vaclav Havel," *Soviet/East European Report* 6, no. 31 (July 25, 1989): pp. 1–2.

45. Judt, "Metamorphosis," pp. 114–15.

EAST GERMANY: THE HARDEST OF
THE HARD-LINERS

As we have seen, among the elements that brought an end to Communism in the countries of Eastern and Central Europe were Solidarity and the Catholic Church in Poland, a "benign" form of Communism and the dark memory of 1956 in Hungary, and a democratic tradition and an eloquent, charismatic leader in Czechoslovakia. But what of the German Democratic Republic, the hardest of the hard-line Communist states? East Germany (the GDR) had no grassroots movement like Solidarity, it was ruled by Stalinist rather than Gorbachevist Communists, and far from having any experience of democracy, it had lived under Nazi and then Communist tyranny for nearly sixty years. But it had one thing that the other Soviet satellites did not have: a sister nation, West Germany, that lived in freedom and prosperity. No other member of the Warsaw Pact was as continuously exposed to the indisputable evidence of what democracy and a market economy can provide a people, and what Marxism-Leninism in the GDR had not. The means by which this evidence was transmitted to East Germans, and in their own language, was essentially the West German mass media, especially television.

With the exception of Dresden and part of Saxony (located in the southeastern corner of the GDR), all of East Germany could receive West German television, mainly due to the relay antennas located in West Berlin. Out of a total population of 16.5 million, about 13.5 million East Germans could receive at least three West German channels: the two national channels, ARD and ZDF, and one of several regional channels. Themselves dedicated propagandists, the East German Communists knew what unrestricted access to West German television could do to minds and wills: "The enemy of the people stands on the roof," Communist Party boss Walter Ulbricht once said of television antennas.[46] In the 1960s, the government sent young Communists house to house ordering that any television antenna be turned away from West Berlin or West German transmitters; sometimes they even broke the antennas. But because West Berlin was located in the middle of East Germany, and Western transmitters were pointed in the same direction as Communist transmitters, the anti-antenna campaign was eventually deemed impractical and abandoned.

46. Elaine Attias, "Liberation on the Airwaves," *Christian Science Monitor*, February 14, 1991.

A STASI STATE

The Communist government shifted to the use of informants; even children in school were asked about their parents' viewing habits. If the parents were watching the "wrong" programs, they were called in by the school principal and told their children would suffer the consequences for such misguided upbringing. Informers working for the *stasi*, the secret police, were directed to denounce people spreading or even commenting on information received over Western television. But by 1980, the East German regime had to resign itself to knowing that most of its people watched West German television; it even took steps, in one instance, to assure its availability. East German workers, even those who were Communist Party members, consistently listed the Dresden area as a region where they did not want to be relocated. When asked for an explanation, they usually referred to the sparse television channels (i.e., West German channels) that could be received there. The government's response was not to increase the number of East German channels but to begin installing in 1983 a cable television system that would include West German transmissions.[47] Like the other Communist regimes in Eastern Europe, the GDR could not grasp the cumulative impact of the foreign mass media. By 1989, according to the German television journalist Werner Sonne, 90 percent of the East German homes with television were capable of receiving West German channels.[48]

The influence of West German television on East German society was reinforced by the fact that the media played a much more dominant role in everyday life in the GDR than in other countries in Central Europe. Studies in the 1980s confirmed that working people in the GDR spent up to 70–80 percent of their free time at home, and what they did at home was to watch Western television programs that contained the message of "a better life, of greater freedom and also of the possibility of actively forging the future."[49] As a result, East Germany, despite the best propaganda efforts of the government, was not a closed but a permeable society that

47. George Quester, *The International Politics of Television* (Lexington, Mass.: Lexington Books, 1990), pp. 127–28; Bornemann, *After the Wall*, p. 136.

48. Werner Sonne, interview by Stephen M. Novak, March 12, 1992, Washington; from an unpublished study by Stephen M. Novak.

49. Helmut Hanke, "Media Culture in the GDR: Characteristics, Processes, and Problems," *Media, Culture and Society* 12 (1990): pp. 175, 177, 182.

constantly compared its political, economic, and cultural way of life with that of West Germany—and found it more and more wanting.

Meanwhile, the SED (the East German Communist Party) continued to direct the country's thirty-nine daily newspapers, with a total circulation of more than nine million, as well as the state-run television and radio channels, with its usual Stalinist efficiency. Guenter Schabowski, a former East German Politboro member, has revealed that editors received daily instructions from the Party as to what was fit to print:

After being issued the Central Committee's "guidelines," the head of the Press Office would summon the chiefs of block newspapers and . . . issue them the "guidelines" which were by then government "recommendations." The editorial departments of the district newspapers were informed of agitation decrees by telex. . . . Those based in Berlin were told by telephone up until the moment before the printing presses started rolling of the news that must be used . . . or had to be given front-page prominence or placed inconspicuously in the inside pages.[50]

The official list of forbidden topics had its Kafkaesque logic: no pictures of fruit baskets on conference tables, for example, because the public might become envious; no reference to sausage kiosks, because people already ate too much meat; no mention of atomic power plants to avoid publicity about a sensitive subject; no mention of home-made flying machines, as otherwise people might contemplate escape.[51]

Given such managed news, which they knew to be incomplete, misleading, or simply false because they had access to alternative news media, East Germans predictably read and watched East German media less and less. Only 3 percent of the East German people routinely watched the GDR's number one television news program, *Aktuelle Kamera,* preferring to tune in either to ARD's *Tagesschau* or ZDF's *Heute*. Also enormously popular was the United States Information Agency's RIAS (Radio in the American Sector), founded by the U.S. military in Berlin in 1947 when Soviet forces refused to share broadcasting time on the only surviving Berlin radio station. RIAS became a major cultural and information medium for Berlin and the rest of East Germany. A 1962 survey of West Berliners and refugees from the east revealed that it was the most popular station in the city for entertainment and information. After German unification, the station received an incredible 3.5 million pieces of mail (the overwhelming

50. Herman Neyn, *Update on Germany: Now Eastern Germany Gets a Free Press* (Bonn: Inter Nationes Bonn, 1991), p. 2.
51. Ibid., p. 3.

majority of them from East Berlin and the five new German states) urging the continuation of "their" radio station. Many listeners expressed their gratitude for the radio's inspiration during a long period of what one German called "economic demise and social disparity."[52]

THE IMPACT OF WEST GERMAN TV

Long before the fall of the Berlin Wall in 1989, some Western observers, like the *New York Times*, had noted that West German television "has had a corrosive, alienating impact on East Germans' attitudes toward their own rulers."[53] How could it have been otherwise? Whereas most of the people in other Communist countries had to depend upon shortwave radio to get the news from the Voice of America, Radio Free Europe, or the BBC, East Germans had easy access to the televised news of West Germany. When Soviet tanks rumbled through the streets of Prague in 1968 or Polish workers struck in Gdansk in 1980 or Moscow tried to explain the Afghanistan war, East Germans could compare the predictable official line of the GDR media with the objective, often understated facts and opinions of West German media. Over the years, exposure to West German media helped forge a politically aware East German population, an essential condition for the revolution of 1989.

Awareness was deepened by the extraordinary amount of coverage that West German television gave to all aspects of life in East Germany. Each week, West German programs like *ZDF-Magazin, Monitor,* and *Report,* moderated by well-known television personalities, presented items about the politics, economics, and culture of the GDR. A concerned East German government retaliated with its own weekly program, the *Schwarze Kanal (Black Channel),* moderated by Karl-Edward von Schnitzler, who spent every Monday evening arguing that Western television was full of propaganda and lies and that life in the West was an unending succession of unemployment, inequality, exploitation, militarism, and crime. Most East German viewers understood which channel was telling lies. The impact of the West German programs was enhanced by their political balance, which ranged from the right (G. Lowenthal on *ZDF-Magazin*) to the left (H. D. Schwarze on *Kennzeichen D*). The GDR audience, deprived of

52. Sonne, interview; *RIAS Program Reaction Survey* (Frankfurt am Main: DIVO, Institute for Economic Research, 1962), p. ii; letter to RIAS Berlin, February 1992, translated by Stephen M. Novak.

53. "Berlin Night and Day," *New York Times,* July 24, 1983.

free political debate in their own country, eagerly followed the spirited discussions in the Federal Republic of Germany. Often the West German moderators would use East German examples to illustrate the abuse of human rights or bottlenecks in the supply of food and consumer goods. The reality of the gray, depressing, and oppressive life in the GDR was revealed again and again over West German television.[54]

West German channels also presented parliamentary debates and official statements from Bonn, filled with references to "our German brothers and sisters in the East," reassuring the average citizen in the GDR that he was neither alone nor forgotten. Every year, the West German chancellor, whether Christian Democrat or Social Democrat, delivered in the Bundestag a nationally televised address on "The State of the Nation in the Divided Land," which described extensively the true situation in East Germany. In addition, there were the televised messages of the FRG president and the chancellor on New Year's Day, on June 17 (the Day of National Unity, commemorating the East Berlin demonstrations of 1953), and on August 13, marking the 1961 building of the Berlin Wall, all encouraging a sense of community, of *ein volk*, between the two Germanys.[55]

DEEPENING DISILLUSIONMENT

Sometimes, Western television goaded the East German government into action, as in the case of the left-wing dissident ballad singer Wolf Biermann. A committed Communist who once delighted in praising Stalin, Biermann became increasingly disenchanted with Communism even as the popularity of his songs and records soared throughout all of Germany. Harassed by the *stasi* and denied an exit visa for years, Biermann was finally allowed in 1976 to travel to Cologne in the west to give a concert. It is estimated that more than half the population of East Germany stayed up to watch Biermann lacerate the GDR for more than three hours with his searing Brecht-like lyrics. He was immediately expelled by the East German Communist Party and denied reentry into the GDR. In his autobiography, published after the opening of the Berlin Wall and triumphal concerts in Berlin and Leipzig, Biermann wrote of his years in exile: "I visited the countries that were poorer and freer than the [GDR], and I had to conclude that Communism was really dead. Nothing could dis-

54. Ivan Denes, interview by author, August 1990. Denes is a veteran Berlin journalist.
55. Ivan Denes, "The Impact of West German TV on the Population of the GDR" (August 1990, photocopy of unpublished paper).

guise it: no tears, no lies in the soul, no injections of foreign capital, and no sad songs. Now the corpse lies in the land and pollutes the atmosphere."[56] Biermann's deep disillusionment and rejection of Communism came to be shared by millions of Germans in the east in the years leading up to the bloodless revolution of 1989.

And then there were all those television commercials that afforded a West German an interlude in which to stretch his legs or get a beer but which for the East German depicted "a world of magical wealth and amusement."[57] The glittering images created in many East Germans an intense longing for material goods and a no less intense hatred for the political party and economic system that made them unobtainable. The same fascination, even obsession, with the good life in the west accounted for the huge audiences of television dramas and comedies: East Germans were attentive not so much to the plot of a program as to the clothes, the furniture, the kitchen equipment, and, above all, the cars that the characters used so casually.

For nearly forty years, the West German media informed East Germans of the reality of everyday life in the west; promoted daily comparison between two vastly different standards of living; encouraged the notion of German solidarity; and provided an appealing political, economic alternative to the deadening life of the GDR. Some of the West German programming was deliberately aimed at the east, such as the parliamentary speeches and debates, but most of the programs were intended for audiences in the FRG. Allowed to operate within a liberal democratic framework, West German media preserved liberty at home and promoted the desire for the same liberty behind the Berlin Wall. In short, without democratic *mediapolitik,* there would have been no bloodless revolution of 1989.

THE IRON CURTAIN BREACHED

The first physical hole in the Iron Curtain appeared on May 2, 1989, when reform Communists in Budapest gave the order to tear down the barbed wire along the border between Hungary and Austria. In the past, Hungarian border guards made sure that East German visitors to their country returned to East Germany; now the rules had changed. While West German television showed pictures of ecstatic East Germans driving

56. As quoted in Marvin J. Lasky, *Voices in a Revolution* (London: Encounter Magazine, 1991), p. 16; Denes, "The Impact of West German TV."
57. William Drozdiak, "The Magnet of Western TV," *Washington Post,* August 19, 1984.

across the Hungarian-Austrian border, East German television carried an official statement criticizing Hungary for the "organized smuggling of human beings." The GDR government might call it "smuggling," but the people knew it was a flight to freedom. Within days, thousands of East Germans who feared to climb the Berlin Wall flooded Hungary in hopes of taking the long road through Austria into West Germany. The same month, embryonic opposition groups based primarily in the East German Protestant churches encouraged people to vote "No"—against the government—in local elections. Although the official count turned up less than a 1 percent no vote, local observers reported that the opposition received about 20 percent nationwide.[58] It was the first significant crack in the electoral invincibility of the GDR regime. Meanwhile, during July and August, hundreds and then thousands of GDR citizens camped out in the West German embassies in Budapest, Prague, and Warsaw, and in Bonn's unofficial embassy in East Berlin. Nothing discouraged their quest for freedom, neither the message from the west that "the boat is full," nor the incessant warnings from the east about West German unemployment, poverty, and animosity.[59]

THE IMPACT OF TIANANMEN SQUARE

A powerful influence on the course of events in East Germany was the development of a pro-democracy movement halfway around the world. When tanks and armed soldiers brutally suppressed the democracy movement in Tiananmen Square on June 4, 1989, their repression filled television screens around the world, but perhaps nowhere with so much effect as in East Germany. One dissident, Pastor Tureck, remembers the impact of those images from Beijing on his parishioners in Leipzig: "We saw Tiananmen Square here in Leipzig on West German television . . . and it influenced our world. Although people were afraid, they were also filled with hope." Many East Germans gathered in Tureck's and other churches to discuss what the events in China meant for their growing protest movement.[60] Party boss Erich Honecker knew how dangerous the virus of democracy was, and ordered East German television not to report the Beijing uprising. But the strategy backfired: West German television enabled

---

58. Daniel I. Gordon and Fred W. Reinke, "East Germany: March 18, 1990," in *The New Democratic Frontier*, p. 23.

59. Naimark, "'Ich will hier raus,'" p. 83.

60. Tara Sonenshine, "The Revolution Has Been Televised," *Washington Post*, October 2, 1990.

East German citizens and leaders to see the inspiring events of Tiananmen Square. When the GDR regime openly supported the bloody crackdown of the Chinese Communist leadership, East Germans were deeply angered.[61] Their sense of frustration was increased by the vivid pictures of liberty that continued to fill their television screens: Poland's Wojciech Jaruzelski standing with Lech Walesa, who made a Solidarity victory salute; soldiers cutting the barbed wire fence along the Austro-Hungarian border; "freedom trains" in Czechoslovakia carrying jubilant East Germans to the west. Television became a window through which the people of East Germany could witness the revolutionary changes all around them. It gave them information and knowledge "with which they could challenge the old ways of looking at the world."[62]

The West German channels ARD and ZDF carried extensive reports about the East German citizens in and around the West German embassies in Budapest, Warsaw, and Prague. They ran dozens of interviews with refugees as well as reports about the negotiations to allow East Germans to enter the west. East German families watched television for hours hoping for a glimpse of a relative or friend risking his life to obtain freedom. When it became clear that the Hungarians were not going to shoot, that refugees were cared for, and that the frontier to Austria was penetrable, people began packing. And when they heard refugees explaining how guides helped them through the fields and forests and how the freedom seekers bribed frontier guards and fended off dogs, thousands of East Germans closed up their apartments, got in their cars, and set off for Hungary. The September 10 announcement by West German Foreign Minister Hans-Dietrich Genscher from the balcony of the West German Embassy in Budapest that Hungary had officially opened its borders to Austria was a highlight in the history of West German television and the collapse of Communism in Eastern and Central Europe.[63]

The East German government was mystified as to why so many citizens, especially young people, wanted to leave. *Neues Deutschland,* the official Communist Party organ, wondered: "There is neither persecution, nor war, nor public disaster nor any other life- or existence-threatening criteria." What *Neues Deutschland* and the Communist regime did not understand was that a guaranteed cradle-to-grave life in the east was no longer enough. "If you put a bird in a cage and give it something to eat,"

61. Ibid.   62. Ibid.
63. Denes, "The Impact of West German TV," p. 6.

said a newly arrived Leipziger on West German television, "it still doesn't feel free." In over 90 percent of the refugee cases, contrary to the expectations of many Western analysts, the two most frequently mentioned reasons for leaving were general political, not economic, conditions and the lack of political freedom, not consumer goods.[64]

Freedom to emigrate had been the first demand, but now East Germans were taking to their own streets and declaring they wanted to remain but in a far different kind of country. In East Berlin, Dresden, and particularly in Leipzig, calls for reform and democratization were raised more and more loudly by larger and larger crowds, whose gatherings were televised by West German cameras and broadcast back into East Germany. Intellectuals, "greens," and church-related activists founded the New Forum and petitioned for legal status; the minister of the interior turned it down because of New Forum's "anti-state platform." Beset on all sides, the Communist government desperately tried to retain control. Foreign Minister Oskar Fischer announced that by October 7, the fortieth anniversary of the GDR and the seventeenth anniversary of Party boss Erich Honecker's rule, the world would see a stablized situation in East Germany. All Eastern bloc leaders including Soviet President Gorbachev were invited to the ceremonies. Anticipating protests, Honecker publicly ordered security forces to crack down on and even shoot demonstrators, if necessary—a command that came to be known as the "China Solution," after the massacre in Tiananmen Square, which, as previously noted, the GDR had officially applauded.[65]

THE LEIPZIG DEMONSTRATIONS

The threats did not work. During the first week of October, rallies were held in various cities of the GDR, including Leipzig, where the first of the weekly "Monday Demonstrations" took place. People sang "We Shall Overcome" and the "Internationale" and shouted slogans like "Legalize New Forum," "We Are Staying Here," and "Gorbi Gorbi," reflecting the socialist inclinations of the participants. The Leipzig demonstrations became the bellwether for the growing sense of community and power that GDR citizens shared in mass meetings throughout the country. The most critical point of the revolution came on October 7 when Gorbachev spoke in East Berlin. Although the Soviet leader only implicitly encouraged re-

64. Naimark, "'Ich will hier raus,'" pp. 85–86.
65. Ibid., p. 88; Bornemann, *After the Wall*, p. 21.

form and reiterated his adherence to the principle of noninterference, he was greeted by chants of "Gorbi, help us" and "*Glasnost* and *Perestroika*." The appeal to the Soviet model of liberalization was telling, as the GDR had long bound itself, economically, militarily, and ideologically, to Moscow. The East German regime had tried to distance itself from Gorbachev's reforms—Honecker's chief ideologist claimed that each socialist country should build its own type of socialism—but the East German government merely succeeded in isolating itself from its own people and the reformers in other Warsaw Pact countries. And now with Gorbachev by his side, Honecker still made no concessions in his hard-line address, concluding with the worn-out slogans: "Work together, plan together, govern together" and "Always forward; never back." Gorbachev warned Honecker, "Life punishes those who come too late," but the East German leader did not listen, nor did he understand the revolutionary fervor that was sweeping the country and being fueled by the Western mass media.[66]

Falling back on traditional Leninist methods, the GDR government unleashed the *volkspolizei* and the *stasi*, who cracked down viciously on demonstrators, particularly in East Berlin. Those arrested were subjected to hours of "neo-Nazi interrogations" that included being made to stand for hours, legs spread apart, half-naked, in unheated rooms. Incensed citizens called for an immediate investigation, and, in an ironic example of *mediapolitik*, a government commission viewed videos of the demonstrations taken by the *stasi*. Although the head of the secret police insisted that the demonstrators had provoked the police to violence, the *stasi*'s own videos revealed a different story: one man was sentenced to six months imprisonment for calling out "No violence" about fifteen times. Through word of mouth and Western television, the extent of police brutality became widely known. And the credibility of a regime "willing to inflict such savagery on its citizens with the left hand, while anointing and garlanding itself with the right," was irreparably lost.[67]

But despite the police brutality in Berlin, fifty thousand determined demonstrators, led by students and church activists, took to the streets of Leipzig on Monday, October 9, in a decisive test of the regime's will. Leipzig emerged as the center of the opposition because it was a university

66. Naimark, "'Ich will hier raus,'" pp. 89–90; Bornemann, *After the Wall*, p. 22; German Information Center, *Focus on the German Unification Process* (New York: German Information Center, 1990), p. 1.

67. Bornemann, *After the Wall*, pp. 23–24.

town, it had a large network of churches, and the *stasi* were not as well organized there as in East Berlin. Not since June 1953, when the angry protests of East Berlin workers forced the Communists to bring in Soviet troops to suppress the riots, had there been so great a display of "people power" in East Germany. An unyielding Honecker gave written instructions to the *stasi* to fire on the crowd, à la Tiananmen Square, if necessary.

Late in the afternoon, the secret police were waiting for the final attack order when leaders of the march, including the world-renowned conductor Kurt Masur, issued an appeal to both sides to "act with prudence so that a peaceful dialogue will be possible." John Bornemann, a Western journalist, recounts that the demonstrators slowly disbanded, and the security forces did not attack, undoubtedly swayed by the size of the crowd, the moral commitment of the people to nonviolence, and the solemn appeal of Masur and the other march leaders. There was also a more practical reason: Egon Krenz, the Politboro member in charge of security, flew to Leipzig that same day and personally cancelled Honecker's order, allowing the protesters to march unmolested.

An uncertain Party leadership debated how to respond to the demonstrators. Using their central propaganda instrument, the television program *Aktuelle Kamera,* they issued a fifteen-minute appeal for socialist solidarity and resistance to the "evil imperialists" in West Germany. They indicated their willingness to engage in a dialogue, welcomed any suggestions on how to build a more attractive socialism, and, most significantly of all, issued no warnings about further demonstrations. Clearly and publicly, the oppressor's will had been broken.[68] The reformers realized that disciplined, peaceful demonstrations in front of TV cameras were their most powerful weapon.

THE COMMUNISTS: TOO LITTLE, TOO LATE

The Monday night demonstrations in Leipzig grew exponentially: on October 9, 70,000; on October 16, 120,000; on October 23, 300,000; on October 30, half a million. Protesters carried posters proclaiming "*Stasi* Out" and "Legalize New Forum." During the fortieth anniversary celebration, the regime had flooded the stores with bananas, rarely available before.

---

68. Ibid., pp. 25–26; "How the Wall Was Cracked—A Special Report: Party Coup Turned East German Tide," based on reporting by Craig R. Whitney, David Binder, and Serge Schmemann, *New York Times,* November 17, 1990, in Gwertzman and Kaufman, *The Collapse of Communism,* p. 216.

One popular banner now read: "Don't Fill Our Mouth with Talk of Reform and Try to Shut Us Up with Bananas." On October 18, the Communist government tried to shore up its rapidly fading authority by ousting Honecker as Party chief, head of state, and chairman of the Defense Council, and dismissing two other hard-line members of the Politboro. Krenz was named the new party leader, but the protests only grew larger, assisted by the regime's placating decision to allow live coverage on East German television and radio. Every reform that the government offered to the people only increased their appetite for more reforms, including the most important of all, an end to Communism.

On November 1, Krenz tried a Gorbachev gambit, flying to Moscow to meet the Soviet president and endorse a version of *perestroika*—economic and social restructuring—for East Germany. Huge crowds marched in Leipzig, East Berlin, Dresden, and other cities while thousands of East Germans resumed their efforts to get into the West German Embassy in Prague. Finally, on November 4, Krenz announced that citizens of the GDR who wanted to settle in the FRG could travel freely through Czechoslovakia. That same day, more than half a million and perhaps as many as one million people demonstrated for democracy in the heart of East Berlin, the largest crowd East Germany had ever seen. At the four-hour rally, Gunter Schabowski, the East Berlin Communist Party chief, tried to strike a note of reconciliation, conceding that "bitter things have been said . . . but only if we speak to each other can we create a new East Germany." The crowd's response was short and to the point: "Shut up!" Among the last speakers was a popular actress, Steffie Spira, who concluded her brief remarks by saying: "I want the government to do what I am about to do. Step down." The government got the message—three days later, the Council of Ministers resigned and called on Parliament to choose a new government; the next day, the Politboro quit.[69] The death rattle of the GDR could now be heard by everyone.

The final action bringing down the Berlin Wall came on Thursday evening, November 9, when Schabowski gave a briefing to reporters which was carried live on both East and West German television. The Communist official announced a new travel law under which East Germans could leave the GDR directly without going through a third country. A journalist

69. Serge Schmemann, "500,000 in East Berlin Rally for Change; Emigres Are Given Passage to West," *New York Times*, November 4, 1989, in Gwertzman and Kaufman, *The Collapse of Communism*, pp. 171–74; Bornemann, *After the Wall*, pp. 28–29; Naimark, "'Ich will hier raus,'" pp. 90–91.

immediately asked: Did the new law also extend to the West Berlin border? A pause and then came the answer, "Yes." Did the new law mean that any GDR citizen could, without a legal passport, travel across the border into West Berlin? Could Germans divided for forty years meet and talk again? Again the answer came, "Yes." Within minutes, hundreds and then thousands of East Berliners were lined up at border crossings.

On the other side, Western television and radio crews waited to record their crossing and capture history. Commanding officers of the border guards, noticing the Western television, overwhelmed by the mobs, unwilling to implement a "Chinese solution," and aware that the world had changed radically in the last month, gave way and opened the gates. After twenty-eight years, two months, and twenty-seven days, and the deaths of eighty people who tried to cross it, the Wall was no more. Western stations, including RIAS, broke into their regular programming to announce the opening of the Wall, bringing tens of thousands of West and East Berliners into the streets for an ecstatic reunion. Western television continued its live coverage throughout the night, helping to create a New Year's Eve atmosphere. Over the weekend, two million people visited the west, bought chocolates, fruit, and souvenirs, and then returned home to a country which would never be the same again. Indeed, it would cease to be a country in less than eleven months.[70]

The nearly bloodless revolution of East Germany resulted from the convergence of the following domestic and regional factors: (1) the impact of liberating events in neighboring countries, especially the emergence of Solidarity in Poland and Hungary's measured moves toward democratization; (2) Gorbachev's consistent rejection of the Brezhnev Doctrine and his pursuit of *glasnost* and *perestroika* in the Soviet Union and other Communist states; (3) the never-abandoned desire of Germans for German solidarity; (4) the emergence of a human rights movement and other reform groups like the Greens; (5) the courageous stand of the Evangelical (Lutheran) Church; and (6) the unwillingness of the Communist leadership to use massive force against the people to maintain Marxism-Leninism. The mass media, especially of West Germany, played a critical part, sometimes encouraging action, sometimes discouraging action, but always contributing to a powerful democratic *mediapolitik* that tore gaping holes in the Iron Curtain and brought down a concrete wall that many thought would stand for decades to come.

70. Bornemann, *After the Wall,* pp. 1–3; "How the Wall Was Cracked," p. 222.

THE IMPACT OF MEDIAPOLITIK

Each of the four Communist countries examined in this chapter—Poland, Hungary, Czechoslovakia, and East Germany—possessed the necessary elements for *mediapolitik:* a significant media infrastructure, a large reading and viewing public, public officials who sought to use the media to their ends, and a mass media that reversed public policy. Each country had a large television viewing audience: Poland, with the largest population of 39 million, had 10 million TV sets. East Germany, with a population of 13.5 million, had 6.2 million sets, one for every two citizens. Czechoslovakia and Hungary had 4.5 million people and 4.2 million sets respectively. There was also high radio penetration, with East Germany, Hungary, and Czechoslovakia having more than 570 radios per one thousand people. The most avid newspaper readers were the East Germans, with a circulation of 552 regular readers per one thousand citizens and the highest literacy rate in the region. Next came Czechoslovakia, with 298 readers per one thousand people, followed closely by Hungary with 254 readers per one thousand, and Poland with 214 readers per one thousand.[71] All these readers and viewers had been exposed for more than forty years to Communist propaganda, and by 1989 their response to its polysyllabic, predictable, bureaucratic language was scorn and indifference. The Communists had built and maintained this extensive infrastructure for the purposes of their internal media, but they created an appetite for news and information which could only be satisfied by underground media (as in Poland) and external media (as in East Germany).

In every one of these Communist countries, the media helped to change the course of history by enabling those struggling for freedom to make their case to the largest possible audience. In Poland, Lech Walesa defeated the head of the Communist trade unions in a televised debate and once again established Solidarity as a political force. In Hungary, television coverage of the funeral and burial of Imre Nagy, the hero of the 1956 revolution, inspired and unified the opposition, enabling it to defeat decisively the reconstituted Communist Party in open elections. In Czechoslovakia, the televising of mass rallies in Prague and a national strike enabled Vaclav Havel to forge a powerful coalition of students, intel-

71. Manny Paraschos, "Europe," in *Global Journalism: Survey of International Communication,* 2d ed., ed. John C. Merrill (New York: Longman, 1991), pp. 119–22.

lectuals, and workers. In East Germany, daily exposure to West German television created an irresistible desire in East Germans to experience the political and economic freedom of their brothers and sisters in the west. In each instance, the most powerful catalyst for change from totalitarianism to democracy was significantly aided by the mass media.

The totalitarian model of *mediapolitik* failed in Eastern and Central Europe because the Communist regimes (1) failed to block external mass media and their message of freedom (although during the cold war, the Soviet Union spent as much as $1 billion annually to jam Western transmissions);[72] (2) did not control absolutely their internal mass media, sometimes even allowing the growth of an effective underground media (as in Poland); (3) admitted they no longer believed in Communism, rendering their propaganda barren and useless; and (4) could no longer call upon the Soviet Union to provide the military might and ideological justification to keep them in power. And so nations which had been Soviet satellites spun off into space seeking their freedom.

Dissidents brilliantly exploited the freedom of the press and the airwaves beyond their borders. Foreign correspondents wrote for their papers, but their stories were translated and broadcast back into the countries where the information was ostensibly banned. The widespread availability of radios and television sets made information more accessible. The official Communist press was forced to provide more information and more truth, or lose what little credibility it had left. People marched and shouted and waved posters, as the journalist Michael T. Kaufman summed it up, and with the security provided by the mass media they exposed forbidden truths and made revolutions.[73]

72. Armin Koessler, "The Transformation of Eastern German Media in the Aftermath of German Reunification" (address presented at the Joint Bank Fund-IMF National Library Week, April 19, 1991), pp. 2–3.

73. Michael T. Kaufman, "Epilogue," in Gwertzman and Kaufman, *The Collapse of Communism*, pp. 352–53.

CHAPTER 6

GORBACHEV'S GAMBLE

IN 1985, MIKHAIL GORBACHEV took command of an empire in deep trouble. Seventy years after the Bolshevik Revolution, Soviet economic growth had stagnated, Soviet farms were unable to feed the people, most Soviet factories never met their quotas or inflated their figures, consumer lines in Moscow and other cities often stretched for blocks, and a distant war in Afghanistan dragged on with no end in sight to the fighting or the deaths of thousands of young Soviet men. Gorbachev knew that without dramatic economic improvement, the Soviet Union's future as a superpower and indeed as any kind of power was exceedingly bleak. He asserted that "only an intensive, highly developed economy can safeguard our country's position on the international stage and allow her to enter the new millennium with dignity as a great and flourishing power."[1]

In his first months, Gorbachev relied upon *uskoreniye* (acceleration) to get the Soviet economy going. He formed new bureaucracies but failed to eliminate old ones. He tried to improve worker efficiency by starting a campaign against alcoholism; the result was a drastic shortage in sugar as thirsty, determined people began making vodka in their homes rather than buying it in state stores. He sought to infuse dynamism into government by firing Brezhnev *apparatchiki* and replacing them with younger men of his generation, but he resisted any basic change in the command system.

When *uskoreniye* failed to make any significant difference in the falter-

1. Hedrick Smith, *The New Russians* (New York: Random House, 1990), p. 177.

156

ing performance of the Soviet economy, Gorbachev instituted a more radical reform, *perestroika* (restructuring), and declared that he would depend upon "the initiative and creativity of the masses" to bring about what he called a "genuine revolutionary transformation" of the country.[2] The Soviet Union would remain Communist, but it would allow decentralization, private enterprise, and other economic reforms that would produce an efficient command economy. Soon Gorbachev was engaged in a great battle with the Party and the *nomenklatura*, the one million or so Party-approved bureaucrats who controlled every institution in the Soviet Union. Throughout 1987 and 1988, Gorbachev passed new laws, moved to decentralize the giant superstructure that ran the economy, and promised more freedom to managers, farmers, and private entrepreneurs, while keeping a tight personal hold on the reins of power. To his dismay, his economic measures met resistance and opposition from almost everyone—turf-conscious bureaucrats, reactionary Party members, nervous people in the street who had never had to worry about job security, advisers who cautioned he was moving too fast, and radical reformers who fumed he was going too slowly.[3]

"NEW THINKING"

To overcome the opposition that confronted him at every level of Soviet politics and society, Gorbachev turned to the mass media. He resolved to marshal public opinion in favor of his economic and political reforms. By introducing such populist concepts as *glasnost* and *perestroika*, Gorbachev made consideration of the people potentially as important as the traditional components of the Soviet state: the Communist Party, the KGB, the Soviet army, and the *nomenklatura*. For his reforms to work, Gorbachev had to replace old ways with new ways of thinking, and that required diversity, debate, and even freedom. He gambled that he could control the virus of freedom he had let loose with *glasnost;* improve the economy and satisfy the consumer desires of the people through *perestroika;* reassure the military and the KGB that he was not jeopardizing their role; persuade the *nomenklatura* to loosen its grip on the Soviet state; secure his own position as general secretary and president; and keep the Soviet Union socialist. Compared with this list of tasks, Hercules had it easy. As he did throughout his life, Gorbachev looked to Lenin and found guid-

2. Ibid., p. 178.
3. Ibid.

ance on how to use the mass media to achieve his objectives as well as a word for the process, *glasnost*. In March 1918, barely five months after coming to power, Lenin had written:

We must transform—and shall transform—the press . . . from being a simple apparatus for the reporting of political news, from being an organ of the struggle against bourgeois mendacity, into an instrument of economic reeducation of the masses, into an instrument for acquainting the masses with the need to work in a new way. The introduction of *glasnost* in this sphere will of itself be an enormous reform and will facilitate the enlistment of the broad masses in self-dependent participation in the resolution of the problems that concern primarily the masses.[4]

In Leninist fashion, Gorbachev promised a new Law on the Press and Information, which would institutionalize *glasnost* as a means of information (i.e., propaganda) and of checking the centralized bureaucracy. The main purpose of *glasnost*, the Soviet leader stressed, was not freedom but *perestroika*, the restructuring of Soviet society to make it a more productive and competitive modern socialist state. Did *perestroika* mean that the Soviet Union was giving up socialism or even some of its foundations? Gorbachev's response in his best-selling book, *Perestroika*, was unequivocal: "We are conducting all our reforms in accordance with the socialist choice. We are looking within socialism, rather than outside it, for the answers *to all questions that arise*" (emphasis added). He reaffirmed his commitment to Communism at every opportunity, as on the seventieth anniversary of the Bolshevik Revolution: "In October 1917, we parted with the old world, rejecting it once and for all. We are moving towards a new world, the world of Communism. We shall never turn off that road."[5] The Gorbachev who wrote *Perestroika* and initiated *perestroika* was a classical Leninist, former U.N. ambassador Jeanne Kirkpatrick wrote, flexible, adaptable, skillful in the pursuit and use of power, committed to socialism and a one-party state.[6]

It was clear to Gorbachev that so massive a social change as he envi-

4. Leonard R. Sussman, *Power, the Press and the Technology of Freedom: The Coming Age of ISDN* (New York: Freedom House, 1989), p. 315.

5. Mikhail Gorbachev, *Perestroika* (Harper & Row, 1987), as excerpted in *Washington Post*, December 6, 1987; BBC *Summary of World Broadcasts*, summary of Mikhail Gorbachev address, November 5, 1987.

6. Jeane Kirkpatrick, "Return to Leninist Orthodoxy," in *Perestroika: How New Is Gorbachev's New Thinking?* ed. Ernest W. Lefever and Robert D. Vander Lugt (Washington: Ethics and Public Policy Center, 1989), p. 49.

sioned could only be effected by the fundamental reeducation of 280 million Soviet citizens through the mass media. The Kremlin had one of the most sophisticated communications networks in the world to call upon. The Soviet Union, for example, had some 8,500 newspapers with a circulation of nearly 200 million published in fifty-five languages. As early as 1918, Lenin had called for a national program to build radio stations, predicting that one day "all Russia will hear a newspaper read in Moscow."[7] Four years later, the strongest radio transmitter in the world, broadcasting with 12,000 watts of power, was built in Moscow. A vigorous policy of "radiofication" was pursued for the next several decades with a high point of some seven million radios produced in 1940. By the time of Gorbachev, there were about 544 radio sets per one thousand population, compared with 570 radios per one thousand people in East Germany. But the medium the government finally came to favor, above all others, was television; here was an instrument that could disseminate instant, uniform propaganda to everyone.

A COMMUNICATIONS REVOLUTION

In 1940, there were only four hundred television sets in the Soviet Union. A decade later, in the waning years of the Stalin era, there were ten thousand sets; but in 1960, as Moscow began to understand that television was much more than a capitalist toy, the number jumped to 4.8 million. In the five years between 1965 and 1970, when Brezhnev consolidated his hold on power, the number of television sets doubled, and by 1976 Soviet industry was producing seven million sets annually. Economic plans projected the annual production of ten million television sets by the early 1990s. Through government planning, a communications revolution occurred: in 1960, only 5 percent of the Soviet population could watch television. By 1986, an estimated 93 percent of the population were viewers, comparing favorably with the 98 percent of the American people who watched television.[8]

Although throughout its history the Soviet Union strove to build a nationwide system of mass communications, the government was never able—until television—to reach everyone. Newspapers tended to be read by only the better educated, while radio, particularly before FM, was at the

---

7. Eli Noam, *Television in Europe* (New York: Oxford University Press, 1991), p. 276.

8. Ellen Mickiewicz, *Split Signals: Television and Politics in the Soviet Union* (New York: Oxford University Press, 1988), p. 3.

mercy of the harsh weather and mountainous terrain that stretched across eleven time zones. "With the development of communications satellites, however," the media scholar Ellen Mickiewicz wrote, "that sprawling inhospitable terrain could be leapfrogged and [television] signals beamed down at relatively low cost."[9] For the first time in Soviet history, the government could present the same message to all the people at the same time. It seemed that Lenin's prediction had been fulfilled, but the Soviets miscalculated human nature.

They believed they could create a new man, and woman, with the proper behavioral mix of education, information, rewards, and penalties, including the Gulag. Having achieved considerable success with newspapers, magazines, and radio, they turned to television as the best means yet of transforming the Soviet people. Their optimism was based on a belief in the "hypodermic model" of communications theory, which maintains that the audience receives all new information instantly and unadulterated from the mass media just as the human body receives medicine or a drug from the injection of a hypodermic needle. The Soviets were not concerned that Western research had discarded the theory, having found that the audience "could not be viewed as an inert element in the communication process."[10] Moscow was only a little disturbed that a survey of an average-sized industrial city in the Russian Republic showed that many citizens (after decades of unrelenting propaganda) did not comprehend basic Marxist terms. About 25 percent did not know what "colonialism" meant; almost half could not say what "imperialism" was. Between 66 percent and 75 percent did not understand the terms "reactionary" and "liberal."[11]

How can such public ignorance or indifference be explained? To begin with, ideology had become so irrelevant in day-to-day Soviet life by the 1980s that very few people, including Communist Party members, believed in it anymore. As a result, Marxist-Leninist polemics were ignored when they were printed or broadcast. Also, many Soviet citizens had been exposed to the West through the use of videocassette recorders (VCRs) and access to Western television and radio, and they did not accept the heavy-handed anti-West propaganda of Gosteleradio and other elements of the Soviet media apparatus. Furthermore, the media scholar Leonard R. Sussman points out, most Soviet citizens seem to have known "the broad outline of what was formally withheld from them." They did not

9. Ibid., p. 4.   10. Ibid., p. 181.
11. Ibid., p. 182.

have statistics on those who died or disappeared under Stalin or how crippled the economy was, but they knew relatives and friends who had been sent to the Gulag, and they stood in lines at food stores that grew longer every year. They watched members of the *nomenklatura* treat themselves to special privileges like food and luxury goods at exclusive shops, free theater seats, large apartments, state-owned dachas, and exclusive health care centers, and their resentment steadily mounted.[12]

"MASTER" PROPAGANDISTS

Despite the contradictory evidence about the impact of television, Soviet leaders proceeded with the "televisionization" of the U.S.S.R., confident that as master propagandists they could make the medium work to their advantage. Marxist in practice if not always in belief, they proclaimed the mastery of science and technology over the human spirit. And there is no denying that television changed the Soviet Union in the three decades between 1960 and 1990. Its messages ultimately reached more than nine-tenths of the population. The amount of time that citizens spent watching television was exceeded only by the time spent working and sleeping.

At first, it seemed that the medium could be "a powerful force for integration" that would forge a national consciousness and a national culture.[13] But *glasnost* brought to the surface ethnic and nationalist aspirations that had long been suppressed by Moscow. In Azerbaijan, for example, protestors sought an Armenian-language television channel; in Moldavia, journalists tried to convert all television broadcasting into Moldavian. Because almost everyone was watching television, the Soviet Union was shrinking and dividing at the same time. Because of the mass media, the collective began to give way to the individual for the first time in Soviet history.

At the center of the growing chaos and uncertainty stood an increasingly beset Gorbachev trying to implement his grand design to alter the mind of a nation. One commentator said that the Soviet leader tried to use the mass media the way that Mao Zedong had used the Red Guards, to destroy the power of the bureaucracy.[14] But as Alexis de Tocqueville once commented, "Experience teaches that the most critical moment for bad

---

12. Sussman, *Power, the Press and the Technology of Freedom*, pp. 105–6.
13. Mickiewicz, *Split Signals*, p. 207.
14. Sussman, *Power, the Press and the Technology of Freedom*, p. 108.

governments is the one which witnesses their first steps toward reform."[15] The Soviet Union in the middle 1980s was a very bad government attempting very radical reform.

We now see that the chances of Gorbachev's successfully implementing *perestroika* and *glasnost* were slim to none. He not only attempted to square a circle (to democratize a totalitarian state) but he tried to manipulate an elemental human force—freedom—that has proved to be the downfall sooner or later of every dictator. Gorbachev kept applying Leninist principles to *glasnost*, insisting that "no one is above control in our country. . . . This applies to the mass media. . . . it should be remembered that a magazine, a publishing house, or a newspaper are not someone's private concern but a concern of the entire Party, of the whole people."[16] But he opened a Pandora's box without knowing what it contained; he turned out to be not the sorcerer but the sorcerer's apprentice. In the end, the mass media helped bring about his demise and the triumph of Boris Yeltsin.

A CRITICAL YEAR

For the Soviet Union, the remarkable year of 1989 began with the withdrawal of Soviet troops from Afghanistan and ended with Gorbachev's beating back attempts by the national Congress to question the Communist Party's constitutional monopoly on power and politics. The Soviet president survived the year, but the promise of free, multiparty elections in Hungary, the election of a Solidarity government in Poland, and the fall of Communist governments in East Germany, Czechoslovakia, Bulgaria, and Romania all had their inevitable impact on Soviet politics. In January 1990, barely one month after adamantly defending the right of the Party to guide the country's destiny, Gorbachev was forced to accept the revocation of Article Six of the Soviet Constitution, which guaranteed the Communist Party the "leading role." In the wake of Article Six's abolition, non-Communist political parties sprang up and assumed power in several Soviet Republics.

The most dramatic result was Yeltsin's election as president of the Russian Republic in the spring of 1990 followed by his exit, and that of many of his supporters in the Russian Parliament, from the Communist Party.

15. Alexis de Tocqueville, *The Old Regime and the Revolution* (New York: Harper and Brothers, 1856), p. 214.
16. Excerpted in *Moscow News*, no. 4, January 31–February 7, 1988.

These new democrats began demanding the restoration of private property and free markets. Parliaments in Russia and the Ukraine declared their
"sovereignty," and in June 1991, Russia held its first completely free popular election. Yeltsin was elected president of the Russian Federation, reflecting the accelerating shift of power from the old Marxist-Leninist system to still evolving democratic institutions. A group of Communist
hard-liners decided they must act to reverse the process while there was
still time, not realizing that it was already too late.

THE AUGUST COUP

There are several reasons why the August 1991 coup attempted by the
Gang of Eight failed: the total absence of public support; the coup plotters' failure to jail Russian President Yeltsin and other key opponents; their
unwillingness to use military force against the opposition; and significant
disagreements within the Red Army and the KGB about the legality of the
coup. But a major cause was undoubtedly the coup plotters' blunder in
failing to control the means of mass communication, internal and external. They did not understand that in the electronic age, political power
flows, not only through the barrel of a gun, but also through the lens of a
television camera.

In vivid contrast, Yeltsin, Mayor Gavril Popov of Moscow, Mayor Anatoly Sobchak of Leningrad (now St. Petersburg), and other members of
the resistance adroitly used the mass media to stall and ultimately defeat
the so-called Committee for the State of Emergency. Rejecting the *realpolitik* represented by Stalin's cynical question about how many divisions
the Pope had, the reformers relied upon liberal democratic *mediapolitik,*
disseminating their message of democracy and constitutional government
through television, radio, telephones, and fax machines. Yeltsin, in particular, understood how important the media were to the cause. In an act of
real courage and unforgettable political imagery, he stood on top of a tank
and exhorted his fellow countrymen to stand firm for freedom and
against the coup. Some seventy-four years earlier in the same city, Lenin
had climbed onto a similar vehicle to announce the coming of Communism. Yeltsin proclaimed that it was ending.

A PROTRACTED STRUGGLE

The coup attempt was the culmination of a year-long struggle between
democratic reformers and neo-Stalinist members of the Soviet establish-

ment who sought to retain the old system of centralized control. As the push for democratization intensified, the resistance of hard-liners like KGB chief Vladimir Kryuchkov, Defense Minister Dmitri Yazov, and Interior Minister Boris Pugo increased sharply, attracting support in the Communist Party, the military-industrial complex, and the large collective farms. There were in fact three coups in 1991. The first came in January when the KGB and the military attempted but did not succeed in bringing down the democratically elected government of Lithuania. At the time, Colonel Viktor Alksnis, the most vocal of the hard-liners in the Supreme Soviet, said that Gorbachev had lost his "will" and warned that the military would go even further, if necessary, to protect the integrity of the Soviet Union.[17]

Six months later, Gorbachev's opponents attempted a "constitutional coup" when Prime Minister Valentin Pavlov asked the Supreme Soviet to give him additional powers because Gorbachev "doesn't have enough hours in his day." Yazov, Kryuchkov, and Pugo openly backed Pavlov, going so far as to suggest that they considered Gorbachev to be "little better than a CIA agent."[18] A seemingly undaunted Gorbachev beat back the challenge and moved ahead with plans for a new union treaty that would have drastically reduced Moscow's political power, but retained his own position as president. The old guard, David Remnick wrote in the *Washington Post,* decided they had to act because they saw in the treaty "the collapse of the union, the fall of a superpower and, perhaps most important, the loss of their own authority."[19]

On Sunday, August 18, 1991, only two days before the new union treaty was scheduled to be signed, Yazov and other coup leaders flew to the Crimea where Gorbachev was vacationing, and demanded that he sign documents declaring a nationwide state of emergency. When Gorbachev rejected the ultimatum, he was placed under house arrest, and steps were taken to isolate the Soviet president, take command of the mass media, and display military strength in key cities. Going by the Leninist textbook, the plotters quickly turned to the mass media. At 6 A.M., Monday, August 19, a television newscaster carefully read a statement that Gorbachev had been replaced by Vice President Gennady Yanayev and a state of emer-

17. David Remnick, "When Fear Died in the Soviet Union," *Washington Post,* August 22, 1991.
18. Ibid.
19. Ibid.

gency had been declared in "certain" regions of the country. The statement explained that an eight-man Committee for the State of Emergency had decided that the Gorbachev reforms had led the country "into a blind alley" and that a "mortal danger" confronted the Soviet Union.[20] Clearly, the conspirators were trying to follow the same plan that had successfully toppled Nikita Khrushchev in October 1964; like Gorbachev, Khrushchev had been vacationing in the Crimea when he was relieved of his position because of "poor health."

Although tanks and armored vehicles immediately moved into cities in the Baltic republics and into the middle of Moscow, there was only a limited display of military strength in the rest of the Soviet Union. In smaller cities like Vologda in northern Russia, the local KGB contented itself with closing down the independent radio stations. Yeltsin and his colleagues realized that the only way to answer the superior power of the plotters (who commanded both the Red Army and the KGB) was to mobilize public opposition wherever they could but particularly in Moscow, Leningrad, and the mining towns of Siberia where the reformers enjoyed widespread support.

To dramatize his defiance, Yeltsin used the top of a tank outside the Russian Parliament to declare that the coup was "anticonstitutional." He urged all Russians to follow the law of the legitimately elected government of Russia. Only a few thousand Muscovites were present, but foreign correspondents were unmolested, satellite television links were not blocked, and nongovernment news services kept operating. Yeltsin's statement was widely distributed and began rallying the people. Following Yeltsin's call for constitutional law and order, General Konstantin Kobets, defense minister of the Russian Republic, made a very brief speech that inspired the assembled crowd and, more importantly, impressed the troops dispatched by the hard-liners. "Soldiers and officers," said Kobets, "I am the defense minister of Russia. Not a hand will be raised against the people or the duly elected president of Russia." A major immediately responded, "We are not going to shoot the president of Russia."[21]

The image of Yeltsin confronting the armed might of the hard-liners was flashed around the world by the Western television networks, especially CNN, again and again. The pictures helped convince President Bush

20. Ibid.

21. Stuart H. Loory and Ann Imse, *Seven Days That Shook the World: The Collapse of Soviet Communism* (Atlanta: Turner Publishing, 1991), pp. 89–90.

(on vacation in Maine) and other Western leaders to condemn the coup quickly and to praise Yeltsin and other resistance leaders. As in China, during the demonstrations in Tiananmen Square, the Voice of America and Radio Liberty broadcast Yeltsin's defiant statements, relayed to them by telephone, back into Moscow, Leningrad, and other Soviet cities where hundreds of thousands of citizens were demonstrating against the coup. The American broadcasts energized the resistance. VOA estimates that the number of its Soviet listeners tripled from the usual thirty million to about ninety million during the attempted takeover.[22] Two Radio Liberty correspondents were inside the Russian Parliament building, feeding reports and interviews to Munich headquarters by telephone. The station's broadcasts in Russian and eleven other languages became a major means by which the opposition got its message to the population. Radio Liberty's normal audience was about thirty-five million and probably doubled during the putsch.[23]

The Emergency Committee then attempted to manipulate the media, televising a late Monday afternoon news conference at which a palpably nervous Yanayev, his hands shaking, explained that the committee was taking over because Gorbachev was too tired and ill to retain command (reporters openly laughed at the explanation); insisted that the coup was constitutional, which it plainly was not; and declared a commitment to continued reform. Rather than convincing those watching that the committee was in firm control of the situation, Yanayev's weak performance raised doubts whether anyone was in charge.

In contrast, Yeltsin never faltered as he asked the people to participate in massive resistance and a general strike on Tuesday. Uninterrupted phone service enabled the anticoup leaders to organize, release statements, and receive and send news. At the height of the crisis, Yeltsin received telephone calls from Bush and British Prime Minister John Major, whom he urged to reaffirm their opposition to the coup as well as their endorsement of his efforts. They immediately complied (Bush by a televised news conference), keeping up the pressure on the faltering Kremlin plotters. At another critical point, Yeltsin phoned a NATO ministers meeting in Brussels and asked them to issue a statement of support, which they

22. *Human Events,* August 31, 1991, p. 4.
23. Leslie Colitt, "Yeltsin's Vital Radio Link with Russian People," *Financial Times,* August 21, 1991; Dirk Schutz, "How Radio Liberty Informed the Soviet Population," *Die Zeit,* August 30, 1991.

did. Still under arrest in the Crimea, Gorbachev smuggled out a video-taped message showing that he was in good health and not a part of the conspiracy. Later, the Soviet leader credited foreign radio stations with keeping him informed of what was happening: "We brought old radios from the servants' quarters and listened to the BBC, Radio Liberty, and the Voice of America."[24]

A COLLAPSING COUP

The standoff in the streets of Moscow between uneasy troops and de-termined protesters lasted from Monday through Wednesday, with Yeltsin's supporters not backing down and the army unwilling to use force against fellow Soviets. The facade of the coup began to crack. Leningrad Mayor Sobchak reported that the local military commander had refused to cooperate with the coup leaders and would not bring tanks into the country's second-largest city. Sobchak telephoned Yeltsin with this impor-tant news and then distributed it to the media. It was no coincidence that at about the same time, tank commanders "defected" in Moscow and set up their vehicles in a defensive circle around the Russian Parliament building (nicknamed the "White House" because of its white marble exte-rior).[25]

If the Kremlin gang had cut all the telephone lines and seized all the broadcast facilities and denied Western television cameras access to the Russian Parliament, where the resistance was headquartered, Yeltsin and his aides would have been isolated and at least partially silenced. Without Yeltsin's charismatic leadership, the resistance would have faltered, and the coup might have succeeded. But even if the eight old apparatchiks, quar-reling and blaming each other for mistakes and oversights, had done all that, their control of Soviet communications would have been far from complete. They also would have had to commandeer the country's 100,000 copying machines, many of which were being used to distribute anticoup statements; 200,000 fax machines that were in contact with peo-ple in the West and around the world; and one million personal comput-ers, which were pressed into service as printing presses. Newspapers like

24. David Hoffman, "Global Communications Network Was Pivotal in Defeat of Junta," *Washington Post*, August 23, 1991; George J. Church, "Anatomy of a Coup," *Time*, September 2, 1991, p. 38; John Hughes, "Moscow Witnesses an Information Revolution," *Christian Sci-ence Monitor*, August 29, 1991; Schutz, "How Radio Liberty Informed the Soviet Popula-tion."

25. Remnick, "When Fear Died."

Nezavisimaya Gazeta (Independent Newspaper) printed their editions on fax and Xerox machines and placed them around Moscow on the walls of subway stations, near major intersections, at bus stops, and in buildings, schools, and churches.[26]

In the end, the Gang of Eight never grasped that the old censorship would not work against the new media. Only the most draconian measures could have controlled the gigantic communications network that the government had painstakingly constructed over a period of nearly thirty years. The Emergency Committee, unlike the Chinese Communists, did not have the will or the resources for so monumental an undertaking. Its members failed to take the most elementary steps to consolidate their position. The KGB of the Russian Federation, for example, shared the same building on Lubyanka Square with Kryuchkov's Soviet KGB, the main institution behind the coup. Yet, the Soviet KGB allowed the Russian KGB to express its public support of Yeltsin. The coup masters did close down most private radio and television stations and pro-reform newspapers when the coup began, and they did order the official state media to disseminate their rationale for the coup. But Western correspondents like ABC's Diane Sawyer and CNN's Steven R. Hurst still worked without restrictions, and television links by satellite were not touched. In contrast, the Chinese Communists cut off satellite access several times to control the foreign coverage of the pro-democracy movement in Beijing.

Throughout the attempted Soviet coup, Interfax and other independent news services operated into and out of Moscow. Yeltsin constantly sent fax messages to a friend in Washington who immediately passed them along to the international media. Pictures on Cable News Network and other Western television networks showed Soviet soldiers and even officers mingling happily with coup resisters. These images, RFE analyst Stephen Foyen pointed out, "undermined any aura of invincibility" the military might have had, and raised early doubts about the Emergency Committee's support. Even if the coup plotters had wanted to, they could not jam Radio Liberty, the Voice of America, and other foreign radio networks, because Gorbachev had sold much of the jamming equipment to the new Russian radio stations for their own use.[27]

26. Don Kowet, "Plotters' Biggest Enemy May Have Been Media," *Washington Times,* August 22, 1991; Frank Wolfe, "Captives Turned to West for News," *Washington Times,* August 23, 1991.

27. John Hughes, "Moscow Witnesses Information Revolution," *Christian Science Monitor,* August 29, 1991; Stephen Foye, "The Failed Coup," *Soviet/East European Report,* September 10, 1991, p. 2; Remnick, "When Fear Died."

"DON'T SHOOT YOUR MOTHERS"

One of the many acts of bravery during the three days of the coup was that of the journalists at the independent radio station, Moscow Echo. On Monday, KGB agents forced their way into the radio station's offices and seized control. With help from the Moscow City Council and the Russian government, the station resumed broadcasting Tuesday afternoon from within the Russian Parliament building. As a result, thousands of mostly unarmed Russians who had set up rough barricades in front of the huge parliament building were able to get news and information. They carried portable radios over which Russian Vice President Alexander Rutskoi and Parliament Chairman Ruslan Khasbulatov urged calm and vigilance. Rutskoi, an Afghanistan war hero, appealed directly to his "brother officers" not to shoot at the crowds because "the interests you are defending are not those of the state, but those of the junta. Nobody will forgive you."[28] Every few minutes, Moscow Echo broadcast bulletins about Soviet troop movements and possible actions against the resistance, as well as statements of support by George Bush, John Major, and other Western leaders.

Among those who listened were a group of women who insisted on forming the front line of the barricade across Kutuzovsky Prospect leading to the White House. The women carried signs that read, "Soviet Soldiers, Don't Shoot Your Mothers." Explaining how important the radio link was, one woman, as ready to die as any soldier in war, said, "I remember Rutskoi and Khasbulatov. They spoke to us very candidly, creating a feeling of unity beyond description. We heard them and they heard us."[29] Despite pouring rain, many citizens stood in front of the Parliament throughout the night. The critical moment of the coup came on Tuesday night, August 20, when tanks were massed on the outskirts of Moscow, ready to force their way into the well-barricaded Russian Parliament building and arrest Yeltsin. Although some violence broke out, during which three Russians were killed, the order to attack was never given, revealing the conspirators "as mediocre men who were incapable of either inspiring or intimidating the society they hoped to control."[30]

Russians watched the struggle between hard-liners and reformers unfold on television. On the second day of the coup, in a remarkable demon-

28. Remnick, "When Fear Died"; Wolfe, "Captives Turned to West for News."

29. David Remnick, "Coup Attempt Created a Crisis of Conscience for Citizens," *Washington Post*, August 25, 1991.

30. Foye, "The Failed Coup," p. 1.

stration of teleplomacy, ABC's Diane Sawyer calmly walked between tanks and around barricades to enter the Russian Parliament and conduct an exclusive interview with Yeltsin. The talk was aired on three separate ABC programs and was picked up by other networks, reaffirming the Russian leader's central role in the resistance and the Kremlin's inability to silence him. The Sawyer interview, remarked one media analyst, emphasized that the outcome of the coup, played out around the world in living color, hinged "not just on who had the most military muscle but on who had the most media, inside and outside Soviet borders."[31] Before meeting Yeltsin, Sawyer paused to talk with broadcasters for Moscow Echo who, she said, were "on the air, urging people to stand firm." Moments later, she asked a Yeltsin supporter: "You think a little broadcasting station downstairs here is going to keep freedom alive?" "Yes," the man replied firmly. Ultimately, that "little broadcasting station" and other mass media did carry the day for freedom and democracy.[32]

In Leningrad, Mayor Sobchak appeared Monday night on the local television station, which, unlike the Moscow TV station, did not shut down, the emergency law notwithstanding. The mayor called for a demonstration the next morning in front of the Winter Palace, which Lenin's forces had stormed in 1917 to begin the Bolshevik Revolution. More than 300,000 turned up to show their support for the constitution and to hear Sobchak declare that the coup was illegal. The people cheered and shouted "Down with the junta!" and "Long live Yeltsin!" and, simply, "Democracy!" There were no tanks in the square because Sobchak had promised the army commander that order would be maintained, and there was no need for a military presence at the rally.[33] Lenin would have understood immediately that the coup was not going to succeed.

The only foreign network providing live, continuous coverage, CNN played a central part in the quick death of the coup. Although its broadcasts were officially limited to hotels, they were routinely picked up by Muscovites who stuck antennas out their windows and aimed them at a huge broadcasting tower. The antennas did not work on Soviet television sets, but more and more people were buying Western sets. Muscovites saw the riveting image of Yeltsin standing on a tank challenging the military might of the old guard, and they relayed that image to their friends and

31. Kowet, "Plotters' Biggest Enemy."
32. Ibid.
33. Anne Husarska, "The Apartment," *The New Republic*, September 23, 1991, p. 16.

neighbors. The crucial impact of television was again proved on the following day when some 150,000 demonstrators filled the square in front of the Russian Parliament to cheer the Russian leader and support his demands that the state of emergency be lifted and the coup leaders arrested.

LIVE FROM MOSCOW

At times, CNN coverage resembled *cinema verité* as it carried pictures from Soviet television that ranged from interviews with people on the street to a Soviet anchor announcing (mistakenly) that prosecutors were "already instituting proceedings against those [plotters] who are guilty." Reflecting its determination to get the story, as it had in Baghdad during the Persian Gulf War, CNN was the only American network with a live satellite hookup from the Russian Parliament. This independent line to the outside world was not challenged by the junta because, evidently, it did not comprehend CNN's political importance. In contrast, when martial law was declared by the Polish Communist government in December 1981, a total news blackout was imposed for three days. In Moscow, government censorship was so loose that the official Soviet television station even offered to lend CNN some camera equipment, an offer which "astonished" the American network. "That was probably the first sign," said a CNN official, "that maybe [the plotters] weren't in control. I expected everyone to be thrown out. I expected China."[34] On Monday evening, August 19, even the government's official news program, *Vremya,* managed to give the impression that it supported Yeltsin and opposed the coup when it showed protest demonstrations in Moscow and Leningrad and interviews with citizens who defended democratically elected leaders.[35]

The Moscow plotters thought that all they had to do was announce their intentions and they would be obeyed. But the Soviet people had lived under the totalitarian rule of Stalin, Beria, and other dictators; they knew that the bureaucrats who made up the junta were not in the same league. Furthermore, the plotters never grasped how teleplomacy has become such an integral part of world politics. An American policymaker in Washington admitted that his first thought on hearing about the Moscow coup was not how to cable instructions to U.S. missions in the field, but

---

34. Howard Kurtz, "For Networks, Drama Turns into a Taut Three-Day Miniseries," *Washington Post,* August 22, 1991.

35. Vera Tolz, "The Soviet Media and the Failed Coup," RFE/Radio Liberty Research Institute, September 15, 1991, p. 2.

how to get a statement on CNN that would shape the response of allies. "Diplomatic communications," he conceded, "just can't keep up with CNN."[36]

There were almost as many telephones as there were rifles on the barricades in front of the Russian Parliament. When VOA reporters were trapped in the crowd, they pulled out their Finnish-made cellular phones and called in reports to their Moscow bureau. The bureau transmitted the reports live to VOA headquarters in Washington, which broadcast them by shortwave back to millions of Soviet listeners. Inside the Parliament building, correspondents for Radio Liberty were sending reports by telephone to their Munich headquarters. Like VOA, Radio Liberty beamed them back into Russia while its sister network, Radio Free Europe, broadcast what was happening in Moscow to the Baltic republics and Eastern Europe. After the coup, Yeltsin said that "Radio Liberty was one of the very few channels through which it was possible to send messages to the whole world." Young people distributed fax copies of the *Independent Newspaper* and other banned publications to the crowd in the square and even to the ostensibly pro-coup military. One young man had an uneasy moment when two policemen approached him as he was giving leaflets to tank crews, but all they asked him was, "Have you got any more for us?"[37] Emergency issues of the independent weekly, *Moscow News,* were distributed, including an appeal by Elena Bonner, widow of Andrei Sakharov, for half a million Muscovites to demonstrate their support for the Russian Parliament in order "to show that we are worthy of the title of citizens of the capital and the state, rather than just a crowd, interested only in sausage."[38]

Even the official newspaper of the Soviet Communist Party was not immune to the democratic fever that swept through Moscow during the three days of the coup. A fierce debate between the Communist chief editor of *Izvestia* and reform-minded printers and other employees ended in the Party organ's not being published on the day after all power had supposedly been transferred to the Committee of the State of Emergency. The printers insisted on publishing Yeltsin's proclamation denouncing the coup; the editor refused. One worker shouted, "You can shoot us, but

36. David Hoffman, "Global Communications Network Was Pivotal in Defeat of Junta," *Washington Post.* August 23, 1991.

37. For Yeltsin quote, see RFE/RL broadcast, August 24, 1991, "Country and World" program; Iain Elliot, "Three Days in August," *Soviet/East European Report,* September 20, 1991, p. 2.

38. Ibid., p. 4.

we're not going to put this paper out without Yeltsin's statement. We live the life of animals, in poverty, and we don't want our children to live the same way." *Izvestia* did not appear that evening. Overnight a compromise was reached, and the paper came out twenty hours late. The front page was devoted to statements from the Emergency Committee while a short-ened version of Yeltsin's statement appeared on page two. The contradic-tory appearance of both pro- and anticoup statements in the Communist Party's official newspaper (one of only eight national newspapers whose publication was authorized by the Emergency Committee) sent a clear message that the plotters were not a reincarnation of Brezhnev, let alone Stalin, and their attempt to seize power would not succeed.[39]

A PANDORA'S BOX

There are multiple ironies in the Moscow coup that swept the Com-munists out of power. It had its roots in a communications revolution be-gun in the Brezhnev era by dogmatic Marxist-Leninists who thought they could use television and the other new technologies as efficient instru-ments of agitation and propaganda throughout the vast country. Gor-bachev sought to use the media to mobilize the masses on behalf of *glas-nost* and *perestroika*. Instead, he unleashed long-suppressed nationalist feelings, provided a platform for populist politicians like Yeltsin, and al-lowed people to express publicly their anger about a system that could no longer feed, clothe, and house them or stifle their desire to live under free-dom.

Gorbachev's gamble failed because he did not comprehend that televi-sion is an individualistic medium that encourages dozens of choices every day—which programs to watch, which not; which products to buy, which not (there had been commercials on Moscow television since the mid-1980s); which candidates to vote for, which not; which news to believe, which not. Gorbachev learned too late that the mass media are not a hy-podermic needle that will inject a message into a passive public body and produce a predictable response, but a megaphone transmitting informa-tion to a diverse audience of many millions who may react in many differ-ent ways to the same message. Neither Gorbachev nor any previous Soviet leader was willing to accept that it was impossible to transform perma-nently the diverse peoples of the Soviet Union into a centralized state and homogeneous society if they did not want to be.

39. Michael Dobbs, "The Inside Story," *Washington Post*, August 26, 1991.

In the end, the coup failed because the plotters did not have the resources or the stomach to do what was necessary to prevail: duplicate
Tiananmen Square and kill hundreds, perhaps thousands, of resolute
Muscovites who had erected a human barricade in front of the Russian
Parliament to defend its most important occupant, Boris Yeltsin. It is possible that the Gang of Eight did not give the order to fire because they
feared it would not be obeyed. Film footage from CNN and other Western
television networks showed that Soviet soldiers, and even officers, were
more willing to mingle with the Russian population than to shoot at it.
The images undermined any aura of invincibility that the tanks and
troops might have possessed, and raised crucial doubts about the Emergency Committee's standing within the army.[40]

Inside the White House, Yeltsin tirelessly used the telephone to warn
the plotters that the price of victory would be a terrible bloodbath; to urge
leaders around the world to condemn the coup and support the resistance; and to coordinate strategy with other freedom fighters in Moscow,
Leningrad, and elsewhere. He and his aides also used radio, television, fax,
and other means of modern communications to inform and direct their
supporters. While it is true that "only" 150,000 people out of Moscow's ten
million residents gathered in front of the Russian Parliament to support
Yeltsin, many of them were prepared to die to save the democratic reforms
that had been initiated—a commitment that lent real weight to the reformers' telephone warnings to the Communist hard-liners that they
could only prevail through the use of maximum force. Again and again,
the people responded to Yeltsin's mastery of words and symbols: his decision to declare his defiance of the coup atop a tank; his dominance of Gorbachev at their joint appearance after the coup; his moving plea to the
parents of the victims of the street violence, at their funeral: "Forgive me,
your president, for my failure—that I could not defend, could not save
your sons."[41] The people supported Yeltsin because they believed in him
and what he represented: a change from imposed tyranny to representative democracy, and perhaps even the creation of a new society.

OF, BY, AND FOR THE PEOPLE

It is a major thesis of this study that technology alone will not produce
freedom; only constitutional guarantees and democratic institutions of,

40. Foye, "The Failed Coup," p. 2.
41. Robert G. Kaiser, "The Revolution That Went Spinning beyond Gorbachev," *Washington Post National Weekly Edition*, September 2–8, 1991, p. 22.

by, and for the people can ensure political and economic freedom. *Media-politik* is not simply the study of how the mass media affect world politics; it is not *realpolitik* in prime time or on the front page. *Mediapolitik* is an examination of the proper balance of media and politics, of a golden mean between these two institutions within the philosophical context of Western democratic values. When the government or the media attain too much power by disregarding or abusing democratic principles, an imbalance occurs, and freedom is threatened.

After having used the mass media during the coup to defend democracy and defeat the hard-liners, Boris Yeltsin subsequently practiced *mediapolitik* in a disturbingly authoritarian way. On August 22, one day after the coup collapsed, the Russian president signed a decree "nationalizing" Communist Party printing presses in Russia, ostensibly to make it easier for non-Party newspapers to be printed. He also closed down six Communist Party papers, including *Pravda* (*Pravda* soon resumed publication without the Order of Lenin Medal on its masthead), and removed the director of the central television and radio service for supporting the coup. Six days later, and without warning, *Vremya* (*Time*), the most watched television program in the Soviet Union, was abruptly taken off the air (it later returned).

As one analyst said, "*Vremya* was mandatory programming on all the national channels—at nine P.M., Moscow time. There was no escaping [it]."[42] While *Vremya* often offered its estimated two hundred million viewers heavy-handed propaganda about tractor-factory openings and smiling collective farmers, the manner of its cancellation raised questions about Yeltsin's commitment to democracy. As the Russian journalist Andrew Yurkovsky pointed out, even Gorbachev at the height of his power in 1989 had failed in his attempt to remove the editor of a single newspaper, the muckraking weekly *Argumenty i Fakty*.

Several critics questioned the constitutionality of Yeltsin's actions, while others protested that there was no proof that everyone at *Pravda* and the other suspended papers had collaborated with the plotters. Quite the contrary, journalists at both Novosti and Tass had reported the people's resistance to the Emergency Committee. Zhores A. Medvedev, a longtime dissident, argued that the Yeltsin camp was "introducing structures that seem to resemble a foundation for authoritarian power more than a framework for democracy." A Western analyst suggested that in some re-

42. Don Kowet, "Party-Line TV Newscast Vanishes from Air," *Washington Times*, August 29, 1991.

spects the Russian leader's actions appeared to be personal rather than ideological and were aimed at newspapers that had strongly criticized him in the past. While conceding that Yeltsin was moving to increase sharply his own power, the analyst stated that it was "too early to say that Yeltsin will become an authoritarian rather than a democratic ruler."[43]

Two years later, in October 1993, when he ordered the shelling of the former Russian Parliament building to defeat a revolt against him, Yeltsin could have been stigmatized as the latest in a long line of Russian despots. Parliament started the conflict, but by using tanks to put down the rebels, Yeltsin weakened the very thing he said he was trying to save—democracy. But his action was supported by Westernized reformers and liberal Democrats like former Prime Minister Yegor A. Gaidar, and once again, Yeltsin escaped permanent political damage.[44] Two days after the fighting ended, Yeltsin went on television to tell the nation: "The principal lesson is that democracy must be reliably defended. The state must use force to counter the threat of violence, the threat to the life and safety of citizens."[45] Commented one Russian human-rights activist, "Communism hasn't won, but democracy hasn't won either."[46] An even greater challenge confronted the Russian president when a Muslim republic one thousand miles south of Moscow declared its independence.

RUSSIA'S LIVING ROOM WAR

In the winter of 1994–95, Moscow's television screens were filled with images never before seen in the Russian capital, not even during the Afghanistan war: wounded soldiers interviewed in field hospitals . . . bloody corpses pulled from a downed helicopter . . . Russian officers refusing to advance . . . women cursing President Yeltsin for trying to stamp out their independence. From their living rooms, Muscovites watched the inept Russian offensive against separatists in Chechnya and increasingly expressed their opposition to an unpopular war. Polls (a new political in-

43. Andrew Yurkovsky, "Russian Journalists on the Barricades," *Christian Science Monitor*, September 9, 1991; Zhores A. Medvedev, "Before the Coup: The Plot inside the Kremlin," *Washington Post*, September 1, 1991; Vera Tolz, "The Soviet Media and the Failed Coup," *Soviet/East European Report*, September 15, 1991, p. 4.

44. Steven Erlanger, "Chechen Conflict Leaves Mark on Yeltsin Presidency," *New York Times*, January 1, 1995.

45. "Hollow Victory," *Newsweek*, October 18, 1993, p. 47.

46. Ibid.

strument in Russia) showed that the public opposed the war by more than two to one.[47]

The shocking images rebutted the Russian government's clumsy propaganda campaign that included Yeltsin announcing, "We must find a political solution," while sending tanks, planes, and thousands of troops into the breakaway region. Deputy Prime Minister Nikolai Yegorov once predicted that Russian troops would occupy the Chechen capital of Grozny "without a fight" and be welcomed as "liberators." Within days, Russian forces were storming Grozny and receiving heavy casualties, all widely reported by the Russian media.[48]

The most compelling footage was aired by the Independent Television Network (NTV), whose audience, however, does not reach much beyond Moscow and St. Petersburg. One broadcast showed an injured Russian soldier whose legs had been amputated, as well as a severely wounded serviceman with tubes running from his nose. NTV also aired pictures of young Russian POWs, clearly frightened, being led into the bomb shelter beneath Grozny's presidential palace, the center of the Chechen resistance. The Russian government threatened to revoke NTV's license to broadcast, but the network ignored the threat and continued its graphic coverage of the Chechen conflict.[49] NTV's news director explained that its pictures were not intended to "sensationalize the conflict" but to substantiate the facts in the face of government propaganda. NTV's firm stand was a victory for liberal democratic and a defeat of authoritarian *mediapolitik*.[50]

Even the state-run television questioned the government's official version of the war. One night the female anchor of *Vremya* (the Russian equivalent of the U.S. networks' evening news programs) reported, with a sardonic tone: "Officially, today, the Ministry of Internal Affairs announced that all roads leading into the center of Grozny were flushed of the Dudayevist bandits, opening the way for a massive humanitarian aid operation directed by the Russian Refugee Association." On screen, a camera panned a street filled with dead Russian soldiers, a tank carrying the

47. Steven Erlanger, "Russians Watch First War on Uncensored TV, to Yeltsin's Alarm," *New York Times*, December 20, 1994; Lee Hockstader, "Brutal Images of Chechnya's War," *Washington Post*, January 4, 1995.

48. Fred Hiatt, "Truth of Chechen War Derails Russian Propaganda Machine," *Washington Post*, January 29, 1995.

49. Hockstader, "Brutal Images of Chechnya's War."

50. Ellen Mickiewicz and Dee Reid, "Russian TV's Freedom Fighters," *New York Times*, January 21, 1995.

green flag of the Chechen secessionists, and a man in an upstairs window shouting, "God is great!"—the Muslim and Chechen battle cry.[51]

The Chechen war confirmed that Russia remains a riddle and a paradox. On the one hand, Yeltsin turned to the military without exploring all possible political solutions to Chechnya's demands; he acted like an authoritarian. On the other hand, Yeltsin did not impose media censorship even though the TV pictures of the debacle in Chechnya seriously damaged his reputation at home and abroad; he acted like a democrat. Perhaps better than any other Russian politician, Yeltsin understood that television is the only national medium the people believe in and its credibility must not be compromised by heavy-handed attempts at government control. When the Russian president suffered a heart attack in July 1995, rumors immediately circulated about the severity of his illness. Within one week, Yeltsin appeared on TV from his Moscow hospital room to reassure everyone that he was recovering and already working four hours a day. Smiling, he promised that he would soon be playing tennis again.[52]

A PARTISAN PRESS

When President Yeltsin ran for reelection in 1996 against Communist Party leader Gennady Zyuganov, he had powerful allies—the country's leading journalists and media executives—who openly argued, reported the *Washington Post*'s Lee Hockstader, that "the stakes [were] too high for them to remain neutral."[53] They cited the threat of a Communist comeback and the potential crackdown on the media to justify their open and decidedly non-Western partisanship. "The Communists are fighting without rules," explained one television journalist. "And if they win, there will be no independence for the mass media at all. . . . We have no choice."[54] All three major TV stations backed Yeltsin's reelection—ORT, of which the government was a majority shareholder; RTR, wholly owned by the government; and NTV, which had often upset the government with its independent reporting but now joined the Yeltsin chorus.

To ensure favorable coverage, the Yeltsin campaign resorted to an old Russian practice—bribes. Gleb Pavlovsky, general director of the Founda-

51. Thomas Goltz, "Russia's Living-Room War," *Washington Post*, January 22, 1995.

52. Alessandra Stanley, "Yeltsin Displays His Health on TV," *New York Times*, July 19, 1995.

53. Lee Hockstader, "Russian Media Stack the Deck for Yeltsin," *Washington Post*, April 3, 1996.

54. Ibid.

tion for Effective Politics in Moscow and a Yeltsin supporter, estimated that as many as one thousand journalists in Moscow alone were "on the take." Included were about fifty elite reporters who received $3,000 to $5,000 a month for writing articles favorable to Yeltsin and other candidates. A top strategist of the Yeltsin campaign confirmed that the campaign was pouring money into what was known as "hidden advertising" in Russian newspapers. "It is done in every campaign by every politician in every country," insisted Vyacheslav Nikonov, a campaign official.[55]

The bribes were so widespread in Russia, observers agreed, because most newspapers had failed to establish an independent financial base, leaving them vulnerable to "advertisers" who were willing to trade "rubles for renown." "We are in the midst of a spree of corruption," stated one member of Parliament, "that involves not only the government and bureaucracy but many other spheres."[56] The campaign's media "investment" paid off. When Yeltsin narrowly defeated Zyuganov in July 1996, experts agreed that massive amounts of money (at least $500 million was spent), "hidden" advertising, and anti-Communist scare tactics had turned the Yeltsin campaign around.

The possibility of a diverse and independent media in Russia suffered another setback in 1998 with the deepening economic crisis. Losses forced entrepreneurs and enterprises to cut back on their legitimate advertising in newspapers and the electronic media. The falloff in advertising required newspapers to close or cut back on their reporting. Less advertising revenue made newspapers more dependent on publisher-owners concerned with achieving a profit and indifferent to journalistic standards. The economic pressures on Russia's privately owned media, wrote the political analyst Paul Goble, might have "the effect of shifting the balance between privately owned and state-owned media" to the latter.[57]

The balance seemed to tilt farther toward the state media in February 1999 with the formation of a new Russian Ministry for Press, Broadcast, and News Media. The government insisted that far from imposing a new censorship, the ministry intended to make relations between the state and independent media as "transparent" as possible. But upon his appointment as head of the new ministry, Mikhail Lesin commented, rather omi-

55. Ibid.
56. Ibid.
57. Paul Goble, "The Economics of Press Media," Radio Free Europe/Radio Liberty commentary, October 13, 1998.

nously, that "the media currently have more opportunities to influence the state than vice versa. Therefore, protection of the state from the 'free media' is a more vital problem today."[58] The ministry followed up on Lesin's analysis in August by warning the heads of television networks that broadcasting interviews with Chechen "gang leaders" was forbidden.

In response to the quickening spread of the Internet throughout Russia, an even more intrusive regulation was attempted by the government. The Federal Security Service (the successor to the KGB) announced that every Internet service provider had to give the FSB without charge a room in its headquarters with the computer and software necessary to monitor all Internet traffic carried by that service. A court challenge was immediately filed by a Russian human rights group, pointing out that the Russian constitution protected the privacy of private communications such as e-mail. The human rights leader Boris Pustintsev was optimistic the court would rule against the FSB regulation but pessimistic about the immediate prospects for democracy in Russia. Building democracy, he said, was a task for "our grandchildren."[59]

But as fragile as press freedom in Russia may seem at the dawn of the twenty-first century, it has survived the enormously difficult years since the dissolution of the Soviet Union a decade ago. And its survival would not have been possible without the support, however erratic, of President Yeltsin. "Whatever else you can say about him," said Mikhail Berger, editor in chief of the daily newspaper *Segodnya*, "during the . . . years of his presidency, Yeltsin has guaranteed independence of the media and freedom of expression in Russia."[60]

THE COMING OF POST-COMMUNISM?

Some conclusions can be drawn about the Russia of the late 1990s. "What we have is post-Communism," said a former Yeltsin spokesman, Pavel Voshchanov, "not democracy." In such a chaotic atmosphere, the strong man on a horse still prevails and democratic institutions like the media play a more limited role than in the West. Unlike America, Voshchanov stated, "our leaders don't depend on public opinion when

58. Charles Fenyvesi, "Protecting the Russian State from the Russian News Media," *RFE/RL Watchlist*, August 26, 1999.

59. Charles Fenyvesi, "Russian FSB Surveillance of Internet Challenged," *RFE/RL Watchlist*, February 25, 1999.

60. Fred Weir, "Media Key to Kremlin Battle Plan," *Christian Science Monitor*, August 9, 1999.

making policy."[61] But unlike Stalin or Brezhnev, the present occupant of the Kremlin cannot ignore public opinion or the media.

Second, most Russians depend for their news on television and regional newspapers that themselves rely on official wire agencies. The majority of the people outside Moscow no longer subscribe to national newspapers like *Izvestia*, which often challenges the government's version of events. ORT, the state-owned TV network, has the largest national audience while the independent NTV dominates in European Russia. The once-firm grip of the central government over TV has been weakened by the creation of privately owned networks like NTV and Moscow's TV6. But in the absence of democratic institutions and legal guarantees, the potential for self-censorship if not outright official censorship of the mass media remains significant.

In elections, the issue of who controls the airwaves becomes critical. Each political party or group wants to put its own man in charge of the mass media. "Their calculation is simple," said a former TV executive, Alexander Yakovlev; "to 'take' the Kremlin, you must 'take' television."[62]

In the end, what the Russian republic becomes depends not on what kind of leader sits in Moscow but what kind of institutions surround that leader. These institutions must encourage the potential for good in people who are private individuals and Russian citizens at the same time. Men, whether American or Russian, are not angels and need government, but government that is not tyrannical. As Madison put it: "In forming a government which is to be administered by men over men, the great difficulty lies in this: You must first enable the government to control the governed; and in the next place, oblige it to control itself."[63] Russia, with its history of a domineering central authority, needs a strong legislature, an independent judiciary, and a free press to guarantee freedom and democracy, and to prevent Zhores Medvedev's warning about structures that lay the foundation for "authoritarian power" from coming true.

61. Steven Erlanger, "Up from Propaganda," *New York Times*, November 13, 1994.
62. Ibid.
63. James Madison, *The Federalist Papers*, No. 51 (New York: New American Library, 1961), p. 322.

CHAPTER 7

THE LESSONS OF
TIANANMEN SQUARE

MAO ZEDONG'S MOST FAMOUS aphorism was "Political power grows out of the barrel of a gun," but the Great Helmsman also believed in the power of the word. His most radical experiment in mass propaganda occurred during the Great Proletarian Cultural Revolution, which lasted from 1966 until 1976 and has been described by the historian John K. Fairbank as China's "ten lost years."[1] Mao was determined to prevent any revisionism of his revolutionary brand of Communism and galvanized a mass movement with slogans like "bombard the headquarters" and "learn revolution by making revolution." Gigantic rallies were held in Peking's Tiananmen Square with the fanatical enthusiasm expressed for Mao at these meetings recalling Hitler's mass rallies at Nuremberg. An estimated ten million students chanted Maoist slogans and waved the little red book, *Quotations from Chairman Mao,* which General Lin Piao had drawn together to indoctrinate the Chinese Red Army. Seeking to wipe out the "Four Olds"—old ideas, old culture, old customs, and old habits—Red Guards roamed the streets, breaking into houses, burning books and manuscripts, humiliating teachers, beating officials, and often killing those who protested or resisted.[2] As a faithful Leninist, Mao used the mass media throughout his life to mobilize (agitate) and educate (propagandize) the Chinese people.

1. John K. Fairbank, *The Great Chinese Revolution: 1800–1985* (New York: Harper & Row, 1987), p. 316.
2. Ibid., p. 328.

For nearly thirty years, until the late 1970s, according to the Communist dissident Binyan Liu, the Chinese Communist Party exercised absolute control over the Chinese media. The Party and its achievements were so glorified that even now few people in China know that as many as thirty million died of starvation in the Communist-made famine of the early 1960s.[3] Chinese journalists experienced their first real press freedom in 1978 when party leader Deng Xiaoping faced a severely weakened economy and needed reforms to save the Communist Party from serious criticism. To persuade his critics that economic (but not political) reforms were necessary, Deng initiated an authoritarian *mediapolitik* and allowed the media to publicize, albeit to a limited extent, the economic devastation caused by "the follies of Mao and his fellow leaders"—much as Khrushchev had allowed his criticism of Stalin at the 20th Soviet Party Congress in 1956 to be published. Both Deng and Khrushchev used the media to excoriate the flawed Communism of the past but insisted on hewing to a new Communism in the future.

In the more open atmosphere, Binyan Liu wrote a searing expose of the most serious public embezzlement since the beginning of the People's Republic of China, exposing the poverty caused by official corruption and abuse of power. The article was published in *People's Literature*, which had a circulation of 1.5 million. The magazine was so much in demand that copies were reduced to tatters as they passed from hand to hand. Newspapers reprinted the expose and provincial radio stations broadcast summaries. In areas where the magazine was not readily available, people would gather and listen to someone read it aloud.[4] Still, Liu's article did not call for an end to Communism, only for its reform—which served Deng's purpose perfectly.

THE TWO CHINAS

To calculate the impact of the mass media in the world's most populous nation, we must remember that China is really two Chinas—the cities, especially the port cities, and the rural villages where two-thirds of the population still lives. Because of mountains, rivers, deserts, and other geographical barriers, regionalism persists. Local dialects hinder nonprint

3. Binyan Liu, "The Impact of Media on Political Change: A Chinese Perspective" (annual Harold W. Anderson Lecture, sponsored by the World Press Freedom Committee in association with the Center for Strategic and International Studies, Washington, November 29, 1990).

4. Ibid.

media like radio, and print media face a low literacy rate. When they came to power in 1949, the Communists immediately took command of all means of communication, determined to use them to help overcome the geographical, linguistic, and other obstacles that had defeated all previous attempts to unify China.

Today all national, provincial, municipal, and district newspapers are controlled by the Communist Party and look "to the [Communist Party's] *People's Daily* for guidance."[5] Besides regular subscribers, rural, factory, and office workers all have access to papers, and passersby can read editions posted on "newspaper walls" near the most frequented parts of cities and towns. Radio in China uses a three-layer system: (1) the national Central People's Broadcasting Station, which broadcasts in Mandarin (in the PRC, the English word "broadcasting" refers to radio, not television); (2) about one hundred regional, provincial, and municipal networks, which translate the central radio's broadcasts into dialects; and (3) grassroots stations that send national programs and local announcements by wire to loudspeakers in communes, marketplaces, fields, and homes. Radio reaches about 95 percent of the Chinese people.[6] It is an essential medium of communication because of China's mountainous terrain and the country's several hundred dialects. Although Mandarin is the official "language" of China, it cannot be understood by many Chinese. Radio became the prime means of mass communication after the Soviet Union and China had a falling out in 1958, and the Soviet advisers who were helping the PRC to start a state-run television system went home.

In the 1970s, Deng gave orders to create a national television network. He decided that he would present his vision of a modern industrialized China to the still largely illiterate Chinese people through television, using its power to inspire as well as inform. He was confident he could control the medium, and all mass media, to serve the goals of the Communist Party and prevent what some of his colleagues feared—the "corruption" of the people through Western images and sounds. Deng dismissed as not relevant the fact that Mao had tried a similar experiment with free speech twenty years earlier with the "hundred flowers" movement, which resulted in students, journalists, and even officials directly attacking the Commu-

5. Anju Grover Chaudhary and Anne Cooper Chen, "Asia and the Pacific," in *Global Journalism: A Survey of International Communication*, 2d ed., ed. John C. Merrill (New York: Longman, 1991), p. 225.

6. Chaudhary and Chen, "Asia and the Pacific," p. 240.

nist Party. Half a million intellectuals and other dissidents were identified during the ensuing "anti-rightist campaign," and many were banished to remote labor camps or executed. Deng reassured his colleagues that he would be more careful with his mass media movement, not appreciating how unpredictable a genie he was setting free. Like all Communists, he was convinced that he could transform humanity and history.

"THE FOUR BIG THINGS"

In 1979, there were only three million television sets in China, most of them primitive black-and-white receivers; that was one set for every three hundred Chinese. By 1987, only eight years later, 116 million television sets were in use (one for every ten Chinese), and nearly twenty million were being produced annually. By the mid-1990s, there was one TV set for every eight people, creating an estimated six hundred million viewers, the largest TV audience in the world. The government spent hundreds of millions of dollars to build the necessary infrastructure of a national television network. In 1979, there were thirty-eight broadcasting centers in China; now there are about four hundred centers, linked by satellite and ground transmitting and relay facilities, so that Chinese Central Television reaches all twenty-nine provinces, including Tibet and Xinjiang.[7] According to the sinologist Nancy Rivenburgh, a television set ranks as one of the "four big things" that a Chinese desires, the others being a refrigerator, a washing machine, and a videocassette player. At $370 for a black-and-white television set or $700 for a domestic color set (a little less than the annual per capita personal income), many Chinese have to share their desire.[8]

Deng's reforms did foster high levels of economic growth throughout the 1980s, but they also created a climate in which interest groups began to challenge the central government. Younger intellectuals tired of Communist shibboleths began looking for new political ideas. Debates on a wide range of policy issues became more prevalent as Western culture, despite Deng's best efforts at ideological censorship, entered and spread across China. Foreign books, periodicals, movies, music, clothes, and radio broadcasts became available, especially in the cities. The government allowed more than one hundred thousand students to study in the West,

7. Mark Hopkins, "Watching China Change," *Columbia Journalism Review,* September/October 1989, p. 35; Chaudhary and Chen, "Asia and the Pacific," p. 301.
8. Ibid., p. 240.

mostly in the United States and in Japan. Every year, over half a million Chinese visited Hong Kong, then still under British rule and a citadel of laissez-faire capitalism. At the same time, hundreds of foreign journalists, thousands of foreign businessmen, and thousands of foreign students and scholars came to the PRC. Millions of tourists, especially overseas Chinese, visited China in the post-Mao era. "This revolution in information," wrote the Chinese analyst Huan Guocang, "created a new generation of Chinese urban youth, one much better informed about the West and eager to modernize and democratize China."[9] In the Soviet Union, by contrast, the information flow from the outside was far more limited. Foreign students did not flock to Moscow; foreign businessmen were not encouraged to set up joint ventures with Soviet companies; foreign tourists numbered in the tens of thousands, not the millions. Even under Gorbachev's *glasnost*, the Soviet Union did not stop jamming Radio Liberty, Deutsche Welle, Voice of Israel, and other foreign news services until November 1988, although the practice cost the cash-strapped Soviet government between $700 million and $1.2 billion a year.[10] Chinese youth were better prepared, intellectually, for democracy than Soviet youth.

For their part, the Chinese news media took an increasingly aggressive tone, particularly in the coverage of official malfeasance; such coverage was consistent with and even encouraged by Deng's campaign to root out the corruption that had become rampant by the late 1980s. Western reporters praised the investigative journalism, one of them writing that he was "amazed to see a Chinese television reporter, mike in hand, standing outside the private home that a provincial official had allegedly built with government funds and trying to question a family member about the allegation as he emerged, stunned and enraged by the report."[11]

BEYOND COMMUNISM

In an atmosphere that encouraged criticism, reformers began to debate publicly what type of political system beyond Communism China might adopt; they called for freedom of the press and democratic decision mak-

9. Huan Guocang, "The Events of Tiananmen Square," *Orbis*, fall 1989, p. 488.

10. Arnold Beichman, *The Long Pretense: Soviet Treaty Diplomacy from Lenin to Gorbachev* (New Brunswick, N.J.: Transaction Publishers, 1991), p. 19.

11. Steven Mark, "Observing the Observers at Tiananmen Square: Freedom, Democracy, and the News Media in China's Student Movement," in *Culture and Politics in China: An Anatomy of Tiananmen Square*, ed. Peter Li, Steven Mark, and Marjorie Li (New Brunswick, N.J.: Transaction Publishers, 1991), p. 261.

ing, seeing the intrinsic connection between free institutions and free media. They wrote hundreds of articles noting China's backwardness compared with that of other countries. By the end of 1988, students and intellectuals were discussing how to exploit two key dates in 1989: the seventieth anniversary of the May Fourth Movement, which marked China's final independence from foreign powers and an end to its feudal politics; and the 200th anniversary of the French Revolution.

Tension between the government and the reformers mounted. A group of leading Chinese scholars in Hong Kong and the United States demanded political reforms, including free elections, free expression, a multiparty political system, and the release of all political prisoners. In February 1989, a group of prominent intellectuals sent a petition to the National People's Congress calling for the release of all activists still in prison for democratic activities during 1978–81. Both documents were widely distributed among Chinese intellectuals and students and were highlighted on VOA and other foreign broadcasts. Wall posters, a favorite communications device of Chinese students, appeared in early March at Beijing universities and in other cities. Preparations began for a huge demonstration on the anniversary of the May Fourth Movement. As one observer put it: "There is a bunch of dry wood; all you need is to light a match."[12]

AN "IRRESISTIBLE" STORY

The match was the sudden death of former Communist Party General Secretary Hu Yaobang, who had been deposed by Deng and the orthodox Marxists for being "too soft on democracy." Intellectuals and students denounced the 1987 "anti-bourgeois liberalization campaign" and demanded Hu's posthumous rehabilitation. On the nights of April 18 and 19, 1989, students clashed with police in front of the Chinese Communist Party headquarters. Tens of thousands of students occupied Tiananmen Square on April 22, offering an irresistible story to the Western media. From this date until the tragic events of June 3–4, the struggle between the pro-democracy movement and the Communist government was dominated by *mediapolitik*.

Each side relied heavily upon the mass media to present its version of what was at stake. For the reformers it was the elimination of bureaucratic corruption and an end to political dominance by geriatric leaders. Most reformers were unquestionably pro-democracy, but they were not anti-

12. Huan Guocang, "The Events of Tiananmen Square," pp. 490–92.

Communist; they believed that the needed reform was possible within the socialist system. For the government hard-liners, the central issue was the preservation of Communism and the maintenance of order and stability; they had to retain a monopoly of leadership. The two sides were debating a classic political question: Who shall rule? The reformers supported the right of the people to help decide the direction of their government through true mass organizations. The hard-liners insisted that only the Party and its "mass" organizations should determine government policy. Although the demands of the student protesters remained essentially the same until the very end—dialogue with the authorities and an official affirmation of the protests—their tactics became more and more provocative, leading the Communist leadership to take extreme measures to stop what it regarded as a serious threat to its very existence. From a Western perspective, the demonstrations in Tiananmen Square were the embodiment of the classic struggle between freedom and repression.[13]

Conscious of the importance of symbols in the media age, the students chose to occupy Tiananmen Square—the center of Communist authority. It was there that Mao had proclaimed the birth of the People's Republic of China in October 1949, and there that all official rallies were held. By seizing the square from the authorities, the students issued a direct challenge to the legitimacy of the Deng regime, and created a powerful image for the mass media. What television gatekeeper would not use film footage of a hundred thousand Chinese shouting antigovernment slogans and demanding democracy? In addition, VOA broadcasts in Chinese carried news of the students' activities to other parts of China, along with messages of the outside world's encouragement. Used to strictly controlling the media, the hard-liners discovered to their dismay that China had became part of a global electronic loop through which news flowed continuously.

DENG'S WARNING

Reverting to old-style totalitarian politics, the government published an editorial in the April 26th edition of the *People's Daily* that denounced the students for a "conspiracy" to "poison people's minds, create national turmoil and sabotage the nation's political stability." By branding the movement an anti-Party and antisocialist conspiracy, the Party issued a clear warning that it was ready to use the full force of its dictatorial powers

13. Mark, "Observing the Observers," p. 260.

to stop the disturbances. Deng was quoted as having said to Party leaders: "We must crack down on these students whatever the cost. I had hoped we wouldn't have to spill blood. But if we have to do so, then we will."[14] Beijing television repeated the warning, but the following day, an estimated 200,000 students broke through police lines and defiantly marched ten miles to demonstrate in Tiananmen Square. They demanded that their movement be recognized as "patriotic" and their elected representatives be allowed to talk directly with the country's Communist leaders. Knowing how vital the media were to their cause, the students insisted that the dialogues be broadcast live over television to the whole country. Deng was infuriated: this was not the purpose for which he had created a national television network.

The Communists' media problems were compounded by their punitive action against the *World Economic Herald*, a 300,000-circulation weekly that frequently challenged the government. When the *Herald* held a forum at which supporters of Hu Yaobang called for a "reappraisal" of the reformist leader and then published a special section about the forum, Shanghai officials stopped the presses and fired the editor, Qin Benli. The government's action angered many Chinese journalists, transformed Qin into a media martyr, and turned the grounds surrounding the *Herald*'s offices into a revolutionary camp where over the next seven weeks students and workers gathered to listen to VOA transmissions broadcast on loudspeakers strung up in the yard.[15]

A CHANGE IN STRATEGY

When Chinese journalists, including one hundred reporters and editors of the *People's Daily*, protested against Qin's dismissal and the blunt *People's Daily* editorial, the government abruptly changed its media strategy, adopting a more conciliatory line. Hu Qili, a member of the Politburo, met with the editors of nine major Chinese newspapers and told them they could report "the actual state of affairs" in Beijing. He insisted that the Party wanted to eradicate corruption along with the students. Two days later, following more demonstrations and the beginning of a student boycott, the government held a televised forum that featured students directing pointed questions at Party officials. While answering a query about

---

14. Steven W. Mosher, *China Misperceived: American Illusions and Chinese Reality* (New York: Basic Books, 1990), pp. 203–4.
15. Mark, "Observing the Observers," p. 264.

freedom of the press, one official revealed his Orwellian state of mind when he insisted that the press was free in China, explaining: "According to the constitution, the press enjoys freedom, but at the same time, it has to be constrained by the constitution and the law."[16]

On May 4, the seventieth anniversary of the May Fourth Movement, more than 300,000 students demonstrated in Beijing, joined by university professors, high school teachers, intellectuals, workers, government employees, and artists. "This marked," one China specialist pointed out, "the first joint street protest between students and others."[17] But it was the participation of some five hundred journalists from Communist Party–controlled publications that had the greatest significance for the students; here was the personal commitment of an organized group that had the power to carry the message of reform to the four corners of China.[18] In addition, hundreds of journalists, Chinese and foreign, covered the demonstrations, which had become a major international story. Intoxicated by the response at home and abroad, the students determined to take full advantage of another historic event: the visit to China of the political leader they most admired in the world.

THE GORBACHEV VISIT

The visit by Soviet President Mikhail Gorbachev should have been a mighty public relations triumph for the Beijing government. It was a symbol, the political analyst Steven Mark points out, of the rapprochement of the world's two greatest Communist nations after thirty years of enmity. It was a political coup for Deng Xiaoping, who agreed to host the summit. But for the Chinese students eager for reform, Gorbachev personified "the idea of political reform within the socialist framework." His policies of *glasnost* and *perestroika* legitimated their desire for more control over their destiny and more freedom for China.[19] The students saw the Soviet leader as an ally in their campaign for reform. For foreign and domestic news media, the Gorbachev visit was an Olympian event. Some 1,200 foreign journalists (including media stars like CBS's Dan Rather) were allowed to join the regular Beijing press corps, as part of the Chinese government's attempt to establish international credibility. Extra satellite privileges were

16. Ibid., p. 265.
17. Huan Guocang, "The Events of Tiananmen Square," p. 494.
18. Tony Saich, "The Rise and Fall of the Beijing People's Movement," in *The Pro-Democracy Protests in China,* ed. Jonathan Unger (Armonk, N.Y.: M. E. Sharpe, 1991), p. 21.
19. Mark, "Observing the Observers," p. 268.

granted to the foreign media, permitting live coverage by American and other television networks. As part of the new policy to report "the actual state of affairs," Chinese television became a powerful source of information for the Chinese people. The hard-liners permitted the more open coverage with the expectation that it would advance their goal of a triumphant socialism. But the new openness produced even more challenges to socialism.

The sympathetic reporting of the students by the media convinced many Beijing citizens that it was all right to demonstrate. On May 17, the government television network broadcast the Tiananmen Square demonstrations, showing people with banners like "The Ministry of Radio and Television Supports Student Hunger-Strikers" and "Oppose the Indifference of the Government." The sound track listed the many organizations and groups supporting the students as the camera panned the huge crowds. Commented the narrator: "Since morning, groups of banner-waving, slogan-shouting people poured into Tiananmen Square from all directions." Viewers could come to only one conclusion: that a popular and peaceful political uprising was under way in the nation's capital. The next day, a message flashed on the television screen: "Important News." General Secretary Zhao Ziyang was shown entering a hospital to comfort students weakened by their hunger strike in Tiananmen Square. Other Chinese leaders were pictured talking with a student who declared that the Communist Party had lost prestige among the people. The following day the scene shifted to the Great Hall of the People, where Premier Li Peng was shown sternly lecturing student leaders. But the students, emboldened by the presence of the television cameras, interrupted Li and lectured him, an unprecedented scene on national television. It was a stunning loss of face for Li, an orthodox Communist, exposed as a mere shadow of Mao. In sharp contrast was the moving coverage of Zhao visiting students in the square, pleading with them to end their hunger strike. "The government will never close the door to dialogue," Zhao promised, tears visible in his eyes, "never. If you have problems we will solve them."[20]

A MEDIA NIGHTMARE

By now, Deng had heard enough free speech to last him a thousand years. His carefully choreographed summit with Gorbachev had been turned into a public debate about his governance that was being broadcast

---

20. Hopkins, "Watching China Change," p. 37; Mark, "Observing the Observers," p. 269.

around the world. He found little solace in the Soviet president's remarks that "we also have our hotheads who want to renovate socialism overnight. But this does not happen in real life, only in fairy tales."[21] Deng was living through a nightmare, not a fairy tale. Gorbachev's official welcome had to be staged at the airport instead of Tiananmen Square, where the students would have mobbed the author of *glasnost* and *perestroika*. Driven by media considerations, Deng had to cancel a visit by the Soviet president to the Forbidden City, the ancient compound of the Chinese emperors, which is located on one side of the square. Even Gorbachev's official news conference was held in a government guesthouse on the city's outskirts instead of in the Great Hall of the People, which also faces the square.

As many as three million people demonstrated throughout Beijing on May 17, including government officials, military officers, and even policemen. Many waved posters demanding an end to "China's dictatorship." Young Chinese held up signs written in English with slogans like "Give Me Liberty or Give Me Death" and "We Shall Overcome." Government television and radio coverage provided a model of protest for the rest of the country—huge pro-democracy demonstrations took place in Shanghai and other major cities. In response, an alarmed Deng held a meeting of the Communist Party's top leadership, at which he called for the imposition of martial law and an end to the "chaos" by "whatever means" necessary. In a classic application of totalitarian *mediapolitik,* he ordered Zhao to appear live on national television and deliver a final warning to the students—desist or else. When Zhao refused, Li went before the cameras and accused the demonstrators of creating chaos and trying to overthrow the Communist Party. The premier then threatened to use the army and security forces against the pro-democracy movement.[22]

But the reformers did not back down because they now viewed the mass media as an electronic security blanket. Student leaders were convinced, wrote the *Washington Post's* Jim Hoagland, that "the presence of a large international press corps here to cover the visit of Soviet President Mikhail Gorbachev helped restrain hardliners in the government who wanted to use the police to restore order, whatever the cost."[23] Students applauded CBS's television cameras when they appeared to cover a rally

21. Robert Delfs, "One Stage, Two Plays," *Far Eastern Economic Review,* May 25, 1989, p. 12.

22. Huan Guocang, "The Events of Tiananmen Square," p. 495.

23. Jim Hoagland, "Blanket Television Coverage Gives Demonstrators a Media Security Blanket," *Washington Post,* May 19, 1989.

on May 16. They quickly learned how to use the news media as an instrument to spread their message of reform and freedom, making themselves available for interviews at every possible opportunity. And they often asked to speak to correspondents from the BBC or the VOA, which, of the foreign radio services, had the largest Chinese audience, an estimated sixty million. During the demonstrations, the VOA's Chinese audience may have grown as large as 400 million.[24]

On May 20, Premier Li declared martial law in the Beijing region, and over 150,000 troops equipped with tanks, cannons, and anti-aircraft missiles moved to the outskirts of the capital. To help control the soldiers, the military command prohibited them from reading newspapers, listening to the radio, or watching television.[25] Some of the most dramatic television pictures now appeared as millions of Beijing residents prevented the troops from moving toward Tiananmen Square. Students, workers, housewives, and the elderly offered food and drink to the soldiers and pled with them not to attack the students. They even stood or lay in front of military vehicles, including tanks, to block their way to the square. It seemed as though the pro-democracy movement had acquired an irreversible momentum.

A GROWING EUPHORIA

Because of their success in stopping the troops and the attendant publicity from the Western media, the reformers' mood in Beijing, Shanghai, and other cities soared. The students demanded the resignation of Li, the retirement of Deng, and an end to martial law. Workers and intellectuals organized: the Beijing Association of Intellectuals formed on May 24, the Beijing Workers' Autonomous Association on May 31. Student leaders continued to communicate with students in other cities by telephone and fax. Two of the students' main support groups came from the private sector: (1) the Flying Tiger Motorcycle Brigade, which provided the students with information about troop movements after martial law was declared and spread information about demonstrations throughout the city; and (2) the Stone Group Corporation, a private computer company that provided students with advanced communications networks.[26]

24. Binyan Liu, "The Impact of Media on Political Change," p. 13; Larry Martz, "Revolution by Information," *Newsweek*, June 19, 1989, p. 28.
25. Huan Guocang, "The Events of Tiananmen Square," p. 496.
26. Saich, "The Rise and Fall," p. 31.

Officers from military colleges caught reform fever and joined the demonstrations. There were rumors of dissension among the political leadership, spawning the hope that the military might try to force the politicians to accede to some of the reforms. But Deng and his aged colleagues were very much in control and determined to restore Communist law and order. They began by tightening the screws of censorship.

On the eve of the imposition of martial law, CBS and CNN interrupted their broadcast of events in China by showing themselves being thrown off the air. The communications link was briefly restored three days later, but live television broadcasts were again halted the following day. Like all totalitarian governments in a time of crisis, China's issued extensive restrictions on all foreign media, forbidding interviews with citizens about the student demonstrations. Although foreign journalists were usually able to evade police surveillance, some were detained and harassed. The foreign media, nevertheless, continued to seek out student leaders who were more than happy to accommodate their desire for information, hard and soft.

Such a symbiotic relationship is familiar in the West, and generally serves the common good, but it had unintended consequences in Communist China when the Western media, caught up in the euphoria, began to predict that the students could defeat the government. During Gorbachev's visit, CBS News quoted a Western diplomat saying, "They'll never put this genie back in the bottle." Bette Bao Lord, a commentator on CBS, told Dan Rather that "the Great Wall has a crack in it." After martial law was instituted—a clear sign the patience of the government was wearing thin—foreign experts predicted not a crackdown but Li Peng's ouster.[27] The wildly optimistic opinions influenced the students, who held so deep a belief in the saving power of the media that they deceived themselves into believing that what the media were saying would surely come to pass. They did not understand sufficiently that democratic ideas require democratic institutions or, like flowers planted in poor soil, they will soon wither and die. Although worn out by nearly six weeks of outdoor living, some ten thousand students, most of them from outside Beijing, remained in the square.

As a symbol of their cause, or perhaps to ward off what some now feared might come, students erected a thirty-three-foot replica of the Statue of Liberty and named it "the Goddess of Democracy." Again and again, television cameras slowly scanned every gleaming white curve, and photographs of the plaster and plastic statue appeared on the front page of al-

27. Mark, "Observing the Observers," p. 272.

most every newspaper in America and around the world. Every Chinese, including the Communist Party leaders, noted that the Goddess of Democracy was so positioned that she stared across the Avenue of Eternal Peace at Mao's portrait over the entrance to the Forbidden City. Military units began moving from the suburbs into the city, creating an unforgettable image: an unarmed civilian stood alone in the middle of the street and, holding out his hand, refused to move. He forced a column of tanks to stop in their tracks. The picture flashed around the world, and commentators noted how in bloody contrast Soviet tanks had run over pro-democracy demonstrators in Hungary in 1956 and Czechoslovakia in 1968.

But even as Western journalists were saying that "in the image contest, the big guys cannot win," the government was preparing for a contest it knew it could win—a contest of raw power.[28] In an effort to recapture the early fervor of the movement, four pro-democracy leaders announced a hunger strike on June 2, sparking a new wave of protests and one final great demonstration of more than one million people in Tiananmen Square. Their demands were live televised dialogue with government leaders and official acknowledgment of the protests, including the retraction of the April 26 editorial, a statement that the protests were not a disturbance, and a positive evaluation of the movement's place in history. To the students and many Western observers, the demands seemed reasonable; to the regime, they constituted a direct challenge to their authority. By the evening of June 3, almost all of the demonstrators had gone home, and most of the foreign media, including Dan Rather and the other U.S. television stars, had departed in pursuit of the next big story.

THE MASSACRE

The regime could have chosen to use the normal instruments of riot control to remove the remaining students from the square, but instead it brought out weapons of war. The massacre stopped the mass protests and buried the pro-democracy movement precisely because the violence was harsh and indiscriminate. The hard-liners decided that the probable loss of international prestige and foreign trade from the massive use of force could be reversed, but their rule might be irrevocably damaged if the demonstrations continued.[29]

28. Walter Goodman, "The Inherent Bias, Good or Bad, of the Mindless Eye," *New York Times,* June 7, 1989.

29. Melanie Manion, "Reluctant Duelists: The Logic of the 1989 Protests and Massacre," in *Beijing Spring: Confrontation and Conflict,* ed. Michel Oksenberg, Lawrence R. Sullivan, and Marc Lambert (Armonk, N.Y.: M. E. Sharpe, 1990), pp. x–xii.

An estimated fifty thousand combat troops, supported by tanks and armored personnel carriers, forced their way through civilian barricades to surround the square. To create excuses for the massacre that was soon to follow, policemen and soldiers provoked fights. Units of the People's Liberation Army launched their attack early Sunday morning, June 4, when they knew only a few reporters would be in the square. Tanks ran over tents, crushing protesters to death while soldiers fired their automatic weapons into the crowds in and around the square. Some students fought back with sticks, rocks, pipes, and firebombs. When the massacre was over, the government initially announced that only three hundred people were killed on June 4, most of them soldiers. Months later, the government figure was lowered to "more than 200," including just 36 students. But BBC and other Western media outlets estimated that as many as several thousand Chinese died in and around the square during the several days of fighting. One Chinese student group cited Chinese Red Cross officials as estimating 3,600 deaths.[30]

The exact figure may never be known, CNN's Beijing correspondent Mike Chinoy later wrote, but "it was substantial." The fact is that the Chinese army, on the orders of Deng and Communist leaders, was "unleashed on crowds of largely unarmed and defenseless demonstrators, most of whom were committed to a campaign of nonviolent protest for political change."[31]

In the best tradition of Edward R. Murrow, a brave Chinese reporter broadcast this commentary:

Remember 4 June 1989. A most tragic event happened in the Chinese capital, Beijing. Thousands of people, most of them innocent civilians, were killed by fully armed soldiers when they forced their way into the city. Among the killed are our colleagues at Radio Beijing.

The soldiers were riding on armored vehicles and used machine guns against thousands of local residents and students who tried to block their way. When the army convoys made a breakthrough, soldiers continued to spray their bullets indiscriminately at crowds in the street. Eyewitnesses say some armored vehicles even crushed foot soldiers who hesitated in front of the resisting civilians.

Radio Beijing's English Department deeply mourns those who died in the tragic accident and appeals to all its listeners to join our protest of this gross violation of human rights and the most barbarous suppression of the people.

30. "A Decade Later, Tiananmen Gets Scant Recognition," *Washington Times*, June 4, 1999.

31. Mike Chinoy, *China Live: Two Decades in the Heart of the Dragon* (Atlanta: Turner Publishing, 1997), p. 288.

Because of the abnormal situation here in Beijing, there is no other news we could bring you. We sincerely ask for your understanding and thank you for joining us at this most tragic moment.[32]

To most Westerners, it seemed that the unwarranted brutality of Tiananmen Square had dealt the Chinese Communist government a serious blow from which it would be a long time recovering. Television had captured and broadcast the awful reality of the massacre; newspapers had reported soldiers firing into crowds and tanks rolling over innocent civilians. Surely the people of China, fearing a repetition of the Cultural Revolution, would rise up in outrage and indignation.

But what these Westerners did not realize was that the great majority of the Chinese people did not know what had happened in Tiananmen Square; all those shocking images and stories had been seen and read in New York, Washington, London, and Bonn, but not in Shanghai, Canton, and Hankow, not even in Beijing. The Voice of America and other foreign radio networks were able to reach only part of the vast populace, for since May 21 the government had been jamming their broadcasts. The Communist leadership, conscious that it faced a critical challenge to its survival, undertook a brilliant if perverted propaganda campaign that turned the massacre into an act of self-defense. Propaganda—*xuanchuan*—has an honored place in Chinese Communist history. When Mao Zedong solidified his hold on the Party in the 1930s, he relied upon slogans and a simplistic catechism to teach party cadres: "What is the Red Army?" "The Red Army is the army of the poor men!" Education, as Mao's guerrillas practiced it, was intended to mold as well as inform.[33]

Employing Goebbels's "big lie" technique, the Deng government proceeded to portray the soldiers at Tiananmen Square as heroes who saved the country from a counterrevolutionary plot. In the face of extreme provocation, it was stated, soldiers had exhibited extraordinary restraint. In fact, declared an official at a televised news conference, "troops did not kill or harm a single person when we cleared the square."[34] Beijing television presented extensive coverage of civilian crowds stoning and burning military vehicles; the tapes and soundtracks were carefully edited to eliminate any evidence that soldiers fired on demonstrators. Deng Xiaoping

32. *Washington Journalism Review,* September 1989, p. 37.
33. Edward A. Gargan, "Seeing Is Not Believing," *Far Eastern Economic Review,* July 13, 1989, p. 57.
34. Robert Delfs, "Repression and Reprisal," *Far Eastern Economic Review,* July 6, 1989, p. 10.

held a televised news conference, surrounded by elderly Party leaders and uniformed military officers, at which he endorsed the brutal suppression of the demonstrators by the People's Liberation Army. While the student demonstrations, Deng explained, started as a "disturbance" by a small minority, they developed into a counterrevolutionary plot intended to "overthrow the Communist Party and the socialist system, subvert the People's Republic of China, and establish a bourgeois republic." In putting down the rebellion, he said, the army and the police showed "very high consciousness and stood up to the test."[35]

A COUNTERREVOLUTIONARY REBELLION

Over the next week, Chinese television produced a torrent of propaganda calculated to inspire pity for the soldiers of the People's Liberation Army and hatred for "the small number of conspirators" who began "a counterrevolutionary rebellion." On just one night, reported the *New York Times,* China's television viewers saw the following:

Scene 1: The camera pans to a large hall where several hundred top officials are listening to an address by Deng. Upon its completion, the prime minister tells the gathering that "Comrade Deng Xiaoping's important speech made a profound analysis of the cause and nature of the counterrevolutionary rebellion and the correctness of the measures we adopted."

Scene 2: The camera opens on a street corner where much of the violence took place in the early morning of June 4. Here a soldier was killed and his body disemboweled and burned by civilians spurred into action when the soldier fired into a crowd. Television news constantly showed scenes of the soldier's charred body propped against a truck or lying flat on its back. The picture switches to Jilin Province, where the soldier's father, mother, and brother live. "I ask his younger brother to learn from the older brother," says his mother, sobbing with sorrow and anger. "Go annihilate the thugs." His father, lying sick in a hospital bed, repeats the theme: "We must resolutely deal with these thugs. They deserve no leniency."

Scene 3: An announcer reports that the public security bureau has received 1,227 letters giving details about "counterrevolutionary thugs."

Scene 4: The camera focuses on a meeting of leaders of China's ethnic minorities who are all voicing support for the government's efforts to "put down the recent rebellion." The announcer quotes one leader as saying: "The scheme of those who wanted to create contradictions and stir up ri-

35. Ibid.

ots among the ethnic groups have failed, thanks to the joint efforts of the minority people."

Scene 5: Two student leaders are seen being led into a police station for interrogation. One of them was arrested in Xian where his family lives. The scene turns to a living room in Xian where the student's older sister and brother-in-law explain why they turned him in to the authorities.

Scene 6: The camera shows an old, heavy-set woman in the Chongwenmen district of Beijing, standing on a bridge covered with wreaths to commemorate the death of a soldier. The old woman says she saw "thugs" kill the soldier by throwing him off the bridge. "I stand in front of the people of this city as a witness," she says. "The People's Liberation Army did not shoot people."[36]

The Communists' propaganda campaign was dominated by television images of students and other young people being arrested, handcuffed, or frog-marched across a police courtyard at gunpoint. The hard-liners' greatest fear, reported the *Far Eastern Economic Review*, was not that the government "would be seen as cruel or unjust but . . . as essentially powerless."[37] The government also moved to take firmer control of the major Party organs, including the *People's Daily* and the Xinhua news agency, which had openly supported Zhao's reformist positions. As we have seen, hundreds of their reporters had participated in the student protests and had even organized demonstrations for press freedom. Premier Li openly acknowledged the key role of the mass media in the pro-democracy movement, commenting: "Due to mistakes in the direction of media work by a small number of comrades in the central leadership who departed from the stand of the Communist Party, some news units gave incorrect guidance to public opinion in the course of suppressing this rebellion. This is the result of the free spread of bourgeois liberalization [i.e., democracy] over a long period."[38] The government also clamped down on public access to computers, telephones, and one other facility the pro-democracy movement used very effectively: the fax.

DISPENSERS OF TRUTH

Although television was unquestionably the most powerful means of communication for the students, the facsimile machine turned out to be

36. Sheryl WuDunn, "Giving the Official Spin: 6 Scenes on Chinese TV," *New York Times*, June 15, 1989.
37. Delfs, "Repression and Reprisal."
38. Ibid., p. 11.

surprisingly important. The machines were widely available in Chinese universities, hotels, and the offices of international businesses. They could be reached by phone to make instant copies of photos, news articles, and Chinese-language newspapers printed in America. The students, *Newsweek* reported, often sent their messages without any firm idea of who might receive them—"the electronic equivalent of a note in a bottle."[39] Office workers, hotel waiters, and others reproduced and enlarged the messages and displayed them publicly. In Shanghai, for example, posters were displayed on scores of city buses that were surrounded by news-hungry crowds when they stopped at major intersections.

One of the most effective dispensers of truth inside China was the Voice of America, which increased its programming in Mandarin to eleven hours a day, adding new frequencies to evade jamming. Its audience soared into the hundreds of millions with possibly as much as one-third of China listening to the VOA, suggesting the potential base for a democratic China. In Nanjing, a crowd of 100,000 gathered in the town square, clustered around students who sat in trees with boom-box radios tuned at peak volume to the Voice of America. Students took notes of the broadcasts and turned them into wall posters that were hung all over the city. News of the protests spread by telephone and personal conversation. Meanwhile, in Washington, the VOA's first television news program was beamed via satellite to about two thousand dish antennas in China, most of them at military installations. VOA Director Richard Carlson explained that the targeting of the military was deliberate: to give the army an accurate account of what was going on and make it less willing to act against fellow Chinese.[40]

WHOM TO BELIEVE?

But whom were the army and the people to believe—the foreign media or their own government, which proclaimed that troops had been attacked by rioters brandishing firebombs and guns financed by "overseas reactionary political forces"? Over and over government televison and radio insisted that the soldiers had exercised maximum self-restraint but were at last compelled to open fire to protect themselves and restore order. Chinese outside the capital with little access to independent information—the VOA has a tiny audience in the interior, where Mandarin is not

---

39. Martz, "Revolution by Information," pp. 28–29.
40. Ibid.

understood—seemed to accept the government's version of events. Most people were relieved, one observer commented, that the nation was not plunged into civil war as it had been during the Cultural Revolution.

For the majority, martial law, the arrest of several thousand students, and a rewriting of history were a small price to pay for the restoration of order. Liberty and justice were undoubtedly important concepts, but not worth the upheaval of their daily lives. As they often had for four thousand years, the Chinese put order ahead of freedom. And perhaps, a university professor in Shanghai suggested, "the truth is too painful to accept"—the truth that the "people's" army had killed hundreds and even thousands of Chinese, young and old, students and workers, in cold blood.[41]

The Chinese authorities could not be budged from the official line. During an NBC television program from Beijing, Tom Brokaw questioned Yuan Mu, a government spokesman, about the events in Tiananmen Square. Brokaw listened to the official deny that a government-led massacre had taken place and then aired videotape showing the army firing on students and bystanders. A grinning Yuan responded that everyone knew that technology could be used to alter images.[42]

The government also relied upon television to demonstrate that it was in firm command. On June 24, CCTV, China's state television, alerted viewers to stand by for "an important message." At 6:30 P.M. (prime time in China), scenes were presented of a Communist Party Central Committee meeting at which General Secretary Zhao Ziyang had been dismissed from all senior Party posts. The camera panned the long dais showing the reorganized Party leadership, including the new general secretary, Jiang Zemin, previously unknown to the Chinese people. Central Committee members raised their hands in agreement that Zhao had split the Communist Party and sided with the pro-democracy movement. Four nights later, television viewers saw an extraordinary performance by Deng Xiaoping, who delivered a passionate talk to army field commanders, praising them for putting down a "counterrevolution." The eighty-four-year-old Deng slashed the air with his hands and shook his fingers in angry gestures.[43] Again, in contrast to the inept Soviet hard-liners, the PRC leadership practiced totalitarian control of the media, understanding fully the ramifications of *mediapolitik* when tied to liberal democracy.

41. Jill Smolowe, *Time*, June 26, 1989, p. 32.
42. Tom Shales, "China: The Networks' Closing Chapter," *Washington Post*, June 21, 1989.
43. Hopkins, "Watching China Change," p. 40.

Unwilling to allow anyone to challenge publicly its version of events, the government expelled two American correspondents, charging them with violating martial-law restrictions. The expulsion of the VOA's Alan Pessin for "creating rumors and . . . inciting and instigating counterrevolutionary rebellion" was significant because of the radio service's key role as a major source of information about Tiananmen Square.[44]

In such a super-charged climate, even listening to foreign radio was dangerous: one citizen was sentenced to prison for putting a radio tuned to the VOA in the window of his restaurant. He was accused of spreading rumors, and the police also complained that the radio drew large crowds that blocked the sidewalk. In Guangdong, the southern province which can receive Hong Kong broadcasts clearly, citizens were ordered to remove their television antennas. And Shenzhen, the special economic zone along Hong Kong's border, banned the sale of Hong Kong papers.[45] The effectiveness of the Communist propaganda blitz can be measured by the experience of an American journalist who spent the night of June 3–4 on Tiananmen Square and wrote about the bloody events that transpired there. But after two weeks of the Chinese government's unrelenting media campaign, she began to doubt the carnage she had herself witnessed. Several weeks later, in Hong Kong, she confessed to feeling relieved after picking up her processed photographs—pictures that "confirmed her memories and her notes of shooting on the square and frantic efforts to care for the wounded."[46]

THE DANGEROUS MEDIA

It is a major theme of this work that the mass media can be used to enslave as well as liberate. This was clearly demonstrated in China, where the Western television transmissions that spread the news about the democracy movement were used by the government to help round up the movement's leaders. ABC News broadcast an eight-second sound bite from Xiao Bin, an eyewitness to the massacre. Five days later, China's state television, CCTV, aired about ninety seconds of the same interview, suggest-

44. Robert Delfs, "Doddering Helmsman," *Far Eastern Economic Review*, June 29, 1992, p. 11.

45. Alan W. Pessin, "Communications and Revolution" (address before the National Association of Government Communicators, December 8, 1989), in *Vital Speeches of the Day*, May 1, 1991, p. 425; Louise do Rosario, "Read All about It," *Far Eastern Economic Review*, June 29, 1989, p. 32.

46. Pessin, "Communications and Revolution," p. 426.

ing that the government had lifted the interview from a satellite feed of raw footage. CCTV followed with its own pictures of Xiao under arrest and his repudiation of his earlier antigovernment views. Although ABC quickly scrambled its satellite signal, and other networks began silhouetting or otherwise disguising the faces of the Chinese who disputed the government's whitewash of the Tiananmen Square massacre, the media were presented with a dilemma: Were they reporters or compassionate human beings? Should they adhere to a libertarian or social responsibility philosophy? Or was it possible for them to follow a responsible, morally based liberal democratic path?

These questions became more than academic when the execution of students began: in Beijing, seven young men and a young woman were executed by a pistol shot to the base of the skull; in Shanghai, three young men who had helped set fire to a train were put to death. The argument for stopping all contact with Chinese seemed compelling, the columnist Jonathan Alter wrote: why risk sending them to jail or even execution? But silence and public acceptance of the "big lie" about Tiananmen Square were precisely the goals of the government. How then could the media protect the identity of those who wanted to talk and still present a believable story? Viewers and readers are understandably less likely to accept anonymous reports. "One of the cruel ironies of journalism," Alter remarked, "is that those who need the least protection often get the most— and vice versa." The American official trying to protect his own interests invariably has his request for anonymity honored. Reporters have gone to jail to protect their sources. But the man in the street, less valuable to the reporter in the future, is far more likely to see his name in print. The China experience suggests that protecting sources should be taken more seriously when a reporter is shielding them from torture and prison than from political accountability.[47]

In another cynical abuse of modern communications, the Chinese government mounted cameras on lamp posts, rooftops, and doorways along streets that foreigners frequent, supposedly as part of a traffic-control system to count vehicles. But the cameras were also secretly monitoring contacts between foreigners and Chinese, including foreign journalists and their sources. Having night vision capability, the automatic cameras were able to record the bloody fighting along the major streets leading to Tiananmen Square. This footage, skillfully edited and replayed constantly

47. Jonathan Alter, "Unwilling Informants?" *Newsweek*, June 26, 1989, p. 29.

on CCTV, showed only aggressive "counterrevolutionary" demonstrators attacking impassive soldiers. Zooming in on individual faces in the crowd, wrote *Time* magazine, the Chinese Communists created "televised WANT-ED posters, complete with telephone numbers for viewers to call to report on the students frozen on the screen."[48]

THE MEDIA AS AGITATOR

One of the most stinging comments about the role of the Western mass media in the Tiananmen Square massacre came from the *Washington Post*'s David Ignatius, who wrote that "we Americans have a nasty habit of encouraging foreigners to rise up and fight for freedom—and then leaving them hanging." This time, however, it was not the U.S. government that played "the outside agitator role," but the news media that brought the protesters onto the global electronic stage and "encouraged them—and us—to imagine that we were all on the barricades of freedom together." Although the students were eager to manipulate the media in any way they could, the media were no less eager to be manipulated. Normally blase anchormen abandoned their customary libertarian pose and allowed their sense of social responsibility and moral righteousness to show. But they got so carried away with what they wished would happen that they began, without sufficient foundation in political reality, to predict that the students would triumph. They turned to diplomats and scholars who supported their overly optimistic view. "China will never be the same. . . . They're clearly going in a direction of a freer society, freer expression," said Winston Lord, former U.S. ambassador to China on NBC's *Meet the Press*. "I think it's unlikely that [the People's Liberation Army] will shoot," said Gaston Sigur, former assistant secretary of state for Asian affairs, on ABC's *This Week with David Brinkley*. "I think the government—Deng Xiaoping and Li Peng—must resign if there's going to be any order brought to this situation," said the Sinologist Kenneth Lieberthal of the University of Michigan.[49]

COMMUNISM'S OTHER FACE

A few observers offered a more sober assessment, but received scant attention. One of them was Dr. Walter H. Judd, a former congressman and medical missionary in China, who at a Washington seminar held only two

48. "Big Brother Was Watching," *Time*, June 26, 1989, p. 33.
49. David Ignatius, "On the Electronic Barricades," *Washington Post*, July 30, 1989.

weeks before the invasion of Tiananmen Square, cautioned that if the demonstrations kept growing "tanks [could] start rolling over people. . . . there would be . . . violence that I think would be almost unbelievable. I hold my breath during these tragic days."[50] Unlike the overly optimistic television commentators, Judd believed that the Beijing government would do whatever was necessary to stay in power, including mass murder, wholesale arrests, and the arbitrary suspension of basic civil liberties, and all without regard for adverse international reaction.

After, but only after, Tiananmen Square, some China watchers came forward with mea culpas. Michel Oksenberg acknowledged that he and others had "sold short the resolve of the octagenarian leaders to defend their life's work." Referring to other campaigns of terror that the Chinese Communists had launched against their enemies, Maria Chang commented: "Like the two faces of Janus, the China of Mao and Deng had been co-existing all along. Mao never really went away, after all." Tiananmen Square profoundly shocked the American people; an overwhelming margin of 87 percent, according to a Gallup poll, held that the army's action against the students was unjustified. The American public's previous high regard for China plummeted, prompting the Chinese author Nien Cheng, who had been imprisoned during the Cultural Revolution, to say: "Americans . . . see the Chinese Communist government for what it really is: a repressive regime with complete disregard for its people and world opinion."[51] This evaluation, however, was not shared by Henry Kissinger and other practitioners of *realpolitik*, who argued that the Communist government had only acted to maintain public order and prevent chaos. Commented Kissinger: "The caricature of Deng Xiaoping as a tyrant is unfair."[52] But Deng's suppression of the pro-democracy movement revealed him to be, in fact, a ready totalitarian. No better demonstration of the essential difference between *realpolitik*, with its shifting amoral center, and

50. Lee Edwards, *Missionary for Freedom: The Life and Times of Walter Judd* (New York: Paragon House, 1990), p. 323.

51. Michel Oksenberg, "Confessions of a China Watcher: Why No One Predicted the Bloodbath in Beijing," *Newsweek*, June 19, 1989, p. 30; Maria Chang, "Mao's Revenge: Totalitarianism Returns to China," *The Asia Column*, May–June 1989, p. 2; Gallup Organization, "Gallup Survey on American Attitudes toward China in the Wake of the June, 1989 Crackdown: Summary of the Findings" (Princeton: The Gallup Organization, July 1989), pp. 11, 14; Nien Cheng, "Massacre in Beijing," *National Review*, August 4, 1989, p. 31.

52. Henry Kissinger, "The Caricature of Deng as a Tyrant Is Unfair," *Washington Post*, August 1, 1989.

liberal democratic *mediapolitik,* with its firm ethical foundation, could be found.

THE ANTI-TIANANMEN SYNDROME

Although Deng Xiaoping called for renewed economic reform in 1992, three years after Tiananmen Square, he did not extend his reform to the mass media. In the summer of 1993, the State Secrets Law was used to sentence a Chinese journalist to life in prison on charges that he sold a copy of a speech by Communist Party General Secretary Jiang Zemin to a Hong Kong reporter a week before the speech was made public. That fall, a mainland reporter for a Hong Kong newspaper and a former editor of a banned Chinese newspaper were arrested under the same law. In December 1994, a pro-democracy activist was condemned to twenty years' imprisonment for distributing four articles on human and workers' rights. Gao Yu, an internationally respected journalist, received a six-year sentence. Remarked an editor of the English-language *China Daily,* "We are like dogs on a leash. A very short leash."[53]

In June 1994, Beijing deployed security forces and interrupted international news broadcasts to prevent commemoration of the fifth anniversary of Tiananmen Square. Hotels in the capital were instructed to unplug their satellite connections to CNN, and TV service in housing compounds reserved for foreign diplomats, journalists, and businessmen was interrupted whenever Western networks broadcast images of the 1989 protests. But despite the tight security, the *New York Times* reported, some expressions of defiance slipped through the information barriers. Using international computer networks accessible in China, Chinese students and professionals on several continents published an electronic file of personal reminiscences of June 3–4. One Chinese student recalled the experience of being run down by a tank on the Avenue of Eternal Peace west of Tiananmen Square. In another act of commemoration that evaded official censorship, Ding Zilin, a professor under house arrest, informed news agencies that she and her husband observed a three-day fast in memory of their seventeen-year-old son who was felled by a soldier's bullet on the night of June 3, 1989.[54]

53. Allison Liu Jernow, "China: The Tight Leash Loosens," *Columbia Journalism Review,* January/February 1994, p. 32; editorial, "Harsh Wind from Beijing," *New York Times,* December 20, 1994.

54. Patrick E. Tyler, "China Tries to Blot Out Memories of 1989," *New York Times,* June 5, 1994.

The tenth anniversary of Tiananmen Square passed unnoticed in Beijing—the square itself was fenced off for resurfacing. There were only two protests near the square, involving a grand total of just two people. On the morning of June 4, 1999, under a large portrait of Mao, a middle-aged man opened an umbrella covered with slogans, including one that said, "Remember the student movement!" He was quickly led away by police. In the late afternoon, at the same location, a young man suddenly threw flyers into the air and began railing against corruption and social division. He was bundled off by police who scooped up the flyers to discover that while they mentioned the need for democracy they said nothing about the student movement of 1989 and ended with the slogans, "Long Live Chairman Mao" and "Down with American Imperialism."[55]

The only public commemoration of the crackdown on Chinese soil was in Hong Kong (no longer a British crown colony) where, at an evening rally, more than 70,000 people held candles, sang songs, and paid their respects to those who had lost their lives at Tiananmen Square. Szeto Wah, a pro-democracy leader, insisted that "nobody has stopped remembering this part of history," but clearly most Chinese had.[56] In addition to the official government line that no Tiananmen massacre had occurred, Beijing launched in the early 1990s a campaign of "patriotic education," intended to increase nationalist fervor and undercut pro-Western sentiment, particularly among young Chinese. School children were taught patriotic songs. University freshmen were required to take a course in modern Chinese history that stressed the achievements of the Communist Party and to visit "patriotic bases" such as Mao Zedong's birthplace. At the same time, influential Chinese thinkers were encouraged by the government to criticize the "excessive love during the 1980s for all things Western."[57]

The campaign seemed to work. By 1995, a survey of ten thousand young people across China revealed that a majority expected to see "major improvements" in the country's political, economic, and military status in thirty years. A Shanghai study showed that patriotism had risen to number two on the list of "important personal values," up from number five in 1984. The challenge, and the danger, to the government, a Western corre-

---

55. Mark Landler, "A Quiet Tiananmen Anniversary in China," *New York Times*, June 5, 1999.

56. Ibid.

57. Henry Chu, "Chinese Students Renew Emphasis on Patriotism," *Los Angeles Times*, June 2, 1999.

spondent, Henry Chu, pointed out, lay in whether Beijing could prevent "nationalism from turning into a threat to Communist rule rather than a tool of it."[58]

Which is why, perhaps, the regime is so adamant in its denials that any such horrific institution as the *laogai* exists in China. But we know from former inmates that there is in fact a vast network of forced-labor camps, the *laogai*, in which several million Chinese, thousands of them political prisoners, struggle to survive. One ex-prisoner was Wei Jingsheng, labeled a "counterrevolutionary" in 1979 for promoting a democratic China by posting a large poster on Democracy Wall in Beijing. Wei was sentenced to the *laogai* for fourteen years, much of which he spent in solitary confinement. China's largest camp, according to a Dutch journal, is located near North Korea; many of the students arrested during the 1989 demonstrations are housed there, under truly Orwellian conditions. Forty inmates are crammed into each cell. Criminals are used to control the political prisoners, who work fourteen hours a day, seven days a week. "Those who do not fulfill their work quota," reported the journal, "are sentenced to overtime instead of meals."[59]

The *laogai*'s best-known ex-prisoner is probably Harry Wu. The son of a wealthy banker, Wu was labeled a "counterrevolutionary" and imprisoned in 1960 for openly criticizing the Communist leadership. He spent nineteen years in various camps, his weight dropping from 155 to 80 pounds, and was finally discharged in 1979. Wu, now a naturalized American citizen, has charged that human rights violations are "more serious in China" than anywhere else in the world. In his books, articles, and personal appearances, he has compared the *laogai* to Hitler's concentration camps, Stalin's gulag, and Pol Pot's killing fields. Wu estimates that China, with 1.2 billion people, has one thousand prisons and camps holding six million people, many of them political prisoners. China, he says, will never reach its full potential as a world superpower "as long as human rights violations are allowed to persist."[60]

THE LESSONS OF TIANANMEN SQUARE

There are several lessons of *mediapolitik* to be learned from Tiananmen Square. First, the mass media have only limited ability to change an au-

58. Ibid.

59. Hans Vriens, "Inside China's Bamboo Gulags," *Intermediar,* reprinted in *World Press Review,* July 1994, pp. 13–15.

60. "Wu Says China Cannot Grow without Human Rights," Agence France Presse, January 23, 1998.

thoritarian country like China. They do not operate in a political vacuum, and if they are not supported by democratic principles and institutions, they cannot *by themselves* create freedom in an unfree country. Whether a society is open or closed depends ultimately upon the people within that society. Technology is the servant, not the master, of the people.

The Chinese students turned to the news media for help and protection in the belief that public opinion could persuade the Communist hard-liners to institute reforms or abdicate. The students underestimated the willingness of Communists to use massive force to retain power, the age-old Chinese tradition of respect for and reliance on elders, and the Chinese people's fear of lawlessness and disorder—reinforced most recently by the chaos of the Cultural Revolution. Both the students and the government used the media to communicate with masses of people, only to discover that its use was both an asset and a liability. The students gained widespread support for their movement, but they terrified the government with the enormity of their success; Beijing had to crush the movement. Deng and other hard-liners lost stature in the eyes of the world with their brutality, but they succeeded in finding and silencing their most active opponents.[61]

Would there have been a pro-democracy movement without the mass media? Almost certainly not. "Never before during four decades of Communist rule," Huan Guocang wrote, "had Chinese students organized an independent political movement, much less had they ever demonstrated by the millions for fundamental changes in the political system and for the resignations of top leaders."[62] Were the mass media responsible for the Tiananmen Square massacre? Clearly, the Western mass media gave the students a false sense of power and protection, encouraging them to raise constantly the political ante: modest demands for more press freedom and a dialogue with the government turned into angry calls of "Down with Deng!" and "Up with democracy!" Fearing that a hundred Tiananmen Squares might erupt all over China, the Chinese government called in the tanks and troops and seized control of what had been so crucial in the rebellion—the mass media.

The government's respect for the crucial importance of the media was revealed in December 1989 when General Secretary Jiang Zemin asserted that "press freedom" was a slogan used to oppose the Party. "In the new period," he declared, "news reporting must serve socialism and serve the

61. Mark, "Observing the Observers," p. 281.
62. Huan Guocang, "The Events of Tiananmen Square," p. 497.

people." The "counterrevolutionary turmoil and rebellion" in May and June, said Jiang, illustrated the chaos that will result "if the tools of public opinion are not tightly controlled in the hands of true Marxists."[63] Can tight control of public opinion be maintained indefinitely? All the dictators of Eastern and Central Europe thought so, including Walter Ulbricht of the German Democratic Republic—and then the Berlin Wall fell.

The second major lesson of *mediapolitik* to be derived from Tiananmen Square is that even in an authoritarian society, the mass media can give the people a taste of freedom, and once tasted, its intoxicating flavor is not easily or soon forgotten. Hundreds of Chinese journalists joined the movement, publishing uncensored articles and broadcasting outspoken commentaries and creating the most liberal period of press freedom since the founding of the PRC in 1949. During the demonstrations, students, workers, and intellectuals organized their own associations based on democratic principles. Leaders were elected, and major decisions were made and approved by majority votes. When Wuer Kaixi, the chairman of PAAUS (the Beijing Autonomous Association of University Students), urged the students to leave Tiananmen Square without consulting other student leaders, a major vote was immediately held, and Kaixi's decision was overturned. Even China's vast network of Party members, police, and informers cannot prevent citizens from using the nation's burgeoning technologies, including the Internet, to explore the possibilities of freedom.

In 1988, for example, six billion letters were delivered and 646 million long-distance telephone calls were made.[64] An estimated forty-five million homes in southern China can receive Hong Kong–based Phoenix Satellite Television, despite laws restricting broadcasts to hotels and foreigners' housing. Since China plugged into the *yingtewang*, as the Internet is known, an estimated five million Chinese have gained access to the Net. Ninety percent of the students at Beijing University have Internet accounts. Concerned authorities have tried to block Chinese Web users from reaching unapproved sites, and a computer entrepreneur was sentenced to two years in jail for selling 30,000 e-mail addresses to a dissident e-mail publication. Such treatment shows, the Internet reporter Greg May wrote, that the government is wrestling with the dilemma of developing a

63. Robert Delfs, "Speak No Evil," *Far Eastern Economic Review*, December 14, 1989, p. 27.
64. Martz, "Revolution by Information," p. 29.

world-class, high-tech economy while maintaining control over information.[65]

Beijing blocks hundreds of Web sites—such as *washingtonpost.com* and *playboy.com*—which it considers potentially harmful to its interests. But it has not yet been successful in stopping people from using proxy servers that allow access to the blocked sites. On June 4, the tenth anniversary of the Tiananmen Square crackdown, several Chinese Internet servers shut down their chat rooms to prevent the dissemination of antigovernment comments. But others such as a popular Web site in the southern city of Guangzhou stayed up.[66]

Many Chinese have been given a new sense of community by the media; no longer do they feel that they are isolated individuals confronting an all-powerful state. As the government depends more and more on the police and the army to assure stability, it "fosters more alienation of the sort that prompted the democracy movement in the first place."[67] Adding to this unstable situation is the government's determination to mix economic freedom and political control. Modern history, including that of China itself, suggests that you cannot allow the former without undermining the latter. Reflecting upon Tiananmen Square and the attempts of the Chinese Communists to rewrite its history, many Chinese remember the words of the great Chinese writer Lu Xun early in this century: "Lies written in ink cannot obscure a truth written in blood."[68]

The third lesson to be drawn from the short life of the pro-democracy movement in China is that in today's interdependent world, no nation, not even the mighty Middle Kingdom, is an impregnable island. Describing his guerrilla army, Mao Zedong used the metaphor of a fish swimming among the people; China, as Orville Schell puts it, is a fish, albeit a giant fish, swimming in the water of the world. The influence of the water which the fish needs to survive is inevitable and continuous.[69] Once Deng allowed the Western media to enter and cover his summit meeting with

65. David M. Lampton and Gregory C. May, *Managing U.S.-China Relations in the Twenty-first Century* (Washington: The Nixon Center, 1999), p. 38; Jaime A. FlorCruz, "Chinese Media in Flux," *Media Studies Journal*, summer 1999, p. 44; Greg May, "Spamming for Freedom," *Washington Post*, February 19, 1999.

66. John Pomfret, "China's Surfers Make Waves," *Washington Post*, June 23, 1999.

67. Huan Guocang, "The Events of Tiananmen Square," p. 499.

68. Nicholas D. Kristoff, "How the Hardliners Won," *New York Times Magazine*, November 12, 1989, p. 71.

69. Orville Schell, "The Great Wall vs. the Fax," *New Perspectives Quarterly*, summer 1989, p. 56.

Gorbachev (who revealed his Leninist colors by carefully saying nothing about the Tiananmen Square massacre), he de facto allowed the mass media, with their liberalizing tendency when coupled with democracy, to become a factor in the politics of the People's Republic of China.

Like Gorbachev, Deng gambled that he could control the foreign media, but he lost the gamble, even though temporarily, when the media fell in love with a million students singing "We Shall Overcome," waving banners that read "Up from Socialism," and building a Goddess of Democracy in front of Mao's image. Despite the subsequent "big lie" campaign and the Orwellian rewriting of history, the intelligentsia know what really happened on June 4. And the Communist regime will always be on the watch for the next Tiananmen Square.

If we consider the five key elements of power in a Communist regime —the Party, the military, the secret police, the bureaucracy, and the mass media—we see that in the instance of Tiananmen Square, all but one were firmly opposed to the pro-democracy demonstrations, enabling Deng and the other hard-liners to take decisive action against the students. Only the mass media were divided in their loyalties, with several hundred journalists joining the protesters and presenting sympathetic coverage of the demonstrations in the square.

In contrast, during the Moscow putsch, some military leaders were clearly reluctant to move against fellow Russians; the Party's official leader, Mikhail Gorbachev, was a victim rather than an instigator of the coup; and the KGB failed to seize all the political and communications centers in many outlying cities. The Soviet mass media were almost entirely on the side of those opposing the putsch. Perhaps the most significant difference between the two pivotal events is that the democratic forces in the Soviet Union had experienced mature leadership in Boris Yeltsin, Anatoly Sobchak, and others, while the pro-democracy students in China had, really, only themselves. In a nation like China that places such high value on age and experience, that was a serious disadvantage.

Although Deng and the other aged leaders were forced to follow a modified authoritarian model of *mediapolitik* for several months, they never seriously considered acceding to the demands of the students for a liberal-democratic model. The Communist regime has since reverted to a strict authoritarian model. It has been argued by some political scientists that political freedom inevitably follows economic freedom, and that therefore some form of democracy must eventually emerge in China, given the economic reforms. Two contradictory celebrations of fifty years of Chinese Communist rule in October 1999, however, suggest that the process will be protracted.

In Shanghai, the journalist John Pomfret reported, Chinese Communists hosted some of the world's wealthiest capitalists in the towering skyscrapers of the city's new business district. The Fortune Global Forum was designed, explained a smiling official, as "a beacon of China's future."[70] But in the capital of Beijing, half a million people, carefully screened for their "love of the motherland," participated in a parade featuring goose-stepping students, soldiers, tanks, rockets, and anti-aircraft weapons. The marchers shouted fifty slogans, all approved by the Central Committee of the Communist Party, such as "Rely on the working class wholeheartedly." Half of Beijing was placed under martial law, one observer wrote, by a Communist leadership caught between a desire for reform and an insistence on "a continued dictatorship and Marxist ideology."[71]

70. John Pomfret, "In 2 Chinese Cities, Celebration and Contradiction," *Washington Post*, September 29, 1999.
71. Ibid.

CHAPTER 8

WHERE THE *KISHA* IS KING

FOR MANY FOREIGNERS, Japan, more so than Russia, is a riddle wrapped in a mystery inside an enigma. It is a small group of resource-poor islands that has became the second most powerful economic nation in the world. It is a constitutional democracy that was led by one political party (the Liberal Democratic Party) for nearly forty years. It is one of the most homogeneous societies on earth but constantly debates controversial issues like the proper role of the emperor, the use of the Self-Defense Forces, revision of the constitution, and the Yasukuni shrine. Its citizens read more newspapers and magazines and watch more television, but have less diversity of information and opinion, than any other developed nation. Why is Japan seemingly as inscrutable as a No play? Lafcadio Hearn, the first Westerner to interpret Japan in modern times, wrote at the turn of the twentieth century of "the immense difficulty of perceiving and comprehending what underlies the surface of Japanese life."[1]

We can begin to unravel the riddle of Japanese politics by understanding that, while Japan's government is based on Western-style democracy, it is in fact a very young Asian democracy, heavily influenced by centuries of non-Western traditions and practices. Unlike the United States, for example, with its emphasis on individual rights, Japan is dominated by a sense of collective responsibility. Americans delight in confrontation while Japanese avoid it, almost always operating by consensus. Although elites

1. Karel van Wolferen, *The Enigma of Japanese Power* (New York: Vintage Books, 1989), p. 14.

undoubtedly wield considerable influence in America, Japan is ruled by a powerful triad: the bureaucracy, the political party in power (the LDP from the 1950s through most of the 1990s), and the business community. This dominant triad is assisted and reinforced by the mass media, which have a major influence on public attitudes about domestic issues and international affairs.[2] Japan practices a form of *mediapolitik* that can be found in no other nation in the world, outwardly liberal democratic but inwardly semi-authoritarian.

The Japanese used to say that they lived under a one-and-a-half party system, meaning that the electoral weight of all the opposition parties did not equal that of the Liberal Democratic Party. The biggest opposition party was the Japan Socialist Party (JSP), which won more parliamentary seats than any other party in the first national elections of 1947. But since then, the JSP has failed to capture a majority in the Diet (Japan's parliament) because its leaders have persisted in taking positions on economic and defense issues far to the left of most Japanese.

As to the LDP, it has been not so much a political party as a confederation of *habatsu,* that is, "factions" or "machines." The primary responsibility of a faction member is to further the political ambitions of his faction head in the Diet. In return, the faction leader places as many of his supporters as he can in positions of influence. As a consequence, the makeup of a Japanese cabinet has usually been determined by hard bargaining among the factions. Although according to the constitution, "the highest organ of state power" is neither the emperor nor the prime minister but the Diet, its actual power is limited. Very little legislation, particularly of the policy- making kind, originates in the Diet.[3]

The most important branch of the Japanese government is its unique bureaucracy, which writes most of the legislation that is submitted to the Diet and nearly all the laws that are adopted. Unlike the United States, the major ministries and government agencies are not run by cabinet members but by administrative vice ministers chosen from the civil service. These bureaucrats are not, however, omnipotent; they must consider the needs and wants of the other members of the ruling triad—the politicians and the business leaders. And increasingly all three groups are required to take into account a relatively new actor in their enclosed world, the mass media.

2. Ibid., p. 41.
3. Robert C. Christopher, *The Japanese Mind* (New York: Fawcett Columbine, 1983), pp. 217–26.

LOYALTY AND CONFORMITY

Although the media are guaranteed freedom from government interference and control under the constitution and often expose governmental and business scandals, they are careful, for several reasons, not to challenge too aggressively the bureaucratic-political-business triad. First, there is the emphasis on the group and consensus rather than the individual and independence, summed up in the proverb, "The nail that sticks up will be pounded down."[4] Loyalty, hierarchy, and conformity in Japanese journalism are institutionalized by the *kisha kurabu,* or press clubs. There are about four hundred *kisha* clubs composed of 12,000 journalists representing 160 media organizations. The clubs are attached to government ministries and agencies and every other important institution in Japan, like the Bank of Japan, the LDP, the police, and corporations. All news about the ministry or institution is presented at *kisha* meetings, which are held several times a day. The process protects member journalists from missing stories and guarantees equal access to information for all members. With few exceptions, every politician, bureaucrat, corporate executive, and other news source releases important information through his *kisha.*[5]

It is the *kisha,* not the government agency or corporation, that arranges all press conferences and briefings and has the power to ban outsiders from the events. In effect, each *kisha* acts as a "journalistic collective": when there is news to report, an informal directorate of the club's senior members decides what is important about a particular story and what is not—and all the members of the club write their story accordingly.[6] The power of the *kisha* is almost unlimited. "Once assigned to a club," says Tetsu Akiyama of the leading newspaper *Mainichi Shimbun,* "a reporter is no longer instructed in what to cover by the paper, but by the club."[7] The journalist must conform to the rules of his *kisha,* or else. A reporter was once suspended from his club for six months because his newspaper published a story which the *kisha* had agreed not to print; the punishment was inflicted on the journalist, although he himself had not been responsible for the appearance of the offending article.[8] But when a political or busi-

4. Jared Taylor, *Shadows of the Rising Sun* (New York: William Morrow and Company, 1983), p. 92.

5. "Kisha-and-Tell: Japan's Subservient Press," *The Economist,* March 18, 1989, p. 96.

6. "Free, Unfettered but Timid," *Far Eastern Economic Review,* June 7, 1984, p. 199.

7. David Brock, "Gentlemanly Press Gets Gloves Dirty," *Insight,* December 4, 1989, p. 8.

8. Van Wolferen, *The Enigma of Japanese Power,* p. 95.

ness scandal occurs and is allowed to be reported by the media, the nation is subjected to a tidal wave of information about it, because many journalists had been aware of the details of the scandal all along.

The *kisha* system has resulted in the routine practice of news organizations' assigning a reporter to a specific politician or high-level bureaucrat, often for life, tying the fate and fortune of the journalist to the official he has been given. What inevitably develops is a classic patron-client relationship in which the reporter receives "gifts" of information and even cash (a carry-over from pre–World War II Japan) while providing the politician with publicity and often public approval. The reporter either writes favorable stories about the politician or refrains from criticism that might endanger their symbiotic relationship. The personal ties and professional dependency created can be so strong as to create "factional struggles" within news organizations that mirror those within the political parties and the bureaucracy.[9]

Foreign correspondents are routinely denied membership in a *kisha*. The respected financial news service Bloomberg Business News won a place in the club attached to the Tokyo Stock Exchange only after a lengthy and often bitter battle. Prior to October 1993, Bloomberg had watched its Japanese competitors routinely receive breaking business news first.[10]

THE INFLUENCE OF KUUKI

Media conformity is intensified by the Japanese system of group writing whereby stories are written by teams of anonymous journalists who seldom receive a byline, although some major newspapers like *Mainichi* and *Yomiuri* are crediting individuals more and more.[11] Given the prevailing ethos of *kuuki* (an atmosphere requiring compliance), there are few complaints and no strikes by journalists against the management of the gigantic media conglomerates that dominate Japan. The last thing that would occur to a reporter would be to write a story critical of his newspaper or television station. On the rare occasion when such media criticism

9. Roya Akhavan-Majid, "The Press as an Elite Power Group in Japan," *Journalism Quarterly* 67, no. 4 (winter 1990): p. 1011; William Nestor, "Japan's Mainstream Press: Freedom to Conform?" *Pacific Affairs* 62 (spring 1989): p. 33.

10. Robert Neff, "The 'Keep Out' Signs on Japan's Professions," *Business Week*, December 1, 1997.

11. See Nester, "Japan's Mainstream Press," p. 34, and Brock, "Gentlemanly Press," p. 8. Also, Takashi Sakamoto of the *Yomiuri Shimbun* and Hitoshi Omae of the *Nihon Keizai Shimbun*, interviews by author, August 15, 1999.

occurs, there is swift retribution. In 1971, the *Asahi Journal*, the weekly magazine of the daily *Asahi Shimbun*, carried a cartoon caricaturing a picture in a prewar primary school textbook in which the sun was rising above the horizon with cherry blossoms in the back. The caption read, "Red, Red, Morning Sun, Morning Sun." *Asahi* means "morning sun" in Japanese. Thus, the cartoon suggested that the mother newspaper, the *Asahi Shimbun* was red or leftist—as indeed it was. After the cartoon appeared, the unamused management of the *Asahi Shimbun* removed the editorial staff of the weekly and a top executive in its own headquarters.[12] In such a closed environment, a journalist does not question the decision of his *kisha* for fear that he will be disciplined, or even expelled and rendered unable to practice his profession.

Such a system is tailor-made for media control by the bureaucratic-political-business triad. In fact, the ruling elite views *kishas* "as information cartels" that supply "limited information in return for the members' promise not to print anything damaging."[13] The Japanese journalist's inability to challenge the *kisha* monopoly is complemented by the fact that Japanese officials are not legally required to provide information about their agency or department. Unlike the United States with its Freedom of Information Act, Japan has several laws restricting the disclosure of various kinds of government information. While the "freedom of newsgathering" is cited as a worthy principle, it is not, like freedom of expression, guaranteed by law.[14]

Control of the media is enhanced by the concentration of ownership in the hands of five giant companies which own newspaper and broadcasting enterprises all over Japan. The five major national newspapers are *Yomiuri, Asahi, Mainichi, Nikkei,* and *Sankei,* with a total circulation of well over thirty million copies a day; these newspapers in turn control Tokyo's five key television stations, NTV, TV Asahi, TBS, TV Tokyo, and Fuji TV. Conformity is furthered by hiring practices: all Japanese journalists joining any of the five national dailies are recruited through a three-stage process of written and oral competition—much like the old Mandarin examinations in imperial China—with rates of success as low as one per 150 applicants.[15] Another component of *mediapolitik* in Japan is the regular

12. Youichi Ito, "Mass Communications Theories from a Japanese Perspective," *Media Culture & Society* 12, no. 4 (October 1990): p. 469.

13. Nester, "Japan's Mainstream Press," p. 39.

14. Akhavan-Majid, "The Press as an Elite Power Group," pp. 1010–11.

15. Ibid., p. 1008.

flow of high-level bureaucrats from departments like the Ministry of Posts and Telecommunications into the media industry. This flow is part of the institutionalized practice of *amakudari* or "descent from heaven," by which every year retiring senior bureaucrats take up executive positions in industries previously under their jurisdiction.[16]

THE PRACTICE OF SELF-CENSORSHIP

There are very few scoops in Japan. Generally, since journalists are not personally credited for investigative reporting, few bother to practice it. The prevailing attitude is summed up by one reporter: "Individuality can get you punished."[17] Such group-think is at variance with the crusading spirit of famous Asian politician-journalists like India's Mohandas Gandhi, who spread his ideas of freedom and nonviolence through his editorship of four weekly newspapers; and China's Sun Yat-sen, who used the mass media of the day to help bring down the Ching dynasty in 1911. For Japanese journalists, any temptation to tell all or even to discover all is controlled by the realization that publication or broadcast without group approval would result in the journalist's expulsion from the *kisha* and his being replaced by a more cooperative and trustworthy member.[18] Therefore, while there is no government censorship, there is deep-rooted, consistent self-censorship by members of the media.

Media criticism of the government, particularly in the policy realm, is also hampered by the widespread public attitude that government officials are "professionals" of policy making, while journalists are only "semi-professionals" who monitor the behavior of professional policy makers.[19] For all their apparent power, then, the Japanese media are guilty of a fundamental weakness: self-imposed conformity in coverage and treatment. According to the scholar Edwin Reischauer, "They commonly come out with headlines and editorials that seem to be almost paraphrases of each other. As a result, tens of millions of Japanese, intellectually armed with the same television and newspaper news and opinion, sally forth to work each day with the same facts, interests, and attitudes in their heads."[20] What is significant, and disturbing, about this conformity is how few people in Japan are concerned about it.

16. Ibid., p. 1009.
17. Brock, "Gentlemanly Press," p. 8.
18. E. G. Seidensticker, "Japan's Timid Media," *World Press Review*, August 1984, p. 61.
19. Ito, "Mass Communications Theories," p. 434.
20. Edwin Reischauer, *The Japanese* (Rutland, Vt.: Charles E. Tuttle, 1977), p. 199.

A MEDIA-SATURATED NATION

The *kisha* syndrome profoundly affects the course of the nation's politics because Japan is a media-saturated country and the Japanese are "news addicts of the deepest dye."[21] Japan has more than 180 newspapers with a daily circulation exceeding forty million. Ninety-three percent of all citizens read newspapers regularly, over half of them the big Tokyo three—the *Yomiuri Shimbun,* the *Asahi Shimbun,* and the *Mainichi Shimbun.* Their readership is the highest in the world (if we except the controlled circulation of Chinese Communist publications) with the *Yomiuri Shimbun* leading with more than twelve million daily readers. The circulation reflects Tokyo's dominance of Japanese politics and economics as well as the simple fact that 10 percent of the nation's 120 million people live there.

Japanese television, which began in 1953 after the American occupation ended, has been led from the beginning by the noncommercial Nihon Hoso Kyokai (NHK), which is modeled deliberately on the British Broadcasting Corporation. NHK's legal autonomy derives from its ability to set and collect its own fees (although the parliament reviews fee proposals), and from its freedom to determine its own programming. Although the government cannot dictate content, however, the prime minister appoints NHK's board of governors, and NHK is an obedient participant in the *kisha* system like every other media organization in Japan.[22] In addition to the two NHK channels, a Tokyo viewer can choose among five commercial channels, several UHF channels with in-school programs, and local news; two NHK satellite channels (requiring a small "dish" receiver); and a pay-TV channel. Some two-thirds of the stations—there are nearly 1,500 VHF and more than 10,000 UHF stations—are operated by NHK, which is largely financed by user fees paid by all owners of television sets. Half of NHK's stations are devoted to educational and cultural programming, while even its "general-interest" stations allot less than 30 percent of air time to entertainment. The 470 VHF and 2,900 UHF privately owned stations are entertainment-oriented, although they are supposed to give 30 percent of their programming to education and culture.[23] Japan has the

21. "Free, Unfettered but Timid," p. 196; Nester, "Japan's Mainstream Press," p. 29.
22. Anju Grover Chaudhary and Anne Cooper Chen, "Asia and the Pacific," in *Global Journalism: Survey of International Communication,* 2d ed., ed. John C. Merrill (New York: Longman, 1991), p. 239.
23. Christopher, *The Japanese Mind,* p. 203.

highest television penetration in Asia, with 563 sets per one thousand people, meaning that only two people ever need to share the same set. This is second in the world only to the United States, which has 793 sets per one thousand people. At the same time, Japan has the highest ratio of newspaper readers in the world, a remarkable 562 copies per one thousand people, compared with a modest 268 newspapers per one thousand people in the United States.[24]

Television news in Japan is much more than a headline service: NHK's regular evening news show is often followed by a half-hour documentary or roundtable discussion on a current topic. Like the United States' C-SPAN, NHK offers the Japanese news junkie live broadcasts of Diet sessions. Perhaps the most impressive part of Japanese television is its cultural and educational programming. It is not unusual for NHK to produce a sophisticated program on philosophy or computers along with an accompanying textbook that sells hundreds of thousands of copies. All these media reflect and at the same time strengthen the conviction of Japan's elites that the Information Age will be as important as the Industrial Age in human history and that Japan is uniquely positioned by its culture and its government-led industry to lead the new age.[25]

THE WORLD'S LARGEST
ADVERTISING AGENCY

A major actor in the mass media, and a key supporter of the bureaucratic-political-business triad, is Dentsu, Japan's largest advertising agency, which does more to mold Japanese popular culture than any other single corporation. In recent years, however, the Hakuhodo agency has increasingly challenged Dentsu's number one position. Dentsu is directly responsible for about one-third of all advertising on Japanese television, monopolizing the scheduling of sponsors during prime time. Some 120 film production companies and more than four hundred graphic arts studios are under its wing. The agency handles about a quarter of all advertising in Japan, placing one-fifth of the ads in the major newspapers and close to a third in the more important magazines. By comparison, the United States' largest advertising agency has a U.S. market share of less than 5 percent. The difference is easily explained: the American company

24. Chaudhary and Chen, "Asia and the Pacific," p. 259.
25. Christopher, *The Japanese Mind,* pp. 205–7.

operates in a fiercely competitive open market while Dentsu receives preferential treatment in a carefully controlled market.

In Western countries, advertising agencies operate as intermediaries between advertisers and the media. In Japan, Dentsu often decides where and how Japanese companies will advertise. The advertising giant often puts pressure on the Japanese media to play down or not report incidents that might hurt the reputation of its clients. A well-known example of the agency's ability to control news occurred in 1955, when news of the arsenic contamination of Morinaga Milk Industry's powdered milk was suppressed. A decade later, Dentsu was able to censor news of deaths caused by a cold medicine produced by Taisyo Pharmaceutical. "Whenever news of a death through that medicine reached us," a reporter recalled, "companies such as Dentsu applied pressure on us not to report it at all, or not to mention the name of the pharmaceutical company. Sometimes they telephoned us; at other times, an executive would visit us."[26]

Another key service of Dentsu is public relations and public opinion polls, carried out by its "ninth bureau," which has sections corresponding to the ministries of construction, transport, agriculture, post and telecommunications, education, finance, and the prime minister's office. The bureau handles the more sophisticated parts of the LDP's election campaigns as well as propaganda about controversial issues like nuclear power safety. During the decades when the LDP controlled Japanese politics, Dentsu's ninth bureau absorbed over one-third of the public relations budget of the prime minister's office and some 40 percent of that of the other ministries. In 1972, shortly after establishing its public relations division, Dentsu published an amazingly candid report which asserted that whereas the LDP maintained advantageous connections with the daily press and television, via the *kisha* club system, relations with important weekly magazines other than those published by the major dailies were not yet based sufficiently on "fixed rules."[27] In the ensuing years, Dentsu did much to "fix" the rules for the LDP.

THE MOST IMPORTANT POLITICAL FORCE?

A survey in the early 1980s of eleven major groups, including business, labor, farm, and media, as well as intellectuals, political party members, and citizen and feminist groups, found that almost every one of them

26. Van Wolferen, *The Enigma of Japanese Power*, pp. 176–78.
27. Ibid., p. 179.

considered the mass media to be one of the most influential groups in Japanese society; today the media have fallen in public esteem because of their close association with the ruling triad. Many politically active Japanese believe, according to Julian Weiss, an Asian specialist, that the media are "institutionally corrupt" and part of an "internal propaganda system."[28]

And yet the Japanese media are quite good at exposing minor political and business scandals. When officials of the International Telephone and Telegraph Corporation were caught smuggling small consumer items into the country, their petty infractions were featured daily in the news until the company contritely promised to lower its exorbitant international telephone rates. The owner of the Hotel New Japan was pilloried in the press when the hotel burned down and was discovered to have lacked some of the mandatory safety features. Society is certainly served when such lawbreaking is reduced or held in check; and the media are able to play a watchdog role because Japanese "strongly fear the consequences of having their reputations blemished."[29] But the media also allow themselves to be used by the establishment, sometimes even creating the illusion that the public interest is being carefully protected when it is not.

In January 1988, for example, the public prosecutor of the city of Osaka decided that a "political donation" was in fact a bribe. The offending politician was a prominent Upper House member of the Komeito ("Clean Government") Party who was indicted on charges of having accepted ten million yen (about $83,000) in return for official favors. The politician's "crime" was to have accepted the money in exchange for recommending to the Transport Ministry a partial revision of measures that discriminated against a national federation of private gravel shippers.

But the charge was legally and politically ambiguous: (1) a private federation cannot take any ministry to court regarding a discriminatory regulation; (2) a Japanese politician is expected to mediate in such cases; and (3) if no LDP member can be found to serve as a mediator, a well-connected member of a minority party will do. Nevertheless, the Komeito politician resigned his seat and apologized for not fulfilling his "ethical responsibility."[30] Had he not done so, the media would have directed the full

---

28. Nester, "Japan's Mainstream Press," pp. 29–30. Also, Julian Weiss, interview by author, July 25, 1999.

29. Van Wolferen, *The Enigma of Japanese Power*, p. 98.

30. Ibid., p. 233.

force of their moral wrath at him. No one bothered to ask why the prosecutor saw fit at that moment to ruin the career of an opposition Diet member. The little morality play enabled the government to act as a vigilant prosecutor, the media to pose as the conscience of the country, the exposed politician to save face by resigning, and the LDP to congratulate itself on deflecting public attention from its own systematic abuse of public trust and misuse of public money reaching into the billions of yen.

Occasionally, even the combined power of the government and the mass media cannot persuade the people to accept a policy that is egregiously political. Such a policy was the normalization of Japanese relations with the Chinese Communist government in 1972; the public was not so much opposed to extending diplomatic relations to Beijing as it was opposed to severing them with the Republic of China on Taiwan. After World War II, Chiang Kai-shek's Nationalist government, unlike other Asian nations, did not insist on receiving massive reparations from Japan. Furthermore, although they had committed atrocities throughout the Middle Kingdom, hundreds of thousands of Japanese troops in China were returned safely home. In contrast, the Japanese troops that surrendered to Soviet forces suffered horribly, being kept in concentration camps in Siberia where many died of malnutrition and subfreezing temperatures.

The Japanese people remembered Chiang Kai-shek's magnanimity and believed that their government should not desert his government on Taiwan for political reasons.[31] Public dissatisfaction with the Sino-Japanese treaty increased when most of the Japanese media, led by the three largest daily newspapers, supinely agreed to write only favorable reports about the Mao Zedong regime in exchange for permission to station correspondents in Beijing. Criticism of the pro-Mao Japanese journalists became so severe during the Cultural Revolution of 1966–76, which resulted in deaths estimated to be in the millions, that several reporters had to resign.[32]

THE RECRUIT SCANDAL

Even in the land of the *kisha,* a reporter can sometimes disregard the rules of Japanese journalism and uncover a scandal that changes the political course of the nation. The story that was to force the resignation of a

---

31. Ito, "Mass Communications Theories," p. 436.

32. Van Wolferen, *The Enigma of Japanese Power,* p. 97; Ito, "Mass Communications Theories," p. 438.

prime minister and create the most serious political crisis in the history of the LDP started routinely. Reporters in the Kawasaki bureau of the *Asahi Shimbun* received a tip from the local police in the spring of 1988 that the deputy mayor of Kawasaki was being investigated for having sold unlisted shares of Recruit-Cosmos, the real estate subsidiary of the Recruit Company, shortly before it went public and jumped 30 percent in value. The shares appeared to be a payoff for the waiver of zoning regulations allowing Recruit to erect an office building. But the police soon stopped the investigation without filing charges and refused to allow any disclosure about their inquiry.

The more senior political reporters accepted the decision of their *kisha* not to publish, but an ambitious young reporter, Keiichi Suzuki, did not. He carefully went through the local records of real estate and stock transactions and tax payments and eventually established that the deputy mayor had indeed granted a special zoning waiver for Recruit in exchange for stock. Suzuki's discoveries were published. When a local politician was later filmed by Asahi TV News being offered hush money by a Recruit executive, the Tokyo bureau of the *Asahi Shimbun* became interested in the story. In September 1988, the Tokyo prosecutor's office launched an investigation, and all the major newspapers began running articles about the growing scandal.[33]

By now, the media were no longer leading the investigation but relying upon leaks from the Tokyo prosecutor, much as Bob Woodward and Carl Bernstein of the *Washington Post* depended upon Deep Throat and other inside sources to advance the Watergate story. The motive of the leakers in each case was the same: carefully timed leaks were the only way the prosecutors could ensure that their superiors would not stop the investigation or prevent it from reaching the higher levels of government.

Why did the Japanese media publish the leaks when they so clearly violated the "go along to get along" philosophy of the *kisha* system? Because many journalists feared an embarrassing repeat of the Lockheed Corporation bribery scandal of the 1970s, when the Japanese media badly trailed the aggressive reporting of the foreign media. The initial Lockheed story was broken by a Japanese monthly magazine that linked Prime Minister Kakuei Tanaka to the receipt of bribes from a Lockheed representative in exchange for promoting the purchase of Lockheed planes by All Nippon Airways. The prestige media ignored the story for weeks until a foreign

33. Brock, "Gentlemanly Press," p. 10.

journalist raised the allegations at a Tanaka news conference. The foreign media continued to dominate the story until Tanaka resigned as prime minister in 1974.[34] The Japanese media determined that they would not be left behind on the Recruit story, no matter who was involved. An important factor—which did not exist in the 1970s—was the twenty-four-hour-a-day presence of CNN.

Ultimately it was revealed that the recipients of Recruit-Cosmos stock included the nation's most prominent public figures, including Prime Minister Noboru Takeshita, former Prime Minister Tanaka (a man who clearly reaped the benefits of public office to the fullest), and three members of the Takeshita cabinet. Besieged by leaks to the press and a determined public prosecutor, Takeshita at last admitted that he had received several hundred thousand dollars in secret donations and loans from Recruit at a vital time in his campaign to become prime minister; he resigned in disgrace in June 1989.[35] Several groups tried to exploit the Recruit scandal. Younger LDP politicians called (anonymously, of course) for a "Recruit purge" that would remove the older corrupt generation. Members of the *keidanren*, a closely knit group of industry leaders, cited the indictment of Recruit chairman Hiromasa Ezoe, a corporate maverick, as a telling example of what happens to those who challenge the "well-ordered corporate hierarchy."[36]

PUNISHING THE LDP

The people also had their say. Angered by the corrupt behavior of politicians who bought highly sought-after homes in the city while the middle class commuted for hours to distant suburbs where they lived in one- or two-room apartments, the electorate voted in the July 1989 elections against the LDP. The LDP lost its majority in the upper house of the Diet to a coalition of the Japanese Socialist Party and a group of small opposition parties. Although the Liberal Democratic Party continued to run the government by reason of its 60 percent majority in the more powerful lower house, Japanese politics received a seismic shock.[37]

Recruit also had a decided impact on Japanese newsgathering, with

34. Ibid., pp. 11–12.
35. David E. Sanger, "Takeshita Undone by System That He Lived by for So Long," *New York Times,* April 26, 1989.
36. Brock, "Gentlemanly Press," p. 11.
37. "Remember the Recruit Scandal?" *Business Week,* January 8, 1990, p. 52; Brock, "Gentlemanly Press," p. 13.

younger reporters in particular becoming more aggressive in investigating leads and leaks. A senior editor complained that his young colleagues were "out of control" and getting their "latest revelations into print before the newspaper's instinctive self-censorship could stop them."[38] In the fall of 1989, Tokyo papers revealed that the lucrative *pachinko* (pinball) industry had given large donations to politicians in both the LDP and Socialist parties. Such donations are legal if they are reported, if they are domestic in origin, and if they do not result in a political quid pro quo. But one paper revealed that some Socialist Party members "acted in ways that favored the *pachinko* industry." Then it was uncovered that pinball parlors had backed the LDP candidacies of three ex-government bureaucrats who supervised the industry.[39]

Far from enjoying their role as muckrakers and frontline opponents of government wrongdoing, however, many Japanese journalists grew uneasy and expressed anxiety about the future of the *kisha* system. A former foreign editor of the *Nihon Keizai Shimbun* (the Japanese equivalent of the *Wall Street Journal*) commented sourly about the new aggressive journalism, "You could call it investigative. I would call it irresponsible." Referring to lurid articles about Prime Minister Sosuke Uno and his relationship with a former geisha, the *Yomiuri Shimbun* editorially deplored the "scandal-mongering" of the press and declared that the nation was on the verge of a "witch-hunt that could seriously damage the body politic." Normally, no one, and certainly not the media, would have paid much attention to Uno's liaison with a geisha. Japan has about 13,000 professional geisha, who are regarded as the keepers of cultural traditions such as classical song and dance and are patronized by the country's political and industrial leaders. But the prime minister put his geisha on the government payroll, which is not the usual practice, and the opposition party raised pointed questions in the Diet that were picked up by the foreign media; the LDP was deep in another scandal.[40] Like his immediate predecessor, Takeshita, Uno abjectly resigned, driven from office in large part by a Japanese press that was reacting to foreign criticism and the strong interest that many women subscribers took in the story.

---

38. "Kisha-and-Tell," p. 96.
39. Brock, "Gentlemanly Press," pp. 13–14.
40. Ibid., p. 12.

THE SHORT-LIVED IMPACT OF RECRUIT

The mystery-riddle-enigma of Japan is superbly demonstrated in the Recruit scandal. Whereas the world was given the impression that the LDP suffered a major defeat with the forced resignation of Prime Minister Takeshita and that law enforcement officials and journalists played a major role in his ignominious departure, the truth is that the Recruit episode was an excellent example of crisis management by the bureaucratic-political-business triad that controls the government, politics, and mass media of Japan. While Takeshita did resign as prime minister, he remained head of the Tanaka faction and therefore the most powerful boss of the LDP. Business leaders used the scandal to halt the career of an upstart entrepreneur, Ezoe Hiromasa, who posed a threat to their well-ordered and profitable existence. Even the Recruit scandal's political impact was short-lived. In February 1990, for the twelfth consecutive time since their party was formed in 1955, the Liberal Democrats were returned to power in the lower house by a decisive majority, making the LDP "the world's best electoral machine." Fourteen of the politicians implicated in the Recruit scandal were reelected, including Takeshita. Kiichi Miyazawa, relegated to the ash heap of politics for his involvement in Recruit, was subsequently elected prime minister in 1991.[41]

The real scandal, the Japan specialist Karel van Wolferen said, was not that some businessman discovered a new way to bribe politicians, but that the impression was created that political bribery was not tolerated in Japan and steps would be taken to prevent its recurrence. Media indignation and exposure were very selective: "No editor made the slightest attempt to trace the more systematic transfers of far greater sums of money from business to some of the most powerful men within the LDP."[42] It has been estimated, for example, that the LDP spent an astronomical $3 billion (dollars, not yen) in the 1990 general elections. The most junior politicians need to raise $1 million a year in a non-election year to pay for everything from handsome presents at the many weddings and funerals they are obliged to attend to an average office staff of fifteen—although the government budget provides for only two. It is estimated that senior leaders spend at least ten times that figure annually.[43]

41. "The Liberal Democrats Face Japan's New World," *The Economist*, December 24, 1990, p. 31.

42. Van Wolferen, *The Enigma of Japanese Power*, p. 437.

43. Joanna Pitman, "Raw and Fishy," *The New Republic*, November 4, 1991, p. 17; "For the Honour of Japan's Politics," *The Economist*, March 18, 1989, p. 13.

When the Recruit chairman stated at his trial that the police had used methods approaching torture in their interrogation of him, no Japanese paper thought it necessary to investigate his charges. The scandal ended with a whimper, not a bang, when the minister of justice declared that the public prosecutor would be punished if it were discovered that he was leaking information to the media.[44] Both prosecutor and press thereupon beat a dignified retreat and returned to uncovering safer scandals.

Rather than a turning point in Japanese journalism, the Recruit incident turned out to be an illustration of the incestuous relationship between the media and their sources and how easily the media can be manipulated to political ends. Before he was forced to resign, Takeshita used the scandal as a red herring to distract public attention from a new consumption tax which he rammed through the Diet in December 1989.[45]

And like journalists the world over, reporters were careful to protect their own, highlighting the many politicians who took money from the Recruit Company but playing down the involvement of the vice president of the *Yomiuri Shimbun* and the president of the *Nihon Keizai Shimbun*. A *Yomiuri* columnist admitted that it was safe for him to write about his colleague's misconduct because the man had already resigned. But if he had first discovered the stock arrangement, he could not and would not have written about the vice president's involvement: "We work as one group so any journalist, any reporter, cannot write any story against his supervisor or his newspaper company."[46]

KOWTOWING TO THE TRIAD

As demonstrated by their coverage of the Recruit and other scandals, most of the mass media of Japan function more like a lap dog than a watchdog, kowtowing to the bureaucratic-political-business triad. They follow neither a libertarian nor a social responsibility philosophy but a pseudo-utilitarian philosophy that enshrines the principle of pursuing the greatest good for the greatest number as defined by the elites that run the country. The media invariably put the national interest, as outlined by the governing elite, before any abstract notion of the public's right to know. They eschew consideration of the philosophical truth that a well-informed and educated public makes for good citizens and a good society.

44. Van Wolferen, *The Enigma of Japanese Power,* p. 437.
45. Ibid., p. 436.
46. Brock, "Gentlemanly Press," p. 11; Mark Fitzgerald, "Recruit Scandal Was No Watergate for Media," *Editor & Publisher,* June 2, 1990, p. 11.

In Japan, economic prosperity and technical competence take precedence over public virtue and justice. Truth is what the triad says it is. Government statements about the economy are invariably published without comment or context.

When an official, for example, of the powerful Ministry of International Trade and Industry (MITI) delivered a speech, every major newspaper dutifully duplicated the *Mainichi Shimbun,* which reported: "Close corporate links between Japanese manufacturers and suppliers enable them to develop new high-tech products within a short period of time, and thus stimulate fierce competition in the market."[47] This was government propaganda, not news. Such supine journalism underscored the fundamental difference between Japanese democracy, with its emphasis on political power and economic stability, and American democracy, with its concern for individual rights and responsibilities.

But an electoral upheaval occurred in July 1993 when the Japanese people, fed up with political corruption and coverup, turned out the LDP, rejected the Socialists, and allowed a seven-party reform coalition to take charge of the Diet. The key symbol of the political tsunami was a grocery cart overflowing with $4 million in illicit cash. Shin Kanemaru, the leading LDP dealmaker and therefore the most powerful man in Japanese politics, admitted receiving an illegal $4 million contribution from a mob-related businessman. The secret payment took so much cash—50,000 separate 10,000 yen bills—that the bagman had to stuff the money into a grocery cart to deliver the payoff to Kanemaru's office. When the establishment tried to let Kanemaru off with a $1,660 fine, Japanese voters reacted furiously. Before their anger—sustained by extensive media coverage—had subsided, Prime Minister Kiichi Miyazawa had lost a no-confidence vote and was forced to dissolve the Diet and call for national elections.[48]

The LDP's fall from power actually began the previous year when, departing from the *kisha* tradition of playing down government corruption, the Tokyo Broadcasting System reported that many of Japan's most important politicians had taken money from a package delivery service, Sagawa Kyubin, known to be connected to Japanese organized crime. This initial revelation led ultimately to Kanemaru's indictment and the disgrace and defeat of the LDP.[49]

47. Brock, "Gentlemanly Press," p. 17.

48. T. R. Reid, "Japan's Political Crisis Sparked by Long-Ignored Average Voters," *Washington Post,* June 20, 1993.

49. Spencer Sherman, "NHK TV Japan," *Columbia Journalism Review,* March/April 1994, p. 35.

Miyazawa's successor as prime minister was Morihiro Hosokawa of the Japan New Party, who tried to implement dramatic political and economic reforms (including a freedom of information law) until he was forced out of office nine months later, the victim, in large part, of intense bickering among a seven-party coalition. Hosokawa's weaknesses as a leader were revealed when he announced and then retracted a tax-reform proposal which would have tripled the rate of the consumption tax—a measure adamantly opposed by the largest party in the coalition. But during his short time in office, campaign financing laws were strengthened.[50]

Taking advantage of the divided opposition, the conservative LDP and the liberal Socialists formed an uneasy coalition that gave them a narrow majority in the lower house of the Diet. They named Tomiichi Murayama, an old pacifist from the left wing of Japanese politics, as prime minister and filled the cabinet with LDP ultra-nationalists. The movement toward major political change halted—"as if the political clock just stopped ticking," the political scientist Eto Jun commented—but the Japanese people's desire for political reform did not.[51] In the spring of 1995, they elected independent Yukio Aoshima, an actor turned citizen-politician, as governor of Tokyo. Like Ronald Reagan, Aoshima has enormous personal charm and a "talent for aligning himself with the popular will," and is regarded as a potential power broker among the competing national coalitions.[52] Tsutomu Hata, the so-called "poster boy" of the political reform movement, uses a white campaign bus to gain TV coverage of his speeches—a publicity tactic politicians in the past would never have resorted to.[53]

The 1996 general election, wrote the economist Robert Alan Feldman, "virtually wiped out the socialists" and gave the LDP a near-majority in the lower house.[54] Many renegades from opposition parties have joined the LDP, but—and there is now always a "but" in Japanese politics—the Liberal Democratic Party has not succeeded in achieving anything like its old dominance. In the summer of 1999, the New Komeito, Japan's second largest opposition party, was supposed to join forces with the LDP to provide Prime Minister Keizo Obuchi with the majority he lacked in the up-

50. Charles Smith, "The Battle to Come," *Far Eastern Economic Review,* April 21, 1994, p. 15.

51. T. R. Reid, "Japan's Voters Disillusioned," *Washington Post,* July 18, 1995.

52. Ibid.

53. Michael Williams, "Japan's LDP Savors Return from Exile," *Wall Street Journal,* August 1, 1994.

54. Robert Alan Feldman, "Sputter, Sputter, Choke," *The Brookings Review,* summer 1998, p. 19.

per house of the Diet. The deal fell through, *The Economist* reported, when the LDP pushed for the official adoption of the *hinomaru* ("Rising Sun") flag and the *kimigayo* ("His Majesty's Reign") anthem. Their use would have become mandatory at all official occasions—"especially in schools."[55]

Although the New Komeito's leadership was willing to go along with the LDP plan, many members of the Buddhist-affiliated party strongly objected, and the bill to make the flag and the anthem official symbols died. Rather than aligning themselves with the LDP, leaders of the New Komeito decided they would stand a better chance in elections if, like the Democratic Party and the Communists, "they make a show of having unwavering principles of their own."[56]

COMFORT WOMEN

In the post-Recruit era, the media have shown a greater willingness to challenge the old order in the most sensitive areas. During World War II, about eighty thousand women, mostly Koreans but including Chinese, Filipinos, Indonesians, Burmese, and Dutch, were forcibly recruited by the Japanese military to provide sexual services to Japanese soldiers as the Imperial Army advanced across Asia. The issue of so-called "comfort women" was buried and denied by the government until Yoshiaki Yoshimi, a history professor at Chuo University, uncovered official evidence of their existence in the library of the National Defense Agency. Yoshimi's findings were published in 1993 on the front page of *Asahi Shimbun*, the same newspaper that broke the Recruit scandal story. Within hours, the chief cabinet secretary expressed Japan's "deep remorse and regret" and publicly admitted for the first time that the Japanese army was "in some way involved" in the administration of the comfort women facilities.[57]

The official veil over Japan's often brutal actions during World War II was lifted further by Kenji Ono, a factory worker turned researcher, who has interviewed former members of the Imperial Army stationed in Nanking in 1937. They revealed details of the infamous "rape of Nanking," during which Japanese soldiers shot and bayonetted thousands of Chinese soldiers. Ono's findings were published in the weekly magazine *Shukan*

55. "Flagging Support," *The Economist*, June 5, 1999, p. 40.
56. Ibid.
57. Louise do Rosaria, "A Quest for Truth," *Far Eastern Economic Review*, February 18, 1993, p. 37.

Kinyobi and reported in the *Asahi* newspaper. In a dramatic departure from past practice, Prime Minister Murayama in 1994 marked the forty-ninth anniversary of Japan's surrender by apologizing for his country's conduct in World War II. "That battle," he said, "brought tragic sacrifices to many people in Asia and the world. Reflecting deeply on the agony and sorrow of these people, I would like to offer heartfelt condolences to them with deep repentance."[58]

JAPANESE MEDIAPOLITIK

Clearly, *mediapolitik* plays a major role in Japanese politics. First, there is a significant media infrastructure in Japan, including two thousand major periodicals (about the same number as in China, but with about one-tenth the number of people to read them—122 million versus 1.2 billion) and thirteen national television channels, plus Cable News Network and a burgeoning cable industry. Second, Japan has an enormous television viewing audience and the highest ratio of readers to newspapers in the world—adult literacy in Japan is 100 percent. But the intellectual quality of even the prestige press is not what it was twenty years ago. An increasing amount of newspaper space is devoted to comics to satisfy the phenomenal cartoon appetite of young Japanese. In 1987, for example, 1.68 billion volumes of *manga*—books or magazines with a cartoon-panel format—were published. *Manga* run the gamut from science fiction and fantasy to adventure, romance, pornography, and how-to manuals.[59]

Third, Japanese public officials and politicians devote a significant amount of time and resources to calculating how to manipulate the media through the *kisha* system, which protects and preserves the bureaucratic-political-business triad that has run the country for decades. Fourth, the Japanese media have materially altered the course of national politics, sometimes in what they have done and more often in what they have not done.

The fate of the young reporter, Keiichi Suzuki, who broke the Recruit scandal story is instructive. Suzuki gained neither fame nor fortune for his enterprise. For him there was no Japanese equivalent of a Pulitzer Prize—the Recruit scandal was not mentioned in the 1989 annual awards of the respected Japanese Newspaper Publishers and Editors Association—no

---

58. Charles Smith, "War and Remembrance," *Far Eastern Economic Review,* August 25, 1994, p. 22.

59. Chaudhary and Chen, "Asia and the Pacific," pp. 229–30.

best-selling book, no award-winning film directed by Akira Kurosawa. He was only a name that elicited shrugs among Japanese journalists in Washington when they were asked about his present whereabouts.

What model of *mediapolitik* best fits Japan: liberal democratic, authoritarian, totalitarian? Unlike other countries that we have studied, Japan is an island nation, far less influenced by foreign media than the People's Republic of China or Eastern Europe. The Voice of America beams sixty hours of Mandarin Chinese programming into the PRC, but zero hours of Japanese into Japan. One reason is political: China is a potential adversary, Japan a longtime ally. Another is technical: the Japanese language is so complex it is often called "the Devil's language," a phrase allegedly coined by St. Francis Xavier, the sixteenth-century Jesuit missionary to Japan. The Japanese, says the author Robert Christopher, rely to a remarkable degree on *haragei*, translated as "visceral communication" or "belly language." It is possible for one Japanese to determine the reaction of another to a particular situation by noting the other's facial expressions, silences, and grunts.[60] Such subtleties of communication cannot be duplicated by the foreign media.

The most culturally and ethnically homogeneous of the developed nations, Japan has been able to Westernize itself, yet still preserve its own special identity. There is no denying that Japan is a parliamentary democracy and that its media are guaranteed freedom of expression under its constitution. But both political and journalistic freedom in Japan are severely constrained because of the incestuous relationship between Japanese politicians and journalists. Furthermore, because the Japanese Supreme Court is controlled by the bureaucrats, whose first duty is to preserve their place in the system, the democratic provisions of the constitution are often not enforced.[61]

Although Japanese citizens may sue the mass media for libel, predictably very few do. The "low rights consciousness of Japanese as individuals," according to the author Kyu Ho Youm, and their high respect for the media as key social institutions discourage such suits.[62] The societal emphasis on loyalty and conformity often results in the self-censorship of stories that might threaten the power structure. While the Japanese media

60. Christopher, *The Japanese Mind,* pp. 39–44.

61. Van Wolferen, *The Enigma of Japanese Power,* p. 310.

62. Kyu Ho Youm, "Libel Law and Freedom of the Press: Judicial Interpretation in Japan," *Journalism Quarterly,* summer 1990, p. 20.

are not authoritarian, they are not liberal democratic as are the American or British media because they do not operate within a framework of moral as well as societal responsibility. Instead, they are dominated by elites who want above all else to retain their entrenched political power.

Certainly, the media have helped to strengthen Japanese democracy since 1945, but so long as the bureaucratic-political-business triad manipulates the media, and the media allow themselves to be manipulated, there will be no true liberal democratic *mediapolitik* in Japan.

CHAPTER 9

THE POWER OF
FIFTEEN MINUTES

WHILE THE POLITICS of most Latin American countries after World War I was characterized by wild swings between reform and revolution, Chile enjoyed political stability and democratic pluralism until the left-wing coalition of Salvador Allende was elected to power in 1970. Many changes occurred in Chile during those fifty years as the country industrialized, urbanized, and modified many of its social and cultural patterns, but democracy was always the political standard by which Chilean governments were judged. By 1960, about 70 percent of the population was living in cities. This urban population was 90 percent literate, while the national literacy rate, including the rural areas, was 84 percent. Large parts of the Chilean population were exposed to radio and television, and newspapers and magazines had a wide circulation.

Prior to Allende's coming to power, the leading party was the Christian Democrats, who sought to win political support from the large number of new voters through mass communications. They succeeded in attracting many voters with their agrarian and social reforms and modernization, always within a democratic context. In the area of communications, President Eduardo Frei's government, just prior to Allende's, established a national television network, created a chain of pro-government radio stations, guaranteed the right of reply in the media, and regulated the access of political parties to privately owned media during elections.[1]

1. Carlos Catalan, "Mass Media and the Collapse of a Democratic Tradition in Chile," in

Chile's peasants and urban poor, however, did not benefit as much as other groups from the many changes, and in 1970 they supported the reform socialist Allende, enabling him to win the presidency in a multicandidate race with only 36.2 percent of the vote. An important factor was the decision of the Catholic Church to take no stand in the campaign, clearing the way for voters to cast their ballots for a socialist. Allende began a program of wholesale nationalization, but more militant members of his Unidad Popular government launched "People's Power": peasant councils seized farms in the countryside, and workers' assemblies occupied factories. Inflation soared to 190 percent, the highest in Latin America. Massive discontent spread as the middle class and then the workers began to strike. Allende ordered the police to contain the extreme leftists, who were smuggling in arms, but also accused the army of planning to overthrow him.

In early September 1973, the embattled president allowed a demonstration of 750,000 people in the capital of Santiago on the anniversary of his election, so alarming the military that a week later General Augusto Pinochet, who had been appointed by Allende, led a coup, with legal backing, of all three branches of the armed forces. It was not a bloodless overthrow: Allende died, probably by suicide, and the official death toll was 2,796.[2] But the majority of the Chilean people were weary of rampant inflation, empty shops, and social chaos, and welcomed the authoritarian rule of Pinochet, expecting that before long Chile would resume its traditional democratic ways. They were to wait far longer than anyone anticipated.

PINOCHET: THE GOOD AND THE BAD

The Pinochet regime was a mix of the economic good and the political bad: serious human rights violations and political oppression existed alongside a free market and a steadily expanding economy. Responding to Chile's century-old democratic tradition, the government at last approved the writing of a constitution in 1980 that mandated a plebiscite in 1988 about the political future of the country. The junta endorsed the constitution, in an attempt to gain legitimacy abroad and in the belief that the people would reward the government for the economic gains and political

Media and Politics in Latin America: The Struggle for Democracy, ed. Elizabeth Fox (London: Sage Publications, 1988), pp. 46–48.

2. Paul Johnson, *Modern Times: The World from the Twenties to the Eighties* (New York: Harper & Row, 1983), pp. 724–25.

stability it had unquestionably provided. After all, the Pinochet regime had privatized state-owned enterprises and social security, deregulated financial markets, passed laws protecting the rights of foreign investors, reduced tariffs, abolished many business regulations, cut government spending and taxes, and reformed labor laws. It had produced, in fact, the freest economy in Latin America. But Pinochet and the other generals did not adequately consider the human desire for political as well as economic freedom, nor did they think that the opposition, divided among sixteen different parties, would be able to forge an effective political organization.

The media were a major consideration on both sides because Chile has a significant media infrastructure: it has, for example, the oldest Spanish-language newspaper in the world, *El Mercurio*. During the Pinochet era, *El Mercurio* and *La Tercera de la Hora* were pro-government newspapers (the latter was financially helped by government loans on several occasions), but by 1987, there were also two opposition dailies, *La Epoca* and *Fortin Mapocho*, as well as several left-of-center weekly magazines. The appearance of an opposition press and the ending of the need to obtain official permission before launching a new newspaper marked the close of the authoritarian period and the beginning of an *apertura* (political opening) under Pinochet, who was reacting to internal and external political pressure.

Always a prominent part of the opposition media were Catholic journals like *Mensaje* (*Message*) and *Solidaridad,* the church's first sociopolitical publication. The Catholic Church also maintained five radio stations, including Radio Chilena, run by the Salesians in Santiago. In predominantly Catholic Chile, the Catholic media made a difference. *Solidaridad,* for example, kept accusing the police of brutality and human rights violations, until Pinochet was forced to appoint a special prosecutor who handed down several indictments. Chile also had outspoken political magazines like *Analisis,* which was consistently critical of Pinochet, a risky practice in an authoritarian state. After a failed assassination attempt on Pinochet in 1987, *Analisis's* foreign editor, Jose Carrasro, was kidnapped and murdered the very next day.[3] Nevertheless, publishers continued to put out articles critical of the regime, with only one taboo: General

3. Michael B. Salwen, Bruce Garrison, and Robert T. Buckman, "Latin America and the Caribbean," in *Global Journalism: Survey of International Communication,* 2d ed., ed. John C. Merrill (New York: Longman, 1991), pp. 277, 287; Manuel Delano, "Paralyzing Fear Gives Way to Hope," *IPI Report,* November 1990, p. 12; Jerry W. Knudson, "Chile's Catholic Opposition Press," *The Christian Century,* December 10, 1986, p. 1122.

Pinochet's family. The broadcast media were a different matter, remaining under the firm control of the Pinochet regime until its final months.

PRIVATE RADIO, PUBLIC TELEVISION

From its birth in the 1920s, radio in Chile was almost entirely a private commercial enterprise, while the control of television was given by the government in the early 1960s to the two universities located in Santiago. Chilean television experienced scant impact or growth until Frei's Christian Democratic administration, which in 1970 authorized a third station intended to promote his party. But the election of Allende and his Marxist regime divided the nation and caught up the media, like everyone else, in a bitter ideological struggle. In August 1973, the Chamber of Deputies, controlled by an anti-Allende coalition, declared that there had been a collapse of democratic institutions, including the mass media, as a result of the Allende government's assumption of total power. This declaration was used as a legal justification for the military coup that soon followed.[4] The Pinochet government left the government-university system of TV ownership essentially intact, even allowing two more universities to establish stations.

Although he was a Latino authoritarian, not a Marxist totalitarian, Pinochet determined, like Leonid Brezhnev and Deng Xiaoping, to make television a primary carrier of government information and propaganda. He was motivated in part by the peculiar geography of Chile: With its many mountains and narrow 2,650-mile-long shape, the country lends itself to electronic and satellite transmissions. Starting in the late 1970s, Pinochet set out to put a television set in every Chilean household. His government subsidized prices to encourage imports and eased credit to facilitate the purchase of sets. By 1988, the year of the plebiscite, between 75 and 80 percent of all families had television. Chile also had one of the largest radio audiences in Latin America, with 1,100 sets per one thousand population.

The final necessary condition for meaningful *mediapolitik* in Chile was confirmed by a 1988 poll, which reported that 41 percent of Chileans considered radio to be the most believable news medium, in large part because of the independent Catholic radio stations. Twenty-seven percent said they considered newspapers and magazines the most believable, and only 14 percent said that of television, which was seen as controlled by the

4. Catalan, "Mass Media and the Collapse of a Democratic Tradition," p. 55.

government. Paradoxically, two-thirds of the same respondents also stated that television was their main source of news and information. "People don't believe the information they get from TV," one analyst said, "but they act on the information they have, which they usually get from television." The same phenomenon occurred in the Soviet Union, where viewers learned to sift through the official televised news to determine who of the top leadership was in or out, what were the economic priorities of the Politburo, and whether the Kremlin considered a particular foreign nation to be a friend or an enemy.

THE GOVERNMENT'S MANY ADVANTAGES

The Pinochet government began its plebiscite campaign with a formidable arsenal of political weapons, including an overflowing war chest, a disciplined cadre of workers, the only nationally known candidate, its excellent economic record, and command of the mass media. Opinion polls also revealed that fear and apathy were strong in a society where political activity had been repressed for nearly fifteen years. The Communists, supported by nearly 40 percent of the voters in the 1970 election which elected Allende, remained banned, while democratic leaders, in the words of one observer, "struggled to regain legitimacy and cohesion after years of dormancy."[5]

In 1987, well in advance of the formal campaign, the Pinochet regime began a daily schedule of "public service" television spots, contrasting the present prosperous and peaceful Chile with the strikes and violence of the Allende era. Dressed in civilian clothes and projecting a grandfatherly image, Pinochet appeared at crowded rallies that were replayed on the evening television news. Like the big city organizations of the United States in the nineteenth century and early twentieth century, the political machines of mayors and governors were enlisted by the Chilean government. Public offices served openly as political headquarters, and people on welfare received letters suggesting they might lose their benefits if the no vote won. Pro-regime workers were offered extra benefits ranging from sacks of flour to bicycles.[6]

The first media breakthrough for the opposition came in March 1988

5. David Marash, "What Television Did to Chile's Election," *Christian Science Monitor*, October 20, 1988.

6. Arturo Valenzuela and Pamela Constable, "The Chilean Plebiscite: Defeat of a Dictator," *Current History*, March 1989, pp. 129–30.

when for the first time in nearly fifteen years of military rule, it was given time on national television to present its views. Calling the government a "dictatorship," four leaders of the Christian Democratic Party urged the country to vote no in the plebiscite in which Chileans would be asked to accept or reject the junta's candidate for president (as yet unannounced, although it was widely assumed it would be Pinochet). The program was presented over the Catholic University station controlled by the Catholic Church, which supported the opposition's demands for greater access to the media. In January, the University of Chile television had begun airing a weekly program of political debates, but that station barely reached beyond Santiago, whereas the Catholic channel had a nationwide audience.[7]

A NOT SO MINOR CONCESSION

The junta made a fateful decision in early August, giving in to internal pressure from the opposition and the Catholic Church as well as external pressure from the United States and the United Nations, when it banned paid political advertising on television but allowed thirty minutes of free time daily during the campaign leading up to the presidential plebiscite. It was announced that the thirty minutes would be shared equally by the Pinochet government and the opposition and would be broadcast by all television channels. From the perspective of the government, it was a minor concession, a way of demonstrating fairness but with little risk. What possible impact could fifteen minutes a day have on a people who had been subjected to a daily diet of government propaganda on radio and television and in newspapers and magazines for fifteen years?

Meanwhile, a national voter registration effort, requiring all voters to obtain a new identity card, was under way. Pinochet's advisers expected, and wanted, fewer than five million of the eight million eligible Chileans to register. Opposition leaders estimated that they needed at least 6.5 million registrants if they were to have a chance; before they were through, they had succeeded in helping 7.4 million Chileans to present their identity papers and register. One of their innovations was registration through rock-and-roll. When it became clear that large numbers of eighteen- to twenty-five-year-olds were not signing up, the Civic Crusade persuaded popular Chilean singers to give a series of rock concerts during July and August. Admission was free to anyone who showed a voter registration

7. "Opponents Present Their Views on Chile National Television," Reuters, March 29, 1988.

card at the concert gate, and interest in performing their civic duty increased dramatically among young Chileans.[8] To discourage voter fraud, the opposition set up parallel computer systems, including a quick-count system run by the independent Committee for Free Elections. This ballot security effort "proved crucial in convincing key government supporters" to accept the results on election night.[9]

In late August, the regime again acceded to demands from Christian Democrats and the Catholic Church, which had long called for democratic reform, and lifted the state of emergency. Pinochet, seeking to project an image of moderation and tolerance, declared that all remaining political exiles—about 430 people—would be allowed to return. It was then announced, with appropriate alarums and flourishes, that General Pinochet would be the government's candidate in a vote to be held on October 5. The military ignored the Catholic bishops' call for a "consensus candidate," as well as the suggestion from conservatives who supported the Pinochet government that a civilian stood the best chance of winning. Over national television, a far-from-humble Pinochet accepted the nomination, arguing that he needed another eight years (which he would have if he won the plebiscite) to complete the task of freeing Chile from Marxism. "Liberty," he warned, "can be an instrument of its own death." Pinochet's nomination and heavy-handed speech were greeted with mass protests, and police fought demonstrators far into the night. The following day, an opposition spokesman, Patricio Aylwin, called Pinochet's nomination a "challenge to the moral conscience of Chileans."[10] The stage was set for what the junta, notwithstanding the widespread demonstrations, thought would be an easy electoral victory and vindication for the benevolent authoritarianism of Augusto Pinochet. A series of powerful fifteen-minute television programs by the opposition soon awakened them to the possibility of a far different result.

THE BATTLE OF THE AIRWAVES

The television camera focused on the tiny middle-aged woman who in her soft voice described the terrible things that had happened to her: "Af-

8. Barbara Boggs Sigmund, "A Lesson in Bravery and Democracy," *America*, October 29, 1988, p. 309.

9. Eugene Robinson, "Gen. Pinochet Came a Cropper According to His Own Rules," *Washington Post*, October 9, 1988; Valenzuela and Constable, "The Chilean Plebiscite," p. 130.

10. Ibid., p. 131.

ter the coup [in 1973] I was kidnapped from my home and taken to an unknown place, blindfolded, where I was tortured. . . . I've never told everything what happened, out of respect for my children, my husband and my
family and out of self-respect. The physical tortures . . . you can erase, but
I don't believe you can erase the moral tortures so easily. For this I am going to vote 'no,' so that tomorrow we can all live together in a free democracy, without hate, with love and happiness." An athletic young man then
entered, tenderly put his arm around the woman, and said he too would
vote no to General Pinochet "because her sentiments are my sentiments
. . . because this beautiful woman is my mother." It was an electrifying moment for the viewing audience: the young man was Carlos Caszely, a famous Chilean soccer player, and only at that instant did the public learn of
his mother's torture and torment. It was, the *Washington Post*'s Eugene
Robinson wrote, "the most memorable three minutes thus far in the battle
of the airwaves" between the "yes" and "no" campaigns.[11]

From the beginning, the opposition's television was sophisticated and
professional, produced by the country's best cinematographers, advertising executives, and producers. Its first broadcast on September 5 opened
with a montage of uplifting scenes reminiscent of the Ronald Reagan political ads of 1980 and 1984. A handsome young man strolled down a country lane; two people in back-to-back telephone booths discovered they
had been talking to each other; a smiling man in a chef's hat turned to reveal a T-shirt with the trademark rainbow of the "no" campaign. In the
background could be heard the campaign theme song, "Chile, Joy Is Coming," which ended, "We're going to say 'No'!"—causing one observer to
suggest that it may be the first time in history that "a dictatorship has been
beaten by a song." Hosting the nightly programs was Patricio Banados, a
respected television anchorman, who had been forced from his job five
years earlier after arousing the ire of the Pinochet regime.[12] The television
spots appeared every night at 10:45 P.M., with "yes" going first one night
and "no" the next; on weekends, the political ads ran at noon. The opposition had a simple and clear message, an authoritative voice, and a powerful medium at its disposal, but was fifteen minutes a night enough to overcome the formidable resources of the government?

11. Eugene Robinson, "Pinochet's Opponents Put Case on Prime-Time TV," *Washington
Post,* September 28, 1988; James F. Smith, "Supporters and Foes of Pinochet Display Contrasting Images," *Los Angeles Times,* September 22, 1988.
12. Sigmund, "A Lesson in Bravery," p. 309; Robinson, "Pinochet's Opponents Put Case
on Prime-Time TV."

With Chile in its third year of 5 percent growth and inflation at less than 20 percent annually, government officials were convinced that their campaign theme of "Chile: A Winning Country" would prevail. However, the initial "yes" television ads were disjointed and predictable, with some parties in the "yes" coalition insisting on presenting separate appeals. In contrast to the seamless quality of the opposition's programs, the government's broadcasts resembled a haphazard patchwork quilt. Business and other leaders complained to Pinochet, and soon the "yes" campaign adopted the opposition's device of an anchor and an opening segment complete with theme song. It also turned sharply negative, warning that a "no" vote was a vote for a return to the violent years of Salvador Allende and Communism.

The government placed ads in newspapers and magazines displaying the word "No" against the black and red flag of Chile's left-wing guerrilla movement, the Manuel Rodriquez Democratic Front. On television, ads would plunge viewers into a dangerous world filled with dark, foggy streets and ominous music. A woman clutching a baby dashed for her car as bands of men waved red banners. A threatening face loomed, a machine gun smashed the windshield, and the camera froze on the young mother's face. "If we return to the past," warned the announcer's voice, "the first innocent victim could be in your family."[13] Other menacing images of the "yes" campaign included:

• A rock thrower, highlighted by a circle, attacked police officers during a demonstration while the announcer urged, "Vote 'yes' so that this man will never govern this country."

• A badly burned victim of a terrorist attack on a bus declared that he would vote yes for peace.

• An old woman reached the head of a line to buy tea only to find there was none—a reminder of the massive shortages under Marxist President Allende. Other women in the line cried while the announcer reminded viewers that in present-day Chile, "We have plenty."

The government used every possible propaganda device. One evening the "yes" program appeared to sign off, and the "no" program began with its theme song, "Chile, Joy Is Coming," along with the campaign's rainbow

13. Valenzuela and Constable, "The Chilean Plebiscite," p. 132; Pamela Constable and Arturo Valenzuela, "Pinochet Trading on Fears of Allende," *Boston Globe*, October 2, 1988; "Chile: Will They Throw Him Out," *The Economist*, October 11, 1988, p. 45.

colors. But suddenly scenes of a riot flashed on the screen.[14] The "no" campaign protested, but the "yes" campaign persisted in its misleading tactics. Another night, the "yes" program highlighted differences within opposition ranks by splicing together taped interviews of Socialist Ricardo Lagos and Christian Democrat Patricio Aylwin. On one half of the screen, Lagos was saying that he had served Salvador Allende's Marxist government with honor, noting, "Of course, I am a socialist." Beside him, Aylwin, in a 1973 interview, praised Pinochet's military coup against Allende and accused the socialists of ruining the country.[15]

MISREADING THE MOOD OF THE PEOPLE

Arrogant and out of touch with the mood of the country he had led for fifteen years, Pinochet believed that he could depend for support on the newly prosperous middle class and the state-dependent poor, both groups vulnerable to the threat of change. But an increasing number of polls showed that for a majority of voters, "the desire to return to civilian rule [was] stronger than the fear of socialism or state reprisal." The people were tired of living in a garrison state, however comfortable most of them were. Each day, and each night, the opposition grew stronger in its televised appeals to those who despised Pinochet, who resented the regime's indifference to Chile's democratic tradition and who had not benefitted under the government's free market approach.[16] The sixteen parties making up the opposition argued frequently and vocally about campaign strategy but closed ranks as the plebiscite drew nearer. The two most fractious members were the still-outlawed Communist Party, which initially called the vote a fraudulent exercise but at last declared its intention to work for a "no" victory; and the rightist National Party, which split over Pinochet's candidacy but then, through its majority faction, joined the campaign against him.[17]

While maintaining its positive campaign theme, "Chile, Joy Is Coming," the opposition also displayed a willingness to confront controversial issues. With less than two weeks to go, one "no" program opened with mothers of the "disappeared" (young people presumably seized and executed by the military) dancing by themselves in a bare hall, with photo-

14. Smith, "Supporters and Foes of Pinochet."

15. "Pinochet Pulls Plug on Foes' Ad," *Chicago Tribune*, September 14, 1988.

16. Constable and Valenzuela, "Pinochet Trading on Fears of Allende."

17. Cynthia Brown, "Democracy vs. Fear and Propaganda," *The Nation*, October 3, 1988, p. 275.

graphs of their sons and daughters pinned on their blouses. It was riveting television. Also broadcast was a concert in Barcelona, Spain, by the British rock star Sting, who sang an ode to the mothers, "They Dance Alone," and told the cheering crowd: "Chileans deserve a democratic life."[18]

In past elections, mass rallies had been a key campaign technique, but with the country's urbanization and Pinochet's campaign to put a television set in every household, television assumed a central political importance. After the plebiscite, a survey by the Center for Public Studies reported that 93 percent of registered voters had watched the programs.[19] Instead of being the means by which the military rulers would shape the future of the nation, television became the means of their downfall. Outside foreign media played only a minor role in the Chilean plebiscite: the Voice of America does not broadcast into any Latin American nation, except Cuba through its Radio Marti; and there is no Latino equivalent of Radio Free Europe or Radio Liberty, even for Cuba. But the opposition brilliantly employed American techniques in their anti-Pinochet pro-democracy programs.

Despite the widespread desire for an end to Pinochet's authoritarian rule, surveys revealed that many voters were uncertain about the competence of the opposition and the safety of a "no" vote. However, nightly evidence that opponents of Pinochet could suggest a democratic future for Chile, without advocating violence or political irresponsibility, "reassured these people and sustained a vote for political change." By allowing the opposition to operate freely in the world of television—although at least one "no" broadcast was pulled when government censors refused to let a respected judge refer to testimony by torture victims—Pinochet gave his opponents political credibility. "In democracy-starved, media-saturated Chile," the journalist David Marash commented, that was an enormous plus for the opposition. Resolving the question of whether it was safe to vote "no" was more difficult. Reports circulated that the police were harassing opposition meetings and seizing voter registration cards. "We all feared that if the 'yes' won," said one "no" leader, "we would have to go into hiding."[20]

In the days leading up to the plebiscite, the far left hurt the "no" cause

---

18. Smith, "Supporters and Foes of Pinochet."
19. Valenzuela and Constable, "The Chilean Plebiscite," p. 131.
20. Marash, "What Television Did to Chile's Election"; Valenzuela and Constable, "The Chilean Plebiscite," p. 132.

and justified the dark warnings of the government by making inflammatory statements, holding street protests in major cities, and calling for a "provisional government" to replace Pinochet. The week before the vote, power stations were dynamited and pamphlets appeared urging the people to take to the streets on election night. Alarmed by extremist tactics that played into the hands of the Pinochet regime, the democratic opposition met with Marxist leaders and obtained an agreement that leftist violence would cease.[21]

THE WILL OF THE PEOPLE

After all the tension, charges, and countercharges, election day came as a relief and a surprise. Many had predicted that the government would never allow the voting to take place, particularly as several polls showed the "yes" campaign running as much as 10 percent behind the "no" campaign. The presence of a large delegation of outside observers from the United States and other Western democracies helped protect the process. The National Endowment for Democracy (NED), founded by the U.S. Congress to foster democracy in foreign countries, spent $1 million to help the Chilean opposition with its registration drive and get-out-the-vote effort. Computers were purchased for independent vote-counting systems, polls were commissioned, and campaign literature was published. American consultants frequently traveled to Chile, but they did not run the campaign: "It was a perfect marriage of their leadership and our experience," commented Kenneth Wollack, vice president of the National Democratic Institute for International Affairs.[22]

Opposition leaders resolved personal jealousies and agreed on a single campaign spokesman—Christian Democratic leader Patricio Aylwin—who handled the responsibility so skillfully that he was later elected president of Chile. Throughout election day, as the historians Arturo Valenzuela and Pamela Constable have recounted, Aylwin used the opposition radio station *Cooperativa* to urge supporters "to vote early, to go home and to stay off the streets until the final results had been confirmed." Aware of the high political stakes, people dutifully voted in the early morning, often dressed in their Sunday clothes, and by midafternoon many polling places were empty. For their part, the armed forces, charged

21. Ibid.
22. Barbara Gamarekian, "How Washington Pros Get Out the Vote in Chile," *New York Times*, November 18, 1988.

with maintaining order at each site, behaved with restraint, and few incidents were reported by the many opposition or independent poll watchers.[23]

As it developed, getting out the vote was one thing and finding out the vote was another. The government had said that it would begin announcing the results as early as 6 P.M., but by 7:35 its spokesman, Alberto Cardemil, had not yet appeared. The "no" campaign, with its own network of poll watchers and vote counters, knew it was winning by a comfortable margin and began worrying about vote fraud. Finally, Cardemil announced results, but only from seventy-nine polling places that showed Pinochet ahead. He promised more figures soon, but an hour passed and then another hour, and Cardemil did not reappear. Opposition leaders had said they would not release any results until at least half a million votes were in, but now they wavered, wondering what the government was up to. It was confirmed later that top aides of the Ministry of the Interior had proposed releasing a false count of one million votes showing the "yes" ahead. This would have inspired "yes" supporters to fill the streets claiming victory, which in turn would have provoked violent counter-demonstrations by "no" supporters. The Interior officials had also asked the police and the military to withdraw from downtown Santiago, hoping that the violence would bring military intervention and even cancellation of the plebiscite.[24]

At this critical moment, the "no" campaign announced that with 200,000 votes counted, it was winning soundly. Caught in a democratic process of its own making and unwilling, with hundreds of foreign observers present, to precipitate a bloody confrontation, the government ordered Cardemil to release more figures showing Pinochet still winning, although by a smaller margin. The opposition immediately responded with a series of announcements, with totals of half a million, a million, and 1.5 million votes, each showing that "no" was winning handily. All along, the government-controlled television stations had been repeating the regime's misleading figures. But Channel 13, run by the Catholic University of Chile, reported the "no" figures as well and described the government's totals as too small to be significant.

The Catholic station then made a crucial programming decision, based

23. Valenzuela and Constable, "The Chilean Plebiscite," p. 132.

24. Robinson, "Gen. Pinochet Came a Cropper"; Valenzuela and Constable, "The Chilean Plebiscite," p. 132.

on the model of liberal democratic *mediapolitik,* that helped tip the scales in favor of the opposition. Shortly after midnight, with the government still unwilling to release additional figures, Channel 13 presented a discussion between Patricio Alwyn, spokesman for the opposition, and Sergio Onofre Jarpa, a former minister of the interior and leader of a conservative party that backed Pinochet. Alwyn gave the latest vote totals, and Jarpa agreed that "no" had won. The reporters interviewing the two politicians began to phrase their questions on the assumption that Pinochet had lost, and the national audience watching the program began to realize that democracy, against incredible odds, had won in Chile.[25]

Public tension increased sharply when Pinochet convened a meeting of the junta and his cabinet at the presidential palace. But on his way into the palace, Air Force General Fernando Matthei, a member of the junta, commented to a reporter that as far as he was concerned the "no" had won. Matthei's statement was definitive and preemptive: no one could ignore an admission of defeat by one of the country's four military leaders. The acceptance of the "no" vote by Pinochet supporters like Jarpa and Matthei and the refusal of police and army officials to withdraw their troops ensured peaceful acceptance of the results. At 2:40 A.M., ashen-faced Interior Minister Sergio Fernandez conceded at a televised news conference that the government had lost, and as the manager of the losing campaign he offered his resignation. The final tally, with 7.2 million votes cast was 54.7 percent, "no," 43 percent, "yes."[26]

WHY PINOCHET LOST

Why did General Pinochet lose? First, he had allowed the plebiscite because he was convinced he would win; he was eager to prove to the world that, in the minds of the Chilean people, his regime was not a pariah but a legitimate government. He and other officials believed their own propaganda about the "new" Chile, which had benefitted many economically, but had not satisfied the deep-rooted desire for political freedom, an integral part of the Chilean tradition. They trusted the always optimistic findings of the regime's dubious opinion polls; as is frequently the case in authoritarian and especially in totalitarian regimes, the pollsters were exceedingly reluctant to report the truth.

Second, the regime's contempt for politics led them to ignore people in

25. Robinson, "Gen. Pinochet Came a Cropper."
26. Ibid.

their camp who had a far better notion of how to run political campaigns. Several members of the military and the business community, for example, felt that a civilian leader rather than the general himself should be the candidate of the "yes" campaign. The *caudillo* scoffed at the suggestion, certain that the people were grateful to him for ending the chaos of the Allende years and producing the prosperity of the last decade. Pinochet made the election a referendum about himself, and given the opportunity, the people voted against an aging, authoritarian general's leading them almost to the end of the century. In allowing the regime to become one man, Pinochet violated the democratic principle of government as a prudent balance of laws and men.

Third, the government allowed the opposition to mount an effective campaign and to install a system to verify the results, making it almost impossible to challenge the electoral process. Each vote was counted in front of opposition representatives, and the "no" campaign prepared three tabulating systems to prevent any Mexico-style tampering. Ironically, after having helped put Pinochet into power in 1973—by playing a pivotal role in toppling Allende—the United States now used its leverage to help remove the general through the ballot box. The Reagan administration put international pressure on the junta by sponsoring a U.N. Human Rights Commission denunciation of Chile in 1986. And through the National Endowment for Democracy the administration funneled more than $1 million to opposition groups to help register voters. In the final days, responding to persistent rumors, the State Department warned the Pinochet government not to delay or cancel the election.[27]

Fourth, the calm behavior of the Chilean voters who voted early and then went home prevented reactionary elements of the government from attempting any scenario based on confrontation. Violence was also prevented when the police and the military did not withdraw but remained in the downtown areas as visible symbols of law, order, and due process.

A fifth element was Chile's legal tradition, which bound 7.4 million voters to follow "an imperfect and dictatorially mandated process" but also compelled Pinochet to "bow to the consequences." Once they realized they had lost, decisively and fairly, neither civilian conservatives nor military officers were willing to abrogate the political contract they had drawn up and publicly signed.[28]

---

27. John Greenwald, "Fall of the Patriarch," *Time,* October 17, 1988, pp. 36–37.
28. Valenzuela and Constable, "The Chilean Plebiscite," p. 152.

DEMOCRATIC MEDIAPOLITIK

One more crucial factor helped make all of the above possible—the mass media. If a democratic model of *mediapolitik* had not functioned during the last month of the 1988 plebiscite, Pinochet would not have been defeated, and democracy would not have been restored in Chile. Although not a perfect liberal democratic model, the *mediapolitik* of the plebiscite was characterized, for example, by a general absence of government censorship. The "no" campaign—except for the one program when a judge was not allowed to discuss the cases of more than fifty people who, he said, had been tortured by Chilean secret police—was allowed to present whatever it wanted on television to persuade the people to vote against Pinochet. The rights of the democratic opposition were protected by the 1980 constitution, approved by the junta. By their participation in the plebiscite, both the government and the opposition were agreeing that politics and the media serve the governed, not the government. The "no" campaign was explicitly committed to democratic principles and institutions. The "yes" campaign, whatever its original intent and however cynical its motivations, returned constitutional democracy to Chile by accepting the results of the plebiscite.

How important were the mass media of Chile? As one "no" spokesman put it, exaggerating as victors are prone to do, "in fifteen minutes' television time, we destroyed fifteen years of government publicity for the dictatorship."[29] Given equal standing with the government on the most powerful medium in the country, the opposition became a credible, then a major, and finally a winning political force. It demonstrated competence and offered a vision of democracy, justice, and joy that won the votes of the Chilean people.

If the government had implemented an authoritarian model of *mediapolitik* in the election, strictly controlling the political content of the media, the "no" campaign would not have been given those magical fifteen minutes every night, and it would not have been able to lay the media foundation for its politically successful campaign. Pinochet, like Gorbachev, was confident that he could use the mass media to his own ends. But his authoritarian brand of *realpolitik* was soundly defeated by a democratic model of *mediapolitik*.

29. Leonard Sussman, *Power, the Press and the Technology of Freedom: The Coming Age of ISDN* (New York: Freedom House, 1989), p. 227.

After the election, Juan Pablo Carnenas, editor-in-chief of *Analisis,* commented that "information is now stronger than any ideology, army or tyrant." To which this caveat must be added: information can be stronger than any ideology *if* the information is transmitted through a mass media protected by laws and a constitution and rooted in democratic principles. The rule of law in democratic *mediapolitik* is essential. The democratic idea and modern media, the political scientist Douglas W. Payne points out, have combined to present "the first serious challenge to the age-old Latin [American] idea that power is more important than law."[30] General Augusto Pinochet of Chile can attest that with all the economic and political power at his command, he could not overcome the nightly impact of fifteen minutes of creative, dramatic, pro-democracy television on the minds, hearts, and votes of the Chilean people.

30. J. Senen Conejeros, interview, *IPI Report,* November 1991, p. 20; Douglas W. Payne, "Latin American Democracy: In Search of the Rule of Law," *Freedom Review,* January–February 1992, pp. 48–50.

CHAPTER 10

THE ENDING OF APARTHEID

ALL SOUTH AFRICAN POLITICS is racial. Blacks and whites have been contesting each other for control of this mineral-rich, fertile land since Dutch settlers first landed in Cape Town in the mid-1600s. The great difference in the twentieth century is that the whites, led by the Boers or Afrikaners, used the law, not just raw force, to create an authoritarian state based upon race. Prior to World War I, strikes by blacks were made illegal, certain jobs were reserved for whites, and the Natives Land Act established the principle of territorial segregation by color. In the 1920s, political institutions were segregated, and the Native Urban Areas Act created all-African residential areas in and near towns. The Native Administration Act gave the white government almost total power to appoint African leaders, define tribal boundaries, move tribes and individuals, and control African courts and land ownership. Section 29 called for punishment of "any person who utters any words or does any other act or thing whatever with intent to promote any feeling of hostility between Natives and Europeans."[1]

In the first post–World War II elections, held in 1948, the Nationalist Party embarked on a reign of power under a series of prime ministers, including H. F. Verwoerd and B. J. Vorster, who turned South Africa into an independent republic outside the British Commonwealth and an authoritarian state based on racial discrimination. To maintain their political and

---

1. Paul Johnson, *Modern Times: The World from the Twenties to the Eighties* (New York: Harper & Row, 1983), p. 521.

economic dominance, the Nationalists adopted a policy of apartheid, which sought to place the black Africans in separate territories, called Bantustans, which would be economically self-sufficient racial enclaves within a South African state ruled by whites. Apartheid was scientifically flawed (even South African scientists admitted that blacks were not biologically inferior to whites); economically unsound (the native areas could never become viable except at an unacceptably high cost to whites); and politically unrealistic (the black majority would inevitably learn what was happening in the rest of Africa and the world and would not accept permanent servitude at the hands of an ever-diminishing white minority). Finally, as Peter Calvocoressi, a British political scientist, points out, proponents of apartheid underestimated how much their policies would force them to rule by violence and repression and thereby attract international attention and condemnation.[2]

The global campaign for economic sanctions against South Africa developed in the sixties but was not then supported by either the American or British governments because of the presence of Soviet power and surrogates in the region. But in the late 1970s, partly through the human rights diplomacy of the Carter administration and partly through congressional initiatives, American policy toward South Africa began to take an openly antiapartheid turn. The Reagan administration sought to reverse this trend through a policy of "constructive engagement," emphasizing moral influence and mutual interests rather than criticism and coercion to bring about regional stability, Cuban and Soviet withdrawal from southern Africa, and internal reform in South Africa. By the end of the Reagan years, a persistent Chester Crocker, assistant secretary of state for African affairs, had succeeded in obtaining an agreement from the South Africans to withdraw their forces from Angola as the fifty thousand Soviet-backed Cuban troops also withdrew. One of the oldest conflicts of the cold war seemed close to being resolved.

Meanwhile U.S. public opposition to the white government of South Africa grew rapidly, fueled by President P. W. Botha's draconian acts against blacks, such as declaring a state of emergency and arresting hundreds of suspected dissidents, including children under the age of eleven. To head off congressionally imposed economic sanctions, President Reagan approved less stringent measures by executive order, describing them as an example of "active constructive engagement." But as the 1980s drew

2. Peter Calvocoressi, *World Politics Since 1945*, 5th ed. (London: Longman, 1987), p. 422.

to a close, the possibilities for peace and reform in South Africa were not promising. The Nationalists were still in power, black African leaders, except for a scattered few like the Nobel laureate Desmond Tutu, were in exile or in jail, and it seemed likely that the authoritarian methods deemed necessary by Pretoria to maintain apartheid would continue for some time to come.[3]

MEDIAPOLITIK AND APARTHEID

Advocates of economic sanctions argue that the South African government finally moved to dismantle apartheid because it could no longer resist international economic and political pressure. While the very real pain inflicted on the South African people, black as well as white, by the global boycott is undeniable, the mass media clearly played a decisive role in the ending of apartheid. Without the extensive coverage by the media, external and internal, Nelson Mandela would not have emerged as the charismatic, even messianic black leader who negotiated on an equal basis with the white leadership about the future of South Africa. The live television broadcast of the freeing of Mandela after twenty-seven years in prison, his first public address in nearly three decades, and similar dramatic events in the early months of 1990 were made possible by a reversal of policy by President F. W. de Klerk, who abandoned government censorship and freed the media in a calculated attempt to change world public opinion that had been running so strongly against his government. No better example of the dynamic interplay of politics and media, of how *mediapolitik* can change the course of a nation, could be found.

For an advanced industrial country, South Africa came very late to television, launching a single state-owned channel in 1976 under the aegis of the South African Broadcasting Corporation (SABC), broadcasting alternately in English and Afrikaans. The government's official explanation for its opposition to television was usually stated in nonracist terms: the medium was too commercial, too addictive, too Hollywood; it was bad for reading, family life, and South Africa's distinctive culture. But the real reason was that U.S. programming would have undercut the policy of apartheid, with its pictures of blacks—Martin Luther King, Jr., Thurgood Marshall, mayors, and congressmen—participating in and often playing a leading role in American politics and society.

3. James A. Nathan and James K. Oliver, *United States Foreign Policy and World Order*, 4th ed. (Glenview, Ill.: Scott, Foresman and Company, 1989), p. 477.

Despite these fears, which proved valid, Pretoria finally permitted television because white South Africans wanted to enjoy its entertainment and information. Consumer choice prevailed over ideological control in spite of the authoritarian nature of the regime. Television was instantly popular, with some three million sets sold within the first three years, outnumbering the total sets in use in all of the rest of Africa.[4] Although the initial channel offered only a "European" program (two black channels did not begin until 1982), a considerable number of black Africans also bought television sets. Data indicated that while whites had more access, blacks watched more television, even the European program. By 1988, almost eight out of ten whites watched television at night while one in ten blacks nationwide tuned in. Since television was rare in rural black areas, the black township figure was undoubtedly much higher.[5]

The low literacy rate among Africans combined with the tradition of oral communication made radio an ideal medium of mass communication in South Africa. Radio transistor sets were inexpensive and could run on batteries, putting them within easy reach of individuals and communities in the cities and the countryside. South Africa was in fact the first African country to introduce radio broadcasting: a station began operating out of Johannesburg in 1920. Theoretically, South Africa's radio system was an "autonomous" public corporation modeled after the BBC, but in practice, its operations were controlled by a board of directors appointed by and subservient to the government. Pretoria had always recognized the importance of radio in the conduct of politics at home and abroad. It underwrote nine full-time services that broadcast in 18 different languages for a total of 2,776 hours per week. One of the services was an all-night external service, Radio South Africa, which broadcast to Africa, Europe, and North America, in English.[6]

In contrast to the strictly controlled broadcast media, most observers, including Africans, agreed that the press of South Africa was—and still is—the freest in Africa. Although all of the daily newspapers were owned and operated by whites, several of them, particularly the English-language papers, consistently opposed apartheid. Taking strong stands against gov-

4. George H. Quester, *The International Politics of Television* (Lexington, Mass.: Lexington Books, 1990), pp. 191–92.

5. Ibid.; House Committee on Foreign Affairs, Subcommittee on Africa, *Media Restrictions in South Africa* (Washington: U.S. Government Printing Office, 1988), statement of John M. Phelan, March 15, 1988, pp. 142–43.

6. L. John Martin, "Africa," in *Global Journalism: Survey of International Communication,* 3d ed., ed. John C. Merrill (White Plains, N.Y.: Longman Publishers, 1995), pp. 181–85.

ernment policies and practices, this critical press was read by more people than the pro–National Party, pro-apartheid Afrikaans press. The opposition press frequently paid a heavy price for its criticism. While the courts were independent and usually fair in their decisions, the police were able to obtain an injunction against a newspaper if they wanted to stop publication of a story they deemed "undesirable." Prior to President de Klerk, the white government constantly sought to manage the press. In 1982, the Steyn Commission of Inquiry into the Media, appointed by President P. W. Botha, recommended to Parliament that journalists be registered and a press council be formed with powers to suspend a reporter's registration.[7] But editors and publishers protested so vehemently that the government did not attempt to implement the recommendations of the Steyn Commission; still, a chilling message had been sent to the South African press.

The media had already been operating under a semi-authoritarian model of *mediapolitik*. The new restrictions, scrupulously debated and approved by Parliament, covered every aspect of political life: (1) the Internal Security Act provided for the "banning" of individuals, preventing them from writing for or being quoted by the media; (2) the Unlawful Organizations Act made it an offense to publish anything that might "further" the aims of proscribed organizations like the African National Congress; (3) the Defense Act limited reporting on the South African Defense Force; (4) the Publications Act empowered a government agency to ban "undesirable" material, including matter considered prejudicial to the safety of the state or the general welfare of the community; (5) the Prisons Act made it an offense to publish false information about prisons without taking "reasonable" steps to ensure its accuracy, while a similar law governed reporting on the police. The measures, according to Tony Heard, a South African editor, "hogtied" the media when they tried to report on a wide range of issues, such as the "police, defense, prisons, official secrets . . . oil supply, nuclear energy, the quoting of banned persons or promoting the aims of banned organizations, remarks held to foster racial hostility, photographing or publishing pictures of prisons or prisoners," including, of course, Nelson Mandela. The Defense Act, for example, was used to keep South Africans from knowing about their army's full-scale invasion of Angola, and an editor was charged under the Internal Security Act for publishing an interview with ANC leader Oliver Tambo.[8] The government insisted

7. Ibid., p. 193.
8. House Committee, *Media Restrictions*, statement of John Oakes, pp. 9–10.

that all it was trying to do was to maintain law and order and prevent revolution and anarchy from destroying the country.

INCREASING BLACK-WHITE CONFRONTATION

But the political turmoil and violence steadily increased as the twenty-five million blacks of South Africa protested more and more angrily against the apartheid policies that protected the rights and privileges of five million whites. Confrontations between security forces and protesters in the black townships became commonplace. In March 1985, police opened fire on a group of funeral marchers in Langa Township in eastern Cape Province, killing nineteen people and igniting a storm of protest and anger in the black population. The slaughter occurred on the anniversary of the 1960 Sharpeville massacre when white police fired on an unarmed crowd of about three thousand Africans, killing eighty-three and wounding some 350, almost all of them in the back. U.S. television networks stepped up their coverage of the South African violence, and pressure began mounting in the U.S. Congress for the imposition of economic sanctions against South Africa. An alarmed Botha decided to clamp down on the violence and, no less importantly, to stop the publication or televising of pictures of white police beating and shooting blacks.

On July 20, 1985, the government declared the first state of emergency since the 1960 Sharpeville massacre, affecting thirty-six black areas in the Johannesburg and Eastern Cape regions. The decree authorized the police to close off any area and to block the publication of any news or comment concerning the state of emergency or its enforcement; it also barred, unless authorized, the publication of the names of detainees without authorization. SABC television understood the part it was to play. After a day of thrown rocks, split heads, and burning tires, in the Alexandra area, close to white Johannesburg, viewers that night saw a school ceremony of little girls dressed in white receiving their awards, only blocks away from the violence. The state of emergency, however, failed to achieve either of Botha's main objectives: August 1985 was one of the bloodiest months in the nation's history, with more than 160 persons killed in politically related violence. And foreign correspondents continued to move freely about the rest of South Africa, filing reports without restriction. That month, ABC, CBS, and NBC broadcast a total of sixty stories about the escalating violence in South Africa, a significant part of their foreign coverage.[9]

9. Ibid., p. 10; Danny Schechter, "South Africa: Where Did the Story Go?" *Africa Report*, March–April 1988, p. 27.

From late 1984 through early 1987, says Bruce W. Jentleson, an analyst at the Brookings Institution, the antiapartheid movement captured the public imagination of America as "no other protest movement had since the Vietnam War." A broad-based coalition of members of Congress, civil rights leaders, mayors, religious leaders, and other prominent citizens joined, in response to the moral dimension of the issue and because, Senate Majority Leader Robert Dole observed, apartheid had become a "domestic civil rights issue." All the necessary analogies were present to enlist the support of the American public: President Botha was the equivalent of Governor George Wallace; Bishop Desmond Tutu was Dr. Martin Luther King, Jr; and the Anti-Apartheid Act of 1985, by which the United States imposed economic sanctions on South Africa, was the Civil Rights Act of 1964. Republicans looking to draw blacks into their party supported the sanctions legislation by margins almost as large as those of the Democrats.

Supported by the coalition and heavy media coverage, the Anti-Apartheid Act of 1985 passed with veto-proof margins in the House, which had a Democratic majority, and in the Senate, with its Republican majority. The White House, which had been resisting economic sanctions, then moved to preempt Congress by issuing an executive order imposing limited trade and economic sanctions. President Reagan also denounced apartheid "as deliberate, systematic, institutionalized racial discrimination." While many Democrats were dissatisfied with the less restrictive provisions of the executive order, the measures were tough enough to prevent Congress from adopting its own sanctions package. The issue, however, was resurrected the following year in the wake of continuing violence in South Africa and the failure of the government to take more concrete steps to abolish apartheid. Congress passed the punitive Anti-Apartheid Act of 1986 by wide margins and in October overrode a Reagan veto, sending a clear warning to Pretoria that it was not moving fast enough to end apartheid.[10]

AN AUTHORITARIAN REACTION

Botha reacted as authoritarian leaders do in a moment of crisis: he tightened restrictions, particularly on the electronic media. On November 2, 1985, he forbade all camera crews, photographers, and radio reporters to report on unrest in areas covered by the state of emergency; print re-

---

10. Bruce W. Jentleson, "American Diplomacy: Around the World and along Pennsylvania Avenue," in *A Question of Balance: The President, the Congress and Foreign Policy*, ed. Thomas E. Mann (Washington: The Brookings Institution, 1990), pp. 158–60.

porters would need police permission. The government justified its censorship by blaming the media for being "part of the violence syndrome," claiming that the presence of reporters contributed to the unrest. Foreign Minister R. F. Botha (no relation to the president) said the action was taken to end the "vicious and venomous coverage by foreign TV crews." He accused the foreign press of ignoring government reform initiatives and presenting a one-sided, distorted picture of South Africa, offering television viewers abroad a "tunnel vision of South Africa aflame."[11]

Once again, however, the township violence did not subside; the number of deaths related to political violence remained high through March 1986, when the state of emergency was lifted. But without the vivid, dramatic pictures they had become accustomed to, U.S. networks curtailed their coverage: in November 1985, ABC, CBS, and NBC broadcast only twenty stories about South Africa. Peter Jennings, the ABC anchor, acknowledged that Botha's media restrictions had "worked."[12] By now there were more than 120 statutory restrictions on the media, enough to fill a thick legal volume that every South African journalist kept on his desk. Facing possible prison sentences of up to ten years and/or fines reaching $8,000, journalists prudently adhered to the laws. But there were still too many media loopholes for Pretoria. On June 12, 1986, four days before the 10th anniversary of the 1976 Soweto uprising that had sparked a year of violence and nearly 600 deaths, President Botha declared a nationwide state of emergency. It was far more comprehensive than the one he had lifted only three months earlier and applied to local and foreign journalists alike.

Photographers, broadcast media, and print journalists were forbidden to cover unrest anywhere in the country. Journalists could not publish or quote any statement deemed "subversive," including anything likely to promote civil disobedience or the objectives of an unlawful organization. The prohibition included any statement that might engender "feelings of

11. C. Anthony Giffard and Lisa Cohen, "South African TV and Censorship: Does It Reduce Negative Coverage?" *Journalism Quarterly,* Spring 1989, p. 4.

12. House Committee, *Media Restrictions,* p. 11; Schechter, "Where Did the Story Go?" p. 27. Also see Eleanor Singer and Jacob Ludwig, "South Africa's Press Restrictions: Effects on Press Coverage and Public Opinion toward South Africa," *Public Opinion Quarterly,* vol. 51:315–34. Singer and Ludwig concluded that the South African government's restrictions on press coverage of protest activities in late 1985–early 1986 did not have the effects predicted: "There was no reduction in violence in South Africa and no reduction in attentiveness or decrease in sympathy for blacks by the American public" (p. 328).

hostility in the public . . . toward any section of the public." Authorities could seize any publication deemed to contain a subversive statement. The very next day, the police confiscated copies of the *Weekly Mail* and the *Sowetan* and later told the *Sowetan* that its use of blank spaces to suggest self-censorship was subversive. Commented the editor of the alternative paper *New Nation:* "They are criminalizing all forms of dissent, and that includes the right to report on dissent."[13]

The government's Big Brother restrictions also prohibited comment or news about the actions of the security forces or those detained without authorization. A newly created Bureau of Information—actually, a Bureau of Noninformation—would be the only agency authorized to disseminate information about unrest. Although court rulings subsequently diluted some of the censorship powers wielded by the executive, in nearly every case President Botha moved quickly to close the gaps and manipulate the flow of news and information. One stratagem briefly used by the American networks to report dissident views was to beam live interviews to the United States or Europe by satellite. If the person being interviewed said something illegal, the news organization could claim it had no control over what he might say. But the government quickly banned live transmission over the satellite, so that if broadcasters taped an interview and then transmitted it, they would be held responsible for what was said.[14]

A GOVERNMENT OBSESSED

During 1986, British Prime Minister Margaret Thatcher wrote several private letters to Botha informing him that she could not hold the line on economic sanctions and urging him to press ahead with internal reform. Thatcher and Reagan agreed that harsh sanctions would not work against South Africa, but in return for their politically unpopular stance, they expected Pretoria to take serious steps toward ending apartheid.[15] Instead the Botha government increased its control over the lives of its people, particularly in the area of news and information. Previously, the government had blacked out news about political violence and what the security forces were doing in the townships. In the weeks before Christmas 1986, an

13. Jim McKenzie, "Combatting Brutal Censorship," *Content*, September/October 1988, p. 33.

14. House Committee, *Media Restrictions*, pp. 11–12; Giffard and Cohen, "South African TV and Censorship," p. 5.

15. Geoffrey Smith, *Reagan and Thatcher* (New York: W. W. Norton & Company, 1991), pp. 202–3.

accelerating campaign of antiapartheid activity, including strikes, boycotts, and anticonscription campaigns, drove Botha into expanding the
news ban to cover nonviolent protest. It was now a violation of law to report on boycotts, "restricted gatherings," and local political structures like
"people's courts." Reporters who happened to be on the scene when violence or any other "subversive activities" happened were literally obliged
to run away, "out of sight." The new decree also broadened the definition
of banned "subversive" statements to cover almost anything that encouraged resistance to the authorities, violent or nonviolent. Any publication
or recording could be banned for up to three months if found to contain
subversive material.

A large step toward prior censorship was taken when news organizations were told to telex articles to the Bureau of Information if, in the censor's judgment, their content might fall under the emergency regulations.
The following month, the Commissioner of Police banned ads and reports that furthered the cause of "unlawful organizations." When a court
voided his decree, the government responded within hours with a new
ruling that empowered the commissioner to ban publications of "any
matter." Seven months later, the government expanded the restrictions yet
again when the home minister assumed the power to suspend or censor
publications that repeatedly published material "supporting revolution."
The phrase encompassed "promoting or fanning the breaking down of the
public order" and "fomenting feelings of hatred . . . toward a local authority or a security force."[16] "1984" had truly come to South Africa.

John M. Phelan, a journalist, offered this striking comparison, which,
although exaggerated, described all too accurately the relationship between the South African government and the mass media in the late 1980s:
Imagine a United States Department of Public Media, which supervised
every radio and television operation in America and made all programming decisions. Next, imagine a U.S. Department of Public Expression,
which could inspect any book, magazine, newspaper, or other publication
and ban its sale or distribution if its contents were deemed to be un-
American, undemocratic, or Communist. Finally, imagine a Federal Media Appeal Board, which would review the censorship of the government,
"now gently chiding the Department as too narrow-minded, now castigat-
ing excessive leniency."[17]

16. House Committee, *Media Restrictions*, pp. 10–12.
17. House Committee, *Media Restrictions*, pp. 107–8.

AUTHORITARIAN CENSORSHIP

At the theoretical core of this censorship was the Leninist belief of the National Party, and leaders like P. W. Botha, that the media should be loyal to the government, help the government achieve its goals, and act, as TASS, Izvestia, and all the other Soviet propaganda organs formerly did, as members of a giant state public relations agency. The media scholar Leonard S. Sussman compared South Africa's press control techniques under Botha with those of Gorbachev during the era of *glasnost*. In both places, *glasnost*, or controlled openness, was expected to advance the interests of the state. Soviet *glasnost* encouraged limited criticism to improve the effectiveness of the centralized economy and society. South African *glasnost* increasingly used the white press to advance government policies that resisted "the sharing of real political power with the black majority." It must be said, however, that for all its calculated attempts to manage the media, the South African government did not, as Iran and Afghanistan did in the 1980s, exclude foreign correspondents completely. With its inherent respect for the law, Pretoria decided to go by the book, allowing correspondents in and then trying to control what they reported. In so acting, the government revealed that it was not a totalitarian but an authoritarian regime. Given the magnitude of the story and the aggressive nature of the foreign correspondents, such a mixed course of action was bound to fail.[18]

The media restrictions had a threefold purpose, according to the journalist John Oakes and other analysts: (1) they were intended to keep whites ignorant of the continuing unrest and violence in the black townships, thereby perpetuating the myth that the Botha government was firmly in control; (2) they deprived foreign publics of the facts about South Africa, defusing international economic and political pressure; and (3) they denied media access to a major political force—black organizations like the African National Congress and the United Democratic Front—thereby distorting political life and tilting the political balance in favor of the white minority.[19] Paradoxically, Percy Qobozo, the late black South African editor, pointed out, whites suffered more from the news blackout than blacks did: "Blacks live in a township where the revolution is occurring. They know by sight and word of mouth what is occurring, but the

---

18. House Committee, *Media Restrictions*, statement of Leonard R. Sussman, pp. 93–94; Giffard and Cohen, "South African TV and Censorship," p. 10.

19. House Committee, *Media Restrictions*, p. 16.

whites in their secure white suburbs do not."[20] Because of government censorship, many white South Africans did not comprehend what was so obvious to ordinary people as well as policymakers in the United States and other countries around the globe: South Africa was in the middle of a revolution.

They therefore endorsed Botha's go-slow, pro-apartheid approach as appropriate policy. But F. W. de Klerk, Botha's successor, determined to expose white South Africans to reality and enlist their support in forging a new South Africa. And to accomplish that, he had to free the media. When the Afrikaners fought and defeated African tribes in the eighteenth and nineteenth centuries, the settlers used the tactic of circling their oxcarts in a protective formation known as a *laager*. In the late twentieth century, the concept of the *laager* served as a metaphor for Afrikaners closing their ranks against the outside world. De Klerk decided to open up the *laager* and adopt a liberal democratic model of *mediapolitik*.

AN UNLIKELY CHAMPION OF CHANGE

Frederik Willem de Klerk was a fourth-generation Afrikaner nationalist born in the northern Transvaal, the most conservative area of South Africa. He grew up steeped in the Afrikaner outlook, which views the world with a proud insularity. He was a member of the Broederbond, a semi-secret society of prominent Afrikaners, which ran the country with a firm hand. De Klerk seemed an unlikely champion of change and radical reform, but when he took office in September 1989, he faced a deteriorating economy at home and continued criticism abroad, both largely traceable to one thing, apartheid.

As early as 1979, even his dour, stiff-necked predecessor, P. W. Botha, had told his fellow Afrikaners to "adapt or die." In 1986, Botha described apartheid as "outdated and unacceptable," but he was never able, or willing, to take the necessary bold steps that would convince South African blacks and the rest of the world that he meant to match deeds and words.[21] In startling contrast, President de Klerk urged his fellow citizens in his inauguration speech to join him in creating a "totally changed South Africa." He pressed the African National Congress to "walk through the open door, take your place at the negotiating table." He knew that the ANC was under increasing pressure to negotiate: its Soviet backers no

20. Ibid., p. 105.
21. Bruce W. Nelan, "Sanctions: What Spells Success?" *Time*, February 5, 1990, p. 31.

longer had the resources or the interest in underwriting revolution thousands of miles away. The peace settlement in Angola had scattered eight thousand ANC guerrillas throughout much of sub-Saharan Africa. De Klerk traveled to Zambia, one of the leading black African nations opposing apartheid, and to London and Bonn, saying he hoped that South Africa's status as an international outcast would soon end.

During the height of political unrest, from 1984–1986, most South Africans never saw the pictures of black protests, stonings, arson, and police violence that the rest of the world saw. Government officials said night after night over SABC television that the unseen violence was caused by leaders of the African National Congress and the Communist Party, who were never shown and were quoted only selectively and rarely.[22] President de Klerk allowed South Africans for the first time to see for themselves the political changes that were taking place in their country. Anglican Archbishop Desmond Tutu, for example, made his first voluntary appearance on SABC television in October 1989, in a debate on religion in politics. Given fifteen unedited minutes in which to make his arguments, Tutu was so encouraged by the new policy that he, who had previously refused to answer questions by SABC reporters, began granting interviews. The government's more open approach to news was graphically illustrated in January, when more than thirty people were killed and millions of dollars of damage done to government-owned railroad equipment. Amid reports of clashes and violence, the black leader of the South African Railway and Harbor Workers Union went on television to give his side of the story—a telling sign of the new more democratic *mediapolitik* in South Africa. In contrast, during a 1987 mine strike, one of the costliest and longest in the country's history, the leader of the black miners union was never heard from until the strike had ended.[23]

DE KLERK'S BALANCING ACT

Finally, on February 2, 1990, after cleverly playing down expectations of what he might say, de Klerk went before Parliament and stunned the nation and the world with a far-ranging package of concessions and reforms, including: (1) repeal of the emergency restrictions on thirty-three opposition groups, including the African National Congress, the South African

---

22. Laurinda Keys, "Change in South African TV Brings Political Shifts to Livingrooms," Associated Press, February 14, 1990.

23. Ibid.

Communist Party, the Pan-Africanist Congress, and the United Democratic Front; (2) lifting of the news blackout, while keeping a rein on photographers and television cameramen; (3) an end to the restrictions on the
movements and political activities of 374 opposition supporters; and (4)
allowing political exiles to return home.[24] Two years earlier, many white
South Africans argued that even talking to the ANC was treason, and now
de Klerk had not only removed the thirty-year-old ban on the black organization, but announced that its leader Nelson Mandela would "soon"
go free. "The season of violence is over," he said. "The time for reconstruc-
tion and reconciliation has arrived."[25] The leader of the far-right Afrikaner
Resistance Movement responded: "God, don't tell me that. No. Oh no. It
can't be true." Reverend Allan Boesak, president of the liberal World Alliance of Reformed Churches, remarked: "If de Klerk had given us any
more, we wouldn't have known what to do with it." That very night, white
viewers listened to televised comments from black activists they had been
taught to regard as their enemies.[26]

De Klerk was playing a delicate balancing act. He had to move fast
enough to satisfy the international community so that it would think seriously about removing economic sanctions against South Africa; far
enough to persuade the African National Congress to begin negotiations
on the political future of their country; but not too fast or too far to provoke the ruling whites into rebelling against him and his reforms. One analyst suggested that de Klerk benefited from what has been called the
"Nixon in China" syndrome, in which "a leader has accumulated the political credentials and capital to act against expectations."[27] Just as Nixon, a
staunch anti-Communist from his first days in Congress, could talk with
Mao Zedong because he would be expected to be firm with the Chinese
Communist leader, so de Klerk, a born-and-bred Afrikaner, could be
trusted to sit down with Nelson Mandela because most whites were convinced that he would protect their political and economic interests.

THE MEDIA: A KEY ALLY

The South African president understood that the mass media, far from
being adversaries as his predecessor had believed, were vital allies in his re-

24. Tom Matthews, "A Prisoner, a President," *Newsweek*, February 12, 1990, p. 28.
25. Ibid., p. 27.
26. Ibid.; Keys, "Change in South African TV."
27. Neil A. Lewis, "An Unpredictable Leader of South Africa," *New York Times*, February
12, 1990.

form campaign. He flung wide the gates to the foreign media so that they could transmit the message that a new South Africa accepted the need for change and a swift end to apartheid. He allowed the domestic media, particularly television, to report fully his actions, both symbolic and concrete, that began to transform the atmosphere of South Africa. His predecessor had imposed a strict authoritarian model of *mediapolitik;* on at least one occasion, Botha had called the SABC newsroom in mid-broadcast to order changes in a program. In his first five months as president, de Klerk dismantled the semi-secret National Security Management System, which controlled the black townships, and downgraded the State Security Council.

Aware of the importance of symbols in the media age, he did away with the plumes and feathers of the presidential guard, ordered municipalities to integrate the beaches, and freed prominent political prisoners like the ANC leader Walter Sisulu. He allowed Sisulu to be interviewed for an hour and a half on SABC television, although technically it was still an act of treason to quote a member of the African National Congress. Alternative newspapers regularly printed "Release Mandela" posters and quoted from ANC broadcasts, without penalty. "The restrictions simply weren't working," commented a government official, "or more precisely, they weren't worth the price we were having to pay in outcry from every direction."[28] All the while, de Klerk was carefully preparing for his most important act of democratic *mediapolitik*—the freeing of Nelson Mandela, martyr, leader, icon.

In December 1989, at the presidential residence in Cape Town, de Klerk and Mandela, still technically a prisoner, held the first of a series of private meetings to discuss convening an *indaba* (Zulu for "negotiations") that would write a new constitution granting blacks the right to vote for a national government. A black leader said that Mandela gained the impression that de Klerk "was a man he could do business with," while the president confided to colleagues that Mandela was "a man of integrity, a man you can trust."[29] Dissimilar in so many ways, both men were lawyers with a respect for the law and a belief in its ability to help find common ground between the ANC demand for one-man, one-vote, black majority rule, and the government's insistence that an equal share for whites be written into the constitution. Mandela publicly underscored his position by leak-

28. Keys, "Change in South African TV"; Mathews, "A Prisoner, a President," pp. 28–29.
29. Scott MacLeod, "At the Crossroads," *Time,* February 5, 1990, p. 28.

ing to newspapers a document he had given to Botha the previous July in which he had stated that white South Africa must "accept that there will never be peace and stability in this country" until the principle of majority rule is accepted.[30] An unruffled de Klerk proceeded with plans to release Mandela, gambling that the black African leader would eschew the rhetoric of revolution and conduct himself as a man who could be trusted by white and black alike. De Klerk anticipated that the mass media would give its full attention to the event, but not even he, for all his shrewd appreciation of the power of the media, was prepared for the apotheosis of Nelson Mandela.

THE FREEING OF MANDELA

On Sunday, February 11, 1990, twenty-seven years, six months, and one week after his arrest in 1962, Nelson Mandela walked out of Victor Verster prison, his passage into freedom televised live throughout South Africa and around the world. The seventy-one-year-old leader, whose picture could not be legally printed in South African newspapers until a few days earlier, was seen by millions of South Africans, white and black, as he marched through the gates of his prison and later as he spoke to a giant rally in Cape Town. In all South African history, no other black man had received such broadcast coverage. The previous Thursday, ABC's Ted Koppel took advantage of the new media freedom and engaged in open teleplomacy by talking via satellite to South African Foreign Minister R. F. Botha in Cape Town, ANC Foreign Minister Thabo Mbeki in London, and Zulu Chief Mangosuthu Gathsa Buthelezi in Durban. Botha appealed to all his "black brothers and friends" to build a new South Africa, while Mbeki expressed restrained hope and Buthelezi welcomed the spirit of conciliation. Although Koppel disingenuously commented that "negotiations don't take place on television programs," both Botha and Buthelezi called for the lifting of economic sanctions against South Africa, prompting Mbeki to respond that "it's still early days" for such an action. Plainly, each of the leaders was talking as much to the world as to each other.[31]

President de Klerk prepared the way for the great event, and made certain that everyone knew who was responsible, by holding a news conference the morning before at which he announced the "open doors" for

30. Ibid.
31. Walter Goodman, "A Strong Step, a Smile: Mandela Floods the Screen," *New York Times*, February 12, 1990.

Mandela. Sitting behind a wooden table in the H. F. Verwoerd Building in Cape Town—named after the white leader who had laid down the first principles of apartheid in the 1950s—de Klerk said that Mandela's release "will bring us to the end of a long chapter," and he appealed to all sides "to prove that we are capable of a peaceful process in creating a new South Africa."[32]

Following his release from prison, Mandela began his first public address in twenty-seven years on the steps of Cape Town's City Hall with the word, "*Amandla!*" ("power" in the Xhosa language), the rallying cry of the black resistance. In a strong unwavering voice, he called for the creation of "a democratic, nonracial and unitary South Africa" as well as "a fundamental restructuring of the economy." He said he hoped that a "climate conducive to a negotiated settlement" would allow the African National Congress to abandon its armed struggle. He referred to de Klerk, watching the address on television at the presidential palace half a mile away, as "a man of integrity," and then added, "Our march to freedom is irreversible."[33]

It was magnificent, moving political television that had veteran U.S. anchors like CBS's Dan Rather and NBC's Tom Brokaw waxing euphoric as they reported the historic event. They were so excited that they got some facts wrong, misstating that Mandela's release from prison and his Cape Town address were not seen live by South Africans, only by an international audience. Brokaw bemoaned that while Mandela was being freed, South African television was showing film of white people at a party; he referred to "the contrariness of this country." Rather for his part announced that Mandela's stirring remarks were not carried live by SABC television; the "big show," he said, was "for international consumption" only.[34]

A NEW MEDIAPOLITIK

Both journalists badly misunderstood de Klerk's new democratic *mediapolitik*, which depended upon widespread coverage of Nelson Mandela by domestic as well as foreign news media. Pretoria needed white South Africans as well as the rest of the world to realize that a new South Africa

32. Tom Mathews, "Free!" *Newsweek*, February 19, 1990, p. 37.

33. John F. Burns, "On Mandela's Walk, Hope and Violence," *New York Times*, February 12, 1990.

34. Tom Shales, "Mandela and the Millions Who Watched," *Washington Post*, February 12, 1990.

with black and white leadership was in the making. Far from banning or delaying pictures of Mandela, SABC scrapped much of its Sunday programming to show the ANC leader's walk to freedom. When Mandela's release was delayed for more than an hour, SABC's chief political reporter filled the time by repeatedly telling South African viewers they were about to watch history in the making. "This is the moment the world has been waiting for," said the South African journalist, caught up in the moment. "The sun is shining on South Africa." The South African network briefly delayed its coverage of Mandela's Cape Town speech, because it began while the regularly scheduled news was on, but it switched live after the news, missing only the opening tributes to the black African leader. The next morning, South African television kept up its extensive coverage of Mandela, providing clips of his endorsement of the armed struggle against the white minority government and lengthy reports from Washington, London, and other major capitals about the generally favorable reaction of foreign governments. Prior to February 2, when President de Klerk lifted the thirty-year ban on the ANC, Mandela's speech would have been illegal, and the SABC would have been prosecuted for broadcasting it.

The center of South African politics shifted from Cape Town to Mandela's single-story brick home on Vilakasi Street in Soweto on the outskirts of Johannesburg. Television vans and satellite equipment surrounded the modest Mandela residence, topped by the ANC flag, illegal only two weeks earlier. More than one thousand requests for interviews from over one hundred countries were telephoned, telexed, faxed, and shouted across the fence. News media stars from the United States, Great Britain, Germany, and Japan filed in and out of the house every fifteen minutes, all remarking that the ANC leader seemed completely at ease, as though he had been on television all his life. Reflecting the new *mediapolitik* of South Africa, SABC television sent two reporters to interview Mandela in his garden, and twenty-five minutes of the conversation ran after the evening news. Images of the man routinely described for decades as a terrorist were beamed into millions of white South African homes as he spoke without bitterness of the injustices done to blacks, his twenty-seven years in prison, and his hopes that whites and blacks could bury the past and agree on majority rule. Mandela credited the media with keeping his cause alive and before the world. He talked with old friends like the journalist Anthony Sampson about the vital role of the press, particularly the alternative press, which pushed the conventional press into taking note of black views. Rejecting a totalitarian view, Mandela remarked that he welcomed media criticism because "a vigorous political movement amongst blacks will arise and be maintained if the press looks at problems objectively."[35]

Barely forty-eight hours after his release from prison, Nelson Mandela had become the most powerful black leader in South Africa, raised to an equal political plane with President de Klerk by an admiring, even adulatory, mass media. By virtue of his decades in prison and his refusal to leave under any conditions but his own, Mandela proved himself to be a man of courage, conscience, and principle. He would also reveal himself to be a skillful, pragmatic politician in the months ahead, willing to sit down at the peace table and negotiate the end of apartheid with the South African government. For his part, F. W. de Klerk displayed a remarkable boldness as well as pragmatism by abandoning a doctrine that had failed. "The National Party has now accepted," he pointedly remarked to an American magazine, "that all South Africans . . . will permanently share power."[36] De Klerk understood that he had set in motion a process of political democratization that might well produce unintended consequences, but there was no alternative other than a prolonged, bloody civil war that was too costly for him and the other pragmatists in the government to contemplate. Both sides accepted the imperatives of liberal democracy.

MEDIA'S MAJOR ROLE

All the necessary conditions were present for *mediapolitik* to play a major role in South Africa. First, there was a significant media infrastructure, with three television channels and twenty-three radio stations serving six million television viewers and twelve million radio listeners out of a total population of thirty million. Responding to South Africa's multilingual audience, two black TV channels broadcast in five African languages while radio services offered programs in twenty different languages. Nearly two-

---

35. Anthony Sampson, "18 Days: A South African Journal," *New York Times*, March 18, 1990; John F. Burns, "Mandela's Day: Exercise and Uproar," *New York Times*, February 15, 1990; John F. Burns, "South Africa Loosens Gag, and the Press Pipes Up," *New York Times*, March 18, 1990. At the 40th annual assembly of the International Press Institute in the summer of 1991, Mandela said: "I am also personally deeply indebted to the international press who kept my name and that of the other political prisoners alive and before the international public. In its way, that assisted in finally achieving our release": Nelson Mandela, "Press Helped to Free Me from Prison," *IPI Report*, June/July 1991, p. 9.

36. David Gelman, "Surprising Statesman," *Newsweek*, February 19, 1990, p. 51.

thirds of the white population of five million watched the evening news programs on television.

Second, white public officials led by President de Klerk as well as black leaders, particularly Nelson Mandela, devoted a major portion of their time to working with the mass media. In the five months between his inauguration as president and his release of Mandela, de Klerk made certain that every careful step he took toward what he called "a new South Africa" was broadcast, often live, and reported in the press without censorship.

Third, and most important, the mass media portrayed the once-banned ANC as a legitimate party and its leaders as a necessary part of the political solution in South Africa. SABC television and other government-controlled mass media abandoned the virulent anti-ANC propaganda that had characterized their reports for decades and presented Mandela and his associates as essentially reasonable men, not Communist revolutionaries, that President de Klerk could negotiate with. They were able to do so because de Klerk deliberately discarded the authoritarian model of P. W. Botha and adopted a liberal democratic model of *mediapolitik* predicated on the principle that politics and the mass media should be free of government influence and control. A new kind of South Africa, de Klerk reasoned, demanded a new kind of mass media.

How radically the media had changed was underscored the following year when the *Weekly Mail*, an antiapartheid newspaper, revealed that the de Klerk government had made secret payments to the Inkatha Freedom Party, a political rival of the African National Congress, shortly after the ANC was legalized and Mandela was freed. The government claimed that the money was for anti-sanction rallies by Inkatha and came from a slush fund reserved for countering economic sanctions and South Africa's international isolation. But documents leaked to the *Mail* and other newspapers made it clear that the money was given to counter the ANC's inroads into Inkatha's political base in various black townships.

In the wake of the scandal, two government ministers were demoted, and de Klerk held an internationally televised news conference at which he insisted that he had not known about the Inkatha funding until he had read about it in the press. He conceded that he should have moved faster to curtail such secret projects. Although key questions were left unanswered—de Klerk could not give assurances that additional funds had not gone to Inkatha—no such public explanation, bordering on an apology, would have been offered by any previous South African white leader. De

Klerk's televised remarks, intended as much for the international community as the people of South Africa, were credited with keeping the dialogue with the black opposition alive. But the ANC reflected South Africa's new politics by commenting coolly to the press that de Klerk's response "evades some very serious issues raised by the exposure of the slush funds and allegations of [government] involvement in violence."[37] Less than two years earlier, such an accusation would never have been published or broadcast and indeed could have led to the banning or imprisonment of the person who said it.

Despite "Inkathagate," de Klerk and Mandela continued to seek a political and economic solution that would satisfy the legitimate demands of the black majority and protect the rights of the white minority. Mandela justified de Klerk's assessment that the two could do business when the ANC abandoned terrorism and committed itself to "the battlefield of ideas and peaceful political activity."[38] In the process, the two leaders kept one eye on each other and another on the mass media, which were no longer puppets on a string pulled by the government but aggressive and independent actors.

LIBERAL DEMOCRACY

In 1994, four years after Nelson Mandela's release from jail, South Africa held its first all-race elections, in which Mandela was overwhelmingly elected president and the African National Congress won a 62 percent majority in Parliament. The predicted uprisings by white racists and Zulu nationalists did not occur, and the de Klerk government calmly surrendered power to the ANC. In office, Mandela continued to talk reconciliation and supervised the drafting and adoption in 1996 of what *The Economist* called "the most liberal constitution in Africa."[39] And all the while, President Mandela and Deputy President Thabo Mbeki strove to solve the four major problems of unemployment, crime, education, and AIDS.

In June 1999, with nine of ten adults voting, Mbeki was easily elected president, succeeding the man described by most as "a transcendent political and cultural figure."[40] The ANC maintained its wide parliamentary

---

37. John Battersby, "Pretoria Disclosures Divide Ruling Party," *Christian Science Monitor,* July 22, 1991; "De Klerk's Response on 'Inkathagate' Fails to Convince His Critics," *Christian Science Monitor,* August 1, 1991.

38. Mandela, "Press Helped to Free Me," p. 10.

39. "Mandela's Heir," *The Economist,* May 29, 1999, p. 19.

40. Jon Jeter, "In S. Africa, a President Replaces an Icon," *Washington Post,* June 17, 1999.

majority. Mbeki inherited the continent's strongest economy, but one rid-
dled with problems. Unemployment among blacks was more than 40 percent, but only 4 percent among whites. Only half of the country's high
school students graduated. The crime rate was soaring, with a murder rate
seven times that of America. Despite construction of more than 600,000
new homes since 1994, there was an acute housing shortage. Health officials estimated that nearly one-fourth of South Africa's forty million citizens were infected with HIV, the virus that causes AIDS.

In 1998, Mbeki told the Parliament that South Africa was "a country of
two nations"—one "white [and] relatively prosperous," the other "black
and poor." He blamed the old apartheid governments and then noted with
approval how, after unification, West Germans had transferred hundreds
of billions of dollars to their less prosperous eastern brothers and sisters.
He contrasted this with the reluctance of white South Africans to pay taxes to improve black lives. But, *The Economist* pointed out, West Germans
are much richer than white South Africans and outnumber East Germans
by four to one, while whites make up only 11 percent of South Africa's
population. "It is simply not possible," stated the international business
weekly, "for the mass of poor black South Africans to prosper through income transfers from whites."[41]

The surer way to prosperity for black and white was through privatization, land reform, good public services at low cost, and a quicker solution
of the pressing problems of unemployment, education, and crime. During
his presidential campaign, Mbeki signaled that he understood this hard
truth when he declared that the ANC would not tamper with the country's liberal democratic constitution. Earlier, he had dismissed the suggestion of a close associate that the ANC should extend its control over every
level of power, from public broadcasting to the judiciary. Against the highest odds and without bloodshed, Nelson Mandela turned South Africa
into a majority-ruled democracy. It is Thabo Mbeki's mission, suggested
The Economist, to "entrench that democracy, not his party."[42]

41. "South Africa's New President," *The Economist,* May 29, 1999, p. 21.
42. "Mbeki's South Africa," *The Economist,* May 29, 1999, p. 14.

CHAPTER 11

THE THIRD SUPERPOWER

IN EITHER A FREE OR AN UNFREE POLITY, the mass media wield enormous influence because they can deliver the same message to many different people at one time. As a result, the mass media have become an essential component of national power, as important to a nation's viability as natural resources, population, economic strength, military might, and political will. Indeed, in our information age, all the other components of national power depend heavily upon the mass media for their effectiveness. Whether a nation is drilling for oil or natural gas, caring for the public welfare, selling stocks and bonds, testing a new weapon, or announcing a new law, the mass media—electronic and print—invariably play a key role. Today, no nation can be a major power without the ability to communicate effectively within and without its borders. It is no coincidence that the two economically strongest nations in the world—the United States and Japan—are also media superpowers.

As a fundamental part of national power, the mass media have affected and even changed the course of world politics for good and for evil, from the triumph of the Bolshevik Revolution and the establishment of Nazi Germany to the end of Communism in Eastern Europe and the former Soviet Union and the spread of democracy around the world. The case studies of this book show that like every other technology developed by man, the mass media can either enrich or enslave the human spirit, depending upon their moral foundation. If the media follow a liberal democratic model, as in the United States, they contribute to a free and just society. If they follow an authoritarian model, as in South Africa before de Klerk and Mandela or in Chile during Pinochet; or a totalitarian model, as in Saddam's Iraq or Castro's Cuba, they perpetuate the regime in power and deny the fruits of freedom and democracy to the people.

I call the interrelationship between mass media and politics *mediapolitik*. *Mediapolitik* examines the reality of media power and its impact on the politics of the nations of the world. But unlike *realpolitik*, with its single-minded emphasis on power, *mediapolitik* argues that politics and media are best served when based on the principles and institutions of representative democracy, as outlined, for example, in the U.S. Constitution. Liberal democratic *mediapolitik* rejects the "realist" view, set forth by the political scientist Hans Morgenthau, that all politics is a struggle for power, that in all domestic and international politics "a political policy seeks either to keep power, to increase power, or to demonstrate power."[1] In politics, power is *not* all; responsibility is also needed to harness power for the common good. Responsibility requires that individuals, particularly politicians and journalists, practice virtues like wisdom, courage, and prudence. *Wisdom,* which comes from the experiences of life, contemplation, reading, debating, and study, gives us purpose and direction in our moral life; it helps us to set goals. *Courage* enables us to pursue those goals and helps us to resist the temptations which might deflect us from the path that wisdom suggests. *Prudence* blends reason with the other parts of human nature such as instinct and emotion; it produces harmony and proportion in our moral life, helping us to avoid fanaticism in pursuit of a goal.[2]

Many politicians and journalists will acknowledge the importance of morality in life in general, but they are uneasy about applying it to their lives in particular. If pressed, some journalists say they believe in a libertarian philosophy that gives them the freedom to report whatever they want without regard for the consequences. They argue that the public *always* has the right to know what its government is planning and doing, even in wartime. But not even the great libertarian John Stuart Mill was a free speech absolutist; he conceded that there are moral limits to freedom. Mill argued that no one should be free to violate wantonly someone else's

1. Hans Morgenthau, *Politics among Nations,* 5th ed. (New York: Alfred A. Knopf, 1978), p. 36.

2. For an early examination of the place of ethics in the mass media, see John C. Merrill and Ralph D. Barney, eds., *Ethics and the Press: Readings in Mass Media Morality* (New York: Hastings House, 1975), especially "The 'Apollonysian' Journalist," by John C. Merrill.

rights, unjustly damage another's reputation, or disclose information when secrecy is vital to the public interest.[3]

Other journalists proclaim their belief in a social responsibility philosophy that obliges the media to provide news and information that encourages their audiences to behave in more responsible ways. But how do you determine what is responsible and what is irresponsible? The American public was undoubtedly persuaded to support the civil rights movement of the 1960s by the mass media's sympathetic coverage of freedom marches in Selma, Alabama, and Oxford, Mississippi, and civil rights leaders like Martin Luther King, Jr. As a result, segregation in the nation was finally eliminated and a more just society emerged.

But when the mass media attempted to present school busing in the 1970s as an extension of the civil rights struggle, their words and images failed to move the American public, because a large majority of parents, black as well as white, opposed school busing. The media dismissed or played down arguments that busing would impair quality education or contribute to school crime and violence. In their laudable but ill-considered desire to be socially responsible, the mass media aligned themselves with social architects in the universities, think tanks, and federal courtrooms who insisted they knew what was best for the American people.[4] The misstep about school busing suggests that social responsibility philosophy is not sufficient for the mass media; they need *moral* principles to guide them on the often slippery slopes of *mediapolitik*. The media scholars Stephen Klaidman and Tom L. Beauchamp insist that a "virtuous journalist" is not an oxymoron but the description of a reporter or editor who seeks truth, avoids bias, and serves the public by rejecting manipulation, inviting criticism, and being held accountable for his work.[5]

When journalists adhere to the virtues of wisdom, courage, and prudence, they make possible a *mediapolitik* based on universal moral principles like liberty and justice. They make impossible the worst political and journalistic sin—the deliberate abuse of power. Liberal democratic *mediapolitik* is not utopian or mindlessly optimistic but seeks a fusion of pragmatism and idealism. It is not a balance of power against power, but a bal-

3. See John Stuart Mill, *On Liberty* (Chicago: Henry Regnery, 1955), chap. 2.

4. For an in-depth analysis of journalism's role in the issue of school busing, see S. Robert Lichter, Stanley Rothman, and Linda S. Richter, *The Media Elite: America's New Powerbrokers* (Bethesda, Md.: Adler & Adler, 1986), pp. 220–53.

5. Stephen Klaidman and Tom L. Beauchamp, "The Idea of Ethics in Journalism," in *The Virtuous Journalist* (New York: Oxford University Press, 1987), pp. 8–10.

ance of necessary power and moral responsibility. It is fundamentally American, deriving from classic documents of the American Revolution like the Virginia Bill of Rights of June 12, 1776, which declared:

No free government, or the blessings of liberty, can be preserved to any people, but by a firm adherence to justice, moderation, temperance, frugality, and virtue, and by a frequent recurrence to fundamental principles.[6]

IN THE GULF

There is no better test of media power and responsibility than in wartime. In the Persian Gulf War, as set forth in Chapter 3, the Bush administration insisted that it adhered for the most part to a liberal democratic model of *mediapolitik,* cooperating with the media to provide the American public with sufficient and timely information about a fast-moving conflict fought thousands of miles from home and thousands of feet above the reporters covering it. Pete Williams, the Pentagon spokesman, applauded the press for giving "the American people the best war coverage they ever had." But many, although far from all, American journalists bitterly protested against what they called controlled access and information management. They vowed they would never again submit to such restrictive and undemocratic rules, such as assigning an officer to accompany reporters to the battlefront and requiring dispatches to be cleared by military censors. Michael Getler of the *Washington Post* deplored what he called "the most thorough and sophisticated wartime control of American reporters in modern times."[7] Driven by bottom-line journalism—the need to maintain the highest possible circulation and audience ratings to enhance profits—and brandishing the First Amendment, media executives complained about censorship by delay, blackouts of the "ugly parts," and leakproof pools. They were also concerned about the profitability of a communications industry that accounts for more than 6 percent of the U.S. GNP and boasts of revenues greater than those of the Pentagon.[8]

The Pentagon, nevertheless, responded to media complaints by adopting, after a year of study, less restrictive war-zone rules for journalists, al-

6. Harry Warfel, Ralph H. Gabriel, and Stanley T. Williams, eds., *The American Mind: Selections from the Literature of the United States* (New York: American Book Company, 1947), p. 148.

7. Hedrick Smith, ed., *The Media and the Gulf War: The Press and Democracy in Wartime* (Washington: Seven Locks Press, 1992), pp. xix, 160.

8. Richard Harwood, "News from the Front," *Washington Post,* February 10, 1991.

lowing wider access, and discouraging the use of small reporter pools. It was an attempt to fuse military pragmatism and journalistic idealism.

But the historic tension between the two institutions is bound to continue, exacerbated by the presence of "an instantaneous, continuous, and international network," CNN.[9] All the talk about less restrictive rules, fewer pools, and more access seems almost irrelevant when television correspondents are broadcasting live from the capital of an adversary or the frontlines of a battle. The debate between exclusion and inclusion can never be totally resolved, but it can be alleviated by a greater sense of responsibility on the part of the media. The rules of conduct proposed by Paul Johnson, a British historian, could help encourage such responsibility. Johnson argues that if journalists "are not moral human beings they cannot be good professionals either." Journalists should always think through the consequences of what they report, says Johnson, asking themselves: "What will legitimately inform, what will needlessly inflame? What will warn, and what will corrupt?"[10]

THE KISHA SYNDROME

Sometimes not even a constitutional framework of democratic principles and institutions produces a democratic *mediapolitik*. Although Japan is a parliamentary democracy that guarantees freedom of the press, journalistic freedom is severely constrained by of the intertwined relationship between Japanese politicians and journalists symbolized in the *kisha,* or journalists' club. As noted in Chapter 8, all important news about the political, economic, and other institutions of Japan is released by the *kisha* attached to that institution. The process protects member journalists from missing a story but also prevents them from printing or broadcasting a story against the wishes of the *kisha.* Media conformity is reinforced by societal conformity, resulting in the self-censorship of stories that would threaten the power of the ruling bureaucratic-political-business triad. The existence of a prominent libertarian journalist is virtually impossible in Japan. While Japanese *mediapolitik* cannot be described as even remotely authoritarian, it is not liberal democratic in the way U.S. or British *mediapolitik* is. A radical utilitarianism usually negates any instinct of the mass media to question government actions and expose public scandals. With rare exceptions, investigative journalism does not exist in Japan.

9. Smith, *The Media and the Gulf War,* p. xxii.
10. Paul Johnson, "Media Morality Function?" *Washington Times,* September 7, 1990.

Is a moral *mediapolitik* possible in Japan? Clearly, references to America's Founding Fathers or ancient Greek philosophers would have little impact on pragmatic, economics-driven Japanese journalists and politicians. There is, however, a philosopher whose wisdom does carry weight in Japan—the ancient Chinese sage Confucius, who declared that a good society is not possible without good men who seek and practice virtue. In his words, "The moral man, by living a life of simple truth and earnestness, alone can help to bring peace and order in the world." Confucius argued that the highest virtue was to be found through "the middle course," often translated as the "Golden Mean."[11] It is one of history's most astonishing coincidences that the philosophers Aristotle and Confucius, living ten thousand miles and two centuries apart, both argued the central importance of the same ethical concept and even used the same words—the Golden Mean.

Virtue, for Confucius, was not an abstract principle but a habit of doing the right thing. He insisted that words must have respect for actions and actions respect for words. "Is it not just this thorough genuineness and absence of pretense," he asked, "which characterizes the moral man?" The normally even-tempered Confucius went so far as to say that he "hated" those who did not follow the Golden Mean, painting a profile of an immoral man that is remarkably familiar in modern times: someone who likes to criticize people or reveal their weaknesses; someone who likes to malign or spread rumors about those in authority; someone who is sure of himself and narrow-minded; someone who knows nothing and yet has not enough wit to speak or behave cautiously.[12]

Among Chinese scholars, Confucianism is known as the religion of *li,* or moral order; it subjects the political order to the moral social order. As Confucius said, "A sovereign who governs a nation by virtue is like the North Polar Star, which remains in its place and the other stars revolve around it."[13] Confucius lived in a time of political unrest and uncertainty, which explains in some measure his repudiation of excess and extremism and his counseling of moderation as a way to order and stability. But his Golden Mean is a timeless method of balancing ethics and politics, maintaining that when good men are present, good government flourishes, but

11. Lin Yutang, ed., *The Wisdom of Confucius* (New York: The Modern Library, 1938), p. 133; also "The Golden Mean of Tsesze," in *The Wisdom of India and China,* ed. Lin Yutang (New York: The Modern Library, 1942), p. 846.

12. Confucius, *The Analects,* in Lin Yutang, *The Wisdom of India and China,* pp. 837–38.

13. Ibid., p. 839.

when good men are gone, good government decays and becomes extinct.[14] In the wake of scandals and resignations by high-ranking Japanese ministers and party officials, the advice of an ancient Chinese philosopher to practice virtue in public as well as private life may strike politicians and journalists alike as precisely what is needed in Japanese *mediapolitik*.

THE MIRACLE YEAR

Sometimes what was a blessing becomes a burden. The mass media, as outlined in Chapter 5, helped to change the course of history in Eastern and Central Europe by sustaining the desire for freedom among its peoples. East Germans learned from West German television how much they were being denied by Communist rule. The underground media of Poland's Solidarity relied upon the West for information. The Velvet Revolution of Czechoslovakia drew inspiration from the Voice of America. The totalitarian model of *mediapolitik* failed in the Communist states of Poland, Hungary, Czechoslovakia, and East Germany because the Marxist regimes (1) failed to block the external mass media with their exhilarating message of choice and freedom; (2) did not control their internal mass media, even allowing, as in Poland, the emergence of a widespread anti-Communist underground press; (3) admitted they no longer believed in Communism, rendering their propaganda useless and their central reason for governing invalid; and (4) could no longer call on the military might of the Soviet Union to keep their peoples in order and themselves in power.

The democratic model of *mediapolitik* prevailed because dissidents exploited the media freedom beyond their borders by listening to Western radio and watching Western television. The stories of foreign correspondents were broadcast back into the countries where the information was supposedly banned. With the Western media as their inspiration, people by the millions demonstrated and distributed formerly forbidden truths and made revolution and freedom possible. But after the revolution came the governing, and in the new democracies, it was discovered that fighting for free speech is often easier than living with it.

In post-Communist Poland, a senior official of the Polish Broadcasting Authority charged that neither the government nor its opponents wanted autonomous radio and television stations that they could not control. In Hungary, the government and the media fiercely debated who should be

14. "The Golden Mean of Tsesze," p. 852.

in charge of public broadcasting; the president of the state-run radio network was fired after calling a parliamentary oversight committee incompetent. Members of the Hungarian Democratic Forum, the largest coalition party in Parliament, favored giving the prime minister wide discretion in hiring and firing the heads of radio and television, both state monopolies. Broadcasters complained that legislators were writing media laws "as if freedom were something bestowed in thimble-sized doses by the state, rather than an inherent right." David Webster of the BBC traced the conflict to the fact that while many politicians and officials recognized the need to build an open, independent broadcasting system, they were afraid that some might take advantage of the new liberties "to endanger the fragile emergence of democracy and to sow discord." Other politicians were more candid: they regarded independent media as a threat to their power and authority.[15]

The International Press Institute, based in Vienna, reported that governments in the Balkan countries, as well as in Russia and Ukraine, retained monopolies over newsprint supply, printing, and distribution, which could be useful weapons against newspapers that become too critical. Helsinki Watch, the human rights group, called Paul Everac, Romania's head of public television, "a man known for his extreme political views and his use of national television to propagate them." Everac's techniques to discredit opposition politicians included "manipulation of camera angles" and "the relegation of . . . opponents to less desirable time slots."[16] Five years after the collapse of Communism, Poland and the Czech Republic were the only former Moscow satellites to allow commercial, nationwide TV stations to compete with the state-owned networks.

One of the most difficult issues in the Czech Republic and in eastern Germany, according to historian Owen V. Johnson, was what to do with the names of people who had allegedly collaborated with the old Communist governments. The lists of names were often inaccurate, containing not only the names of dead people but the names of people whom the police had tried and failed to enlist—like Vaclav Havel. Those who favored publication argued that government suppression of important information was wrong and that anyone who was mistakenly included on the lists would be able to clear his name. The issue was complicated because some politi-

15. Glenn Frankel, "Uneasy Listening," *Washington Post.* May 25, 1992.

16. Rick E. Bruner, "Dark Information Age in Eastern Europe," *The World & I,* June 1994, p. 83.

cians urged publication to further not freedom of the press but their political career—hoping to damage their opponents.[17]

In the fall of 1999, a decade after the fall of the Berlin Wall, the New York–based Freedom Forum published a survey of media freedom in former Warsaw Pact countries. In the Czech Republic, reported the media analyst Joel Rubin, "political influence still colors the media." A new press law failed to guarantee media access to the government and to protect the confidentiality of a reporter's sources. It was not until July 1997 that the state monopoly of national broadcasting was broken in Hungary. Since then two Western-led companies have received broadcast permission, and cable companies are developing a digital, Internet-integrated system. Foreign investors also play "a major role in Polish media." By 1996, foreign money held a 56 percent share of Poland's daily newspapers and more than 50 percent of the magazines. Polish law, however, prohibits foreign interests from controlling more than 33 percent of the country's broadcast media. Rubin concluded that the mass media of Eastern and Central Europe are coping, often unevenly, with "the remains of a break from an authoritarian past that was dramatic but far from clean."[18]

In the midst of such pressures, said Rick Bruner, a reporter based in Budapest, many journalists are at a loss on how to use the freedoms they have gained. In addition to being underpaid, overworked, badly trained, and under constant pressure from politicians and advertisers, reporters in the East usually do not have the support or guidance of more experienced colleagues. In the past forty years, "no one has had legitimate experience with a free press." The result, very often, is self-censorship.[19] "We are all sick," remarked a legislator in the Armenian Parliament, "sick with the Communist bacillus. We were raised into Communism, and it's very hard for us to imagine a new way of life."[20]

FUNDAMENTAL QUESTIONS

The new Eastern democracies are debating fundamental questions: What authority, if not the party or the government, should decide what

17. Owen V. Johnson, "East Central and Southeastern Europe, Russia and the Newly Independent States," in *Global Journalism: Survey of International Communication*, 2d ed., ed. John C. Merrill (New York: Longman Publishers: 1991), p. 163.

18. Joel Rubin, "Transitions—A Regional Summary," *Media Studies Journal*, fall 1999, pp. 61, 63, 66–67.

19. Ibid.

20. Fred Hiatt, "Many Ex-Soviet Republics Find Democracy Elusive," *Washington Post*, June 8, 1995.

news may or may not be published and broadcast? Who is to determine if the potential harm from the publication or broadcast of information outweighs, or does not outweigh, the public's right to know that information? Are the mass media mature enough to be given almost unlimited freedom and therefore almost unlimited power?

As he has done so often, Vaclav Havel went to the heart of the matter, telling a Prague conference of foreign and local journalists—to their discomfiture—that freedom of the press "is only one side of the coin"; the "other side is represented by responsibility."[21] Havel's press secretary, Michael Zantowsky, explained that the Czech government would not hesitate to encourage responsibility by all appropriate legal means. One journalist, for example, wrote that more alcohol had been consumed in Hradcany Castle during the first six months of the Havel administration than by the previous governments in ten years. Uncertain of the facts, officials of the Havel government carefully checked invoices over the preceding decade and discovered that their drinking habits were quite modest—they had in fact drunk more soft drinks than hard liquor or wine, unlike previous administrations. In the United States, the White House might have demanded a correction, which would have been printed on an inside page of the errant publication. Taking media responsibility more seriously, the Havel government sued the offending journalist for libel, demanding as a sentence that he apologize in public in the same place in the newspaper where his false report first appeared.[22]

The Prague conference examined the rights and wrongs of publishing false information, focusing on an incident that sparked the beginning of the Velvet Revolution. When students began demonstrating in Prague on November 17, 1989, they were attacked by riot squads and secret police. Zantowsky, then a Reuters correspondent, received a telephone call from Peter Uhl, a Civic Forum activist, saying that a student had been killed by the police. Assured that the information came from an absolutely reliable eyewitness, Zantowsky filed a story on the killing which was immediately broadcast by Voice of America. As much as any other single incident, the student's death sparked the huge demonstrations of 200,000 people on November 20 which in short order brought down communism in Czechoslovakia. Although Communist officials vehemently denied that any student had died, no one after forty years of Marxist-Leninist propa-

21. Benjamin C. Bradlee, "The Shock of the Press," *Washington Post*, July 15, 1990.
22. Ibid.

ganda believed them. But the story *was* false: no student had been killed by the police or anyone else. For reasons that are unclear to this day, a secret policeman lay on the ground and pretended to be dead. Zantowsky admitted that technically Uhl should have been jailed for deliberately providing false, inflammatory information, but instead the onetime Civic Forum activist was appointed head of the Czechoslovak News Agency.[23]

How should a democracy reward a journalist who is responsible, at least partially, for making that democracy possible? Does a moral end sometimes justify immoral means, or never? How would Zantowsky treat a journalist who came to him with a story about a student who was killed by a policeman of the Havel government? It may be that Uhl truly believed the eyewitness and was only guilty, as was Zantowsky, of not confirming the student's "death" by a second source—a standard procedure in journalism for so explosive a story. It may be that Uhl and Zantowsky did not take the extra step because they anticipated and wanted the incendiary impact of the government's brutal action on an already aroused populace. At the very least, in acting as they did, the men became participants in, rather than observers of, the revolution.

Yet, the importance of the incident should not be exaggerated. While the "killing" was a catalytic event, mass demonstrations had already begun, Havel had emerged as a charismatic leader, and the revolution was under way. Communism would have fallen in Czechoslovakia, perhaps not so quickly, without the false story. Yet the incident points up the awesome power of words in the media age to lead or mislead. Havel himself said just a few weeks before the Velvet Revolution began: "Words that electrify society with their freedom and truthfulness are matched by words that mesmerize, deceive, inflame, madden; words that are harmful, lethal even."[24]

Most journalists and politicians agree that the one thing that will bring about permanent liberal democratic *mediapolitik* in Eastern Europe is time. "We just expected too much," says Johann Fritz, the head of the International Press Institute. "You can't overcome history which shaped people in Russia for 70 years, in some of the East European countries for 40 or 50 years, in just two or three years."[25] Hanna Suchocka, who served as

23. Ibid.

24. Vaclav Havel, "The Chance That Will Not Return" (acceptance speech for the Peace Prize of the German Booksellers Association), as quoted in *U.S. News & World Report*, February 26, 1990, p. 38.

25. Bruner, "Dark Information Age," p. 84.

prime minister of Poland from July 1992 to September 1993 and a member of the Parliament from the Freedom Union, explains that in 1989, the Polish people had two expectations. The first, political freedom, was quickly fulfilled when censorship was abolished and the "pillars of democracy" were laid. But the people's material expectations were not realized, taken as they were "straight out of reruns of *Dallas.*" What few Poles understood, admits Suchocka, "was that not everyone in the West shops at Saks, and the amount of hard work that is needed to create wealth."[26]

In a democracy, the mass media are best controlled by themselves and by society within an ethical or moral, not simply legal, context. Laws, statutes, and regulations are not sufficient. What is needed, again in Havel's words, is a commitment by all members of society—politicians, journalists, and ordinary citizens—to "spiritual values, humanistic ideals and intellectual integrity." Such a society is not an impossible dream because, Havel reminds us, Europe is "the old continent" (extending back to ancient Greece) with the qualities of many, though not all, older people: "Wisdom, tolerance and understanding." With these qualities, he argues, the new Europe will become a community of many different but equal people who will "share individual responsibility for the welfare of the community."[27] In the quest for a journalistic code that would help ensure a liberal democratic model of *mediapolitik,* what better qualities could there be than wisdom, tolerance, and understanding?

A TALE OF TWO COMMUNIST COUNTRIES

Why did the totalitarian model of *mediapolitik* succeed in China but fail in the Soviet Union? Because the Chinese Communists were better Leninists than their colleagues in Moscow. Deng Xiaoping did not hesitate to use massive force to retain power, sending in the army to kill hundreds, perhaps thousands, of pro-democracy Chinese students in and around Tiananmen Square, while in the Soviet Union the Gang of Eight failed to employ even moderate force—only three Muscovites died during the attempted coup—to control the people and the mass media.

In China, students used the media to communicate with masses of people, with mixed results. The students gained widespread support for their movement, but they terrified the government with the enormity of their

---

26. "Voices of Hope and Disquiet: Bread and Butter, Armies and the Future," *New York Times,* September 30, 1994.
27. Havel, "The Chance That Will Not Return."

success; Beijing felt obliged to crush them. The mass media gave the students a false sense of power and protection, encouraging them to raise constantly the political ante. Fearing that Tiananmen Squares might erupt all over China, the Chinese government called in the tanks and troops and seized control of what had been so crucial to the success of the rebellion—the mass media. The government's Leninist attitude toward the media was spelled out in December 1989, six months after the Tiananmen Square massacre, when the general secretary of the Communist Party declared that in "the new period, news reporting must serve socialism and serve the people" (i.e., the Communist Party). He added that what he called the "counterrevolutionary turmoil and rebellion" of the preceding May and June illustrated that chaos will inevitably result "if the tools of public opinion are not tightly controlled in the hands of true Marxists."[28]

His statement raises the question: Can tight control of public opinion be maintained indefinitely? All the dictators of Eastern and Central Europe thought so. But even in an authoritarian society like the People's Republic of China, the mass media can give the people an intoxicating taste of freedom. During those two months of protests, students, workers, and intellectuals organized their own associations based on democratic principles. China's vast network of Party members, police, and informers could not prevent citizens from using the nation's burgeoning communications network. In today's interdependent world, no nation, not even the mighty Middle Kingdom, is an island. Once Deng allowed the Western media to enter and cover his summit meeting with Mikhail Gorbachev, he allowed the mass media to become a prime factor in the politics of the People's Republic of China.

Will there be another pro-democracy movement in China? Is liberal democracy possible in China? Some Sinologists argue that China must first break "the grip of the past," essentially agreeing with Mao that the "four olds" (old culture, thought, habits, and customs) held China back from modernization, particularly in the economic sphere. Deng took much the same position with his call for economic liberalization.[29] But other analysts suggest that the traditions of China can help form the basis for a liberal democratic society. First, there is the Confucian concept that

28. Robert Delfs, "Speak No Evil," *Far Eastern Economic Review,* December 14, 1989, p. 27.

29. John K. Fairbank, *The Great Chinese Revolution: 1800–1985* (New York: Harper & Row, 1987), pp. 361–68.

human nature is essentially good and sustained by education. Until the Communist era, all Chinese school children read from a primer, written in the Sung Dynasty of the twelfth century, which began:

In the beginning,
Man's nature is good,
And near to one another naturally.
Men are set apart by practice.
Without education,
Nature degenerates.[30]

Second, there is the justification of rebellion against a tyrannical government. Mencius, the great Chinese philosopher of the fourth century b.c., whose relationship to Confucius was like that of Plato to Socrates, wrote: "When a ruler treats his subjects like grass and dirt, then the subjects should treat him as a bandit and an enemy."[31] Third, there is the concept that subordinates have a sacred duty to criticize and oppose the wrongdoings of their superiors. Confucius said in the "Book of Filial Piety": "In the face of a wrong or unrighteousness, it is the duty of the son to oppose his father, and it is the duty of the servant to oppose his ruler."[32]

These ancient philosophical ideas do not contradict but complement modern political ideas like limited government, equality of opportunity, freedom of speech and of the press, an independent judiciary, and the right of the people to dismiss incompetent, corrupt, or tyrannical regimes. Tiananmen Square was not an isolated incident. Since 1900, aside from the 1930s and 1940s when China was resisting Japan's brutal invasion and occupation, every succeeding generation of Chinese has demanded more political freedom; there were nine separate democratic movements in China in the twentieth century—in 1908, 1911, 1917, 1919, 1957, 1968, 1976, 1980, and 1989. Despite the Chinese Communists' antidemocratic campaign, the students and intellectuals who led the 1976, 1980, and 1989 uprisings have not given up; they will continue to press for the political freedom they believe is their natural right as Chinese and as human beings.

---

30. Dimon Liu, debate before the Oxford Union Society, June 4, 1992. I am endebted to Dr. Liu for much of the following analysis.
31. Lin Yutang, *The Wisdom of India and China*, p. 744.
32. As quoted by Dimon Liu, Oxford debate.

THE FIRST LADY IN CHINA

That the Chinese government is determined to suppress political liberty, regardless of the circumstances, was proved in its intimidating treatment of the Fourth World Conference on Women, held in Beijing in September 1995. At the official U.N. event as well as the parallel nongovernmental meeting in the northern suburb of Huairou (attended by an estimated thirty thousand delegates), Chinese security agents "tailed visitors, photographed gatherings, searched rooms and bags, confiscated documents and videotapes, stopped peaceful protests [and] detained some journalists."[33] Several delegates, including exiles from Tibet and leaders from the Republic of China on Taiwan, were denied visas to attend the U.N. conference as well as the NGO meeting. The proceedings of a "global tribunal" on human rights for women halted when Chinese interpreters ceased translating as the secretary general of Amnesty International, which had been openly critical of China, began to speak.[34]

In response, First Lady Hillary Rodham Clinton brought the U.N. delegates to their feet with a litany of abuses that have afflicted women around the world and with sharp criticism of China for trying to limit free and open discussion of women's issues. "It is a violation of human rights," Mrs. Clinton declared, "when babies are denied food, or drowned, or suffocated, or their spines broken, simply because they are born girls. . . . or when women and girls are sold into slavery or prostitution for human greed."[35] She did not have to spell out the offending nation. China has been widely criticized for forcing women to be sterilized or have abortions as part of a one-child family policy. And there have been wide reports of female infanticide by parents who want a son.

Mrs. Clinton admonished her hosts for their antidemocratic behavior, commenting that "freedom means the right of people to assemble, organize, and debate openly. It means respecting the views of those who may disagree with their views of their governments. It means not taking citizens away from their loved ones and jailing them, mistreating them, or

33. James Walsh, "Spirit of Sisterhood," *Time*, September 18, 1995, p. 79.

34. Patrick E. Tyler, "Meddling by China Is Seen as Marring Meeting on Women," *New York Times*, September 2, 1995. Tyler also reported that a Chinese publishing house that had agreed to provide press facilities for a special newspaper at the U.N. meetings reneged on its agreement once the newspaper staff arrived in Beijing.

35. Patrick E. Tyler, "Hillary Clinton, in China, Details Abuse of Women," *New York Times*, September 6, 1995.

denying them their freedom or dignity because of peaceful expression of their ideas and opinions."[36]

Her remarks were cheered by delegates from more than 180 countries, praised by critics left and right, and featured on every evening telecast in the United States and the rest of the world, except for one country. The official Chinese press was under orders to ignore the First Lady. Her speech was summarized in one line at the bottom of a *Peoples' Daily* report. It was blacked out on official television and radio. Turning reality upside down, Beijing TV kept reporting how pleased the U.N. delegates were with Chinese hospitality. CNN carried daily special reports on the conference, but its coverage was reduced through new government controls. Ordinary citizens were prohibited from coming near the conference site. Even for women interested in the conference, it was impossible to obtain a draft of its "Platform for Action," a U.N. document freely available inside the hall. The most striking fact about the U.N. conference in Beijing, observed the *New York Times* correspondent, was how "sealed off" it was from the rest of China, where nearly a quarter of the world's women live.[37]

Three days after the First Lady delivered her powerful but unpublicized address and after she had left the country, the Chinese Communist government retaliated with a blistering attack on U.S. treatment of women. "The position and conditions of Chinese women," asserted the New China News Agency, "are in no way inferior to the situation of the women in the United States and are indeed much better on the whole." As proof, the government organ stated that American women only won the right to vote 144 years after the United States' founding, while Chinese women won suffrage with the founding of the People's Republic of China in 1949. As for Mrs. Clinton's charges about forced abortion, the agency brazenly denied them, stating that "China prohibits forced abortions or forced sterilization, and has adopted a lenient birth policy."[38] In Orwellian China, the truth is what the Communist government and the Communist Party say it is.

SINCE THE PUTSCH

The August 1991 coup in Moscow failed for several reasons, including the widespread hostility of the Russian people to the coup and the plot-

---

36. Ibid.

37. Patrick E. Tyler, "Between U.N. Meeting and Chinese, a Wall," *New York Times,* September 11, 1995.

38. Jane Macartney, "Beijing Says Women Fare Better in China Than in U.S.," *Washington Post,* September 9, 1995.

ters' failure to jail key opponents like Boris Yeltsin. But a major cause was clearly the failure of the plotters to control the mass media and to allow Boris Yeltsin, Mayor Popov of Moscow, Mayor Sobchak of Leningrad (now St. Petersburg), and other pro-democratic leaders to mobilize public support within and without the Soviet Union. If the Committee for the State of Emergency had silenced its opponents and prevented the holding of rallies and other public demonstrations, it might have succeeded in re-instituting Brezhnev-style Communism, although for how long is problematical. After more than seventy years of Communism in all its forms, including the reformist version of Gorbachev, the Soviet people were fed up and ready to try something new—like democracy without centralism and an economy without commands.

In the end, the coup collapsed because its instigators did not have the will to duplicate Tiananmen Square and kill hundreds, perhaps thousands, of resolute Muscovites who had erected a human barricade in front of the Russian Parliament to defend its most important occupant, Russian President Yeltsin. It is quite possible the members of the committee did not give the order to fire because they feared it would not be obeyed. In China, the mass media gave pro-democracy students a false sense of security that was shattered when Deng and the other hardliners sent in the troops and tanks. In the Soviet Union, the mass media strengthened the resolve of Yeltsin and his supporters, who quickly discovered that the plotters were not men of steel like Stalin, but men of butter like the Russian novelist Goncharov's famous non-hero, Oblomov.

Since the putsch, the mass media of Russia, like their counterparts in Eastern and Central Europe, have not had easy going. Under Soviet President Gorbachev, most media received state or Communist Party subsidies; Russian President Yeltsin withdrew state support for most newspapers and magazines, although he continued to underwrite two major television stations, Russian Television and Ostankino Television. Largely because of the increase in subscription prices, necessitated by the loss of subsidies, eighteen of the most popular Russian newspapers and sixteen magazines had twenty-five million fewer subscribers in 1992 than in 1991.[39] By mid-1995, daily circulation of Russian newspapers had fallen to about eight million (from a high of ninety-six million a decade before). Even the highly respected *Moscow News* was in financial trouble but, clinging to its inde-

---

39. Vera Tolz, "The Plight of the Russian Media," *RFE/RL Research Report*, February 28, 1992, p. 57.

pendence, refused to take subsidies from the state.[40] There was recurring concern about censorship. When Yeltsin attempted to close down several major Communist newspapers after the 1993 coup attempt, he was sharply criticized by the Russian media and liberal intellectuals. Aleksandr Yakov-lev, a leading architect of *glasnost* and *perestroika,* lamented that Russia was "regenerating in itself the vices of the past in new wrappings."[41]

Are the anti-Communist "democrats" now in power recreating the un-democratic system of the Communist past? Is it true, as one observer charged, that "the junta has been defeated but democracy is in danger?" Another critic pointed to the many state-owned television and radio sta-tions and the state-run monopolies of newsprint and postal and distribu-tion services and asserted: "In Russia today, as in the Soviet Union in the past, power rests with those who are in charge of distribution of scarce goods."[42] Are the Russian people doomed, as some maintain, to consume all the news that's fit for the government? In such an uncertain climate, there is clearly a role for foreign media, like Radio Liberty, which opened a bureau in Moscow from which it dispenses not only news but suggestions on how to make democracy and a market economy work. Russians have never had to answer questions like: How are prices set? How does a stock market function? How do you establish a social security system? Radio Liberty director Enders Wimbush states that it will take "at least another generation" for Russia to find the answers; "until then," he says, "we are surely needed here."[43]

Amid all the charges and countercharges about press freedom, Yeltsin's consistent response was that the government had no desire or plan to in-fringe on the rights of the media. Yeltsin met with a group of journalists and promised to help publishing houses and the media in general weather the problems caused by the economic crisis. His minister of information pointed out that since the creation of his ministry, 1,700 independent, pri-vate publications as well as almost the same number of publishing houses and dozens of television and radio stations and information agencies had been established. To demonstrate its commitment to pluralism and satisfy

40. Steven Erlanger, "Russian Press Is Free, Free to Go Broke," *New York Times,* July 6, 1995.

41. Julia Wishnevsky, "Russia: Liberal Media Criticize Democrats in Power," *RFE/RL Re-search Report,* January 10, 1992, pp. 6, 8.

42. Igor Sedykh, "All the News That's Deemed Fit," *Christian Science Monitor,* February 21, 1992.

43. Dirk Schutz, "How Radio Liberty Informed the Soviet Population," *Die Zeit,* August 30, 1991.

conservative critics, the press ministry partially subsidized ultra-right-wing publications like *Sovetskaya Rossiya* and the anti-Semitic nationalist paper, *Den,* which have not only criticized the Yeltsin government but called for its overthrow and the restoration of Soviet power.[44]

When the parliamentarian Ruslan Khasbulatov suggested that the newly independent *Izvestia* be made an organ of the Russian Supreme Soviet, Yeltsin registered his firm opposition and publicly reaffirmed his commitment "to defend the mass media." The Russian president kept his word by supporting a new law on the press which ensured no censorship by specifically omitting any provision for funding censorship agencies. The law also stipulated that the media have the right to request information on the activities of state bodies, organizations, public associations, and their officials. Refusal to provide information is possible only if a state, commercial, or other secret specifically protected by law would be exposed.[45]

The unbalanced nature of Russian *mediapolitik* was confirmed when the president's press secretary was asked in an interview whether there had been "cases of the press changing Yeltsin's attitude toward various problems." He responded, "No."[46] But the Russian leader did not hesitate to change media personnel, as when he abruptly fired Yegor Yakovlev, director of the Russian state television company, because of his objective coverage of ethnic conflict in Russia. In another example of media tampering, Yeltsin abolished the St. Petersburg Television Company after its director, whom he had personally chosen, joined the ranks of the Russian nationalists.[47] Since confrontation between the government and the mass media is to be found in the United States and other mature democracies, it is not surprising that the two institutions should find themselves at loggerheads in new democracies like Russia.

In May 2000, the newly inaugurated Russian President Vladimir Putin admitted that "the construction of a democratic society [in Russia] has not been completed," and asserted that "we have to preserve and develop democracy."[48] Many observers in and out of Russia were willing to take

44. Tolz, "The Plight of the Russian Media," p. 54; Jamey Gambrell, "Moscow: The Front Page," *The New York Review,* October 8, 1992, p. 59.

45. Ibid., pp. 60–61; Edith Oltay, "The Russian Media after Glasnost," *Post-Soviet East European Report,* October 22, 1992, p. 6; Vera Tolz, "The Plight of the Russian Media," p. 57.

46. Ibid., p. 59.

47. David Hoffman, "TV's Role in Fostering Democracy," *Christian Science Monitor,* December 18, 1992.

48. Daniel Williams, "Putin Vows to Build Democratic Society," *Washington Post,* May 8, 2000.

Putin (plucked from political obscurity and named prime minister by President Boris Yeltsin) at his word.

But they pointed to the creation of a Press Ministry to oversee the media and the government's exploitation of the state-run media before the Duma elections in December 1999 as possible signs of a more restrictive society. And they noted that the private television station NTV was thrown out of the press pool in January 2000 for reporting that Russian casualities in Chechnya were five times what the Kremlin admitted.[49]

Perhaps most worrisome was the role of television in Putin's winning presidential campaign. Although Putin waived his free air time, he received "the lion's share of news coverage on all television networks." Putin was often shown surrounded by groups of enthusiastic supporters. On the last day campaigning was allowed, Putin taped a three-minute address urging citizens to vote that was broadcast in full at the beginning of every newscast over the two major television channels—Russian Public Television (ORT) and Russian Television (RTR).[50]

There is no proof that Putin or his campaign staff ordered ORT or RTR to cover the presidential campaign as they did. But their news coverage, according to the Russian media analyst Laura Belin, "followed the general script of Putin's campaign."[51] If President Putin is sincere about his pledge to build a democratic society in Russia, he must not make a practice of manipulating the media as he apparently did in his presidential campaign.

Is the antagonism inevitable or can it be ameliorated? Are there steps, political, legal, economic, and moral, that can be taken to produce a more liberal, more democratic form of *mediapolitik* in Russia? A major obstacle to the building of democracy in Russia and other post-Communist countries, says the Radio Free Europe analyst Paul Goble, is that many people appear to be more interested in what their governments can give them than in how they go about it. A September 1999 poll by the All-Russian Center for the Study of Public Opinion revealed that most Russians ranked entitlements like education, medical care, and pensions as far more important than free speech or the right to information. Such an attitude, Goble suggests, could encourage leaders to deliver the goods de-

49. Jamie Dettmer, "Putin Revives Soviet-Style Media Curbs in Russia," *Washington Times,* February 27, 2000.

50. Laura Belin, "Russian Election Report: News and Analysis of the 2000 Russian Presidential Election," RFE/RL broadcast, April 7, 2000.

51. Ibid.

manded by the people while violating democratic norms "with impuni-
ty."[52]

So, to borrow from Lenin, what is to be done? First, and above all, there
must be a clear separation of executive, legislative, and judicial powers,
with no one branch of government able to dominate the others. Second,
there must be a resolution of conflict through the rule of law and not executive fiat. Third, the government should continue to encourage private
television channels and radio stations. Fourth, the Russian media must
abandon its preference for commentary based on the French model, and
take up factual reportage patterned after the American model. The media's
highly politicized approach is viewed by many as harmful and antidemocratic. They want straightforward reporting so that they can draw their
own conclusions. Fifth, journalists must accept the responsibility to confirm the information they receive and avoid the use of unproved asser-
tions, no matter how provocative.

Dmitry Avraamov, who teaches journalism ethics at Moscow University, insists that the freedom of choice that Russian journalists now enjoy
also requires individual morality. That is a difficult step, he concedes, in a
country where the notion of personal ethics, with its emphasis on individual responsibility and moral behavior, runs counter to the old Soviet mass
media's collectivist ethic.[53] But personal ethics and morality are not inconsistent with historic Russian values rooted in Orthodox Christianity,
which is enjoying a strong revival in Russia, especially among those under
thirty years of age.

Individual morality must be cultivated by journalists and politicians to
protect the liberties won and prevent the return to power of Leninist demagogues. Andrei Sakharov wrote in his historic proposal for democracy,
justice, and freedom, smuggled from the Soviet Union and published in
the West seven years before he received the Nobel Prize for Peace in 1975:

Intellectual freedom is essential to human society—freedom to obtain and distribute information, freedom for open-minded and unfearing debate, and freedom from pressure by officialdom and prejudices. Such a trinity of freedom
of thought is the only guarantee against an infection of people by mass myths,
which, in the hands of treacherous hypocrites and demagogues, can be trans-

52. Paul Goble, "Entitlements, Rights and Democracy," Radio Free Europe/Radio Liberty analysis, September 30, 1999.
53. Marcel Dufresne, "A Soviet Press Code," *Washington Journalism Review,* July/August
1990, p. 30.

formed into bloody dictatorship. Freedom of thought is the only guarantee of the feasibility of a scientific democratic approach to politics, economy, and culture.[54]

THE POWER OF THE DEMOCRATIC MODEL

At first glance, it might appear that the liberal democratic model of *mediapolitik* played a somewhat similar role in Chile and South Africa, enabling the Chilean opposition to bring down a military dictator, Augusto Pinochet, and the South African opposition to force the release of its imprisoned, charismatic leader, Nelson Mandela. In both instances, the mass media played a decisive democratic role, in the absence of which General Pinochet might still be president and Mandela still in prison. But there was a fundamental difference between the political philosophy of the leaders of the two countries. Pinochet was a Machiavellian who believed that he could use the mass media as a means to his authoritarian ends, i.e., to remain in power. De Klerk was a constitutional democrat who believed that the mass media could be used to democratic ends, i.e., to share power. The Chilean *caudillo* did not understand the innate liberalizing power of the media in a democracy. Despite all their economic and political resources, Pinochet and his administration could not overcome the nightly impact of fifteen minutes of pro-freedom, pro-democracy television on the minds and votes of the Chilean people. Information rooted in democratic principles and disseminated through a media protected by a constitution bested propaganda based on fear and demagogy.

In contrast, de Klerk used the media to persuade his white supporters that they should share power with the black majority. Government-controlled media presented Mandela and other black leaders as reasonable men, not Communist revolutionaries, that the government could negotiate with. De Klerk deliberately abandoned the authoritarian model of his predecessor and adopted a liberal democratic model predicated on the principle that politics and the mass media should be free of government control. A new kind of South Africa, de Klerk reasoned, required a new kind of *mediapolitik*.

The defeat of Pinochet through constitutional means renewed the traditional faith of the Chilean people in democracy. Chile found it comparatively easy to resume practicing freedom of assembly, speech, and the

---

54. Andrei Sakharov, "Thoughts on Progress, Peaceful Coexistence, and Intellectual Freedom," in *Without Force or Lies: Voices from the Revolution of Central Europe in 1989–90*, ed. William Brinton and Alan Rinzler (San Francisco: Mercury House, 1990), p. 4.

press while retaining the free market and other economic reforms instituted by the Pinochet government. The Chilean government, however, has proposed that a reporter have a journalism diploma to ply his trade. Some journalists see the seeds of a state-controlled media in the proposal. They also note with concern the new constitution of its northern neighbor, Colombia, which ensures the "right to honor" for citizens, a right that could be interpreted to protect politicians from public—i.e., media—criticism.[55] They worry that a similar provision might be introduced in Chile.

For all their anxiety, Chilean journalists know their independence is far greater than that of their Mexican colleagues. In Mexico, reporters' low wages are often supplemented by under-the-table government payments known as *embutes*. It is also a common practice for newspapers to give reporters a 15 percent sales commission on advertisements placed by government ministries that the reporters cover. The practice has a predictably inhibiting effect on investigative journalism in Mexico. Withholding advertising is a weapon that the government has used to punish unfriendly media. It is a powerful weapon: many newspapers receive 40 to 60 percent of their advertising revenues from state corporations or agencies. As a result, newspapers and radio and television stations are careful not to offend the wrong public official; and news broadcasts by Mexico's commercial network, Televisa, have a reputation of being more progovernment than the state-run Imevision.[56] The solution, as emphasized in these pages, is a solid framework of democratic laws and institutions within which both politicians and journalists operate. To his credit, former President Carlos Salinas de Gortari took several steps to extend media freedom in Mexico, including the formation of the National Commission on Human Rights, an ombudsman agency which investigates human rights violations; the importation of newsprint which has diminished the potential control of the state newsprint agency over critical publications; and the privatization of some state-owned television and radio stations.[57]

THE PRISM OF RACE

As with everything in South Africa, the interrelationship of politics and media is dominated by race. Leading up to the 1994 elections, de Klerk

55. Julia Michaels, "Despite Democracy, the Free Press Is under Fire in Latin America," *Christian Science Monitor,* November 5, 1991.

56. David Clark Scott, "Mexico's Press Guards Its Freedom," *Christian Science Monitor,* September 26, 1991.

57. Ibid.

knew that retaining political and economic rights for the white minority in a new multiracial society depended in large measure on the media's reporting and supporting the reasons for such rights. To demonstrate his commitment to multiracial media, de Klerk appointed Madala Mphahlele, a black executive, to head the South African Broadcasting Corporation's second channel, which alternated between English and five African languages. Mphahlele saw his job as devising a strategy for programming that would unite the country's ethnic groups. But many black leaders who suffered for decades under apartheid were not very interested in whites' rights and expected the mass media, particularly the black media, to support black majority rule without any restrictions. There were disturbing acts of black on black censorship, including threats of "necklacing" (burning a tire around someone's neck) and organized campaigns to stop stores from stocking the "wrong" newspaper. An editor of the black-oriented *Sowetan* commented: "We have now reached a point where a journalist is told, 'You are either for us or against us.'"[58]

Nevertheless, media owners and journalists praised the media charter released by the African National Congress, which called for freedom of the media, the free flow of information and the scrapping of all censorship laws, removal of the South African Broadcasting Corporation from government control, and diversity of media ownership. But they pointed to worrisome phrases in the charter such as "democratization of the media," "media monitoring and regulating," and the "assurance of diversity of ownership," all of which have elements of government compulsion.[59] One observer wrote that black journalists in South Africa faced conflicts with "their readers, their paymasters, the political groups they cover—and work in a climate of violence few American journalists could even contemplate."[60] In such a climate, press freedom needs guarantees like those in the First Amendment to the U.S. Constitution. In fact, they already exist in the "African Claims," a remarkable human rights document written during World War II by black African politicians and intellectuals, including the then-president of the African National Congress, A. B. Xuma. The document declared that:

58. Phillip van Niekerk, "'Mau Mauing' South Africa's Media," *Weekly Mail,* reprinted in *World Press Review,* October 1991, p. 54.

59. Raymond Louw, "ANC Media Moves Welcomed, But . . ." *IPI Report,* February 1992, p. 13.

60. Juliette Kayyem, "The New Censors," *The New Republic,* January 27, 1992, p. 19.

• All governments must derive their authority from the consent of the governed.

• No person or group of persons should be subjected to oppression and domination by virtue of his or her race, gender, ethnic origin or religion.

• All persons should enjoy the right to life, unfettered by impositions from either secular or clerical authorities.

• All persons should have the right to hold and express whatever opinions they wish to subscribe to, provided that the exercise of that right does not infringe the rights of others.[61]

With these ideals as a foundation, a democratic South Africa respectful of every citizen's rights regardless of his color is possible. Such a country was significantly advanced by the national election of April 1994, when millions of South Africans—three-fourths of them black and voting for the first time—elected South Africa's first democratic government. The mass media continued to be an important factor in the transition to democracy. In a televised debate with Mandela prior to the election, de Klerk stated, "The ANC and the National Party promise the same thing. The real test is who has a plan to achieve it."[62] Mandela, who did not even see television until the 1970s, revealed once again his mastery of the media by grasping de Klerk's hand at the end of the debate, which, all observers agree, he won. Mandela said he would be proud to work with his opponent. He was, as ever, gracious, gentlemanly, and in command.[63]

Sixty percent of South Africans picked the plan of the ANC and the leadership of Nelson Mandela, who, seeking consensus, asked de Klerk to serve as a deputy president in his government of national unity. De Klerk accepted, commenting about the peaceful transition of power, "I feel a sense of achievement."[64] From his first day in office, Mandela sought to reassure white South Africans, whose cooperation and capital he needed to reach his economic and political goals. Quoting from his speech at his trial for treason thirty years before, Mandela said, "I cherish the idea of a new South Africa where all South Africans are equal, where all South Africans work together to bring about security, peace and democracy in our country."[65]

61. Nelson Mandela, "Press Helped to Free Me from Prison," *IPI Report,* June/July 1991, p. 11.

62. Bruce W. Nelan, "Time to Take Charge," *Time,* May 9, 1994, p. 30.

63. Richard Stengel, "Portrait of a Leader," *Time,* May 9, 1994, p. 38.

64. Ibid.

65. Ibid.

Most of the media remained initially in the hands of the white minority. In 1994, for example, all but ten of the sixty-one managers of the South African Broadcasting Corporation were white, and almost all spoke Afrikaans, not English, as a first language. The head of SABC's news department once said that he would not hire any reporter who did not speak Afrikaans, eliminating almost every black candidate whose first language is tribal and whose second language is usually English.[66] But in 1994, the head of the SABC, Gert Claassen, vowed that the corporation's staff would be 50 percent black and 50 percent female by 1997—and he very nearly succeeded. The principle driving the transformation, explained a senior general manager, was that SABC would "reflect South African society rather than become the tool of any government."[67]

In that spirit, the black majority government must be careful not to do in the future what the white minority government did in the past. "Whenever we criticized the [white] government," said one prominent black political reporter, "the ANC cheered. Now they will be the government. Will they cheer when they are criticized?"[68] There is a danger, commented Allister Sparks, the former editor of the *Rand Daily Mail,* that the wrong kind of press "could easily breach a nervous government's tolerance threshold and invite the 'remedy' of press control."[69] The ANC-led government must not only "honor" the rights of journalists and a free press but institutionalize those rights through laws. In so acting, the government will match deeds with words and strengthen the democratic foundation for the new South Africa.

THE "THIRD SUPERPOWER"

The power of the mass media is inexorably increasing around the world. Infrastructure alone tells much of the story: more than 1.2 billion television sets now dot the globe (an average of one set for every fifth person), a 50 percent jump over the last five years. The number is expected to continue growing by 5 percent annually, and more than twice that in Asia, where half the world lives. Television sets are more common in Japan than

---

66. Adam C. Powell III, "Johannesburg Spring," *American Journalism Review,* June 1994, p. 39.

67. Kimberly J. McLarin, "The Voice of Apartheid Goes Multicultural," *New York Times,* July 25, 1995.

68. Powell, "Johannesburg Spring," p. 38.

69. Allister Sparks, "For the Media, the Opportunities of Pretoriastroika," *Media Studies Journal,* fall 1993, p. 109.

flush toilets; almost every Mexican household has television but only half have a telephone.[70] The total number of portable radios is nearing 2.5 billion, a 100 percent increase in the last fifteen years. Although most of the world's radios can pick up international programs via short wave, few television sets could until the 1980s. But with the development of satellite television and individual receiving dishes—the size of a pizza and the cost of a radio—national borders are disappearing and individuals rather than governments are increasingly controlling the flow of information, except in countries like Iraq and North Korea.

Political leaders, democratic and nondemocratic, are obliged to spend more of their time coping with what Timothy Garton Ash, an Oxford University political scientist, calls "the third superpower"—the mass media. Diplomats in Libya, for example, say television is weakening the regime of Muammar Qadhafi by exposing the country's impoverished population to the tempting consumer products seen in Italian commercials. Rather than resisting borderless television, many goverments are leasing or launching their own satellites. Like ambitious nations that want to join the nuclear club and be one of the big boys, "a country today barely ranks as a world-class power unless it lofts a satellite bearing its own acronym." Examples include Asiasat, Aussat, Turksat, Thaicom, Arabsat, Insat, Indonesia's Palapa, and Spain's Hispasat. The overriding reason is almost always political sovereignty, not economic rationality: "Each country," explained Meherro Jussawalla of the East-West Center, "wants to control its own satellite system for domestic purposes."[71]

The mass media have changed the practice of politics in countries—democratic, authoritarian, and totalitarian—as the case studies in this book about major nations have demonstrated. Smaller nations are no less affected. The royal family of Thailand, for example, used television to halt large-scale public unrest that included several deaths and resulted from a struggle between the military-dominated government and the democratic opposition. In a satellite television interview from Paris, where she was visiting, Princess Maha Charki Sirindhorn urged Thai citizens to end their fighting. Then, King Bhumibol Adulyedej, a universally revered figure in Thailand, held a televised audience with two feuding generals. Pictures of the uniformed, decorated leaders shuffling up to the king on their knees as

70. John Lippman, "How TV Is Transforming World Culture and Politics," *Los Angeles Times*, October 20, 1992.

71. Ibid.

he scolded them were broadcast across the country and around the world, demonstrating royal power and humiliating the generals, who agreed to stop fighting and name a nonmilitary prime minister.[72] In this instance, a monarch used television to advance democracy in a country that follows an authoritarian model of *mediapolitik*.

THE NEW WORLD INFORMATION ORDER

The third world has long resented seeing the rest of the world through the West's eyes, a fact made inevitable by American and other developed nations' ownership of global news organizations like the Associated Press, BBC, and Agence France Press. The emergence of satellite communication makes cultural imperialism a real possibility for many third world nations. In addition, few developing countries have much sympathy for the Western concept of a free press. The Indian author S. Nihal Singh says that most third world countries, justifying their self-perceived need for a censored and even government-controlled press, "mixed their genuine grievances with dubious self-interest" to endorse enthusiastically what came to be called the New World Information and Communication Order (NWICO).[73] The philosophy of NWICO was that each nation should become self-reliant in mass communications and not be dependent on other nations. Each nation has the right to determine its own communications system and to decide what should be communicated and why. Implicit in NWICO was the view that developed and less-developed nations have different communications objectives and that the latter wish to use the mass media to promote national economic growth, develop and preserve national culture, and create a national identity among diverse ethnic and religious groups.[74]

The 1978 general conference of UNESCO (United Nations Educational, Scientific and Cultural Organization) accepted NWICO as an official goal and helped place it on the agenda of the United Nations, which that same year adopted a resolution requesting UNESCO's director general to "draw up a model for cooperation and assistance in the application and improvement of national information and mass communication systems for social progress and development."[75] For Western, especially American,

---

72. Tyler Marshall, "TV a Star Player on the World's Political Stage," *Los Angeles Times,* October 20, 1992.

73. S. N. Singh, *The Rise and Fall of UNESCO* (Ahmedabad, India: Allied Publishers, 1988), p. 75.

74. Robert G. Picard, "Global Communications Controversies," *Global Journalism*, p. 82.

75. Ibid., p. 85.

journalists, the language conjured up Big Brother images and threatened the freedom of the press.

The McBride Commission, chaired by Sean McBride, winner of the Nobel and Lenin Peace Prizes, submitted a final report on the New World Information and Communication Order to the 1980 UNESCO general conference. The reaction of the U.S. delegate was surprisingly mild, expressing some reservations but stating: "My government was particularly pleased to find an unequivocal affirmation of freedom of the press and full access to news stories."[76] But prominent nongovernmental organizations like the International Press Institute and the World Press Freedom Committee were greatly disturbed by the McBride Commission report and asked UNESCO to suspend its work in the field.

The two most controversial issues related to the "right to communicate" and the "protection of journalists." The right to communicate was proposed as a new human right in the information society. That sounded reasonable, but a UNESCO document about NWICO principles talked of communication "both as a right of the individual and as a *collective right* [emphasis added] guaranteed to all communities and nations." That language set up an inevitable conflict between the liberal democratic philosophy of individual-oriented Western societies and the more authoritarian philosophy of group-oriented third world societies. To Western journalists, "collectivist" seemed only a short distance from "collective." Concern spread that the "right to communicate" might lead to a normative code drawn up by some international body like UNESCO, which appeared to be moving farther and farther from its democratic origins.

The issue of protection of journalists rose out of the Indo-China war, with meetings first held by various U.N. and other bodies. There was talk of issuing "safety cards" to journalists who covered wars and other conflicts. Consistent with its liberal democratic principles, the United States objected to giving the United Nations—an agency of mixed governments, democratic, authoritarian, and totalitarian—the power to issue or withdraw safety cards. When it was not invited by UNESCO to attend a 1981 international meeting on the protection of journalists, the World Press Freedom Committee convened its own meeting and issued a statement calling on UNESCO to "abandon attempts to regulate news content and formulate rules for the press."[77] Belatedly, UNESCO officials realized how

76. Ibid., pp. 87–88.
77. Ibid., pp. 90–91.

provocative the NWICO proposals were to Western journalists and governments and began backing off.

At the 1983 general conference, NWICO was described as an "evolving process" rather than a set of principles. UNESCO's new director general, Federico Mayor, went much farther, declaring in 1988 that plans for the New World Information and Communication Order "no longer" existed because they violated human rights clauses in the organization's charter. "UNESCO," Mayor declared, "must guarantee the free flow of information."[78] But such palliatives were too little and too late for the United States, Great Britain, and other Western nations, whose skepticism about UNESCO's true intentions was reinforced by a lavish 1989 conference in the Ivory Coast. Under the title "Peace in the Minds of Men," conferees discussed the responsibility of media decision makers and "the overhaul of the role and the messages of the mass media" through the prism of the state rather than the individual journalist.[79] It was evident, at least to most Western nations, that the world would have to look somewhere other than the United Nations or UNESCO for guidance about the proper balance between politics and the mass media.

TELEDEMOCRACY

Over the last three decades, almost all the parliaments of the industrialized democracies have been opened to television, subjecting the legislative process to public examination as never before. Many legislators have been reluctant to acknowledge that the media millennium is at hand. In Great Britain, members of Parliament voted eight times over twenty years before finally admitting cameras into the mother of parliaments in 1988. Sometimes television can galvanize the public into unanticipated action. In Japan, a parliamentary committee approved the overseas deployment of noncombat troops in 1989 for disaster relief and U.N. peacekeeping activities—the first use of Japanese forces outside the country since the end of World War II. Many Japanese leftists and pacifists strongly opposed the measure. The committee vote sparked a brawl in which television cameras showed members of the Buddhist Komei (Clean Government) Party fighting alongside ruling Liberal Democrats—a scene that so angered Komei

78. Jim Hoagland, "Europe's New Romance with Ecology," *Washington Post,* March 28, 1989.

79. D. Kinnane-Roelofsma, statement before UNESCO Oversight Hearing, Senate Foreign Relations Committee, April 19, 1989.

members, most of whom opposed overseas deployment, that the party abandoned its support for the bill. It took Prime Minister Kiichi Miyazawa weeks of careful politicking, and the imposition of more restrictions on the use of the troops, to persuade the Komei party to help enact the bill.[80] In this instance, the ruling LDP significantly altered important legislation because television forced the party to pay more attention to an essential element of democracy that it often ignores—the people.

As we have seen in Chile, television has the ability to turn the course of campaigns and the outcome of elections in a more democratic direction. But television can produce nondemocratic outcomes, even in a democracy. Before being elected president of Brazil, Fernando Collor de Mello was an attractive but little-known state governor with a modest record of success and the backing of a new, small political party. But in the 1989 presidential election Roberto Marinho, owner of Rede Globo, which produces 70 percent of all Brazilian television, enthusiastically supported the forty-year-old Collor and his free-market plans to modernize Brazil. Marinho is probably the most influential man in Latin America's most populous nation, "the president with no term of office," in the opinion of *Imprensa* magazine, Brazil's main journalism review.[81] With Marinho's backing and the power of Rede Globo, the charismatic, telegenic Mellor defeated the other better-known candidates from larger parties. But seasoned politicians understand that you need more than the media to govern—you must have a broad-based program, a consistent philosophy, and a national constituency, especially in times of crisis. When a financial scandal subsequently caused Collor's removal from office, several political observers laid his downfall not so much to the release of an incriminating report but to Marinho's decision—and Globo's—to give prominent coverage to street rallies calling for his impeachment. The lesson of Collor's rapid rise and fall was not lost on Brazilian politicians. Among the first people the new president of Brazil met was *mediameister* Roberto Marinho.[82]

What all our case studies suggest is that where there are weak democratic institutions there will inevitably arise strongmen eager to seize power but exceedingly reluctant to give it up. In the hands of such demagogues, the mass media are not a technology of choice but of control —not of freedom, but of slavery.

80. Ibid.
81. Julia Preston, "Brazil's Power of the Press," *Washington Post*, December 9, 1992.
82. Ibid.

CHAPTER 12

THE MILLENNIUM OF
THE MEDIA

THE MASS MEDIA, particularly what are called "the new media,"
continue to change the politics of the oldest democracy in the world—the
United States. John F. Kennedy was the first television president in 1960,
Ross Perot the first talk show presidential candidate in 1992. Both used television to address the voters directly—Kennedy in his televised news conferences, Perot mostly on cable television programs—without being fil-
tered—that is, mediated—through the critical judgment of traditional
journalists and politicians.

In *The Electronic Commonwealth*, Jeffrey Abramson, Christopher Arte-
ton, and Garry Orren provide examples of the "new" media: cable television, satellites, computers, teleconferencing, videocassette recorders,
videotext, laser discs, and fiber optics; and the "old" media: broadcast television, radio, newspapers, magazines, telephones, and telegraph. The authors describe six characteristics of the new media: they "explode" previous limits on the volume of information; they make it possible to
exchange information without regard for time and space; they increase
consumer control over the kinds of message received; they increase the
sender's control over which audiences receive which messages; they decentralize mass communications; and they give interactive or two-way capability to television.[1]

1. Jeffrey B. Abramson, F. Christopher Arterton, and Garry R. Orren, *The Electronic
Commonwealth: The Impact of New Media Technologies on Democratic Politics* (New York:
Basic Books, 1988), pp. 4–5.

THE FASTEST GROWING MEDIUM

The Internet is not, the political scientist Richard Davis points out, as new as many assume: it was established in 1969 at the University of California for purposes of national defense. Private online services began in the 1970s, with CompuServe the first to offer online access service to customers late in the decade. With the introduction of the World Wide Web in the mid-1990s, a "network of [private] computer access providers," writes Davis, "became the backbone of the Internet."[2] The newest medium is different from the old media in that Internet users can send and receive messages. The Net integrates text, audio, and visual presentations on the same site. The Internet is, in fact, "a range of mediums all in one."[3] And it may be the fastest growing medium in mass communications history: it took the telephone thirty-eight years to reach a market penetration of 30 percent of households, something the Internet did in seven years. In early 1993, about 90,000 Americans had access to the Internet; in January 1999, the figure was eighty-one million adults, an increase of 900 percent.[4]

After some initial hesitation, old-line media organizations began using the Internet to expand their audience, particularly among younger Americans. In early 1997, more than 1,500 newspapers had electronic issues, including major dailies like the *New York Times* and the *Washington Post.* C-SPAN has put its broadcast programs on its home page; talk radio is available through Internet sites. By 1998, according to Richard Davis, 93 percent of news organizations were using the Internet to gather news, while 86 percent of journalists said they used the Net to find sources. And the Internet has ratcheted up the already swift process of news gathering and delivery—for every news organization, there is now "the challenge of 24-hour news updating."[5]

That sometimes results in a "feeding frenzy," to use the political scientist Larry Sabato's term, as it did in January 1998. *Newsweek* had been preparing a long story about the sexual relationship between President Bill Clinton and a young White House intern named Monica Lewinsky, and decided to delay the article for a week, looking for more verification. Someone from *Newsweek,* leaking with the same sense of purpose as an

2. Richard Davis, *The Web of Politics: The Internet's Impact on the American Political System* (New York: Oxford University Press, 1999), pp. 34–35.

3. Ibid., p. 36.

4. James P. Lucier, "Goodtimes.com," *Insight,* July 19, 1999, p. 13.

5. Davis, *The Web of Politics,* p. 56.

outraged government official, called an Internet columnist named Matt Drudge (who wears an old-fashioned Walter Winchell fedora). Without bothering to check the facts, Drudge went online, boasting of a "World Exclusive!" Instantly, wrote Richard Reeves, an author and journalism professor, "the nation was wading through minute-to-minute multimedia reportage of rumors, affidavits, oaths, depositions," melding traditional journalism and Internet technology.[6] The end result of this uneasy marriage was the impeachment but not the conviction of President Clinton.

Most elected officials, nevertheless, have embraced the new technology. Every U.S. senator and about half the members of the U.S. House of Representatives have Web pages. Every major Republican presidential contender had his own page in 1996, as do the leading candidates in 2000 (Governor George W. Bush put the names of all his contributors online). Independent Jesse Ventura had no party structure or endorsements in 1998 when he sought Minnesota's governorship—all he had was his name, a libertarian program, and the Net. There is a move in California to allow voting online. The Library of Congress in 1995 established an online system offering all legislation considered and passed by Congress. Some enthusiastic politicians—like Vice President Al Gore—have predicted that the Internet will spread "participatory democracy" and create a global conversation "in which everyone who wants can have his or her say."[7]

But only about half of U.S. households have a personal computer, and Internet users, especially those who use the Net for political news and information, are—so far—not representative of the general population. Internet users tend to have higher incomes and more education and, according to a Pew Research Center survey, to be more politically active. Missing from the "electronic commons," one analyst stated, are the poor and minorities.[8] And as a practical matter, media analyst Bruce M. Owen says, "using the Internet is far from being as cheap, easy, and reliable as watching TV."[9] What the Internet can do better than any other medium is tailor

6. Richard Reeves, *What the People Know: Freedom and the Press* (Cambridge, Mass.: Harvard University Press, 1998), p. 120.

7. Albert Gore, speech to the International Telecommunications Union, Washington, March 21, 1994.

8. Davis, *The Web of Politics*, p. 26.

9. Bruce M. Owen, "The Internet Challenge to Television," *AEI Newsletter*, August 1999, p. 3. Owen delivered the lecture at the American Enterprise Institute, Washington, on July 8, 1999, based on his new book, *The Internet Challenge to Television* (Harvard University Press, 1999).

information to the individual requesting it, stimulating a new and potentially powerful grassroots politics—as Ventura's gubernatorial victory proved.

As might be expected, some countries do not welcome such activism. The Paris-based Reporters sans Frontiers identified in August 1999 twenty nations that forced subscribers to use a state-controlled Internet service provider or censored Web sites. The worst offenders were the Communist regimes in China, Cuba, North Korea, and Vietnam, followed by the authoritarian governments in Burma, Iran, Iraq, and Libya. China, for example, closed three hundred cybercafes in Shanghai and sent a computer user to jail for two years for providing the e-mail addresses of thirty thousand Chinese to a dissident Web site.[10] But, the management theorist Peter Drucker and other analysts argue, the Internet operates without regard for national or political borders: it has created a global marketplace and politics beyond the power of the state to control.[11]

The clash of new and old media has produced a paradox. In 1998, the combined audience of the three oldest networks—ABC, CBS, and NBC—in prime time (8 to 11 P.M.) was only 25 percent of households with television. By adding the newer broadcast networks like Rupert Murdoch's Fox, UPN, WB, and PAX, the figure reached 32 percent.[12] But during the same period, increased advertising rates produced record profits (ABC reported an 84 percent increase in profits one year) and billion-dollar bids for the networks by bottom-line-conscious conglomerates. Analysts point out that the "webs" (as the broadcast networks are known) still offer free, over-the-air entertainment and information that blanket the country. Although 98 percent of U.S. households are wired for cable, only 70 percent subscribe. "Most advertisers," says *Variety*'s Max Robbins, "would still rather send one message to a large audience one time, than run a commercial ten times to ten smaller audiences on cable."[13] Robbins's observation also holds true for national politics, where Republican and Democratic candidates spend more than two-thirds of their budgets on broadcast television.

10. Paul Goble, "An Internet Enemies List," Radio Free Europe/Radio Liberty analysis, August 12, 1999.

11. See Peter F. Drucker, "Beyond the Information Revolution," *The Atlantic Monthly*, October 1999, pp. 47–57.

12. Robert J. Samuelson, "Network Fadeout," *Washington Post*, January 13, 1999.

13. Alexandra Marks, "If TV Networks Are Dinosaurs, Then This Is Still the Jurassic Age," *Christian Science Monitor*, October 23, 1995.

"OLD" AND "NEW" MEDIA

Sometimes, the difference between the new media and the old is not that great. Walter Wriston, the former chairman of Citicorp, has described personal computers as electronic throwbacks to the Committees of Correspondence during the American Revolution, which kept patriots advised of the latest developments in the war with England. Today, private PC users communicate through thousands of electronic bulletin boards on the Internet that carry news about everything from personal experiences to political messages.[14] "Old" media like CBS and the *New York Times* will continue to have an impact on politics and campaigns for many years to come, but with satellites, says James M. Perry, a political reporter, candidates can hold rallies in different parts of the country at the same time. Campaign strategists in separate cities and states can meet in teleconferences. Direct mail is being supplemented by videocassettes sent to targeted voters—a tactic that the television evangelist Pat Robertson used in the 1988 Republican primaries and Republican Senator Richard Lugar of Indiana (normally thought of as an old-style politician) emulated in the 1996 primaries.[15] In the 2000 elections, campaigns are using the Internet to disseminate information, gauge public opinion, get out the vote, and raise funds.

Amid all the media fireworks, nothing was more controversial than Ross Perot's suggesting, during the 1992 campaign, the establishment of an electronic town hall in which voters would replace their elected representatives in deciding public policy—a continental impulse of the moment that would delight Jean Jacques Rousseau and disturb James Madison. After the president, members of Congress, and various experts had presented on national television some proposed legislation or policy, voters would register their opinion with a button on their television set or by telephone or even postcard. As Perot explained to his favorite talk show host, CNN's Larry King, "It's either up or down or sideways," prompting the question: Was he referring to the fate of the legislation or of representative democracy? In the opinion of the futurist John Naisbitt, that is a moot question because "we have outlived the historical usefulness of representative democracy."[16]

14. Guy Halverson, "Wriston Sees Information Era Diffusing Power," *Christian Science Monitor,* October 16, 1992.

15. James M. Perry, "Call It New Media, Teledemocracy or Whatever, It's Changing the Way the Political System Works," *Wall Street Journal,* June 24, 1992.

16. Ibid.; John Naisbitt, *Megatrends* (New York: Warner Books, 1984), p. 177.

Lawrence K. Grossman, former president of NBC News and PBS, has predicted that the day is fast approaching when, thanks to the new electronic technologies, we will achieve "plebiscite democracy." As evidence, he cites state ballot initiatives, the demand for national referenda, and talk radio. The people, he says, will become "the fourth branch of government, alongside the president, the Congress and the courts."[17] But Grossman seriously misreads American political history. From the beginning of the Republic until the present, the people have been the trunk of our government, with the presidency, the Congress, and the judiciary branching out from them. Our most successful political leaders have been guided by the will of the people, from Abraham Lincoln (preserving the Union) and Franklin Roosevelt (overcoming the Great Depression) to Harry Truman (containing Communism) and Ronald Reagan (reducing the size of the welfare state). When presidents ignored the people or misrepresented their best interests—as Lyndon B. Johnson did on the Vietnam War and Richard Nixon with Watergate—they either left office or were removed from it.

Grossman argues that the old system of checks and balances carefully crafted by the Founding Fathers will be replaced by an "electronic republic." At the center of this cyberdemocracy will be "an informed, engaged, public-spirited electorate."[18] But such an electorate would not be new: it is at the very heart of the republic envisioned by the Founders. Madison, Jefferson, and the others expected the press (what we now call the mass media) to inform the people regularly about their government and their elected representatives so that the people would remain engaged in their workings. The result was to be a public-spirited people and nation. American history confirms that the system of checks and balances created by the Founders has generally worked well throughout our history, particularly in time of crisis—as during the Civil War, the Great Depression, and the cold war. Where the American system has failed has been due to a lack of leadership by our politicians and our journalists, as during the Vietnam War and the Bill Clinton–Monica Lewinsky scandal.

A more subtle criticism of representative democracy is made by Alvin Toffler, a futurist often quoted by former House Speaker Newt Gingrich. In *The Third Wave* and other works, Toffler and his wife Heidi argue that

---

17. Lawrence K. Grossman, "Beware the Electronic Republic," *USA Today*, August 29, 1995.

18. Ibid.

we are in the middle of a "third wave" in human history—the information revolution—that is replacing the "second wave," the industrial revolution, which in its turn replaced the "first wave," the agricultural revolution. In the third wave, argue the Tofflers, we must build a new political system based on three principles: (1) minority power rather than majority rule, which is becoming obsolete; (2) semidirect democracy, in which we will shift from depending exclusively on representatives to representing ourselves on many occasions; and (3) decision division, in which we put more decisions where they belong—at the state or local, rather than the national, level. The Tofflers insist that the issue "is not 'either/or' in character." They are proposing a *combination* of direct and indirect democracy. "But we must," they say, "begin thinking outside the worn grooves of the past three hundred years."[19]

Despite the Tofflerian rhetoric, most political scientists believe that representative democracy has not outlived its usefulness. Because electronic town halls and similar feed-back mechanisms can be easily manipulated, American politics needs deliberation and discussion, in and out of Washington, to prevent American democracy from becoming a crudely majoritarian system. A demagogue could misuse television to create an electronic mob; historical antecedents that come to mind are Huey Long and Father Charles Coughlin in Depression-era America, Hitler in Nazi Germany, and Lenin and Stalin in the Soviet Union. Almost certainly, electronic referenda would further weaken political parties, increase voter volatility, and expand single issue politics. Although some scholars continue to be intrigued by the possibilities of "real-time participation" in public affairs, even Perot has had second thoughts, saying that what he really meant was using interactive television to allow millions of Americans to participate, symbolically, in the legislative process.[20]

THE CNN PHENOMENON

Cable television, and especially the Cable News Network (CNN), deserves a special place in any discussion of *mediapolitik*. What a computer does within an office, CNN does around the world, giving millions of viewers on different continents the same information at the same mo-

19. Alvin and Heidi Toffler, *Creating a New Civilization: The Politics of the Third Wave* (Atlanta: Turner Publishing, 1995), p. 99. Also see Alvin Toffler, *The Third Wave* (New York: Bantam Books, 1980), pp. 419–34.

20. Hugh Carter Donahue, "Ross Perot as Master of the Media," *Christian Science Monitor,* June 24, 1992; Perry, "Call It New Media."

ment. "It has become the common frame of reference for the world's power elite"—from Boris Yeltsin and Jiang Zemin to Bill Clinton and Saddam
Hussein.[21] One British foreign secretary stayed only at hotels that carried
the network. When the name of his country was omitted from a news quiz
about the nations participating in the Middle East peace talks, King Hussein of Jordan directed palace officials to call and complain to CNN's Am-
man office. The terrorists who held Terry Anderson hostage in Lebanon
used CNN to release a videotape of his appeal for help. Even its most fierce
competitors openly acknowledge CNN's central importance in world
news and politics. Don Hewitt, founding producer of CBS's award-winning *60 Minutes*, concedes that CNN has become *the* source of knowledge
in a crisis, particularly an international crisis. It has come closer than any
other network so far to creating the global village that Marshall McLuhan
spoke of, because "now the minute that anything happens [we] all run to
CNN and think, 'The whole *world* is sharing this experience with me.'"[22]

Although it is rooted in American democracy and the free market,
CNN presents itself as a global network that must remain politically neutral. Its journalistic philosophy is a haggis of social responsibility and libertarianism mixed with the do-good impulses of its ego-driven founder,
Ted Turner. An ardent environmentalist, Turner founded the Better World
Society to educate people about pollution, hunger, and the arms race. His
heroes are Martin Luther King and Gandhi; they used to be Alexander the
Great and Napoleon. Turner is a hands-on chief executive, accounting for
the network's often unpredictable programming. On the one hand, CNN
enabled Boris Yeltsin to transmit his message of hope and freedom during
the Moscow putsch, advancing democracy in the former Soviet Union. On
the other hand, the network broadcast a sycophantic interview with Fidel
Castro which ignored the many real violations of human rights and
democracy in Communist Cuba.[23]

During the Persian Gulf War, the controversial Peter Arnett obtained
an exclusive interview with Saddam Hussein, during which the Iraqi dictator thanked Americans who were demonstrating against the war and
characterized the conflict as a "Zionist war" being fought with American
blood. Many Americans, especially those with relatives fighting in the war,

---

21. William A. Henry III, "History as It Happens," *Time*, January 6, 1992, p. 24.
22. Ibid.
23. Priscilla Painton, "Man of the Year," *Time*, January 6, 1992, p. 39; Henry, "History as It Happens," pp. 25–26.

strongly criticized CNN for broadcasting what they called Iraqi "propaganda." A CNN producer, Robert Wiener, subsequently revealed that it had been necessary to engage in self-censorship to obtain the Saddam exclusive. Wiener and a CNN crew were taken to Kuwait City, where they saw the devastation caused by the "Iraqi gang rape" of the city. Weiner planned to report what had happened to Kuwait City, but was warned by Iraqi officials that to do so would jeopardize the Saddam interview. The eyewitness account of conditions in the Kuwaiti capital never aired.[24] Most journalists would agree that CNN paid too high a price for an interview with the dictator of an aggressor nation with which the United States and most of the rest of the world were at war.

CNN's importance is significantly strengthened by its willingness to spend millions of dollars on its international coverage—24 foreign bureaus in 1999—when the broadcast networks are severely reducing their overseas news budgets. CNN International can reach 150 million households worldwide, not including 78 million households in the United States that CNN reaches. Its major global competitor is the British Broadcasting Corporation, whose BBC World service reaches about 60 million homes outside the United Kingdom. Since 1997, CNNI has depended heavily upon a "regionalization" strategy. Instead of one international network, it utilizes four "international" networks—one for Europe, the Middle East, and Africa; one for Asia; one for Central and South America; and one for the United States. CNNI, wrote the media analyst Nicholas Varchaver, is thus able "to tailor, albeit only in broad strokes, shows for different parts of the world."[25]

Ninety-eight percent of CNNI's audience, says its president, Chris Cramer, is non-American, "affluent," and "influential." Which explains in part why CNN is willing to spend ever larger sums on international news and to develop a worldwide brand recognition comparable to that of Coca-Cola.[26]

A POPULIST REACTION

Many Middle Americans who feel left out or who are alienated by what they call the "elite" media, like National Public Radio and the New York City–based commercial networks, have found a happy, if noisy, home in

24. Peter Arnett, interview with Saddam Hussein, Cable News Network, January 30, 1991; Robert Wiener, *Live from Baghdad* (New York: Doubleday & Delacorte, 1991), pp. 129–35.
25. Nicholas Varchaver, "CNN Takes Over the World," *Brill's Content*, June 1999.
26. Ibid.

talk radio. Talk radio became politically important in 1987, the journalist Alexandra Marks points out, when the Federal Communications Commission eliminated the "fairness doctrine." Until then, national talk radio was usually limited to late nights (and low ratings), when personalities like Larry King conducted lively but noncontroversial conversations with celebrities and sometimes politicians. When the Reagan administration lifted the regulations requiring radio and TV programs to be balanced politically, "the lid was ripped off the talk."[27]

Concurrently, new satellite technology enabled radio producers to beam, and stations to receive, talk shows across the country. This technical development coincided with FM's finally replacing AM as the dominant source of music for listeners. AM radio stations had to come up with a new format to survive. Millions of people began talking and listening and connecting. "I think that talk radio functions," says David Brudnoy, a Boston-based talk-show host, "as the last neighborhood in town."[28]

The undisputed "king" of the neighborhood is Rush Limbaugh, whose Monday-through-Friday afternoon program is heard weekly by some twenty million listeners. His daily critiques of the Clinton administration and his calls for support of the Republicans' Contract with America are credited by some analysts with helping to bring about the historic GOP win in 1994. Michael Harrison, editor and publisher of *Talkers* magazine, argues that talk radio "doesn't create the public's mood; it reflects it."[29] Whether Limbaugh and his many imitators lead or follow their audience, no one in national politics disputes that talk radio has become and is likely to remain a major influence in American *mediapolitik,* loud proof of the people's deep dissatisfaction with politics as usual. Although highly critical of television and radio talk shows, Howard Kurtz, a media reporter, nevertheless conceded in his book *Hot Air* that the programs "spur a national conversation, offer a voice to the powerless, [and] provide an outlet for anger and frustration."[30]

THE RESPONSIBILITY OF POWER

Lincoln understood how essential the press is to politics and government, commenting: "With public sentiment, nothing can fail; without it

27. Alexandra Marks, "Talk Radio's Voice Booms across America," *Christian Science Monitor,* November 1, 1995.

28. Ibid.

29. Ibid.

30. Howard Kurtz, *Hot Air: All Talk All the Time* (New York: Times Books, 1996), p. 363.

nothing can succeed. Consequently he who molds public sentiment, goes deeper than he who enacts statutes or pronounces decisions."[31] Given this power to affect success or failure, the standards and decisions of journalists warrant as much attention as those of lawyers, physicians, business leaders, union leaders, or academicians. It will not suffice for journalists to glibly promise fairness, balance, and accountability. It must be asked: What philosophy is going to guide their fairness and sustain that accountability, not just to readers, viewers, sources, peers, and employers, but to society?

The answer will not be found in the Statement of Principles of the American Society of Newspaper Editors, with its predictable references to responsibility, freedom of the press, truth and accuracy, impartiality, and fair play. The ASNE statement is all fat and no muscle, with not a hint of how a journalist might be reprimanded or penalized for violating one of the "principles." The Code of Ethics of Sigma Delta Chi, the Society of Professional Journalists, uses the word "ethics," but in the most utilitarian way, stating that journalists should avoid gifts, favors, and political involvement; substantiate claims from private sources and at the same time protect their sources; and seek news "that serves the public interest"— while not defining "public interest." The SPJ code deserves credit for acknowledging that "journalists should be accountable to the public for their reports," although as with the ASNE Statement of Principles, there is no suggestion of what should be done when journalists fail in their responsibilities, beyond the vague words, "the public should be encouraged to voice its grievances against the media."[32]

The hollow rhetoric of these two codes suggests that the media believe they have a special right to freedom under the First Amendment of the U.S. Constitution. So they have, but that right is not an end in itself, the political scientist James W. Carey points out, but was justified in order that the media might serve a liberal democratic society. The media do not exist simply to inform or educate the public but to help sustain a virtuous public, the very foundation of democracy. Carey maintains that the First Amendment enumerates not so much the rights of individuals or corpo-

31. *Collected Works of Abraham Lincoln*, vol. 3 (New Brunswick, N.J.: Rutgers University Press, 1953), p. 27.

32. American Society of Newspaper Editors, "Statement of Principles," and Sigma Delta Chi, Society of Professional Journalists, "Code of Ethics," in *Responsibility in Mass Communication*, 3d ed., by William L. Rivers, Wilbur Schramm, and Clifford G. Christians (New York: Harper & Row, 1980), pp. 289–94.

rations or the state but the rights of "a certain kind of public"—a public possessing the virtues of wisdom, courage, and prudence.[33]

The urgent need for a moral code for the mass media was underscored by the results of a 1992 survey of American journalists by two political scientists, David Weaver and C. Cleveland Wilhoit. When asked whether a reporter should use confidential business or government documents without authorization, 80 percent said yes; 63 percent approved the use of a hidden microphone or camera, and 28 percent would not prohibit actors from recreating or dramatizing news. The last revelation was particularly disturbing, condoning as it did the mixing of fact and fiction and therefore reality and fantasy.[34]

THE THIN-SKINNED MEDIA

How reluctant the media are to accept criticism, even from their peers, can be seen from the short unhappy history of the National News Council. Established in 1973 by a group of well-known journalists and public figures, the council was intended to be a forum for independent appraisals of the fairness of media performance. Its findings were released to the public, but aside from the power of publicity, the council had no way of enforcing its recommendations. Major U.S. media like the *New York Times* and CBS opposed the council and refused to fund it or cooperate in its inquiries, claiming that such a watchdog organization was unnecessary, since they had their own self-correcting mechanisms. Although media councils have earned respect and approval in Great Britain and Scandinavia, the National News Council achieved only marginal status in America, and died in 1984, unremarked and unlamented by most of the media.[35] Its demise was inevitable, not only because of media indifference and even hostility, but because of public indifference. There must be a moral consensus among all major social institutions for there to be morality in our politics and in our mass media. The media can no more operate in a moral vacuum than a human being can breathe without oxygen.

Among the few scholars who have seriously considered the interrelationship of the mass media and classical philosophy is John C. Merrill. In *The Imperative of Freedom,* Merrill emphasizes the central importance of

33. James W. Carey, "The Press and Public Discourse," *Kettering Review,* Winter 1992, pp. 15–16.

34. Joann Byrd, "Extraordinary Techniques," *Washington Post,* November 22, 1992.

35. Doris A. Graber, *Mass Media and American Politics,* 3d ed. (Washington: CQ Press, 1989), pp. 369–70.

freedom, both institutional and existential, in journalism, drawing upon Locke, Mill, and Jefferson. The book is strongly libertarian and would have been lauded by the radical individualist Ayn Rand. But in a later book, *The Dialectic in Journalism*, Merrill suggests that there should be a balance between freedom and ethics, a "merger of Platonic social responsibility with Aristotelian political individualism." Freedom, he argues, clashes with ethics to gain more flexibility and individualism while ethics conflicts with freedom to temper personal desires with social concern. Neither, he believes, ever wins the battle nor is vanquished; instead, a reconciliation, a "dialectical synthesis," results that is the "best solution to many of the problems of mass communication."[36]

CIVIC JOURNALISM

One strong response to the decline in civic life in America, and the mass media's acknowledgment that they are at least partially responsible for the decline, is a new movement called "civic journalism" or "public journalism." Public journalism's goal, according to the journalist Alicia Shepherd, is to "reconnect" citizens with their newspapers, their communities, and their politics, with newspapers playing the role of community organizer. Under such journalism, "professional passivity is passe; activism is hot. Detachment is out; participation is in. . . . Readers' voices must be heard."[37]

Although only a decade old, public journalism is being adopted in dozens of newsrooms and broadcast stations across the country, led by the Knight-Ridder newspapers. Its components include a newspaper or radio or TV station asking its readers what stories a paper should cover, and how; being an active player in, not simply an observer of, the community; lobbying for changes in government and society on the news pages; finding sources "whose voices are often unheard"; and strengthening its bonds with the community. At the heart of public journalism is the idea that "a newspaper [or broadcast station] should act as a catalyst for change."[38]

Skeptics ask, "Isn't public journalism what first-rate newspapers and stations have been doing all along?" Then again, if readers are able to dic-

---

36. John C. Merrill, *The Dialectic in Journalism: Toward a Responsible Use of Press Freedom* (Baton Rouge: Louisiana State University Press, 1989), pp. 1–3; John C. Merrill, *The Imperative of Freedom* (New York, 1974).

37. Alicia Shephard, "The Gospel of Public Journalism," *American Journalism Review*, September 1994, p. 29.

38. Ibid., pp. 29–30.

tate what a newspaper or station should or shouldn't publish, they add, isn't the newspaper or station abrogating its responsibility? Says Leonard Downie, Jr., executive editor of the *Washington Post*, "No matter how strongly I feel about something that's going on out there, my job is not to try to influence the outcome."[39]

Davis (Buzz) Merritt, Jr., editor of the *Wichita Eagle*, and Jay Rosen, a professor at New York University, the acknowledged founders of public journalism, argue that public journalists must not engage in mere consciousness-raising. They must be willing to get involved in their community as facilitators and referees, although not necessarily as partisans. One example: the *Charlotte Observer* in 1992 created an election coverage model that abandoned horse race reporting and concentrated on the issues that mattered most to voters, according to a series of surveys and town meetings. Reporters asked questions at news conferences that had been submitted by readers. National Public Radio was so impressed with the *Observer* model that it merged traditional narrative with the voices of voters in its election-year coverage so that listeners could hear citizens thinking through issues.[40]

In 1994, one of the nation's largest foundations, the Pew Charitable Trusts, created the Pew Center for Civic Journalism, which began holding conferences, publishing books, and producing videos with the stated purpose of stimulating "citizen involvement in community issues."[41] At a Washington symposium on civic journalism, the keynote speaker, David Broder of the *Washington Post* admitted that the bonds of trust holding together our system of representative government "are badly frayed." As a result, Broder said, there was a powerful movement to substitute some form of direct democracy (like national initiatives and referenda) for the kind of government "we have had in this country for over two centuries." Such a movement, the veteran political reporter stated flatly, "poses a genuine threat to all forms of liberty, including the freedom of the press."[42]

Symposium participants argued that more "voter-oriented news coverage" would reduce public frustration and hostility concerning electoral politics and slow down the movement toward direct democracy. Rick Thames, the public life editor of the *Charlotte Observer*, urged reporters to stop filling their news reports with unsubstantiated attacks by candi-

---

39. Ibid., p. 30.   40. Ibid., pp. 31–32.
41. *Civic Catalyst*, Pew Center for Civic Journalism, October 1995, p. 16.
42. Ibid., p. 6.

dates, internal squabbles within political parties, the latest horse race polls, and "investigative" reporting about something a candidate did twenty years ago. Instead, suggested Thames, "devote the majority of your resources" to stories that "explore the issues, explain how they affect voters' lives and reveal what the candidates propose to do" about those issues.[43]

Despite the good works that could be created by civic or public journalism, traditional journalists worry that public journalists will become so involved in the political process they will lose their editorial balance and news objectivity. Howard Schneider, managing editor of *Newsday*, believes that once a newspaper or broadcast station begins to lead the parade rather than cover it, its credibility is in danger. "The whole point of American journalism," says Marvin Kalb of the Shorenstein Center on the Press, Politics and Public Policy at Harvard University, "has always been detachment from authority so that critical analysis is possible."[44] Can a newspaper or a TV station analyze objectively a situation it helped create? More disturbing is the possible degeneration of public journalism into something akin to the yellow journalism of the late nineteenth century when egocentric publishers like William Randolph Hearst used their newspapers to champion their personal causes and political candidates.

For the most part, though, the impulse of the public journalists is worthy—to improve the community in which they live. But the impulse will go astray if it is based only on what the community wants or the journalists' sense of social responsibility. Whatever the form of journalism—public or private, print or broadcast, commercial or non-commercial—a *moral* sense of right and wrong must be present to help a reporter or editor make correct decisions as to what is published or broadcast.

HOW THE MEDIA SEE THEMSELVES

In the spring of 1995, as related in the Introduction to this work, the author mailed a three-page questionnaire to selected editors, reporters, ombudsmen, and media critics across the country, inviting them to comment on the current state of American journalism and its future role in global politics. Responses arrived from ninety-five print and broadcast journalists, including representatives of the *New York Times*, the *Washington Post*, the *Los Angeles Times*, *USA Today*, and more than thirty other daily news-

43. Ibid., p. 2.
44. Ibid., p. 34.

papers, *Time, Newsweek, U.S. News & World Report,* ABC News, CBS News, NBC News, National Public Radio, the *New Yorker, American Journalism Review, Forbes, Reader's Digest, Quill,* the Nieman Foundation, the Institute on Religion and Public Life, and the Media Research Center. (See Appendix 1 for a complete tabulation of the results.) The quotes that follow here were taken from the questionnaires returned by the journalists.

Their responses can be summarized as follows: We acknowledge that public confidence in us has declined sharply. We admit our cynicism, our arrogance, our penchant for the sensational. We resolve to do a better job of matching media responsibility with media power in the years ahead.

The first question quoted the latest University of Michigan survey about the lack of public confidence in the press and asked: "Why do you think the news media no longer enjoy the public's full confidence?" The explanations offered varied from "too left-wing elitist" (Michael Barone of *U.S. News & World Report*) to "too cynical and adversarial and too superficial and sensationalized" (David Shaw of the *Los Angeles Times*) to "we are living in a distrustful and cynical society" (Richard Harwood of the *Washington Post*) to "because the news media no longer confine themselves to reporting the news" (Emerson Stone, formerly an editor for CBS News).

Hal Bruno, the highly regarded political director of ABC News for twenty years, offered a five-part answer: "(1) We're telling [the public] things they don't want to hear; (2) an increase in irresponsible, undisciplined and sensationalized reporting; (3) [public] ignorance due to poor education; (4) lazy minds, and (5) a 'cry baby' generation." Along with several others, Nina Totenberg of National Public Radio agreed with Bruno's point about the public's intellectual laziness, saying that people do not read newspapers but "watch tabloid TV" and other "ratings-driven products" that are becoming "less and less substantive."

Bill Monroe, who for many years hosted NBC's *Meet the Press,* asserted that public confidence in the media had declined sharply because the media "increasingly try to tell people what to think instead of just informing them." Echoing the findings of Stanley Rothman's and Robert Lichter's *The Media Elite,* Monroe stated that journalists "have attained celebrity status" and "have become, in too many cases, arrogant, feeling superior to those they report on. All of these things, inevitably, cause resentment and distrust." The *Washington Post* media critic Howard Kurtz listed the media's flaws as "arrogance, sensationalism, too many high-profile errors and a tendency to become too cozy with the political establishment."

Lawrence Barrett, a veteran *Time* reporter and editor, suggested four reasons for the public's lack of confidence in the mass media:

(1) The public has lost confidence in *most* institutions, and the press isn't immune from that.

(2) The frontier between news and entertainment is now almost non-existent and this causes confusion. Also, the float of political consultants into quasi-journalism causes confusion.

(3) The world is a very complex and frightening place. Has been for many years. The press has difficulty in explaining the complexities and frequently *over-emphasizes* the negative or frightening part.

(4) There are too many factual errors in print and on the air.

Ann Compton, a Washington correspondent with ABC for over twenty years, thought that the public had *"always"* lacked confidence in the media about political issues on which it has an opinion. At the same time, the public retains a very high level of trust in information about events of which it knows little, such as the Gulf War, the Oklahoma City bombing, or natural disasters. Harmful to the media at present, said Compton, is tabloid journalism, "which . . . pushed the mainstream media too far in its coverage of O. J. Simpson." Bill Kovach of the Nieman Foundation stressed the "bottom line" philosophy of network, newspaper, and station owners, stating that the media's "goal is less to inform than to gain an audience as large as possible to maximize profits."

John Corry, former TV critic of the *New York Times* and now a writer for *The American Spectator,* commented on the public's inability to distinguish between "the press" and the "media." He acknowledged that the public's confusion is compounded by the fact that "old-fashioned reporters" and tabloid journalists like Geraldo Rivera now cover the same story. Corry also noted "the schism" between the public and the elite media, saying that the public's perception of an issue is not the same as that of a $6 million anchorman like Peter Jennings. Like ABC's Compton, Elliott Negin, senior editor of the *American Journalism Review,* argued that the media have never enjoyed the public's "full" confidence. But he went on to say that the media's image suffers from "their obsession" with political horse races and mudslinging, with entertaining their audiences, with sound bites, and with "official" sources who wind up dominating the debate.

Joann Byrd, who served as the *Washington Post*'s ombudsman, summed up the media's flaws this way: "The media seem self-serving, distant, and divorced from the old public-service ethic. The public thinks the media are a business."

CYNICAL, NOT SKEPTICAL

Addressing the problem of media attitude, the questionnaire quoted Kathleen Hall Jamieson of the Annenberg School of Communications at the University of Pennsylvania about the damage that journalistic cynicism can do to journalism and society. The American public, Jamieson explained, expects the news media to keep it informed about the wrongdoings of government; such reporting requires a healthy skepticism. But the public does not expect the news media to characterize *every* doing of government as wrong; such reporting, nevertheless, is prevalent in Washington and other media capitals. "If you cover the world cynically," warned Jamieson, "you invite your readers and viewers to reject journalism as a mode of communication because it must be cynical too."[45] Journalists were asked whether they agreed or disagreed that "many journalists have become cynical rather than skeptical." An overwhelming 72 percent agreed with Jamieson's assessment, while only 27 percent disagreed.

Asked whether the media have "lowered standards in pursuit of greater circulation and higher ratings," nearly three-fourths of the respondents— 73 percent—agreed that standards have been "significantly" lowered, while only one-fourth—26 percent—disagreed. This is a remarkable and damning admission: the great majority of the journalists polled—all leaders in their profession—conceded that the pursuit of profits and the bottom line has replaced a commitment to fairness and even accuracy. The Founders' intention that the press would act as an impartial middleman between the people and their government, as a guarantor of liberal democracy, is now mocked by trash TV programs and even establishment newspapers unable to resist disseminating one more lip-smacking speculation about Hillary Rodham Clinton's future or George W. Bush's past.

"NEUTRALITY" VS. NATIONAL INTERESTS

Stating that the old ideal of objectivity has been challenged by a new standard of "neutrality," the questionnaire asked whether a foreign correspondent should be "neutral" or consider "national interests" in his war

45. William Glaberson, "Raking Mud; The New Press Criticism: News as the Enemy of Hope," *New York Times,* October 9, 1994.

and foreign reporting. The respondents split almost evenly, with 45 percent saying that a foreign correspondent should be neutral, 39 percent saying that he should consider national interests, and 6 percent saying he should do both.

It is a core argument of this book that American journalists have a solemn obligation, under the First Amendment, to practice moral responsibility based on the virtues of wisdom, courage, justice, and prudence. Wanting to discover how journalists felt about such a proposition, the questionnaire asked if "there is a place for moral (as distinguished from social) responsibility in journalism." Specific reference was made to the British historian Paul Johnson and his "ten commandments—rules of moral conduct" for those who exercise media power and influence. Almost nine-tenths of those responding—87 percent—said there was a place for moral responsibility in American journalism; only 8 percent said there was not. Five percent had no opinion.

Such near unanimity on the rightful place of morality in journalism confirms that many leading American journalists are deeply disturbed by the prevailing cynicism, arrogance, and sensationalism of their profession. There is clearly a strong desire to reform journalism and win back the public's confidence and respect. But how does one go about such a difficult and demanding task? The questionnaire asked which of the following reforms the respondent favored:

• A nongovernmental National Media Council to evaluate public complaints about media performance. Yes: 54 percent. No: 45 percent. (Several emphasized that any council must be private and not run by government.)

• Ombudsmen at all TV networks and regularly scheduled "letters to the editor" in prime time. Yes: 80 percent. No: 20 percent.

• Free TV network time for major political candidates running for national office. Yes: 57 percent. No: 43 percent.

• More exacting standards for political advertising, especially negative ads. Yes: 50.6 percent. No: 49.4 percent.

• Restrictions on outside income, like speaking honoraria, for journalists. Yes: 44 percent. No: 56 percent.

• Abolition of shield laws (which allow journalists to protect the confidentiality of their sources). Yes: 14 percent. No: 86 percent.

• Restrictions on the use of leaks (once suggested by Ben Bradlee of the *Washington Post*). Yes: 16 percent. No: 84 percent.

As can be seen, the reform that received the greatest support (80 percent) was the installation of ombudsmen at all TV networks and the scheduling of "letters to the editor" in prime time. At present, not one of the broadcast networks has such a person or allows for regular public comment or criticism on the air. CNN has a weekly half-hour program that discusses the news media, but no ombudsman per se. Perhaps one of the reasons why CBS's *60 Minutes* has been one of the top-rated programs for several decades is that it regularly broadcasts viewers' reactions to its reports. Many of National Public Radio's shows, including its popular "All Things Considered," have frequent "letters to the editor."

The other reform to receive solid support (57 percent) was the proposal to provide free TV network time to major political candidates—a longtime practice in Great Britain and other Western democracies. That barely 50 percent favored more exacting standards for political advertising and that less than 50 percent endorsed restrictions on outside income suggest that journalists still shy away from the tough, demanding steps required for serious reform.

TWENTY-SIX WAYS TO IMPROVE
THE NEWS MEDIA

The next question was, "What one reform would you like the news media to adopt?" As might be expected, the answers were as varied as the institutions and the backgrounds of the respondents. They ranged from the philosophical ("I wish," said former ombudsman Joann Byrd, "that [the media] had more respect for readers") to the practical ("More accountability for blind, unattributed quotes," Matt Roush, *USA Today*).

Here are twenty-six suggestions culled from the responses that would help produce a more responsible journalism:

• "Greater responsibility about and less interest in private lives of public people. But it won't happen."—Ann Compton, ABC News.

• "Reestablish *accuracy* as a cardinal standard."—Lawrence Barrett, *Time*.

• "Refrain from publishing unsubstantiated rumors simply because they have been reported elsewhere."—Howard Kurtz, *Washington Post*.

• "Acknowledge errors and biases."—Brent H. Baker, Media Research Center.

• "Respect privacy more—following older guidelines in that area—than they seem to today."—Jane Weston, *New York Times*.

• "Stop reporting all events through political prism of 'liberal' and 'conservative.' But that won't happen."—Richard J. Neuhaus, *First Things*.

• "I believe the restrictions on outside speaking fees, which turn journalists into hypocrites, should be adopted by news organizations."—Julia I. Keller, *Columbus Dispatch*.

• "Be more accountable—more open to criticism and adjustment, not always so defensive and self-righteous."—Brian L. Steffens, *Quill*.

• "Free TV time."—Jonathan Alter, *Newsweek*.

• "Use news reporting more vigorously to combat sound-bite politics and misrepresentations in political advertising."—John Carman, *San Francisco Chronicle*.

• "Fewer anonymous sources."—Paul Greenberg, *Arkansas Democrat Gazette*.

• "I oppose any attempt to interfere in the free working of the press. Vigorous competition is the best shield against bias."—Thomas J. Bray, *Detroit News*.

• "Ban on the use of paid sources."—Ginny Holbert, *Chicago Sun-Times*.

• "Ombudsmen and letters."—Bill Monroe, formerly NBC News.

• "Better on-the-job training, more discipline on young reporters, stronger leadership from news executives."—Hal Bruno, ABC News.

• "(1) Tighter control on the use of unnamed sources. (2) More corrections of the sort the *New York Times* publishes under the 'Editor's Note' rubric."—David Shaw, *Los Angeles Times*.

• "Have greater respect for the personal privacy and dignity of men, women, and children. This means less obsession with their sex lives and financial peccadilloes."—Adam Meyerson, *Policy Review*.

• "Try to forget Hollywood for five minutes."—James Wolcott, *The New Yorker*.

• "Stop that namby-pamby New Age hogwash called 'public journalism.'"—Mike Duffy, *Detroit Free Press*.

• "Ethics education for all staff, especially management, [including] college courses, mid-career training seminars, in-house 'conversations,' etc."—Jay Black, University of South Florida.

• "We need to decrease our addiction to celebrity, gossip and spurious trend stories and do more serious analysis of what's important."—Phil Kloer, *Atlanta Constitution*.

• "Ombudsmen at all major media outlets."—John Sweeney, Wilmington (Del.) *News Journal*.

• "Stop pretending that [the news media's] current performance is objective. Admit to being biased and admit that their work-product is affected by that bias."—William A. Rusher, The Claremont Institute.

• "Free TV network time for major political candidates thereby reducing the influence of money. I also feel we sorely need a redefinition of the meaning of 'news.'"—Carl Jensen, Sonoma State University.

• "One reform won't do it; a dramatic change in thinking and conviction is needed."—William Murchison, *Dallas Morning News.*

• "To understand that journalistic ethics and practices are not some sort of decoration to add to reporting at the last minute, but the centrality of what we are and from which all else must flow."—Emerson Stone, formerly CBS News.

WHICH ROLE FOR THE MASS MEDIA?

The last question quoted James Q. Wilson, a political scientist who has stated that the U.S. news media play the role of "gatekeeper, scorekeeper and watchdog," and asked, "Which role(s) do you think the news media should play in the American politics of the 21st century?"[46] A little more than one-third (37 percent) responded "watchdog," while less than one-fourth (21 percent) replied "all three—gatekeeper, scorekeeper and watchdog." Only 10 percent answered "scorekeeper," while just 2 percent said "gatekeeper." Twenty-nine percent offered other answers, ranging from "accurate reporting" to "explicator" to "let people be their own scorekeeper."

The diverse responses suggest that there is no consensus among these leading journalists as to what the mass media's role should be. The 37 percent who favored a "watchdog" role come closest to the Founders' concept of the press as a middleman—an honest broker of information—between the people and their representatives. The 21 percent who opted for a "gatekeeper-scorekeeper-watchdog" role represent the New Journalism with its emphasis on the journalist as an active participant in and even creator of news.

The lack of consensus reinforces the difficulty of reform. Also of concern is the resigned attitude of ABC's Compton and others who, after offering a sensible reform, comment, "But it won't happen." Are they saying that it is *impossible* to reform the mass media? Are the members of the

---

46. James Q. Wilson, *American Government: Institutions and Policies* (Lexington, Mass.: D. C. Heath and Company, 1980), p. 239.

mass media salaried automatons who only do what they are told, or do they have the intelligence and the determination to change the course of their profession and therefore the course of the society in which all of us live? If each of the leading journalists who responded to the survey undertook to carry out just *one* reform, *mediapolitik* in America and around the world would be significantly altered and for the better: it would be brought more into conformity with liberal democratic principles. In short, reform of the mass media is possible if enough journalists of good reputation and high resolve determine it is necessary. If journalists, however, do not carry out a program of self-correction, an impatient public could well demand that the government take corrective action against the mass media.

Given the major role of the media in the conduct of U.S. politics at home and abroad and the leadership of American media around the world, it would seem that American journalists have little choice but to undertake liberal democratic reforms like appointing ombudsmen at all the major networks and cable systems, a nongovernmental national media council, higher standards for political advertising, and the inculcation of ethics and moral philosophy among reporters and editors.

There are increasing signs that reform is on the way. Following the 1996 election, executives of the major TV news organizations met in New York to discuss future election coverage. A prominent proposal that emerged was to devote one hour of free time during each of the last nine weeks of the fall campaign to an intensive discussion of a single, important issue. CBS's Walter Cronkite and former *Washington Post* political writer Paul Taylor have proposed that all the networks offer "a few minutes a night of free air time" to the major candidates in the final month of the fall campaign. The format: "talking-head presentations . . . no tricky images . . . no unseen narrators. Just the candidate, making his or her best case to the biggest audience America assembles every night." "Today," says Reese Cleghorn, president of the *American Journalism Review* and dean of the University of Maryland's College of Journalism, "the press relentlessly exposes its own bad performance."[47]

A major player in helping the press criticize itself is the Freedom Fo-

---

47. Doris A. Graber, "Whither Televised Election News? Lessons from the 1996 Campaign," *Press/Politics*, spring 1998, pp. 112, 118; Walter Cronkite and Paul Taylor, "Politics in Prime Time," *Washington Post*, March 6, 1996; David S. Broder, "Policing the News Business," *Washington Post*, September 9, 1998.

rum and its predecessor, the billion-dollar Gannett Foundation. At its New York headquarters and at the Newseum, located in Northern Virginia across the Potomac River from Washington, the Freedom Forum sponsors a river of publications, seminars, conferences, and events about a free press and free speech. David Shaw, a media critic, suggested at a Freedom Forum seminar that reporters were making more mistakes today because they were trying to hold on to news consumers distracted by competing media. "You wind up," said Shaw, "with people taking chances, taking risks that they didn't take before." David Broder of the *Washington Post* urged his colleagues to put aside cynicism so that they could recognize good news. "When we have the chance," said Broder, "to explain to people [about honorable practices] in government, we should not pass that up." Robert Shogan, the national political correspondent for the *Los Angeles Times*, asserted that the impact of character on nearly every national public office and institution was growing, not shrinking. "Character and values," Shogan said, "are the most powerful tools we have for political communication. Whether they are good or bad depends on how they are used—or abused."[48]

Some large-scale TV advertisers, according to Karl Zinsmeister, editor of *The American Enterprise*, are beginning to say enough is enough. Dissatisfied with programming options, Proctor & Gamble and other advertising heavyweights like Johnson and Johnson, Sears Roebuck, Ford, and IBM are organizing to encourage "more winsome, less decadent shows" in prime time. Media critics can protest loudly without any certainty of effect, but if major advertisers begin pushing their money in different directions, "there will be noticeable results."[49]

THE NEED FOR ETHICS

Journalists must accept the responsibility of power and believe in the power of responsibility. They must steer a middle course between the Scylla of libertarianism and the Charybdis of social responsibility. Their guiding principle should be the Golden Mean, founded on the precepts of

48. "Reporters' Risk-Taking Behavior Leads to More Mistakes, Critic Says," *The Freedom Forum and Newseum News*, November 1998, p. 1; "National Reporters Can Learn from Local Colleagues, Broder Says," *The Freedom Forum and Newseum News*, January/February 1999, p. 6; "Fellow Examines 'Character Issue' in Politics," *The Freedom Forum and Newseum News*, July 1998, p. 8.

49. Karl Zinsmeister, "Taking Out the TV Trash," *The American Enterprise*, March/April 1999, p. 5.

wisdom, courage, justice, and prudence. Plato says that life can be symbolized as a man driving a chariot pulled by two horses. One of the horses is sluggish and needs to be spurred on; the other is high-spirited and needs to be reined in. The driver represents reason, which has the duty to moderate the passion and aggression of the one steed and not to give in to the sloth and weakness of the other. It is reason, Plato says, that leads us to the Golden Mean, the middle way between two extremes.

For the journalist, the middle way would lie between lying to get a story and depending upon a government handout. For a politician, it would fall between supporting or opposing legislation depending on the wishes of financial contributors and supporting or opposing legislation depending on the polls. For a voter, it would be between not voting at all and voting the straight party ticket. Moral reasoning does not take place in a vacuum but within a culture. Most decent people in the world have never had a course in ethics or moral philosophy nor have they needed one. They have made the right decisions in their lives because of institutions like their family, school, church, community, and government. Because of the moral education provided by their culture, most people, at least where there is adequate political and intellectual freedom, have little difficulty in making moral decisions. Their decisions, according to Jesse Mann, a Georgetown University philosophy professor, are the natural outflow of courage, common sense, self-control, fair-mindedness, love, and care—"the qualities important to any culture that wishes to survive."[50]

In his provocative work *News and the Culture of Lying,* the magazine editor Paul H. Weaver states that liberal democracy "isn't automatic"—it requires a commitment throughout society to classical liberal notions like individual responsibility and limited government. It requires sacrifices and the practice of "active citizenship." Weaver praises C-SPAN, with its potential audience of sixty million households, for practicing what he calls "constitutional journalism," presenting events without commentary and allowing the viewer to make up his own mind about their importance and relevance.[51]

Cokie Roberts, cohost of ABC's Sunday morning program *This Week with Sam Donaldson and Cokie Roberts,* has urged the mainstream media

50. Jesse Mann, "Moral Reasoning and Newsgathering," in *Journalism Ethics: Why Change?* ed. Doug Ramsey and Dale Ellen Snaps (Los Angeles: Foundation for American Communications, 1986), pp. 18–19.

51. Paul H. Weaver, *News and the Culture of Lying: How Journalism Really Works* (New York: The Free Press, 1994), pp. 216–20.

to do "a better job" of explaining the institutions of government, particularly Congress, to the American public. While conceding that politicians must shoulder "a very heavy burden of the blame" for the lack of public trust in the system, Roberts insists that "so must we." In the annual Theodore H. White Lecture at Harvard University, she argued that "all we have defining us, as a nation, is our commitment to the Constitution and the institutions that it created. . . . To undermine those institutions is a real recipe for disunion."[52]

A GLOBAL TURNING POINT?

We are at a global turning point, say scholars like Francis Fukuyama and Dankwart Rustow, because democracy has become a seemingly irresistible force. Since World War II, Gulags and genocide along with economic failure and corruption have brought crashing down almost every rightist and leftist totalitarian regime. "This is the first time in history," says Rustow, "when there is no legitimate alternative to democracy."[53] The process of democratization has been advanced by mass communication. The computer, the fax machine, and satellite television have erased national borders, breaking governmental monopolies over communication while inspiring aspirations for freedom. Fukuyama argues that other forms of government—monarchy, fascism, communism—all failed because they were imperfect vehicles for freedom; liberal democracy triumphed because it allowed the greatest possible freedom. But liberal democracies, he says, are not self-sufficient: "the community life on which they depend must ultimately come from a source different from liberalism itself."[54]

The Founders of the American Republic would agree; they were not isolated individuals motivated solely by economic self-interest but members of communities bound by a common moral code and belief in God. Liberal democracy of any century requires societal consensus, a people who agree as to what constitutes good politics, fair economics, and responsible media, and who demand a *mediapolitik* founded, at least in part, on these words of John Adams:

52. Cokie Roberts (fifth annual Theodore H. White Lecture, The Joan Shorenstein Barone Center on Press, Politics and Public Policy, John F. Kennedy School of Government, Harvard University, November 17, 1994).

53. George D. Moffetti III, *Christian Science Monitor*, May 23, 1991.

54. Francis Fukuyama, *The End of History and the Last Man* (New York: The Free Press, 1992), pp. 326–27.

Public virtue is the only foundation of republics. There must be a positive passion for the public good, the public interest, honor, power and glory, established in the minds of the people, or there can be no republican government, *nor any real liberty.*[55]

But let us be clear: Public virtue depends on *private* character. And for the best definition of the American character, we must turn to the historic embodiment of America, George Washington. Throughout his career, our *pater patria* maintained that the inalienable rights that Americans enjoyed required a commitment to moral duty and civic virtue. And a crucial aid to the achievement of those objectives, he wrote to the printer Matthew Carey, were "periodical Publications." Washington declared: "I consider such easy vehicles of knowledge, more happily calculated than any other, to preserve the liberty, stimulate the industry and meliorate the morals of an enlightened and free People."[56]

Washington always sought, the political historian Matthew Spalding points out, to inculcate maturity and moderation in the conduct of America's domestic and international affairs. In his Farewell Address, Washington expressed the modest hope that his advice would be remembered "now and then" so as to "moderate the fury of party spirit, to warn against the mischiefs of foreign intrigue, [and] to guard against the impostures of pretended patriotism."[57]

Maturity and moderation, whether in 1796 when Washington uttered those words or in 2000 when these words are being written, encourage reason rather than emotion in our *mediapolitik.* They reject instant analysis and sound-bite journalism. They do not pander or appeal to the prurient. They lead a journalist to admit that he can make mistakes and to acknowledge publicly his mistakes. They produce responsibility and honor accountability. They accept the truth, expressed by the political philosopher Michael Novak, that "as human lungs need air, so does liberty need virtue."[58]

55. John Adams to Mercy Warren, c. 1776, in *Novus Ordo Seclorum: The Intellectual Origins of the Constitution,* Forrest McDonald (Lawrence, Kan.:University Press of Kansas, 1985), p. 72.

56. George Washington to Matthew Carey, June 25, 1788, in *The Writings of George Washington,* vol. 30, ed. John C. Fitzpatrick (Washington: U.S. Government Printing Office, 1931–1944), pp. 7–8.

57. Matthew Spalding, "George Washington, Father of His Country" (paper presented at the annual meeting of the American Political Science Association, Chicago, August 1995), pp. 23, 25; also see George Washington, "The Farewell Address," in Fitzpatrick, *The Writings of George Washington,* vol. 35, pp. 214–38.

58. Michael Novak, "Awakening from Nihilism: In Preparation for the 21st Century:

Where the family and the churches and the schools have failed, suggests the historian Paul Johnson, journalists high and low must now encourage a sense of morality and a commitment to ethics among themselves and the readers and viewers whom they serve. They can turn for guidance to thinkers like Michael Novak, who, borrowing from Lord Acton, stated that "liberty is not the freedom to do what you wish; it is the freedom to do what you ought."[59]

The twentieth century was the century of scourges—the Great Wars, the Great Depression, the Great Purges, Auschwitz, the Gulag, the Cultural Revolution, the killing fields of Cambodia, racism, abortion. But in the twenty-first century, most of mankind has abandoned totalitarianism and turned to liberal democratic institutions and Judeo-Christian values. How principled, how moral, how free, the *mediapolitik* of this century will be depends on what *individual* politicians, journalists, and ordinary citizens do.

The model need not be Saint Paul, who tried to convert all the pagans of the ancient world, but Dino Corbin, the manager of a Chico, California, television station, who abruptly cancelled several high-rated trash talk programs. "You don't have to hit me with a two-by-four," explained Corbin. "The talk shows have been trying to outdo each other in sinking deeper and deeper into the gutter and I did not contract for that."[60] What is required, in the words of one observer, are "small but steady changes for the better which, over a period of time, bring immense and welcome transformations."[61]

Four Lessons from the 20th" (the Templeton Address of 1994, London, May 5, 1994), as reprinted in *First Things*, no. 45, August–September 1994, p. 6.

59. Novak, "Awakening from Nihilism," p. 21. For an exposition of Lord Acton's ideas about conscience and liberty, see Lord Acton, "The History of Freedom in Christianity" (lecture, London, May 1877), in *Essays in the History of Liberty*, ed. J. Rufus Fears (Indianapolis: Liberty Fund, 1985), pp. 29–53.

60. *CBS Evening News with Dan Rather*, November 9, 1995.

61. Paul Johnson, "How the Media Can Make the 21st Century Principled, Civilized and Safe" (address before the World Media Association, Moscow, April 1990).

APPENDIX

The following questionnaire was mailed to more than 200 editors, reporters, ombudsmen, and media critics in print and broadcast journalism in April 1995. Follow-up telephone calls were made to about fifty key journalists, asking them to fill out and return the questionnaire. Ninety-five journalists responded during the months of April, May, and June 1995. In addition to the questionnaire, several respondents sent back articles, speeches, and even books they had written about the state of American journalism. Responses were received from representatives, past and present, of the following news organizations:

New York Times, Washington Post, Chicago Tribune, Chicago Sun-Times, Los Angeles Times, USA Today, Wall Street Journal, Washington Times, Dallas Morning News, Fort Worth Star-Telegram, Newsday, New York Daily News, New York Post, San Diego Union Tribune, San Francisco Chronicle, Columbus Dispatch, Detroit Free Press, Detroit News, St. Louis Post-Dispatch, Philadelphia Inquirer, Arkansas Democrat Gazette, Atlanta Constitution, Seattle Times, The Oregonian, The Daily Oklahoman, Richmond Times-Dispatch, Hartford Courant, Rocky Mountain News, (Wilmington, Del.) News Journal, Birmingham News, Colorado Springs Gazette Telegraph, and *Fort Wayne News-Sentinel.*

Time, Newsweek, U.S. News & World Report, ABC News, NBC News, CBS News, National Public Radio, NET, Radio America, WBZ-TV Boston, Radio-Canada, Scripps-Howard News, *The New Yorker, The (Montreal, Canada) Gazette, El Pais (Madrid, Spain), The Washingtonian, Reader's Digest, Forbes, Quill, American Journalism Review, First Things, Policy Review, Human Events,* and *The American Spectator.*

The full text of the questionnaire, with the responses, follows.

MEDIAPOLITIK QUESTIONNAIRE

Your candid response will help us present the opinions of the most influential members of the U.S. news media about the current state of journalism and its future role in global politics.

It should take you no longer than 10 minutes to answer all questions. We are most grateful for your cooperation.

1. According to the annual University of Michigan survey, the American public has lost much of its confidence in the press and TV. In 1993, 39 percent of the public had hardly any confidence in the press, while 37 percent had hardly any confidence in TV.
    Why do you think the news media no longer enjoy the public's full confidence? Various answers; see chapter 11.

2. Social scientists Robert Lichter, Stanley Rothman, and Linda S. Lichter state that today's journalists are politically liberal and do not observe traditional norms and institutions. Do you:
    Agree 45%
    Disagree 55%
    No opinion less than 1%

3. Kathleen Hall Jamieson, head of the Annenberg School of Communications at the University of Pennsylvania, has warned that "journalists are now creating the coverage that is going to lead to their own destruction. If you cover the world cynically . . . you invite your readers and viewers to reject journalism as a mode of communication because it must be cynical too."
    Do you agree or disagree that many journalists have become cynical rather than skeptical?
    Agree 72%
    Disagree 27%
    No opinion less than 1%

4. Critics charge that the media have significantly lowered standards in pursuit of greater circulation and higher ratings. Do you:
    Agree 73%
    Disagree 26%
    No opinion less than 1%

5. Most journalists follow either a libertarian or a social responsibility philosophy. Libertarians say they must be free to report whatever they can discover—the public has a right to know almost everything. Socially responsible journalists consider the impact of what they report—they seek to influence social behavior and thought for a common good.
    Which philosophy do you generally follow?
    Libertarian 27%
    Social responsibility 31%
    Both 12%
    Other 30%

6. In war and foreign reporting, the old ideal of objectivity has been challenged by a new standard of "neutrality." A reporter is supposed to stand midway between two opposing sides, even when one of the sides is his own. Should a foreign correspondent:
    Be neutral 45%
    Consider national interests 39%

Both 6%
Other answer 10%

7. British historian Paul Johnson has proposed ten commandments—rules of moral conduct—for all who exercise media power and influence. Is there a place for moral (as distinguished from social) responsibility in modern journalism?
Yes 87%
No 8%
No opinion 5%

8. Do you favor any of the following media reforms?

—A nongovernmental National Media Council to evaluate public complaints about media performance.
Yes 54%
No 46%

—Ombudsmen at all TV networks and regularly scheduled "letters to the editor" in prime time.
Yes 80%
No 20%

—Free TV network time for major political candidates running for national office.
Yes 57%
No 43%

—More exacting standards for political advertising, especially negative ads.
Yes 50.6%
No 49.4%

—Restrictions on outside income, such as speaking honoraria, for journalists.
Yes 44%
No 56%

—Abolition of shield laws.
Yes 14%
No 86%

—Restrictions on use of leaks.
Yes 16%
No 84%

9. What one reform would you like the news media to adopt?
Various answers; see chapter 11.

10. Do you agree or disagree that the news media wield too much power in American politics?
Agree 17.5%
Disagree 74.4%

Other 3.5%
No opinion 4.5%

11. Political scientist James Q. Wilson asserts that the news media play the roles of gate-keeper, scorekeeper, and watchdog in our political system. Which role(s) do you think the news media should play in the American politics of the twenty-first century?
Gatekeeper 2%
Scorekeeper 10%
Watchdog 37%
All three 21%
Other 29%

BIBLIOGRAPHY

NEWSPAPERS AND MAGAZINES

America
American Journalism Review
(formerly Washington Journalism
Review)
The Atlantic Monthly
Boston Gazette
Boston Globe
Broadcasting and Cable
Business Week
Chicago Tribune
The Christian Science Monitor
Columbia Journalism Review
The Economist
Editor & Publisher
Far Eastern Economic Review
Insight
International Herald Tribune
Los Angeles Times

Media Studies Journal
Moscow News
The Nation
National Review
New Perspectives Quarterly
The New Republic
New York
The New York Times
Newsweek
Time
TV Guide
USA Today
U.S. News & World Report
The Wall Street Journal
The Washington Post
The Washington Times
The World & I

BOOKS

Abramson, Jeffrey B., F. Christopher Arterton, and Garry R. Orren. *The Electronic Commonwealth: The Impact of New Media Technologies on Democratic Politics.* New York: Basic Books, 1988.

Alexander, Alison, and Jarice Hanson. *Taking Sides: Clashing Views on Controversial Issues in Mass Media and Society.* 3d ed. Guilford, Conn.: Dushkin Publishing Group, 1995.

Altschull, J. Herbert. *Agents of Power: The Media and Public Policy.* White Plains, N.Y.: Longman Publishers, 1995.

Arlen, Michael. *The Living Room War.* New York: Viking Press, 1969.

Auletta, Ken. *Three Blind Mice: How the TV Networks Lost Their Way.* New York: Random House, 1991.

Banac, Ivo, ed. *Eastern Europe in Revolution.* Ithaca, N.Y.: Cornell University Press, 1992.

Black, Jay, Bob Steele, and Ralph Barney. *Doing Ethics in Journalism: A Handbook with Case Studies.* Birmingham, Ala.: EBSCO Media, 1993.

Bliss, Edward, Jr. *Now the News: The Story of Broadcast Journalism.* New York: Columbia University Press, 1991.

Boller, Paul F., Jr. *Presidential Campaigns.* New York: Oxford University Press, 1984.

Borneman, John. *After the Wall: East Meets West in the New Berlin.* New York: Basic Books, 1991.

Braestrup, Peter. *Big Story: How the American Press and Television Reported and Interpreted the Crisis of Tet 1968 in Vietnam and Washington.* Garden City, N.Y.: Anchor Books, 1978.

Brinton, William M., and Alan Rinzler, eds. *Without Force or Lies: Voices from the Revolution of Central Europe in 1989-90.* San Francisco: Mercury House, 1990.

Brzezinski, Zbigniew. *The Grand Failure: The Birth and Death of Communism in the Twentieth Century.* New York: Collier Books, 1989.

Burden, Hamilton T. *The Nuremberg Party Rallies: 1923-39.* New York: Praeger, 1968.

Calvocoressi, Peter. *World Politics since 1945.* 5th ed. London: Longman Publishers, 1987.

Carpenter, Ted Galen. *The Captive Press: Foreign Policy Crises and the First Amendment.* Washington: Cato Institute, 1995.

Cater, Douglas. *The Fourth Branch of Government.* New York: Vintage Books, 1959.

Chamberlin, William Henry. *The Russian Revolution: 1917-1921.* New York: Grosset & Dunlap, 1935.

Chinoy, Mike. *China Live: Two Decades in the Heart of the Dragon.* Atlanta: Turner Publishing, 1997.

Christians, Clifford G., John P. Ferre, and P. Mark Fackler. *Good News: Social Ethics and the Press.* New York: Oxford University Press, 1993.

Christopher, Robert C. *The Japanese Mind.* New York: Fawcett Columbine, 1983.

Cohen, Bernard C. *The Press and Foreign Policy.* Princeton, N.J.: Princeton University Press, 1963.

Cohen, Elliot D., ed. *Philosophical Issues in Journalism.* New York: Oxford University Press, 1992.

Creel, George. *How We Advertised America.* New York: Harper & Brothers, 1920.

Darnton, Robert. *The Literary Underground of the Old Regime.* Cambridge, Mass.: Harvard University Press, 1982.

Davis, Richard. *The Web of Politics: The Internet's Impact on the American Political System.* New York: Oxford University Press, 1999.

Dennis, Everette E., George Gerber, and Yassen N. Zassoursky. *Beyond the Cold War: Soviet and American Media Images.* Newbury Park, Cal.: Sage Publications, 1991.

de Tocqueville, Alexis. *The Old Regime and the French Revolution.* New York: Doubleday, 1955.

Diamond, Martin. *The Revolution of Sober Expectations.* Washington: American Enterprise Institute, 1974.

Donovan, Robert J., and Ray Scherer. *Unsilent Revolution: Television News and American Public Life.* New York: Cambridge University Press, 1992.

Edwards, Lee. *Missionary for Freedom: The Life and Times of Walter Judd.* New York: Paragon House, 1990.

Emery, Edwin, and Henry Ladd Smith. *The Press in America.* New York: Prentice-Hall, 1954.

Erikson, Robert S., and Kent L. Tedin. *American Public Opinion: Its Origins, Content and Impact.* 5th ed. Boston: Allyn and Bacon, 1995.

Fairbank, John K. *The Great Chinese Revolution: 1800-1985.* New York: Harper & Row, 1987.

Fox, Elizabeth, ed. *Media and Politics in Latin America: The Struggle for Democracy.* London: Sage Publications, 1988.

Fukuyama, Francis. *The End of History and the Last Man.* New York: Free Press, 1992.

Garber, Larry, and Eric Bjornlund, eds. *The New Democratic Frontier: A Country by Country Report on Elections in Central and Eastern Europe.* Washington: National Democratic Institute for International Affairs, 1992.

Garment, Suzanne. *Scandal: The Culture of Mistrust in American Politics.* New York: Anchor Books, 1991.

Gilder, George. *Life after Television.* New York: W. W. Norton, 1992.

Gorbachev, Mikhail. *Perestroika.* New York: Harper & Row, 1987.

Gordon, George N. *The Communications Revolution: A History of Mass Media in the United States.* New York: Hastings House, 1977.

Graber, Doris. *Mass Media and American Politics.* 3d ed. Washington: CQ Press, 1989.

Gwertzman, Bernard, and Michael T. Kaufman, eds. *The Collapse of Communism.* New York: Times Books, 1990.

Halberstam, David. *The Powers That Be.* New York: Alfred A. Knopf, 1979.

Hale, Oron J. *The Captive Press in the Third Reich.* Princeton, N.J.: Princeton University Press, 1964.

Hamilton, Alexander, James Madison, and John Jay. *The Federalist Papers.* New York: New American Library, 1961.

Hiebert, Ray Eldon, ed. *Impact of Mass Media.* 3d ed. White Plains, N.Y.: Longman Publishers, 1995.

Hitler, Adolf. *Mein Kampf.* Boston: Houghton Mifflin, 1943.

Hohenberg, John. *Foreign Correspondence: The Great Reporters and Their Times.* 2d ed. Syracuse, N.Y.: Syracuse University Press, 1995.

Jensen, Carl. *Censored: The News That Didn't Make the News — and Why.* New York: Four Walls Eight Windows, 1995.

Johnson, Paul. *Modern Times: The World from the Twenties to the Eighties.* New York: Harper & Row, 1983.

Klaidman, Stephen, and Tom L. Beauchamp. *The Virtuous Journalist.* New York: Oxford University Press, 1987.

Kurtz, Howard. *Hot Air: All Talk All the Time.* New York: Times Books, 1996.

Ladd, Everett Carll, and Karlyn Bowman. *What's Wrong: A Survey of American Satisfaction and Complaint.* Washington: AEI Press, 1999.

Lambeth, Edmund B. *Committed Journalism: An Ethic for the Profession.* 2d ed. Bloomington, Ind.: Indiana University Press, 1992.

Langguth, A. J. *Patriots: The Men Who Started the American Revolution.* New York: Simon and Schuster, 1988.

Lasky, Melvin J. *Voices in a Revolution.* London: Encounter Magazine, 1991.

Lefever, Ernest W., and Robert D. VanderLugt, eds. *Perestroika: How New Is Gorbachev's New Thinking?* Washington: Ethics and Public Policy Center, 1989.

Lenin, V. I. *Collected Works.* Vol. 5. Moscow: Foreign Languages Publishing House, 1961.

Lichter, S. Robert, Stanley Rothman, and Linda S. Richter. *The Media Elite: America's New Powerbrokers.* Bethesda, Md.: Adler & Adler, 1986.

———. *Prime Time.* Washington: Regnery Publishing, 1994.

Linsky, Martin. *Impact: How the Press Affects Federal Policymaking.* New York: W. W. Norton, 1986.

Loory, Stuart, and Ann Imse. Introduction by Hedrick Smith. *Seven Days That Shook the World: The Collapse of Soviet Communism.* Atlanta: Turner Publishing, 1991.

Madison, James. *Letters and Other Writings of James Madison, Fourth President of the United States.* Vol. 3. Philadelphia: Lippincott & Co., 1865.

Manchester, William. *The Last Lion, Winston Spencer Churchill: Alone 1932-1940.* Boston: Little, Brown and Co., 1988.

Mann, Thomas E., ed. *A Question of Balance: The President, the Congress and Foreign Policy.* Washington: Brookings Institution, 1990.

McDonald, Forrest. *Novus Ordo Seclorum: The Intellectual Origins of the Constitution.* Lawrence, Kan.: University Press of Kansas, 1985.

McLuhan, Marshall. *Understanding Media: The Extensions of Man.* New York: Signet Books, 1966.

Merrill, John C., and Ralph D. Barney. *Ethics and the Press: Readings in Mass Media Morality.* New York: Hastings House, 1975.

Merrill, John C., ed. *Global Journalism: Survey of International Communication.* 3d ed. New York: Longman Publishers, 1995.

———. *The Dialectic in Journalism: Toward a Responsible Use of Press Freedom.* Baton Rouge, La.: Louisiana State University Press, 1989.

Methvin, Eugene. *The Riot Makers.* New Rochelle, N.Y.: Arlington House, 1970.

Mickiewicz, Ellen. *Split Signals: Television and Politics in the Soviet Union.* New York: Oxford University Press, 1988.

Mill, John Stuart. *On Liberty.* Chicago: Henry Regnery, 1955.

Miller, Judith, and Laurie Mylroie. *Saddam Hussein and the Crisis in the Gulf.* New York: Times Books, 1990.

Morgenthau, Hans. *Politics Among Nations.* 5th ed. New York: Alfred A. Knopf, 1978.

Mosher, Steven W. *China Misperceived: American Illusions and Chinese Reality.* New York: Basic Books, 1990.

Mott, F. L. *American Journalism: 1690-1960.* 3d ed. New York: Macmillan, 1960.

Naisbitt, John. *Megatrends.* New York: Warner Books, 1988.

Nathan, James A., and James K. Oliver. *United States Foreign Policy and World Order.* 4th ed. Glenview, Ill.: Scott, Foresman and Co., 1989.

Neustadt, Richard E. *Presidential Power: The Politics of Leadership from FDR to Carter.* New York: John Wiley & Sons, 1980.

Neyn, Herman. *Update on Germany: Now Eastern Germany Gets a Free Press.* Bonn: Inter Nationes Bonn, 1991.

Noam, Eli. *Television in Europe.* New York: Oxford University Press, 1991.

Oksenberg, Michael, Lawrence R. Sullivan, and Marc Lambert, eds. *Beijing Spring, 1989: Confrontation and Conflict.* Armonk, N.Y.: M. E. Sharpe, 1990.

Padover, Saul K. *Thomas Jefferson on Democracy.* New York: Penguin Books, 1939.

Popkin, Jeremy D., ed. *Media and Revolution: Comparative Perspectives.* Lexington, Ky.: University of Kentucky Press, 1995.

Press, Charles, and Kenneth Verburg. *American Politicians and Journalists.* Glenview, Ill., Scott, Foresman and Co., 1988.

Quester, George. *The International Politics of Television.* Lexington, Mass.: Lexington Books, 1990.

Ramsey, Doug, and Dale Ellen Snaps, eds. *Journalism Ethics: Why Change?* Los Angeles: Foundation for American Communications, 1986.

Reagan, Ronald. *An American Life.* New York: Simon and Schuster, 1990.

———. *Speaking My Mind.* New York: Simon and Schuster, 1989.

Reeves, Thomas C. *The Life and Times of Joe McCarthy: A Biography.* New York: Stein and Day, 1982.

Reischauer, Edwin. *The Japanese.* Rutland, Vt.: Charles E.Tuttle, 1977.

Rivers, William L., Wilbur Schramm, and Clifford G. Christians. *Responsibility in Mass Communication.* 3d ed. New York: Harper & Row, 1980.

Sabato, Larry J. *Feeding Frenzy: How Attack Journalism Has Transformed American Politics.* New York: Free Press, 1991.

Schama, Simon. *Citizens: A Chronicle of the French Revolution.* New York: Alfred A. Knopf, 1989.

Severin, Werner J., and James W. Tankard, Jr. *Communication Theories: Origins, Methods, and Uses in the Mass Media.* 3d ed. New York: Longman Publishers, 1992.

Smith, Geoffrey. *Reagan and Thatcher.* New York: W. W. Norton, 1991.

Smith, Hedrick, ed. *The Media and the Gulf War: The Press and Democracy in Wartime.* Washington: Seven Locks Press, 1992.

———. *The New Russians.* New York: Random House, 1990.

———. *The Power Game: How Washington Works.* New York: Random House, 1988.

Stephens, Mitchell. *A History of News: From the Drum to the Satellite.* New York: Viking, 1988.

Summers, Harry G., Jr. *On Strategy: A Critical Analysis of the Vietnam War.* New York: Dell, 1984.

Sussman, Leonard R. *Power, the Press and the Technology of Freedom: The Coming Age of ISDN.* New York: Freedom House, 1989.

Taylor, Jared. *Shadows of the Rising Sun.* New York: William Morrow and Co., 1983.

Toffler, Alvin. *The Third Wave.* New York: Bantam Books, 1980.

Toffler, Alvin, and Heidi Toffler. *Creating a New Civilization: The Politics of the Third Wave.* Atlanta: Turner Publishing, 1995.

Unger, Jonathan, ed. *The Pro-Democracy Protests in China.* Armonk, N.Y.: M. E. Sharpe, 1991.

van Wolferen, Karel. *The Enigma of Japanese Power.* New York: Vintage Books, 1989.

Vermeer, Jan P. *In "Media" Res: Readings in Mass Media and American Politics.* New York: McGraw-Hill, 1995.

Warfel, Harry, Ralph H. Gabriel, and Stanley T. Williams. *The American Mind: Selections from the Literature of the United States.* New York: American Book Co., 1947.

Wattenberg, Ben J. *The Good News Is the Bad News Is Wrong.* New York: Simon and Schuster, 1984.
Weaver, David H., and G. Cleveland Wilhoit. *The American Journalist: A Portrait of U.S. News People and Their Work.* 2d ed. Bloomington, Ind.: Indiana University Press, 1991.
Weaver, Paul H. *News and the Culture of Lying: How Journalism Really Works.* New York: Free Press, 1994.
Wiener, Robert. *Live from Baghdad.* New York: Doubleday, 1991.
Wilson, James Q. *American Government: Institutions and Policies.* Lexington, Mass.: D. C. Heath and Co., 1980.
Wolfe, Bertram. *Three Who Made a Revolution.* New York: Dial Press, 1948.
Yutang, Lin. *The Wisdom of Confucius.* New York: Modern Library, 1938.
———. *The Wisdom of India and China.* New York: Modern Library, 1942.

ARTICLES

Akhavan-Majid, Roya. "The Press as an Elite Power Group in Japan." *Journalism Quarterly* 67 (winter 1990).
Bean, Walton E. "The Accuracy of Creel Committee News, 1917-1919: An Examination of Cases." *Journalism Quarterly* 18 (September 1941).
Bernstein, Carl. "The Holy Alliance." *Time,* February 24, 1992.
Carey, James W. "The Press and Public Discourse." *Kettering Review* (winter 1992).
Corry, John. "TV News and the Neutrality Principle." *Commentary,* May 1991.
Denniston, Lyle. "In Defense of Journalistic Competence." *The Long Term View* 1 (summer 1992).
Dufresne, Marcel. "A Soviet Press Code." *Washington Journalism Review,* July/August 1990.
FlorCruz, Jaime A. "Chinese Media in Flux." *Media Studies Journal* (summer 1999).
Gambrell, Jamey. "Moscow: The Front Page." *The New York Review,* October 8, 1992.
Giffard, C. Anthony, and Lisa Cohen. "South Africa TV and Censorship: Does It Reduce Negative Coverage?" *Journalism Quarterly* (spring 1989).
Glaberson, William. "The New Press Criticism: News as the Enemy of Hope." *New York Times,* October 9, 1994.
Graber, Doris A. "Whither Televised Election News? Lessons from the 1996 Campaign." *Press/Politics* (spring 1998).
Guocang, Huan. "The Events of Tiananmen Square." *Orbis* (fall 1989).
Hanke, Helmut. "Media Culture in the GDR: Characteristics, Processes and Problems." *Media, Culture and Society* 12 (April 1990).
Hopkins, Mark. "Watching China Change." *Columbia Journalism Review,* September/October 1989.
Ito, Youichi. "Mass Communication Theories from a Japanese Perspective." *Media, Culture and Society* 12 (October 1990).
Jakubowicz, Karol. "Musical Chairs? The Three Public Spheres of Poland." *Media, Culture and Society* 12 (April 1990).
Knudson, Jerry W. "Chile's Catholic Opposition Press." *The Christian Century,* December 10, 1986.

Kristoff, Nicholas D. "How the Hardliners Won." *New York Times Magazine,* November 12, 1989.

Maitre, H. Joachim. "How the War Was Covered." *Bostonia,* May/June 1991.

McAuliffe, Kevin. "Kosovo: A Special Report." *Columbia Journalism Review,* May/June 1999.

McKenzie, Jim. "Combatting Brutal Censorship," *Content,* September/October 1988.

Matusow, Barbara. "Abroad: The White House Writes the Lead." *Washington Journalism Review,* September 1984.

Nester, William. "Japan's Mainstream Press: Freedom to Conform?" *Pacific Affairs* (spring 1989).

Payne, Douglas. "Latin American Democracy: In Search of the Rule of Law." *Freedom Review,* January/February 1992.

Robinson, Daniel N. "Races and Persons." *The World & I,* February 1992.

Schechter, Danny. "South Africa: Where Did the Story Go?" *Africa Report,* March/April 1988.

Schell, Orville. "The Great Wall vs. the Fax." *New Perspectives Quarterly* (summer 1989).

Seidensticker, E. G. "Japan's Timid Media." *World Press Review,* August 1984.

Shepherd, Alicia C. "The Gospel of Public Journalism," *American Journalism Review,* September 1994.

Sigmund, Barbara Boggs. "A Lesson in Bravery and Democracy." *America,* October 29, 1988.

Singer, Eleanor, and Jacob Ludwig. "South Africa's Press Restrictions: Effects on Press Coverage and Public Opinion toward South Africa." *Public Opinion Quarterly* 51, no. 3, 1987.

Spalding, Matthew. "George Washington, Father of His Country." Paper delivered at the annual meeting of the American Political Science Association, Chicago, August 1995.

Thompson, Loren B. "The Press and the Pentagon: Old Battles, New Skirmishes." *The American Enterprise,* January/February 1992.

Tomlinson, Kenneth Y. "Freedom's Victory: What We Owe to Faith and the Free Market." *Imprimis,* December 1991.

Tunstall, Jeremy. "Are the Media Still American?" *Media Studies Journal* (fall 1995).

Valenzuela, Arturo, and Pamela Constable. "The Chilean Plebiscite: Defeat of a Dictator." *Current History,* March 1989.

Varchaver, Nicholas. "CNN Takes Over the World." *Brill's Content,* June 1999.

Wilson, James Q. "Stagestruck," review of *Picture Perfect: The Art and Artifice of Public Image Making,* by Kiku Adatto. *The New Republic,* June 21, 1993.

Youm, Kyu Ho. "Libel Law and Freedom of the Press: Judicial Interpretation in Japan." *Journalism Quarterly* 67 (winter 1990).

Zinsmeister, Karl. "Taking Out the TV Trash." *The American Enterprise,* March/April 1999.

INDEX

Mediapolitik: How the Mass Media Have Transformed World Politics was designed and composed in Minion by Kachergis Book Design, Pittsboro, North Carolina, and printed on 60-pound Glatfelter and bound by Sheridan Books, Ann Arbor, Michigan.